Digitizing Identities

This book explores contemporary transformations of identities in a digitizing society across a range of domains of modern life. As digital technology and ICTs have come to pervade virtually all aspects of modern societies, the routine registration of personal data has increased exponentially, thus allowing a proliferation of new ways of establishing who we are. Rather than representing straightforward progress, however, these new practices generate important moral and socio-political concerns. While access to and control over personal data is at the heart of many contemporary strategic innovations and domains as diverse as migration management, law enforcement, crime and health crisis prevention, "e-governance," internal and external security, new business models, and marketing tools, we also see new forms of exclusion, exploitation, and disadvantage emerging.

Irma van der Ploeg is Senior Research Fellow at UNU-MERIT at Maastricht University Economic and Social Research Institute on Innovation and Technology.

Jason Pridmore is an Assistant Professor in the Department of Media and Communication at Erasmus University in the Netherlands.

Routledge Studies in Science, Technology and Society

1 **Science and the Media**
Alternative Routes in Scientific Communication
Massimiano Bucchi

2 **Animals, Disease and Human Society**
Human–Animal Relations and the Rise of Veterinary Medicine
Joanna Swabe

3 **Transnational Environmental Policy**
The Ozone Layer
Reiner Grundmann

4 **Biology and Political Science**
Robert H. Blank and Samuel M. Hines, Jr.

5 **Technoculture and Critical Theory**
In the Service of the Machine?
Simon Cooper

6 **Biomedicine as Culture**
Instrumental Practices, Technoscientific Knowledge, and New Modes of Life
Edited by Regula Valérie Burri and Joseph Dumit

7 **Journalism, Science and Society**
Science Communication between News and Public Relations
Edited by Martin W. Bauer and Massimiano Bucchi

8 **Science Images and Popular Images of Science**
Edited by Bernd Hüppauf and Peter Weingart

9 **Wind Power and Power Politics**
International Perspectives
Edited by Peter A. Strachan, David Lal and David Toke

10 **Global Public Health Vigilance**
Creating a World on Alert
Lorna Weir and Eric Mykhalovskiy

11 **Rethinking Disability**
Bodies, Senses, and Things
Michael Schillmeier

12 **Biometrics**
Bodies, Technologies, Biopolitics
Joseph Pugliese

13 **Wired and Mobilizing**
Social Movements, New Technology, and Electoral Politics
Victoria Carty

14 **The Politics of Bioethics**
Alan Petersen

15 **The Culture of Science**
How the Public Relates to Science Across the Globe
Edited by Martin W. Bauer, Rajesh Shukla and Nick Allum

16 **Internet and Surveillance**
The Challenges of Web 2.0 and Social Media
Edited by Christian Fuchs, Kees Boersma, Anders Albrechtslund and Marisol Sandoval

17 **The Good Life in a Technological Age**
Edited by Philip Brey, Adam Briggle and Edward Spence

18 **The Social Life of Nanotechnology**
Edited by Barbara Herr Harthorn and John W. Mohr

19 **Video Surveillance and Social Control in a Comparative Perspective**
Edited by Fredrika Björklund and Ola Svenonius

20 **The Digital Evolution of an American Identity**
C. Waite

21 **Nuclear Disaster at Fukushima Daiichi**
Social, Political and Environmental Issues
Edited by Richard Hindmarsh

22 **Internet and Emotions**
Edited by Tova Benski and Eran Fisher

23 **Critique, Social Media and the Information Society**
Edited by Christian Fuchs and Marisol Sandoval

24 **Commodified Bodies**
Organ Transplantation and the Organ Trade
Oliver Decker

25 **Information Communication Technology and Social Transformation**
A Social and Historical Perspective
Hugh F. Cline

26 **Visualization in the Age of Computerization**
Edited by Annamaria Carusi, Aud Sissel Hoel, Timothy Webmoor and Steve Woolgar

27 **The Leisure Commons**
A Spatial History of Web 2.0
Payal Arora

28 **Transparency and Surveillance as Sociotechnical Accountability**
A House of Mirrors
Edited by Deborah G. Johnson and Priscilla M. Regan

29 **The Fukushima Effect**
A New Geopolitical Terrain
Edited by Richard Hindmarsh and Rebecca Priestley

30 **Digitizing Identities**
Doing Identity in a Networked World
Edited by Irma van der Ploeg and Jason Pridmore

Digitizing Identities

Doing Identity in a Networked World

Edited by Irma van der Ploeg and Jason Pridmore

LONDON AND NEW YORK

First published 2016 by Routledge

2 Park Square, Milton Park, Abingdon, Oxfordshire OX14 4RN
52 Vanderbilt Avenue, New York, NY 10017

Routledge is an imprint of the Taylor & Francis Group, an informa business

First issued in paperback 2020

Library of Congress Cataloging-in-Publication Data
Names: Ploeg, Irma van der editor. | Pridmore, Jason, editor.
Title: Digitizing identities : doing identity in a networked world / edited by Irma van der Ploeg and Jason Pridmore.
Description: New York : Routledge, 2016. | Series: Routledge studies in science, technology and society ; 30 | Includes bibliographical references and index.
Identifiers: LCCN 2015035987
Subjects: LCSH: Online identities. | Identity (Psychology) | Information technology—Social aspects. | Identification.
Classification: LCC HM851.D5485 2016 | DDC 303.48/33—dc23
LC record available at http://lccn.loc.gov/2015035987

ISBN: 978-1-138-79463-4 (hbk)
ISBN: 978-0-367-59765-8 (pbk)

Typeset in Sabon
by Apex CoVantage, LLC

Contents

Figures

Table

Acknowledgements

This book results from several years of pleasant and fruitful cooperation among many people. At its origin lies the work we conducted within the DigIDeas project team, consisting of Vlad Niculescu-Dinca, Karolina La Fors-Owczynik, Isolde Sprenkels, Jason Pridmore, and Irma van der Ploeg.

In addition, two international workshops, one held in Amsterdam in November 2011 and one in Maastricht in June 2013, provided us with the invaluable input of many much-appreciated colleagues, some of whose work is presented in this volume alongside our own.

All this was made possible by a generous Starting Grant provided by the European Research Council, and by the COST-Action Network Living in Surveillance Societies, which we gratefully acknowledge.

Irma van der Ploeg
Jason Pridmore

Introduction

Digitizing Identities

Irma van der Ploeg and Jason Pridmore

DIGITIZATION OF IDENTITY

With digitisation and automation processes pervading virtually all aspects and domains of society over the past two decades, the routine registration of personal data has increased exponentially. When in numerous contexts technologically mediated and automated interaction started to replace physical and face-to-face encounters, depriving the interacting partners of traditional, trusted ways of establishing to each other who they are, a strong need for new identification practices emerged.

Securing interactions, controlling access to buildings or information, providing personalised services, assessing rights and entitlements, and tracking movements of people, goods, and data all led to an increasing reliance on information technology (IT)–based technologies for automated recognition of individuals. Thus a wide range of systems and methods has been developed and implemented during the previous decennia, constituting a specialized field within IT and information and computer science called 'identity management (IDM),' Some of these methods are based on something a person knows, like a PIN code or password; another set relies on something a person has in possession, like a smartcard or (electronically enhanced) document, and a third set is based on inalienable traits like physical features, such as fingerprints, iris patterns, or a facial image. Such front-end mechanisms are connected to elaborate back-end systems and databases, connecting the identifiers with personal files, track records, or enabling access to services. All these new mechanisms thus involve registration and storage of personal data in the 'identity management' part of the IT system, rendering individuals 'known' to the system and recognizable as such in subsequent interactions and exchanges.

Today our lives are full of identification and authentication systems like these; whether we do our online banking, book a flight, access the parking lot at work, cross an international border, or apply for a visa, we have to prove who we are—or more accurately, we have to prove that we are who we claim to be, and therefore entitled to engage in that particular (trans-)action.

But the digitization of identities involves more than using information and communication technologies (ICTs) for establishing who someone is. Through the mere growth of digital communications, interactions, and transactions, vast amounts of personal data are registered, because the technology is designed to log information on every action, thus generating and storing details of people's behaviours. When we use identifiers like person-name-records (PNRs), biometrics, registration numbers, IP addresses, or electronic product codes (EPCs), these data can be linked and connected to track individuals or produce personal profiles unprecedented in detail, availability, and durability. Such more elaborate profiles also constitute digital identities, in the sense that they tell a story about who one is: past choices, movements, preferences, connections, and personal history can be assembled from a range of different domains to form a more or less detailed 'picture.' It is in this sense of digital identity that, as one authority in IDM research reminded us, 'digital identities always grow, never shrink' (Pfitzmann, 2007), meaning that what is registered about a person (the number of attributes), in however dispersed systems, only increases over time; once registered, such attributes are virtually impossible to erase. Thus, one's digital identity, or *digital persona* (Clarke, 1994), can cast long shadows over one's life (Blanchette and Johnson, 2002). Digital identities in this sense can be retrieved from numerous databases that may be connected and subjected to algorithmic searches and analyses to find correlations and patterns, from which to define groups and categories. Thus, as much as a unique, individual profile, such digital identities also serve to define and allocate one to a group or category that can be targeted within specific risk-management, marketing, or prevention-policy strategies. Digital identities are created and maintained for their predictive capabilities. Law enforcement agencies looking for suspects, health organizations and researchers looking for risk indicators, and businesses wanting to 'know' their customers are among the most eager to avail themselves of these data.

Clearly, access to and control over personal data is at the heart of many contemporary strategic innovations, ranging from migration and border management, law enforcement, crime and health prevention, 'e-governance,' and internal and external security to new business models and marketing tools. The awareness that these developments come with great potential risks and challenges to fundamental rights like privacy and non-discrimination, however, has increased as well, as evidenced in an increasing number of reports and opinions published by international authoritative bodies like UNESCO, the OECD, the Article 29 Data Protection Working Party of the EC, and the European Group on Ethics in Science and New Technologies. It is also central to the work of a growing number of civil society and activist organizations concerned with 'digital rights,' privacy, and surveillance issues, such as Bits of Freedom, Privacy International, and the Electronic Frontier Foundation to name but a few examples. Further, continuing efforts towards legal regulation are central to how digital identities can and perhaps 'should' be done, something culminating in revised legislation on the European Union (EU) level regarding personal data.

Feeding into these increasingly widespread concerns is the immense popularity of social media, where people voluntarily present detailed textual and visual accounts of their lives to mass audiences. Through personal profiles, blogs, uploading of pictures, and sharing experiences in online communities, individuals voluntarily 'share' extensive accounts of their personal and professional lives with chosen circles of 'friends,' but as often with less-defined audiences and little awareness of the potential for secondary use, surveillance, and other adverse consequences to them. This too qualifies as construction of digital identities, in the sense that it often involves a careful and conscious effort to experiment with and shape one's image to oneself and others. These technologically enabled new practices have received a lot of scholarly attention as well, starting with the first seminal studies of still text-based online social communities like 'MUDs (multi-user dungeon)' end 'MOOs (MUD-object oriented)' in the 1990s, up to the numerous analyses of today's nearly global and ubiquitous online presence of hundreds of millions of people through platforms such as Facebook, Twitter, Instagram, Pinterest, LinkedIn, and more.

Posing the question in what ways new information technologies and digital media mediate and transform identities in the information society, this book connects with the fact that 'identity' is also a key concept in contemporary social theory and in contemporary conceptualisations of the relation between technology and society, ethics, and normativity. Thus, a field of enquiry emerges at the crossroads of theoretical, technological, and societal developments, representing opportunities for frontier research.

THEORIZING IDENTITY

Clearly, the phenomena we are describing here have taken on such enormous proportions that they sometimes appear to be defining of our time and age. Moreover, they seem to affect not only how, where, and when we establish to others who we are but also how we think about ourselves and others, how we know ourselves and others know us, how we form and sustain relationships of various kinds, and how we act and enact our plans and projects. In other words, this wide-ranging digitization touches upon our very identities in numerous ways.

But which theoretical resources do we need to make sense of it all? Are we really talking about one phenomenon here, or are there significant differences that the much-, if not over-used term 'identity' fails to differentiate sufficiently? What do we mean when we talk about identities and identification anyway?

In addition to the public ethical, legal, and political concerns about digital identification, academic interest from the social sciences and humanities has been triggered by the sudden prominence of 'identity' in our highly technologized society as well. Of course, within these scholarly traditions, 'identity' has been a recurring, much-theorized theme predating the 'information revolution' and our current mobile communication-technology-saturated everyday-life by decades. Psychologists, social theorists and philosophers have been working on the question what constitutes identity, how it comes about, and why it matters for a long time and in many different ways.

Much commented upon already is the wide range of angles, disciplines, and traditions that over many years have been brought to bear on understanding identity. Unsurprisingly, this now vast literature yielded not one but a range of more and less diverging concepts of 'identity.' During the late 20th century, for instance, it became central to various strands of social theory, including post-colonial, feminist, and queer theory, where it got deeply connected with social politics. Next to these strands of social theory, it figures as a key term in psychology in various ways, including psychoanalysis and social and developmental psychology. Philosophers, in their attempts to bring more analytical clarity to the concept, have, paradoxically, contributed to the proliferation of different understandings of 'identity' as well.

All this yields a vast range of different accounts of what 'identity' consists of, how it comes about and is known, and where and to whom it matters. Over the past decade, the coming together of the digitization of society and the prominence of issues of identity has opened up a new space for research on 'digital identities' in all the fields mentioned, giving rise to a surge of new, often interdisciplinary scholarship that builds on these older traditions in various ways.

We will refrain from attempting to provide a complete overview of the many approaches to 'identity' one finds here but, instead, briefly explain the ones that played a key role in the research that led to this book. We will thus briefly explain what 'identity' looks like from the respective 'schools of thought' associated with identity management discourse, sociology, surveillance studies, and science and technology studies. But before that, and in order to better be able to characterize these different takes on identity, we will highlight three key distinctions we found helpful in understanding these various approaches and the differences among them.

THREE DISTINCTIONS

Overall, there are three key distinctions that account for many of the differences one finds among the various notions of 'identity.'

The first is the distinction between 'identity' in a narrow sense and a broader understanding of it; thus in many contexts, 'identity' simply refers to someone's name and a few other attributes such as age, gender, and nationality. Knowing someone's identity can then be achieved by simply taking a look at that person's passport, for example. This is the concept of identity one finds in law enforcement practices and national ID-card schemes, for example. In contrast to this stand a notion of identity that encompasses a much wider range of other elements, including, for example, one's tastes and preferences, one's belief system, one's lifestyle, profession or position in society, one's life story, up to one's deepest dreams and desires. Getting to know a person's identity in this sense involves a lot more then mere checking of identity papers; in fact, there is hardly a limit to what can be considered relevant to this notion of identity.

This distinction resonates with a key philosophical distinction one finds, for example in the work of Schechtman (Schechtman, 1990), who explains how philosophers, when analysing 'identity,' have tended to be occupied with the question of re-identification, which involves 'spelling out the necessary and sufficient conditions for saying that a person at t1 is the same as a person at t2' (Schechtman, 1990, p. 79), resulting in in criteria of personal identity over time. This she opposes to identity 'self-knowledge,' which involves reference to the beliefs, values and desires that are 'expressive of who one really is.' Thus, whereas the first concept provides an answer to the question 'What makes a person the same as herself through time and space?' the second answers 'What makes a person unique and different from others?' A similar distinction can be found in the work of Ricoeur, who articulates it as the distinction between 'idem' and 'ipse' identity (Ricoeur, 1990).

It can be argued that most of the time when 'identity,' 'identification,' and in particular 'verification' are mentioned in relation to digital systems, it is the first, narrow conception, the re-identification, or the 'idem identity' that is concerned: usually the aim of identification systems is merely to establish that someone is the same person that first applied for the service, created the account, got issued the new passport, or got allocated some benefit. Moreover, it is the second concept, the 'ipse' or 'self-knowledge' variety of 'identity,' that is probably the socio-politically and morally far more significant one, because it pertains to this idea of who one 'really' is in terms of highly personal characteristics, choices, and values. It may therefore be important to look closely at which of the two is concerned in any specific case to make sure what exactly is at stake. However, this does not mean that they are completely unconnected. To take the example of someone's identity being verified in the context of social benefit payment: While on one level this constitutes merely establishing that this person is the same one that was enrolled in the programme earlier, at the same time, the very act of verifying their identity does establish them as 'social benefit recipient,' which, on another level, is a significant socio-political and morally charged identity aspect in the wider sense.

The second distinction is related to this but is different, as it relates not so much to 'content' of identity but rather to the perspective from which it is conceived. This concerns the difference between identity as something attributed *to* someone by others and identity as some kind of private self-understanding. These two notions are sometimes played out against each other in the sense that the validity of the one may be denied by referring to the other. This occurs in particular in relation to the act of identification: Here the distinction between the first- and the third-person perspective may cover a world of difference. For instance, a person's public image may be deeply contrasting with their own sense of their 'true self.'

A lot of the early work on 'digital identities' in relation to individuals' appropriation of personal computers (PCs), the Internet, and participation in online communities, such as Turkle's (Turkle, 1984, 1995), is characterized by an emphasis on opportunities to experiment, play around anonymously, or carefully shape and manage one's online personal 'profile,' so that concerned mainly this first-person notion of identity as one's own self-understanding. In contrast, those working towards what later became known as 'surveillance studies' concerned themselves above all with the third-person perspective involved in the type of identification involved in personal data gathering and monitoring of people by others (e.g. Gandy, 1993; Lyon, 2003).

But in most social-theoretical approaches that include some form of this distinction, a dependency between the two is assumed, in the sense that an individual's private sense of self and identity is not thought to be independent of 'the social' or vice versa. Usually, both are seen as somehow mutually influencing each other, with the theory providing ideas about the mechanics of this connection.

The third distinction we want to highlight here is that between conceptions of identity that see it as something that is essentially 'there' and that can be known, expressed, registered, proven, faked, and so on versus a conception that sees it as the *outcome* of processes, practices, social interactions, on-going construction, enactment, or performance. This distinction cuts through the other two, in that the essentialist version can come in the narrow and the broad variety and in the attributed-by-others as well as the first-person form. Similarly, the other version—let's call that the constructed one—can be perceived as personal endeavour, mainly done from a first person perspective, but also as that which results from others' actions, attributions, and classifications; it can be restricted to the narrow version or include the wider variety. Thus, to take the most counter-intuitive case: 'Identifying myself' in the narrow sense, as this person with a particular name, gender, date of birth and nationality, may be seen as merely stating a basic, objective fact about myself. But it can also be shown to be a result of a series of actions and a set of historically and culturally contingent practices involving naming, birth registration, kinship definitions, producing ID documents, and so forth.

Most concepts of identity one finds in the literatures and discussions on digital identity can be characterized by the way they are positioned with regard to these three distinctions. The tricky thing, and the reason to elaborate these distinctions here, is that more often than not, it remains quite implicit what variety of 'identity' is concerned when digital identities are discussed. Consequently, a lot of confusion, paradoxical claims, miscommunication, and controversy occur, causing some to argue that the concept has become analytically useless (e.g. Brubaker and Cooper, 2000; Gutwirth, 2009).

However one feels about that assessment, it can hardly be denied that in one form or another, 'identity' remains very much central to a wide range of socio-politically controversial and ethically sensitive discourses and practices today. In particular, if one wants to make sense of the way digital technologies have been and are involved in these, 'identity' and 'identification' often are prominently there, whether one likes it or not.

In this volume, we have gathered a series of contributions that approach the topic of digital identities in a number of different ways. Within this diversity, and broadly speaking, four key discursive practices can be found as informing the notion of identity in each of these; in what follows we will briefly characterize these.

IDENTITY MANAGEMENT

The first concerns identity as it is encountered in digital practices of identification. In particular, the growth of 'e-commerce' and 'e-government' rendered the anonymity of interacting partners as a problem that needed to be solved to enable the establishment of trust relations required for economic exchange over the net and governmental services to assess entitlements. An entire new industry surrounding digital identity, identification, and 'identity management' started booming by developing all kinds of means to 'identify' people when interacting with and through an information system.

This industry generated a discursive and technological practice that dealt with 'identity,' in the first instance specifically in the narrow sense: names, connected to home or IP addresses, Social Security numbers and bank accounts, were what mattered here. Moreover, *verifiable* identities were what mattered, thus leading to the very opposite of the celebrated anonymity and freedom to playfully experiment briefly enjoyed by MUD and MOO enthusiasts during the 1990s. Moreover, as 'certified identity,' this typically concerns identity and identification from a third-person perspective and of the pregiven, essentialist variety. Elaborate infrastructures involving usernames, account numbers, PIN codes, tokens, smartcards, security mechanisms, and biometrics have been developed over the past decades to ascertain whether someone really is the person they claim to be and, therefore entitled to access bank accounts or government or social services or buy and sell online.

It is in these identity-management practices that the notion of identity mentioned briefly at the beginning of this introduction and exemplified by the quote from Pfitzmann originates. Here, 'an identity' has come to denote a specific dataset pertaining to an individual user of a particular IT system, like an account number connected to a name, possibly including address, date of birth, a biometric, a picture, or an ID number, and so on. This kind of 'identity' looks like a thing, a dataset, a commodity, a file, an 'account' in an IT system; it can be exchanged, moved about, sold, stolen, be provided or revoked by an 'identity provider,' and must be 'managed' by the owner of the system.

Clearly, in many respects, this notion is very much at odds with the way philosophers, social scientists, and other theorists have, through long and respectable intellectual traditions, come to talk and think about identity. Nonetheless, through the prominence of 'identity management,' whenever people interact with systems, authorities, or services through digital systems, this concept of identity has tended to spread elsewhere. Thus, for example, governments have come to perceive themselves as 'identity providers' because of their traditional role in issuing passports and other state-certified identity papers (Barnard-Wills, 2012).

But it is also in more traditional practices like policing and law enforcement or migration and border management that these identity-management systems and identification practices are prominent. Identifying a suspect or checking passports at border-crossing points is also premised on this notion of identity, as it increasingly involves the use of IT–based systems developed within this IDM frame.

But the very spread of this particular, if not peculiar, concept of 'identity' is a reason for caution for academics. In the context of a collection of studies of 'digitisation of identity,' this concept of identity is the *object* of study rather than a theoretical, interpretative resource as such. For that, the next three identity discourses are the ones most prominent in this collection.

SOCIOLOGICAL THEORY

Sociological theory has long been concerned with the production of identity, albeit alternatively discussed as the production of 'selves' or 'subjectivities.' This is, as indicated in our second distinction, largely done in relation to how personal identity is understood in relation to the attribution of identity by others. For instance, Charles Horton Cooley (1902) articulated the 'looking-glass self' as an internalization of others' perspectives—or at least the personal interpretation of what those perspectives might be. This was further reflected in later symbolic interactionist thought, most notably of George Herbert Mead (1932) and Herbert Blumer (1969), who saw identity—again, in their case, a notion of self-understanding—as largely a reflective process. Most importantly, their work began to describe how identity could be seen as part of a process of meaning making that occurs between individual persons and others in the course of day-to-day social life. The reflective processes that this is seen to inherently entail was further developed by Anthony Giddens in his description of 'late modern' identities (1991). For Giddens, identity is produced through a process of continual self-monitoring in light of and in contrast with social structures and practices. In his perspective, identity is a continual process of reflexivity—though we may retain certain identifying attributes, sociological theory largely reflects the narrative production of identity through a broad definition connected to life stories, beliefs, and personal histories.

This highlights the contrasts between self-knowledge and the external attribution of identity by others; however, each of these perspectives is predicated on the idea that identity is a product of interactions between persons and social groups. Erving Goffman's work drew inspiration from symbolic interactionism, but his dramaturgical focus on social contexts was one of the most prominent early works to discuss how identities are performed (1959). By using notions such as 'face' and an understanding of selves produced through 'scenes,' Goffman's flexible conceptualization of identity gained significant interest as more essentialized notions of identity became less appealing in light of more complicated social and political dynamics of the 1960s and 1970s. Of course, concerns about the performativity of identity were extended into later work as well, most notably that of Judith Butler. Butler's understanding of identity is clearly focused on how performance processes work together to produce an identity (1990). However, in contrast to Goffman, there is no sense of inner desires or propensities to act. Butler describes (gendered) identities as produced over time through repeated performances. It is an illusion of identity that is produced in a continual acquiescence to the workings of power.

Butler's work is in line with and draws on Foucauldian perspectives on the production of subjectivity. Both Foucault's understanding of disciplinary power (1979), the focus of his earlier work, and the focus of his later work on confessionary technologies of the self (1988) indicate that identity is largely a by-product of the workings of power upon 'docile bodies' in the first instance and self-reaffirming relationships to power through personal examination in the second.

Though some sociological theory pays attention to materiality—such as Goffman's references to 'props' and Foucault and Butler's concerns with performances on and of the body—in large measure, these descriptions are primarily discursive in their focus. The focus in this collection on digital technologies, however, requires an account of both the material and the discursive. Though some sociological theory points us in this direction, the incorporation of materiality in understandings of identity and identification is more explicit and better accounted for in the next theoretical approaches.

SURVEILLANCE STUDIES

Another key discourse on identity informing the chapters in this volume is that of surveillance studies, an interdisciplinary (though heavily inclined towards sociology) field of research focussing explicitly on information technologies, in particular on practices of digital monitoring of people in the broadest sense of these terms. Studies in this field, with topics ranging from police using closed-circuit television (CCTV) in public spaces, managers monitoring workers in call centers, health organizations collecting patient data, to big data analysis of consumer data by marketers, and much more, are deeply concerned with the societal, socio-political, and theoretical meaning, impact, and significance of such practices of 'surveillance.' Taking their cue from the work of, amongst others, Michel Foucault, these studies have tended to emphasise the way in which ICTs are contributing to phenomena like social sorting, automated discrimination, categorical suspicion, and panoptic surveillance (Norris and Armstrong, 1999; Lyon, 2003; Monahan, 2006).

The problem of identity is one of the central issues of surveillance studies for at least two reasons. One is that many surveillance practices come in the guise of identification practices and technologies, such as described above, thus putting the notion of identity centre stage empirically. Another is that a key insight from its Foucauldian discourse-theoretical roots is that surveillance, through its intricate micropolitical power mechanisms, produces subjectivities and identities.

How these two lines of thought and research are related, however, is not a straightforward matter at all. The key terms, 'surveillance' and 'identity,; tend to have different meanings in each, as well as different levels of abstraction, different relations to contemporary technological developments, different practical articulations, and different socio-political significance. But they *are* related in important and complex ways that are rendered even more opaque by frequent conflations and shifts of meaning in both academic and general public discourses on 'surveillance.'

Nonetheless, with its fast-growing body of both theoretically and empirically rich and robust descriptions, the field of surveillance studies has become increasingly influential in focusing academic research, policy, and various publics on the issues, incidents, and inequalities that have arisen from the proliferation of digital monitoring and registration practices and technologies.

SCIENCE AND TECHNOLOGY STUDIES

In the conceptualizations of identity described so far, one aspect remains rather elusive, and that is the role of technology. Because we are concerned here with the digitization of identities, that is, the involvement of various forms of information and communication technologies in contemporary transformations of identity, this is particularly problematic. Of course, digital technology, in the form of various IT–based identification systems and online platforms, figures prominently in the approaches discussed so far, but more often than not, these technologies are represented there as black-boxed tools, whose effects follow inevitably from their intended functions, without much attention to the materialities and particularities of these systems themselves or how these play out in specific, localized practices.

The field of science and technology studies (STS), though not specifically focussed on issues of identity, does offer an approach that enables inclusion of these material technological, contingent, and local (f)actors in the analysis. Deeply committed to an anti-essentialist and empirical constructivist epistemology, STS approaches to digital identities and identification technologies emphasize the need to study situated instances of implemented technologies to make sense of their transformative agency.

In particular, approaches more or less loosely based on actor-network theory (ANT) provide useful theoretical and methodological resources to articulate the way various technical systems are involved in contemporary transformations of identity. If one goes along with the notion that identities are constructed or enacted rather than pregiven essences, and differently so with the uptake of digital technologies, it makes obviously more sense to take an approach that provides an account of how technologies are implicated in this process.

Thus, in this field, 'identity' has been theorized as something that is produced or 'performed' in the very interaction among technology, persons/bodies, discourses, institutional arrangements, and practices or, put differently, within hybrid socio-technical configurations (Law, 1991; Haraway, 1991; Latour, 1993; Mol, 2002).

ANT distinguishes itself from other approaches precisely by the agency it grants to technology in these construction processes. Far from resorting to technological determinism, it stresses the distributed nature of this agency over the socio-material configurations, the 'networks' or 'hybrid collectives' through which a range of different 'actants' jointly perform identities (Akrich and Latour, 1992). In order to conceptualize and analyse the active role of technology in this in a non-deterministic way, the notion of 'script' has been introduced, thus highlighting how technology enables and invites certain actions and behaviours by 'users' without fully determining these (Akrich, 1992). With the help of additional key concepts like 'enrolment' and 'translation,' this approach makes it possible to analyse the tranformative role of technologies in today's digital identification practices.

Clearly, this approach comes with an elaborate vocabulary of its own, which renders combinations with other approaches less than straightforward, but it has the huge advantage of providing the best theoretical and methodological resource available today to account for technologies' transformative capabilities in an empirically sound, non-reductionist, and non-determinist way.

Another highly relevant perspective developed within STS is the one focussing on classification and its consequences (Bowker and Star, 1999). One curious aspect of identification is that it usually is not just about determining unicity but also about assigning category. Thus, if we show you our passports, this not only establishes our unique personal identities but simultaneously our nationalities, our genders, and so forth. In fact, the very possibility of establishing a unique identity with a passport is based on this passport's status as official national document establishing the category of citizenship. In similar vein, if a police detective identifies a suspect by matching a latent fingerprint with a database-registered one, this simultaneously shows this unique suspect to be a member of the class of registered criminals. Thus, identity and classification are intrinsically connected, which makes the analysis of categorization and classification schemes, the 'scaffolding' of most IT systems and databases, highly pertinent to our topic.

This phenomenon has received attention from surveillance studies scholars through the concept of 'social sorting,' but there it figures mostly as a conclusion, where the analysis stops. The STS approach highlighted here takes classification and its 'social sorting' effects as the starting point of the analysis and subsequently aims to deepen understanding by unravelling which contingencies went into the design of classification schemes and categorizing systems in the first place. Moreover, it emphasises that in order to assess effects, one needs to study how classifications are appropriated and used in specific contexts, where local, contingent factors shape the way categorization and classification play out on the lives and fates of those being subjected to such systems.

ORGANIZATION OF THIS VOLUME

A common element in the contributions to this book is the empirical approach to the topic: All chapters are based on empirical research of a domain or practice in which digital identities and identification are, one way or another, prominent. Moreover, while most contributions focus on some form of identification in the narrow sense empirically, the over-arching concern is how new modes of 'doing identity' digitally affect identities in the wider sense, as socio-politically significant and often ethically problematic phenomena. Thus, throughout, an anti-essentialist perspective on identity is maintained but one with the serious awareness that 'if technology defines situations as real, they are real in their consequences.'

We have clustered these contributions by the type of identification practice and the types of identities involved. Thus, Part I consists of a cluster of chapters concerned with today's wide take-up of social media and 'sharing' personal experiences with peers. This *Sharing and Connecting* section examines more fully the production of 'friends' and 'consumers' as identities of particular interest.

Anders Albrechtslund and Anne-Mette Albrechtslund begin this section by offering an exploratory and interpretive study analysing the activities on social media in terms of 'touristic practices.' Their text suggests a direction in which identity performances via online social networking practices are potentially translatable and useful in relation to practices of online sociality. Touristic practices then become a way of thinking about and through the expansion of digitized identities on social media.

Following this, Jason Pridmore examines the way in which identity attributions and personal biographies become increasingly sharable. His chapter focuses on application programming interfaces (APIs) that serve as the basis for how particular sets of data move from one place to another—specifically how applications (apps) rely on certain protocols and requests for personal data. As these 'market devices' become increasingly prolific, understanding of the potentials for and dangers and difficulties posed by digital identities becomes increasingly clear.

Daniel Trottier then looks closely at the work and cultivation of identities on social media, looking specifically at experiences with Facebook. His chapter discusses the uncertainty and tensions inherent in caring for a 'digital self,' combining issues of exposure with the proactive management of a public self. The visibility of Facebook produces a convenient platform to connect, but one rife with concerns about creeping and stalking. This early look at Facebook adoption continues to resonate and helps frame the navigation of purposeful identity development and its surveillance. Finally, Isolde Sprenkels and Irma van der Ploeg look specifically at how children's digital identities are produced and enacted in the very process of identifying these children. This chapter shows how the categorizations and characterizations of children that online marketing surveillance practices produce are simultaneously called upon to legitimate these practices. The empirical focus of this chapter is on 'advergaming,' the uncomfortable amalgam of branded online games blending childhood fun with commercial interests. This chapter's specific focus on children provides the transition to our next section.

Part II, *Growing Up: Children and Guardians*, centers around digital practices involving children. Growing up in a digitized society, most children today are highly involved in various new forms of online social interaction and, as such, are often considered much better informed and skilled in using these new forms of digital communication than are earlier generations. On the other hand, however, they are also considered naive and vulnerable, in need of care, surveillance, and protection. At the one end of this spectrum, children as users of digital media and systems are seen as the 'avant garde' in whose practices and preferences the future of learning, participation, and sociability can be gleaned. At the other end, they appear as the objects of increasingly elaborate, extensive registration and risk-assessment systems, through which they are preformed at once as potential victims and potential perpetrators, requiring pre-emptive identification and preventive intervention.

The chapters in this section focus on this double-edged relationship of children to digital systems and the identities this brings along. Based on extensive interview data gathered in the context of the Media Smart's Young Canadians in a Wired World research project, Valerie Steeves tells a rich story about adolescents' experiences with online visibility, surveillance, and their strategies for 'identity management.' Taking issue with a one-dimensional view on young peoples' relation to social media and digital environments, Steeves paints a colourful picture of the aware and complex nature of their views and negotiations with peers as well as with parents and other authorities to guard their 'online persona' and enjoy the freedoms this brings.

The contribution by Isolde Sprenkels and Sally Wyatt traces the emergence and development of 'media wisdom' as a policy issue in Europe and in the Netherlands. The chapter analyses this concept's translation into a range of initiatives in which the Internet and social media appear alternatingly as opportunity and as threat to children's development into healthy, engaged, and educated citizens. Using the concept of 'boundary object,' the chapter shows how 'media wisdom' has been appropriated by various actors to eventually produce a whole industry of educational initiatives and courses directed at children. The authors conclude that, even if these initiatives show variation in the extent to which digital media are seen as threat or opportunity, they tend have in common a particular distribution of responsibilities: Through a common neglect of the agency and affordances of particular features and designs of online media and the way these shape children's chances to understand and engage with them, it is the children who invariably get the task of learning, adapting, and becoming 'media wiser.'

The chapter by Karolina La Fors-Owczynik and Govert Valkenburg looks at children's identities from the opposite direction, that is, at systems in which they figure not as users but as the objects of data gathering, elaborate registration, and risk assessment. Starting with systems recently implemented in Dutch youth care, the chapter then traces information-sharing practices and connections to other actors involved in risk identification in relation to children, such as police departments dealing with juvenile delinquency. It argues that, with the proliferation, sharing, and communication of 'risk indicators' and 'profiles' and the emphasis on prevention and preemption, risk identities of children come to include ever more aspects and extend further and further in time and (social) space. In the process, this renders being seen *at* risk interchangeable with being seen *as* risk and these risk identities increasingly impossible to ever grow free from.

Part III focuses on digital practices connected with potentials for criminality or deviant behaviour. This section on *(Mis)Behaving: Suspects and Deviants* sees the application of digital technologies in the on-going process of identifying persons or practices deemed subversive or problematic. It is not surprising then that a fair bit of focus both in practice and in these collected chapters examines children and youth as a key concern. They are of a particularly intensive involvement in today's digitization of identification, and the first two chapters in this section are both on 'problem youth.'

Francisca Grommé's description of Burgcity and their pilot study into data mining examines in context the processes and problems of finding problem youth through the combination of various data sources. She looks specifically at the process of focusing or 'zooming in' on these problem youth that, as a metaphor, remains problematic. She argues that this metaphor both reinforces the need for ever more data collection and maintains embedded and problematic normativities inherent in data-mining practices. What emerges clearly from her analysis is how the digital practice of 'zooming in' requires 'situated improvisations' to become meaningful, resulting in the creation rather than (closer) observation of that object of concern, 'problem youth.'

Vlad Niculescu-Dinca, Irma van der Ploeg, and Tsjalling Swierstra's chapter then continues this focus on normative issues by looking at technological developments and policy transformations in contemporary policing. For years now, the Dutch police have prioritized the issue of 'problem youth,' and this chapter examines how this increasingly has come to involve monitoring and 'mapping' of youth groups of concern with geographical information systems and social media monitoring technologies. The authors show how these technological practices play a constitutive role in the ways in which youth groups are performed as 'problematic' and even in the definition of what counts as a 'group.' The authors note that in this context, the police use the notion of 'crime displacement' to explain why they see fewer 'problematic groups' on the streets while justifying more intensive monitoring and data collection; thus these practices are seen to perform new forms of 'suspects' and 'suspicious behaviours.'

Shifting away from the issue of problematic youth, Peter Lauritsen examines new practices involving the use of CCTV and the identification of criminal perpetrators. Lauritsen looks at the idea that more crimes will be solved at a low cost because of the cameras as a 'folk theory'—something that, although it lacks empirical support, still serves as an engine for future action. In his chapter, Lauritsen further questions the effectiveness of CCTV in police work by using the concept of 'oligopticon' to interpret the empirical findings, noting how the surveillance process envisioned by folk theories of CCTV is always dependent upon limited and fragile networks. What emerges from this study of CCTV use is that it does not provide a holistic view of criminal activity or an effective prevention strategy but is rather about establishing a vision that occasionally may help the police to identify a suspect.

Each of these chapters looks at how digital technologies are used to establish particular persons and groups of persons as suspicious and carefully analyses the less-than-straightforward way this happens. 'Zooming in,' 'crime displacement,' and 'folk theories' are the concepts used to make sense of these practices and to highlight their normative implications, given their significance for police interventions and actions.

Finally, Part IV *On the Move: Migrants and Travellers* focuses on an area of digital identification dense with global socio-political, legal, and ethical tension: (international) mobility. For all the many and diverse reasons people may travel, be it as tourists, refugees, labor migrants, or displaced by natural disasters, governments are exerting themselves to keep track of their movements. The desire to control cross-border mobility, to know who enters the territory, and to separate the trustworthy from potential threats, the ones needing protection and help from the ones requiring to be stopped and apprehended, has engendered elaborate digital identification and monitoring infrastructures.

The chapter by Peter Adey and Philip Kirby starts with a special form of mobility relatively neglected in the scholarly literature so far: evacuees from natural disaster–stricken areas. After briefly outlining the historical emergence of disaster-management systems in the Second World War, they describe how the catastrophically failed emergency management during the Hurricane Katrina disaster gave rise to a new generation of evacuation-management systems, from which emerges 'the digital evacuee.' While the authors document the disastrous results from failing to adequately track and trace people on the move—an aspect receiving little attention from surveillance scholars—they also point out how a highly abstracted representation of evacuees within even the new systems fails to perform them as embodied social beings, with highly problematic consequences.

Next, Dennis Broeders and Huub Dijstelbloem take on the more general issue of international migration policy, specifically in the European context. They observe how a range of technological developments, which they characterise in terms of 'datafication,' have changed not merely the way policies are executed but the process of policy making itself, including the nature of the actors involved in that process, as well as the perception and definition of the problems to be addressed. Using actor-network theory's notion of 'centers of calculation,' they address the question how the role of the state, as key responsible actor in migration and mobility management, changes as a result.

Karolina La Fors-Owczynik and Irma van der Ploeg, finally, look into the way these same systems play out locally when used by immigration, border management, and other law enforcement authorities. Describing three specific risk-assessment systems migrants may come into contact with in the Netherlands, the authors analyse how their design and operation affect the needs and rights of those subjected to them. On the basis of these empirical examples, they conclude that these systems contribute to an erosion of the distinction between perceptions of migrants as potentially being at risk and posing a risk, while an over-optimistic belief in these technologies' functionality simultaneously exposes these already vulnerable groups to new types of hazards.

The overall aims of this book are to increase understanding and awareness of the more problematic aspects of digital identification practices and to contribute to the quality of academic and policy debates about social and ethical acceptability of these technological developments. We hope to achieve these goals by bringing together the work of a set of exemplary scholars, using insights gained from several disciplines to bear on contemporary developments in digital identification, thus offering novel ways to identify and articulate the issues concerned. With this series of chapters reporting empirical studies on a range of domains in which digital identification is at the centre of innovation efforts, the book offers state-of-the-art, fine-grained knowledge of the ways digital technologies of identification are implicated in contemporary transformations of identity.

REFERENCES

AKRICH, M. (1992) The De-scription of Technical Objects. In Bijker, W. E. & Law, J. (eds.) *Shaping Technology/Building Society—Studies in Sociotechnical Change*. Cambridge (MA): The MIT Press, 205–224.

AKRICH, M. & LATOUR, B. (1992) A Summary of a Convenient Vocabulary for the Semiotics of Human and Nonhuman Assemblies. In Bijker, W. E. & Law, J. (eds.) *Shaping Technology/Building Society—Studies in Sociotechnical Change*. Cambridge (MA): The MIT Press, 259–264.

BARNARD-WILLS, D. (2012) *Surveillance and Identity. Discourse, Subjectivity, and the State*. Farnham: Ashgate.

BLUMER, H. (1969) *Symbolic Interactionism: Perspective and Method*. Englewood Cliffs, NJ: Prentice-Hall.

BLANCHETTE, J.-F. & JOHNSON, D. G. (2002) Data Retention and the Panoptic Society: The Social Benefits of Forgetfulness. *The Information Society*, 18(1). p. 1–13.

BOWKER, G. C. & STAR, S. L. (1999) *Sorting Things Out. Classification and Its Consequences*. Cambridge, MA, London: MIT Press.

BRUBAKER, R. & COOPER, F. (2000) Beyond Identity. *Theory and Society*, 29(2000). p. 1–47.

BUTLER, J. (1990) *Gender Trouble: Feminism and the Subversion of Identity*. New York: Routledge.

CLARKE, R. (1994) The Digital Persona and Its Application to Data Surveillance. *The Information Society*, 10(2). p. 77–92.

COOLEY, C. H. (1902) *Human Nature and the Social Order*. Scribner: New York.

FOUCAULT, M. (1979) *Discipline and Punish: The Birth of the Prison*. Harmondsworth: Penguin.

———. (1988) *The History of Sexuality, Vol. 3: The Care of the Self. Vol. 3*. New York: Random House LLC.

GANDY, O. H. (1993) *The Panoptic Sort: A Political Economy of Personal Information*. Boulder (CO): Westview Press.

GIDDENS, A. (1991). *Modernity and Self-Identity: Self and Society in the Late Modern Age*. Stanford (CA): Stanford University Press.

GOFFMAN, E. (1959) *The Presentation of Self in Everyday Life*. New York: Anchor Books.

GUTWIRTH, S. (2008) Beyond Identity? *Identity in the Information Society*, 1(1). p. 123–133.

HARAWAY, D. J. (1991). *Simians, Cyborgs, and Women: The Reinvention of Nature*. London: Free Association Books.

LYON, D. (Ed.) (2003). *Surveillance as Social Sorting: Privacy, Risk, and Digital Discrimination*. London/New York: Routledge.

LATOUR, B. (1993) *We Have Never Been Modern*. Cambridge (MA): Harvard University Press.

LAW, J. (Ed.) (1991) *A Sociology of Monsters: Power, Technology and the Modern World*. Oxford: Basil Blackwell.

MEAD, G.H. (1932) *Mind, Self and Society from the Standpoint of a Social Behaviorist*. Chicago: University of Chicago Press.
MOL, A. (2002) *The Body Multiple: Ontology in Medical Practice*. Durham (NC): Duke University Press.
MONAHAN, T. (Ed.) (2006) *Surveillance and Security: Technological Politics and Power in Everyday Life*. New York: Routledge.
NORRIS, C. & ARMSTRONG, G. (1999) *The Maximum Surveillance Society. The Rise of CCTV*. Oxford: Berg.
PFITZMANN, A. (2007) *An Introduction to Digital Identity*. Keynote lecture. OECD Workshop on Digital Identity Management. Trondheim, Norway, May 8–9.
RICOEUR, P. (1990) *Time and Narrative. Vol. 1*. Chicago, London: University of Chicago Press.
SCHECHTMAN, M. (1990) Personhood and Personal Identity. *Journal of Philosophy*, 87(2). p. 71–92.
TURKLE, S. (1984) *The Second Self: Computers and the Human Spirit*. New York: Simon and Schuster.
TURKLE, S. (1995) *Life on the Screen: Identity in the Age of the Internet*. New York: Simon and Schuster.

Part I

Sharing and Connecting

Friends and Consumers

1 The Touristic Practice of Performing Identity Online

Anders Albrechtslund and Anne-Mette Albrechtslund

INTRODUCTION

Since the early days of the social Internet in the 1990s, scholars have been concerned with how we perform identity and make sense of ourselves online. Observing how communication in online settings is always dependent on some form of symbolic mediation, usually text and images, it appears that identity needs to be created and "composed", as Sherry Turkle has put it (see 2002, 101; see also Albrechtslund, 2010). The idea of multiple, fragmented identities which online personas permit as something useful and liberating, undermining many traditional ideas about identity, connects to Donna Haraway's famous myth of the cyborg as a hybrid identity in a utopian reality where people are "not afraid of permanently partial identities and contradictory standpoints" (1991, 154).

However, although Turkle argued for the intimate connection between what we do online and what we do in real life, she still represents a view on the Internet, especially prevalent in early Internet studies, which separates virtuality and reality, when writing, for example: "We can use the virtual to reflect constructively on the real" (2002, 109). This tradition sees possibilities for expressing and exploring multiple identities in 'cyberspace', the famous term coined by William Gibson in his novel *Neuromancer* (1984). Cyberspace as metaphor designates a frontier-like abstract space, removed from the real, physical world as we know it, an exotic, mythologized space where users could be free of the limitations of the body, time, geographical boundaries, and so on (Finnemann, 2005, 11). Such utopian perceptions of cyberspace have been criticized from several angles as different Internet researchers have taken a more nuanced view on cyberspace. For example, Annette Markham has demonstrated an understanding of the many different ways people perceive what it is to be online, identifying a continuum of experiencing cyberspace as a tool to a place to simply a way of being (1998, 87). Following Markham's distinctions, we might say that today, the Internet has become a way of being, or perhaps even more accurate, the Internet has become an integrated element in our way of being and cannot be isolated in the form of 'cyberspace'.

Even though communities and social networks are relatively new phenomena in relation to the Internet, there already exists a large volume of studies about activities, technologies, services, communication, and critical issues. These Internet studies are diverse in approach, scope, and focus. However, most studies share an interest in concrete practices of Internet users. Our current study connects to this interdisciplinary field, as it draws on qualitative and analytical methods to investigate online social networking practices. Here, we offer an exploratory and interpretive study focusing on the typical activities related to the use of social media. By analysing these activities in terms of touristic practices, we hope to contribute to the understanding and conception of identity performance via online social networking practices.

In this chapter, we explore and analyse online sociality as a touristic practice to provide a new way of understanding how identity is produced and performed in a network of diverse and dynamic actors. Online sociality mainly unfolds within peer-to-peer social networking services, such as Facebook, Twitter, and Foursquare, as well as Internet communities centred on common interests, such as online games, music, or sports. There are at least two reasons for applying this approach. First, a number of similarities between practicing online sociality and practicing tourism can be readily identified. These include both technologies such as the camera and practices such as 'postings' (as in Facebook status updates and postcards, respectively). Second, by exploring these similarities further, our ambition is to emphasize certain dynamics in online social practices which are otherwise not immediately recognizable. For instance, the tourist engages in a range of activities (sightseeing, photographing, sending postcards, etc.) which appear "in some sense unnecessary" but can be seen as part of a meaningful exchange between everyday life and the vacation (Larsen, 2008; Urry and Larsen, 2011, 1). Correspondingly, the user of social media typically performs seemingly unnecessary activities (sharing mundane moments, photos, thoughts, and links) which nonetheless can be interpreted as a catalysing practice producing meaning and identity (A.M. Albrechtslund, 2011). This approach can help us better understand the popularity of social media and the easy incorporation of such practices into everyday living in spite of the many perceived dangers (e.g. privacy invasion, online predators) and negative consequences (e.g. time waste, corporate exploitation; A. Albrechtslund, 2008). As such, our purpose is to situate social media practices and the performance of digital identity in existing cultural practices by pointing out similar dynamics.

In the following, we introduce an analytical framework by characterizing a number of key features of the dynamics of touristic practices, drawing on insights from the academic literature and observations of tourism in Paris. The complementarity of online sociality and touristic practice then forms the basis for our key analytical points. Finally, we use these points to explore the production and performance of identity across different sites of online sociality, and we conclude with a discussion of some of the issues emerging from the results of our approach.

DYNAMICS OF TOURISTIC PRACTICES

The study of modern mass tourism includes a wide variety of theories, concepts and empirical focal points, and in this section, we draw especially on tourism studies influenced by cultural and sociological theories, in particular John Urry's *The Tourist Gaze* (Urry and Larsen, 2011) as well as Roland Barthes's *The Eiffel Tower* (1983). We will elaborate on four selected phenomena of special interest: the sight, the tourist, the camera, and the postcard. These constitute key elements of the touristic experience, which are all interrelated and very useful for building our analytical framework.

The Sight

Surfacing from the Trocadéro underground metro station in Paris's 16th arrondissement, the first thing which catches the eye is a colourful kiosk selling tourist artefacts, pancakes, and ice cream, surrounded by people with cameras and faces generally turned in one specific direction; it is actually possible to see the tourist attraction prior to it appearing before your eyes. After turning left around one wing of the Palais de Chaillot onto the crowded paved platform, the Eiffel Tower, more than 500 meters away, appears as a spectacular and overwhelming sight. A closer look reveals that many of these people are in fact not looking at the tower but have their backs turned towards it; they are posing in front of a photographer who is working to include both the person and the tower in an all-encompassing picture. As one continues towards the attraction down the stairs and through the Jardins de Trocadéro, passing more tourists and ice cream stands, the tower grows before the eyes, and it becomes increasingly difficult to capture it in a single gaze. Finally, the tourists arrive at the foot of the Eiffel Tower.

The curious thing is that there is no real *inside* to visit, as Roland Barthes concludes (1983). In fact, it might be said that the monument is "utterly useless" (238), as it does not serve any reasonable purpose other than to attract tourists. This has been the case since its construction in the 1880s, when Gustave Eiffel himself found it necessary to defend the contested usefulness of the tower, including different kinds of scientific research and meteorological observations. However reasonable these claims are, "they seem quite ridiculous alongside the overwhelming myth of the Tower, of the human meaning which it has assumed throughout the world" (239). In other words, the Eiffel tower and other sights have no useful function such as a road or an airport, but this does not imply that the tourist sight is meaningless. The distinction between usefulness and meaning is important, because it anticipates the point that the tourist attraction is more than just an object to see; rather, the sight is a catalyst for a more complex tourist experience.

This corresponds to John Urry's characterization of modern mass tourism as essentially *unnecessary* (Urry and Larsen, 2011). Urry compares the relation between everyday life and tourism with Michel Foucault's study of the relation between normality and illness in *The Birth of the Clinic* (1973), where studying deviation at the same time provides a perspective on normality. In a similar way, the study of tourism—where people are separated from their ordinary circumstances—gives insight into everyday life as well as society, since tourism is at the same time in opposition to and a product of everyday life. Accordingly, tourism is meaningful as a part of modern experience, even though it is unnecessary, and tourist attractions are essentially useless.

"Then why do we visit the Eiffel Tower?," Roland Barthes asks, and he answers:

> No doubt in order to participate in a dream of which it is (and this is its originality) much more the crystallizer than the true object. The Tower is not a usual spectacle; to enter the Tower, to scale it, to run around its courses, is, in a manner both more elementary and more profound, to accede to a view and to explore the interior of an object (though an openwork one), to transform the touristic rite into an adventure of sight and of the intelligence. (Barthes, 1983, 241)

Tourism thus encompasses a ritualistic practice in the sense that sightseeing can be a form of appropriation. In the case of the Eiffel Tower, this attraction is an "obligatory monument" (247) for the tourist to see Paris. As Barthes puts it, the tourist must perform an "initiational tribute" (248) when visiting the city for the first time to be able to claim to have *seen* Paris. There is a double meaning to 'seeing Paris' here, as the view from the tower obviously provides a great panorama of the city; however, the ritualistic practice of visiting the tourist attraction involves a translation into knowledge on a more symbolic level of apprehending a certain meaning of Paris.

The Eiffel tower, one of the most-visited and famous monuments in the world, can be understood as the archetype of a tourist attraction. What constitutes this as a *sight*—irrational, useless, but certainly meaningful—is its facilitation of the touristic experience, the tourist's participation in a dream, as Barthes puts it. Thus the sight is nothing without the sightseeing; the tourist's job is to perform it through a specific set of actions.

The Tourist

When you enter the Rue des Francs Bourgeois in Paris's Marais district, it feels like stepping onto a trail towards something. The intimate, quiet atmosphere of the small streets of this neighbourhood are intersected by more populated stretches connecting to the Place des Vosges, the oldest square in the city, celebrated for its architectural beauty, its famous historic residents and literary associations, including Alexandre Dumas's three musketeers. People yielding cameras and backpacks are immediately recognizable as tourists, many studying maps and guidebooks. The tourist trail towards the Place des Vosges is not an official, designated route to the tourist attraction. However, the crowds seem to follow some invisible road signs that organize the Marais into sections that are crowded and others almost left alone by tourists.

The figure of the tourist is a well-known stereotype with a broad variation of local flavours. For example the 'American tourist,' loud-speaking adults wearing shorts, baseball caps, and Hawaiian shirts, or the 'Japanese tourist,' travelling in large groups, always snapping photographs. Although these stereotypes of course rarely correspond directly to reality, tourists do tend to stand out in street life due to certain conducts, appearances, and activities. Not to imply that any single feature immediately identifies a person as a tourist; however, a number of little things often indicate something separated from the mundane practices of locals. For example, a man entering a Parisian bakery wearing his backpack on his front so as to avoid pickpockets might display a certain unfamiliarity with his surroundings. Or a family moving slowly, side by side, down the sidewalk of a crowded street, not adapting to the polite, observant, and fast-paced rhythm of the Parisians.

This is, of course, not to say that tourists are unaware of appearing 'touristic' and, essentially, not being local. Self-conscious and playful attitudes towards the practice of sightseeing itself can often be observed to the point at which it is possible to talk about a kind of post-tourism (Urry and Larsen, 2011, 13). This connects to another characteristic of the modern tourist experience: that it can hold both the genuine and the tacky. On the one hand the tourist's ritualistic practice is a search for the experience of something true or authentic, for example 'the romance of Paris'; however, the very same dream can just as well become part of the cliché of Paris, reproduced in tourism advertisements. The authentic and the inauthentic can be sought after or enjoyed by the tourist even as part of the same experience, and both can be part of the production of meaning.

When tourists gather on the Place des Vosges or take in the view of the Eiffel Tower from the Palais de Chaillot, they tend to do a number of things: They either move slowly or linger in the same spot, they study guidebooks and maps, interact with their travel companions, and display a blend of focused seriousness and light-hearted playfulness. A noticeable activity is, of course, the posing and photographing—or, to put it another way, the searching for and selecting motifs and angles that adequately capture the experience. In his book, Urry develops an understanding of the "tourist gaze" as a particular way of looking at the world which translates certain things into sights (Urry and Larsen, 2011). This gaze is not an individual perspective but is a product of many working actors, including guidebooks, others' experiences, local presentation, cultural signs, and general social patterning (4). Importantly, it is also a product of its relation to its opposite, such as the mundane activities of everyday life, indicating that the tourist gaze is always dependent on historical and societal circumstances.

The Camera

When one steps onto the Pont de la Tournelle towards the Ile Saint-Louis between the Latin Quarter and the Marais district, a beautiful view of the Notre Dame cathedral appears. This is a spot where especially tourists stop to take in the view. It seems as if the bridge has dynamic invisible fields into which tourists and accidental passers-by try to avoid stepping. These fields are constituted by the line between a photographer and one or more tourists posing in front of the view towards the attraction. Interestingly, such invisible fields seem to be generally respected as a private space, indicating that this is an important moment not to be disrupted. The photographer, the sight, and the poser(s) are all part of a network performing a ritual consisting of three acts. First, the spectacle is composed, poser(s) are arranged, and the right angle is found. Second, the photo is taken, mostly including several clicks, and third, the photographer and poser(s) gather to look at the picture(s) just taken, as if previewing the vacation photo album in the making. However, when this ritual has been performed, the invisible field disappears, and everything moves on again.

Modern mass tourism has been characterized as being a visual culture (Urry and Larsen, 2011, 14). Thus, photography has always been a central practice in the tourist experience, with the classic Kodak camera as iconic device (West, 2000). Like any other technology, the tourist camera has developed significantly through the decades; however, the change to digital photography in the last few years has arguably been the most important. At least, the third act of the ritual mentioned above is only made possible by the viewing display of the digital camera, just as it generally facilitates a wide range of sharing and distribution opportunities. Accordingly, the advent of digital photography in tourism has further emphasized the social aspect of taking pictures, making it a group activity. Interestingly, the recent explosion in the use of different types of camera phones and smartphones has apparently not yet eliminated the classic companion of the tourist, the single-purpose camera around the neck, although the types of devices are many, ranging from the semi-professional SLR models to the more compact pocket versions. This choice of technology seems to be reflected in the practice of photography, as taking tourist pictures does not seem to have the light, casual air to it as everyday smartphone use.

The tourist experience in all its phases is filled with pictures: studying guidebooks, brochures and online resources when planning where to go or researching the chosen destination. At the vacation spot, personalized pictures of tourist attractions and leisure activities are taken. After returning home to everyday life, the pictures are arranged and displayed in albums

(Larsen, 2005, 431). An obvious question to ask might be: Why take pictures of tourist attractions that have been photographed countless times already and are perhaps even on the cover of the brochure that launched the idea of going in the first place? Susan Sontag (1977) argues that photography is a way of grasping the world: "To photograph is to appropriate the thing photographed. It means putting oneself into a certain relation to the world that feels like knowledge—and, therefore, like power" (4). Taking pictures of the Notre Dame cathedral is therefore rarely about discovering a novel perspective or creating an original aesthetic work. Rather, the picture taking is a necessary act of appropriation both as a more abstract knowledge/power relation and as a concrete documentation of a moment for later retrospection.

The tourist photo is usually part of a collection of photos chronicling the vacation, and this collection always has a potential audience. The photo album thus serves as a point of departure for a narrative structured around the events or sights which the selection of photos has emphasized as the most important. As such, the individual photo is always part of a larger network consisting of other pictures, memories, stories, other people, and so forth. This also means that the tourist vacation is connected to everyday life through pictures:

> "Tourist photography and everyday life are not separate worlds but bridges constantly traversed by photographing tourists on the move. It is a form of photography intricately bound up with performing social relations and picturing co-travelling 'significant others', which also means that many otherwise 'ordinary' places are transformed into dramaturgical landscapes" (Larsen, 2008, 431).

The tourist album is the key element in this bridging between vacation and everyday life, and, today, it comes in a variety of forms. As another consequence of the change to digital photography, the photo album can be shared with selected friends, family, or networks where a co-narration can take place through comments, shares, and 'likes' (Facebook). Accordingly, the social aspect of tourist photography has been brought to the foreground by the emergence of online social networks.

The Postcard

Arriving at the Funiculaire Gare Haute, the upper station of the little tram line that helps you get up the many stairs of the Montmartre, the Sacré-Coeur Basilica appears on your right hand. The imposing church is one of the major tourist sights in Paris, but, like the Eiffel Tower, it also attracts tourists because it offers a great panoramic view of the city. After visiting this site, many tourists pass along one side of the church and then turn left on the Rue du Chevalier de la Barre, where a noticeable tourist trail towards the Place du Tertre begins. This surrounding area is densely packed with restaurants and shops selling tourist merchandise, collectibles, souvenirs, and postcards. Most often, the postcards are displayed on stands outside the shops and are, thus, a very eye-catching part of what tourists experience walking in these streets. Some stop to browse through these postcards, which are mostly inexpensive and can be hand picked from the stands or bought in preselected packages at a discount.

The postcard is not confined to being a phenomenon of mass tourism, as it has been an important aspect of modern communication needs since the early 20th century (Rogan, 2005, 3). A postcard is a single piece of paper or thin cardboard meant to be written and mailed without an envelope. However, the touristic postcard most often features a glossy photograph of a sight or location at the destination from which the tourist is mailing the card: for example, at the Place du Tertre many postcards present a photo of the Sacré Coeur Basilica. Other postcards feature images more symbolically connected to the destination, for example by alluding to the city's colourful past with reproductions of famous Toulouse-Lautrec posters such as 'Le chat noir.' Yet another type of postcard can offer more playful motifs, such as a simple black background with the generic text 'Paris by night.' The postcard is thus obviously a part of the visual culture of mass tourism but is also distinguished from photos, souvenirs, and so on by its emphasis on written communication.

As a communicative object, the touristic picture postcard is remarkable for its blending of private and public spheres. It contains a private message between a sender and a receiver familiar with each other, usually friends or family, but the open format makes this message potentially readable for anyone handling the card between the tourist and the recipient—for example, mail workers, other household members, and so forth. Moreover, the recipient conventionally displays the postcard in the home for guests to see and even sometimes read, emphasizing the semi-public nature of this type of communication. Like the tourist experience in general, the postcard is essentially unnecessary. The genre does not invite an intimate correspondence and, therefore, the content is often generic. However, sending a postcard is a meaningful action for the tourist as well as the recipient by being mailed from the vacation spot to friends or family, thus connecting the tourist to his everyday life and maintaining this relation as a communicative performance. This location-specific mailing of the postcard is what makes it meaningful, as the act of conveying the message that the tourist is currently vacationing and having experiences makes the communication phatic in nature (Jakobson, Pomorska, and Rudy, 1987; Rogan, 2005).

TOURISTIC PRACTICES AS ANALYTICAL FRAMEWORK

In the previous section we studied sights, tourists, cameras, and postcards and found certain characteristics that prevailed throughout these dynamic touristic practices. As Urry (and Larsen, 2011) has noted, tourism is essentially unnecessary but maintains a complicated and meaningful relationship with the 'real' life of the everyday (1). In this sense, the tourist vacation is not so much seen as an escape from reality or from what really matters but as something which is distinguished from but also created by everyday life. The tourist sight is rarely in itself a meaningful object but rather has a catalysing function similar to the 'MacGuffin,' a narrative plot device used especially in thrillers and whodunits (Truffaut, Hitchcock, and Scott 1985, 138). In such stories, this is usually an object desired and pursued by the protagonist; however, the reason for its desirability is rarely explained in detail,[1] but it remains an obligatory object motivating the moving forward of the plot. Like the Eiffel Tower in Barthes's analysis, the tourist sight is often in itself a 'useless' monument, but it plays a central role as a catalyser for the 'dream' in which the tourist wants to participate, that is, the modern mythology or popular story of Paris as the city of romance, art, and good living.

Just as the film spectator may be aware of the emptiness of the MacGuffin while still enjoying the thrill of the plot, the tourist often displays a quite self-conscious and sometimes even playful attitude towards sightseeing and the sight itself. At the same time, the tourist makes sure to uphold the acts of the touristic ritual, that is, taking pictures, lingering, and gazing at the view. Indeed, the photographing activities at the tourist site are rarely connected to aesthetic ambitions but are part of this catalysing process. Tourist photography, for instance, can function as a way of reaffirming significant social relations, both in the act of taking pictures of each other at the destination and of sharing them after having returned home (Larsen, 2005).

Another characteristic feature of touristic practices is that they serve as bridging mechanisms between seemingly distinct spheres. The photo album links the vacation experience with the context of everyday life by being a medium both for own reminiscence and for communicating the experience to others. The photo album is thus not only an example of tourism as constituting a primarily visual culture, it also highlights the social nature of most touristic practices. Further, the bridging mechanism can also produce a blending of public and private, as the semi-public nature of the postcard illustrates. When tourists appropriate attractions by taking personalized pictures, this practice is an example of something public becoming private by the creation of 'invisible fields' between poser and photographer which are respected as tiny private spheres in an otherwise very public space. These photos are again made semi-public when the photo album communicates the private experience to a broader audience through sharing with family, friends, or a network.

These two mechanisms, catalysing and bridging, are not simply accidental side effects of tourism but are central to the dynamics of the touristic practices we have studied and their production of meaning. In the following, they are used as analytical concepts to explore the practice of performing identity in online social settings with a special focus on posting, photo sharing, and location check-ins.

PERFORMING DIGITAL IDENTITIES

Engaging in online social activity can be said to always involve posting as a general activity which includes text communication, sharing of photos and other images, and, as a newer development, indicating a specific location at the time of posting. As such, posting something is the basis of online communication on diverse platforms such as blogs, message boards, and social network sites—the latter seeing a dramatic increase in user activity in recent years (Madden and Zickuhr, 2011). Focusing on the practice of posting rather than a more specific social network site activity is therefore productive for analysing the performance of online identity, as it offers a way to maintain a general perspective on online communication. We structure the following study around the two central features of our analytical framework, catalysing and bridging, as it is difficult to separate these diverse types of online activities.

The Useless as Catalyst

In their influential article from 2007, boyd and Ellison developed a definition of social network sites which emphasizes a semi-public profile, a list of connected users, and ability to browse and interact with this egocentric network of users. The personal profile thus plays a central role in this definition, as it was typically the point of reference in the design of the site, but today, it seems that the importance of the profile has diminished in favor of the flow of live updates from users in the network (A. Albrechtslund, 2011). This live content stream of 'statuses,' 'tweets,' or 'check-ins' is the de facto interface to social network sites such as Facebook, Google+, Twitter, and Foursquare.

In the section on tourist practices above, we discussed how the tourist engages in a range of activities (sightseeing, photographing, sending postcards, etc.) that seems essentially unnecessary but is part of a meaningful exchange between everyday life and the vacation. The tourist sight, as epitomized by the Eiffel Tower in Barthes's essay, is characterized by its inutility, something which seems to "escape reason" but is "something other and something much more than" (1983, 238) the object in itself. The question of why we visit these 'useless' monuments can be seen as addressing the same consternation regarding the use of online social services, where the user of social network sites typically performs seemingly unnecessary or superficial activities (sharing mundane moments, photos, thoughts, and links). While the type of content may vary across sites, postings are typically characterized by being compact, quick observations, descriptions, or opinions meant for continual reading. Although longer texts are allowed and produced on social network sites, Twitter's famous 140-character limit sets a standard for the genre of the status update. The content of the live stream, produced by users posting to the network, is rarely profound or thought provoking in itself. However, performing these activities can be interpreted as a catalysing practice producing meaning and identity.

If we understand identity as something performed (Butler, 1990) or continuously narrated (Ricoeur, 1988), a person's actions and statements in all aspects of life, such as clothing, hairstyle, general appearance, and behaviour, all contribute to both self-understanding and outward personality. Performing identity online is thus not to be seen as isolated from the general identity work but rather as an integral part of it. However, online social networking does offer a distinct way of connecting these identity performances that, in turn, produces something new.

To read and contribute to the live content stream involves a set of practices that produce a certain way of 'seeing' and understanding. Like the tourist gaze frames the experience of something as a sight to visit, online social networking produces a certain 'gaze' which translates experiences into something sharable which might attract 'likes' and comments. For example, a parent sharing a baby picture with a cute caption is an active and selective construction of a certain moment, which is different from a passive registration of the complete activities during a certain timespan. This is not to say that such postings are necessarily a rosy presentation of a moment, for example leaving out the baby screaming, diaper changes, and the like. The capture is an actively constructed depiction of this moment, produced not only by the individual perspective of the poster but rather as the result of a co-creation involving, for example others' comments, likes, the design of the site, and general experience with the genre of (baby photo) posting. Just as tourists can exhibit an ironic, self-aware attitude towards practicing the tourist gaze (cf. the so-called post-tourist), it is entirely possible—and quite common—to play around with the conventions of posting, but this awareness is also an affirmation of the existence of a certain 'gaze,' or what could be called "The Facebook Eye" (Jurgenson, 2012).

The social Internet space consists of diverse discourses and data. In the context of social network sites, the live content stream is primarily[2] constituted by postings from a given user's network of contacts, shaping the communicative space in which the user participates. While other kinds of social sites such as web forums and blogs are not usually customized to the individual user in this way, they similarly provide a specific framework for social interaction. It is a distinctive feature of social network sites that, for example, baby photos, links to news articles, photos of silly cats, discussions about sports, and location specifications blend together in a continual flow. Meaning is produced across these various discourses as the practice of online sociality unfolds. Postings from both private and professional life may form part of an ongoing production of identity in which each contribution to the content stream can have a catalysing function. The specific framework for such a meaningful identity online can be described as a co-constructed way of understanding and performing sociality (Larsen and Ryberg, 2011). In other words, our social life is also experienced under the conditions of a certain gaze resembling that of the tourist. This gaze is totalizing because it assembles a variety of actors and circumstances into a composite vehicle for continuous identity performance and narration.

Bridging the Gaps

Reminiscent of the way in which the tourist leaves behind everyday life and goes on vacation, online socializing involves a range of conceptual divisions and dualities such as online/offline, private/public, real/virtual, professional/personal—an issue which has remained a central matter in Internet research for many years (Silver, 2000; boyd & Ellison, 2007; Baym, 2010). As mentioned, identity is produced through many different elements in the practice of online sociality, as both posting updates, photos, and links and taking part in different interactions constitute a continuous circulation of information. Identity performance online thus always unfolds in relation to a hybrid and transient totality. In the following, we will elaborate on this dynamic and discuss how the individual engages in a constant interpretation and negotiation, bridging the gaps experienced as a result of these perceived divisions and dualities.

Seemingly distinct spheres are constantly bridged in the practice of online sociality. The division between public and private spheres, for instance, is at the heart of much discussion, confusion, and concern relating to Internet use. The more or less extensive sharing of personal information on social websites—activities, beliefs, preferences, whereabouts, family relations, and so on—creates a hybrid space in which public and private life is continually traversed and negotiated (Albrechtslund, 2008). Similarly, distinguishing between online and offline domains often entails a complex process of sorting out yet other divisions and dualities, including real/virtual, authentic/inauthentic, and natural/technological. The separation of such concepts often proves to be difficult when engaging with actual use, as Petersen (2007) has demonstrated in his study of the interweaving of materiality and online life, describing it as mundane cyborg practices in reference to Haraway (1991). While engaging in online sociality does not involve departing from the physical circumstances of everyday life as it does for the tourist on vacation, both practices share the persistent involvement with devices that maintain the social relations, context, and significance of everyday life and thus bridges these gaps.

The central touristic device of the postcard embodies the blending of spheres that are often perceived as separate, connecting vacation and everyday life as well as public and private communication. Reminiscent of this dynamic is the key practice of posting updates to online social sites. Seen as a bridging activity, the posting of any kind of content to, for example, Facebook's News Feed is an act of performing identity within the context of a network consisting of various social relations. Like the postcard, the status update is rarely about profound content but has more to do with the act of communicating and connecting in itself. Just as the postcard functions as a device to embed the vacation experience in the context of everyday life, the status update achieves meaning because it is part of a person's reality as a whole, not removed from it. Furthermore, the importance of mailing the postcard on location, and, correspondingly, posting the thought, comment, anecdote, and so on to the online network in a more or less immediate connection to the given situation is a testament to the way the meaning created by these acts results from a hybridity of physical and virtual space and of present and absent actors.

The same dynamics can be said to be at work in the practice of online photo sharing. This activity has become an increasingly significant element of posting in recent years and is manifesting in various interesting and playful ways, as the rise of services such as Instagram, Pinterest, and Snapchat show. Sharing personal photos online is thus a key bridging activity and an important catalyst for meaning production as well. The coalescence of intimacy and exhibition is similar in the practices of tourist photography and photo sharing, which are both characterized by transforming "configurations of the fields of cultural production in the context of new media, for which 'art', 'folk' and 'popular', as well as 'artist', 'professional' and 'amateur' are inadequate" (Burgess, 2007, 29). The creation of photo albums is at the same time a construction of a personal archive, driven by a sort of "nostalgia for the present" (Jurgenson, 2011) in which meaning is produced by "slicing out this moment and freezing it" (Sontag, 1977, 15), and a central device in the social dynamics of identity performance, producing and displaying social relations (Larsen, 2005).

CONCLUSION

It is important to stress that we do not claim any direct identification between online social networking and tourism such as a superficial statement that online social networking is 'the same' as tourism. Nor do we pretend that users of social media are 'everyday tourists' or even that tourism and online social networking can be reduced to a single type of practice carried out by a specific type of actor. Here, tourism purely serves as an analytical framework providing a point of departure that allows for a productive way of thinking about the everyday practices of social media.

What we have set out to do in this chapter is to identify the dynamics that are at play in the cultural practice of tourism in general and then to show how these dynamics are translatable and useful in relation to practices of online sociality. As these new practices emanate from and are embedded in our traditional cultural habits, it is hardly surprising that we are able to connect online sociality to a phenomenon such as mass tourism. Facebook,

Foursquare, and other social networking applications are new technologies that let us connect to our social networks in new ways. However, as we have shown, the dynamics driving these services look very familiar. There are a number of immediately apparent similarities between tourism and social media practices which inspired us to explore the connection further, namely the interesting blending of public and private spheres and the complex role of gratuitous activities in the mundane context of everyday life. Further analysis led us to articulate two concepts, catalysing and bridging, as a way to grasp how the seemingly unnecessary or even useless activities of online socializing are integrated in a meaningful performance of digital identity. In other words, when users of social media engage in what appears to be time-wasting, gullible, or escapist activities, they are also actively taking part in a meaningful enactment of identity in a network of social relations. This also means that identity performance is not understood as a fabrication or staging of the self,[3] where the 'real' or 'authentic' is somehow located behind the mask of social conduct.

Another pertinent similarity when considering touristic practices and online sociality is the political and economic issues; tourism is a major commercial industry, and so are social media. As such, the experience of vacation as well as online social networking is obviously embedded in a larger ideological framework which enables and shapes these practices. However, these structural issues alone do not answer the question of why we engage in these practices. Our study offers a way to understand the motivation behind them and thus what makes the industries possible in the first place. A narrow focus on ideological issues can have the unfortunate consequence of infantilizing the subject taking part in these activities and reducing the complexity of the meaning-producing practice of performing digital identities to an exploitative power relation. Rather, a closer look at these practices as an experience which is meaningful for the individual opens up a trajectory of thinking that provides new insights into the everyday life with the Internet.

NOTES

1. Famous examples include the 'secret microfilm' in Alfred Hitchcock's *North by Northwest* (1959), and the 'Maltese Falcon' in John Huston's film (1941).
2. Other content includes ads, promoted posts, and site updates.
3. Only if understood in Goffmanian terms (1959). Our understanding of identity in this chapter corresponds to Goffman's dramaturgical model of social interaction, which describes identity as a performance with varying degrees of social strictures and codes.

REFERENCES

ALBRECHTSLUND, A. (2008) Online Social Networking as Participatory Surveillance. *First Monday*, 13(3).

ALBRECHTSLUND, A (2011) Socializing the City: Location Sharing and Online Social Networking. In Fuchs, C., Boersma, K. & Sandoval, M. (eds.) *Internet and Surveillance The Challenges of Web 2.0 and Social Media*. New York: Routledge, 187–197.

ALBRECHTSLUND, A.M. (2010) Gamers Telling Stories: Understanding Narrative Practices in an Online Community. *Convergence: The International Journal of Research into New Media Technologies*, 16(1) (February). p. 112–124.

ALBRECHTSLUND, A.M. (2011) Online Identity Crisis: Real ID on the World of Warcraft Forums. *First Monday*, 16(7).

BARTHES, R. (1983) *A Barthes Reader*. New York: Hill and Wang.

BAYM, N.K. (2010) *Personal Connections in the Digital Age*. Cambridge: Polity Press.

BOYD, D. & ELLISON, N. (2007). Social Network Sites: Definition, History, and Scholarship. *Journal of Computer-Mediated Communication*, 13(1). p. 210–230.

BURGESS, J.E. (2007) *Vernacular Creativity and New Media*. Brisbane: Queensland University of Technology.

BUTLER, J. (1990) *Gender Trouble: Feminism and the Subversion of Identity*. New York: Routledge.

FINNEMANN, N.O. (2005). *Internettet i mediehistorisk perspektiv*. Copenhagen: Samfundslitteratur.

FOUCAULT, M. (1973) *The Birth of the Clinic*. London: Tavistock.

GOFFMAN, E. (1959) *The Presentation of Self in Everyday Life*. Garden City (NY): Doubleday.

HARAWAY, D. (1991) A Cyborg Manifesto: Science, Technology, and Socialist-feminism in the Late Twentieth Century. In *Simians, Cyborgs and Women: The Reinvention of Nature*. New York: Routledge. p. 149–182.

HITCHCOCK, A. (1959) *North by Northwest*. MGM Pictures.

HUSTON, J. (1941) *The Maltese Falcon*. Warner Bros.

JAKOBSON, R., POMORSKA, K. & RUDY, S. (1987) *Language in Literature*. Cambridge: Harvard University Press.

JURGENSON, N. (2011) The Faux-Vintage Photo. *Cyborgology*. Available from: http://thesocietypages.org/cyborgology/2011/05/14/the-faux-vintage-photo-full-essay-parts-i-ii-and-iii/. [Accessed 10–10–2012]

JURGENSON, N. (2012) The Facebook Eye. *The Atlantic*. Available from: www.theatlantic.com/technology/archive/2012/01/the-facebook-eye/251377/. [Accessed 12–10–12]

LARSEN, J. (2005) Families Seen Sightseeing: Performativity of Tourist Photography. *Space and Culture*, 8(4). p. 416–434.

LARSEN, J. (2008) Practices and Flows of Digital Photography: An Ethnographic Framework. *Mobilities*, 3(1). p. 141–160.

LARSEN, M.C., & RYBERG, T. (2011) Youth and Online Social Networking: From Local Experiences to Public Discourses. In Dunkels, E. & Fraanberg, G.M. (eds.) *Youth Culture and Net Culture: Online Social Practices*. Hershey (PA): IGI Global, 17–40.

MADDEN, M. & ZICKUHR, K. (2011) *65% of Online Adults Use Social Networking Sites*. PEW Internet & American Life Project. Washington (DC): PEW Research Center.

MARKHAM, A.N. (1998) *Life Online: Researching Real Experience in Virtual Space*. Lanham (MD): Rowman Altamira.

PETERSEN, S.M. (2007) Mundane Cyborg Practice: Material Aspects of Broadband Internet Use. *Convergence: The International Journal of Research into New Media Technologies*, 13(1). p. 79–91.

RICOEUR, P. (1988) *Time and Narrative. Vol. 3*. Chicago: University of Chicago Press.

ROGAN, B. (2005) An Entangled Object: The Picture Postcard as Souvenir and Collectible, Exchange and Ritual Communication. *Cultural Analysis*, 4(1). p. 1–27.
SILVER, D. (2000) Looking Backwards, Looking Forward: Cyberculture Studies 1990–2000. In Gauntlett, D. (ed.) *Web.studies: Rewiring Media Studies for the Digital Age*. Oxford: Oxford University Press. p. 19–30.
SONTAG, S. (1977) *On Photography*. New York: Macmillan.
TRUFFAUT, F., HITCHCOCK, A. & SCOTT, H. G. (1985) *Hitchcock*. New York: Simon and Schuster.
TURKLE, S. (2002) Our Split Screens. *Etnofoor*, 15(1/2). p. 5–19.
URRY, J. & LARSEN, J. (2011) *The Tourist Gaze 3.0*. London: Sage.
WEST, N. M. (2000) *Kodak and the Lens of Nostalgia*. Charlottesville: University of Virginia Press.

2 A Social API for That
Market Devices and the Stabilisation of Digital Identities

Jason Pridmore

INTRODUCTION

The mechanisms for transmitting and receiving data on the Internet have shifted. While early protocols and the use of hypertext transport protocol (http) remain in use, web browsers to mobile devices to operating systems increasingly rely upon applications to function. This chapter focuses on the process whereby data has been made accessible and usable by external applications—that of application programming interfaces (APIs). At the most basic level, APIs are the means by which different technologies are enabled to communicate with each other. They have been in use for many years, as they standardize the protocols for the information that can be retrieved, used, and amended by applications from an external resource. In a number of cases, and more importantly for the context of this book, increasingly this resource comes in the form of *social media* data. This chapter argues that these relatively obscure and unseen APIs, particularly those connected with social media, have significant implications for the conceptualization and development of digital 'identities' in our contemporary world. As social media is infusing itself into numerous aspects and domains of everyday life, these social media APIs are arguably becoming default arbitrators and mediators of 'identity.'

The increased popularity and availability of social media itself can in part be attributed to publicly available APIs, or rather, the applications that have been made to work on or through these interfaces (see Dix, 2011). The relatively recent orientation to applications, or apps as they are better known (popularized by a 2009 Apple iPhone advertisement with the phrase "There's an app for that"), have received significant attention from consumers and the media. However, the APIs they are based upon have received significantly less attention, despite the fact that an increasing number of APIs are available for a divergent number of sites, services, and resources (see Bodle, 2011). APIs are focused on potentials for interoperability and include commonly used 'tools' such as Google search, resources such as videos with YouTube or photos with Flickr, or social media like Twitter and LinkedIn. All of these allow their content or data to be 'embedded' onto an independent website or application through the use of their open API. One of the first and longest-lasting API successes, the Google Map API, became very popular as it allowed a number of different applications to integrate Google maps as a resource for their own purposes (Dix, 2011). More recently, Facebook's success as a platform (at least in historic terms of growing its user base and popularity over MySpace) has largely been attributed to its *public* API, particularly as it allowed for the implementation of third-party applications and the more recent development of what they call an 'Open Graph' protocol (Bodle, 2011; Jung and Lee, 2010; Dix, 2011).

The shift towards the development and use of *social media* APIs has happened more recently (concurrent with the growth of social media). The predominant use of APIs previously centred on developing tools and games that relied on data separated to some degree from individual persons. These include maps, images, and keywords. Yet the increased presence of social media and their publicly available APIs have allowed for the development of applications that can extract a variety of more personally identifiable information. APIs—as market devices (see what follows)—provide access to data in various forms, from more "transactional" data to "archives of the everyday" (see Beer and Burrows, 2013). They give certain but easily measurable and quantifiable sets of attributes, characteristics, practices, and more of those persons engaged in social media. These are records connected to a social media 'profile,' which can be seen as tantamount to a 'bricolage' of digital identity: status updates, relationships, friends, location, tagged photos, searches, reposts, 'likes,' and more are the 'materials at hand' in the intermingling of 'identity' production with digital technologies. This connection between identity and technology is inclusive of the idea that at the very least, identity is seen as some form of a fluctuating collection of *attributes (voluntarily) indicated to others* and those *characteristics attributed to and expected of us by other agents* (see Jenkins, 2008). Identity in this form is seen as *contingent* and *relational*, marking a transition from rather static notions of identity inherent in identity documents and identity provisions. Instead, social media allow for both indications and attributions to be collected and analysed in digital form, and it is APIs that have made this increasingly accessible.

The argument of this chapter is that APIs are market devices that stabilize the dynamic and constantly updated data of social media and serve to connect a number of different actors. They allow applications to access significant details about social media users and can act in a person's place, extending and amplifying their actions, relevance, and relationships in ways previously unknown. They make the dynamic constitution of identity measurable and quantifiable and continually updatable. Yet all the while these APIs remain out of sight and are only hinted at within the confines of a potentially singular encounter in which a social media participant grants permission to an application to access their personal profile. The chapter explores the relationship between the use of APIs and how this connects with the personal production or performance of identity through applications. APIs are key components in the socio-technical configuration of persons, social media databases, and applications that define and determine the technological transfer of data in ways hidden from people that use these various social media–'powered' applications. Though applications are most often convenient, engaging, and entertaining tools or resources, the relationship between information available through APIs and the production of contingent and relational digital identities needs to be made clearer.

The following sections in this chapter begin to do just this. First, this chapter describes APIs as 'market devices' that bring together people, activities, and technologies. Second, the permission process on the side of both developers and social media users of these market devices is shown to indicate the extent of identifiable data that becomes accessible through a singular acceptance 'click.' Though there are a number of relevant social media APIs, this section focuses specifically on the permission process by two of the largest social media providers, those of Facebook and Twitter. Next, given the availability of data from this process, the chapter highlights some of the analytical convergence of technology, consumption, social media, and identity in contemporary discussions. It notes that social media are important platforms upon which both self-identified and externally identified categorisations are created, produced, and imposed. This information yields a number of (partial) digital 'identities' that serve as representations for particular persons in particular contexts. The chapter then concludes by arguing that APIs are increasingly important and necessary components in socio-technical configurations of identity. The stabilize access to continually shifting and augmented digital 'identities' by allowing access to the dynamic and rich mixture of data and associations of social media participants. These can be seen as neither fully owned nor controlled by persons or a given system. Instead, a digital identity—or perhaps digital identities—are themselves contingent and relational and enacted in various social and technical ways that are beyond the range of either human or technical agency.

CONSUMPTION AND MARKET DEVICES

Social media are objects of consumption, yet their use has significantly shifted understandings of consumption towards cultural forms being seen as processes of 'prosumption.' This concept is at the very least a reaction that "the analytic distinction between consumption and production has often been overdrawn by social scientists" (Beer and Burrows, 2013, 49). Historically, descriptions of material or cultural production and consumption have reinforced rather mechanical and binary descriptions of markets—such as depictions of 'cultural dupes' and 'consumer choice.' The former—in the vein of Frankfurt School theorists—have focused attention on culture industries and the latter—in a more 'post-modern' vein—viewed consumption as a means of producing personal identity. These have largely ignored the co-constitution of consumption subjects and objects (see Miller, 1987) in their focus either on corporate power (through advertising, for instance) or assertions of consumer expression through the use of goods (in either anticipated or unanticipated ways). These descriptions have often disregarded the fluid and nuanced ways in which consumers and producers interact. Prosumption, in part, begins to point out the overlap already present in many areas of consumption and production, but most specifically it does so in connection with social media (Ritzer and Jurgenson, 2010).

More importantly for this chapter, there has been very little recognition of the role of *technology* in these 'prosumption' interactions. This chapter draws from an actor-network theory approach that "invites us to notice the broader networks that tend to include myriad sociotechnical devices" (Bajde, 2013, 10). Within networks, devices serve to stabilize a given configuration and reinforce certain sets of practices as valued and valuable. In this case, APIs as devices are better understood as market devices. *Market devices* "play a pivotal role in deploying and stabilizing special and temporal configurations" through which "consumption subjects and objects can come into being and relation" (ibid., 10). That is, in this case, APIs set the parameters around how information about social media participants can be accessed and produced within the 'marketplace' of social media data. They make this information both quantifiable and useable by simplifying interoperability and standardizing categories of activities in order to ease applications access and to reinforce and perpetuate social media use. Gerlitz and Helmond (2013) describe 'like' buttons in similar terms, noting how these have the capacity "to both metrify and intensify user affect and engagement by turning them into numbers" (1361).

Though market devices have increasingly been looked at in relation to market studies (Araujo et al., 2008), there have been limited analyses of these devices in connection with studies of consumption (Badje, 2013). By describing APIs as market devices, the focus here is on how these sets of protocols and categories can be seen as technical instruments that serve to bring together technologies, people, and activities. APIs are part of a configuration of activities that serve to construct an economic, social, and technical space. Within this space, everyday practices are documented and digitized, and APIs make this process accessible. This is largely for commercial purposes, if not on the part of the application that uses this data, certainly on the part of the social media corporation. As market devices, APIs are "material and discursive assemblages" that, given the position social media occupies in the various forms of contemporary capitalism, "intervene in the construction of markets" (Muniesa et al., 2007, 2). APIs can be seen to have fundamentally shifted the usefulness of social media by creating an accessible and systematically categorized dynamic archive of data. Some applications themselves are material and discursive assemblages and, as such, can be seen as market devices as well. However, they are predicated on APIs that allow data to make sense—to be categorized and classified in ways deemed useful.

For example, an application relies on an API to gain access to a user's posts or status updates on social media. This allows the owner of the application to learn the activities of social media users—whether they take notice of promotions, make references to a particular brand or company, or indicate an activity in which they regularly participate. A fitness company, for instance, can gain data through an application that tracks a participant's exercise routine and the posting of this on a social media. Or a media company can quantify the number of times a subscriber references their publications and begin to quantify the spread of a given story. This information is determined by the classification and categorization of activities deemed relevant by the social media, and its APIs 'ascribe' (see Akrich, 1992) a particular way in which this information is conceived of *and* retrieved. This information is constantly updated and made accessible so that the social media participant can be assessed historically and dynamically. Additionally, given their interactive capabilities, APIs similarly ascribe how an application may produce data on behalf of the user, such as posting updates, from articles read to exercise activities to personal location. As a marketing device, the ascription process for an application allows that application to see and produce "certain (but not all) things very well" (Badje, 80).

As market devices, APIs are objects with agency—these articulate the means by which applications can act and set the parameters around those actions (Muniesa et al., 2007, 2). They create an open architecture for sharing content and data between communities and applications that are increasingly seen as valuable. More specifically, in a context in which social media is increasingly integrated into everyday life, APIs stabilize the interactions among organizations, applications, and the dynamic practices of social media users. They are not simply intermediaries, but devices that determine the architecture of these interactions. In order to understand a bit better what this architecture looks like, we will look in the following section more specifically at the developer options and the permissions process seen by users.

APIs IN PRACTICE

As market devices, APIs sit at the intersection of social media participants (their activities, posts, and aspirations), technology developers and their platforms, and those that seek to use the information being produced within social media for particular goals. This latter group includes marketers, politicians, social activists, social scientists, and more. The normative expectations embedded into system design (see Madrigal, 2013), anticipated by users and shaped through everyday consumption of and within social media, are becoming an increasingly crucial resource for understanding and arguably guiding people's everyday lives. This resource allows for the interpretation of social media user profiles into various forms of social, economic, political, and geographic categories (as well as many others). APIs are the means by which this information is made accessible and continually updateable.

There is a proliferation of APIs across a variety of technologies—currently more than 11,000—with a number of applications or 'mashups' that rely on multiple APIs to accomplish certain integrated technology and software goals (see www.programmableweb.com). Not all of these APIs are forms of social media; in fact, most are focused on less 'social' data, such as maps or statistics, for instance (the Google Maps API remains the most widely used API). However, this chapter focuses on social media and, specifically, two of the largest social media providers, that of Facebook and Twitter.

While a majority of social media 'enhanced' interactions are dependent upon APIs, some are simply part of the internal social media environment itself. Along with and integrated into APIs, these tools allow for extended information gathering and dissemination through social media. They make it possible to allow people to keep up with the latest trends, information, products, and services offered by a number of brands, for instance via the 'like' button on Facebook, 'following' an organization on Twitter, the "check in" feature of Foursquare, the 'pin-it' feature for Pinterest, and more generally the ability to share content with others. The information produced and distributed by these are dependent on the way in which social media have set up the interface between users and these organizations, but most of this occurs internally.

However, to access and use relevant data produced by and about social media participants (including the internal features) beyond the enclosed social media environment, websites, organizations, and marketers rely on applications that interface with social media data. The API determines the mechanics of accessing data.

For most APIs, after an initial agreement, the more 'technical' aspects of the connections among the social media participant, the application, and the social media provider, quickly disappear. None of the technical complexity that underpins these devices is evident. Once activated, the agreement to 'connect' or 'log in' (or other mechanisms that rely on APIs) permits consumer access to specific branded content, features, and services that are available both on social media and proprietary websites. In many cases, this permission process also allows these organizations significant and continual access to the user's social media profile and the ability to alter these profiles, post 'messages' or 'status updates' for them, geographically locate them, and more. It is this initial moment of application request and user acceptance that is of particular interest for this chapter.

The singular 'click' that indicates a user accepts the terms and conditions for the application, including what an application can access or do in relation to the social media profile, is the initial moment through which software components and data are enabled to communicate with each other. These are based on the protocols or rules set out within an API (for further information, see 3 Scale 2011: "What is an API? Your Guide to the Internet (R)evolution" and Anonymous 2014: "API versus Protocol"). For social media, the relevant data held by providers is connected with external applications and systems that can make use of this information. The permission process through which an application can access and produce data is crucial; from this point forward, applications appear to be seamlessly integrated with social media resources, and the permission request only appears again in very limited circumstances.

So what does this primary access look like—how does it appear? What is the process by which an application obtains a social media participant's permission to access and amend his or her data? And what data is available? As the API is predetermined by the social media platform, there are two main processes through which an application begins to interact with social media data—either accessing user data or amending their profile. On the one side, the application developer has to select certain features and requirements for the social media participant to accept, and on the other side this person must accept these requirements by granting permission to the application to access their data. What follows details both the application developer's view and the consumer acceptance process for both Facebook and Twitter. Though the uses of their APIs are not always the largest by volume, they are perhaps the best-known *social* media APIs.

Application Developers' View

In the case of Facebook, an application may require the social media to act as a form of 'identity' verification (sign-in), be used for a particular game portal, allow for personalized content, or produce certain consumer analytics. By default, applications that are given access (permission) receive the following pieces of basic data: 'id name,' 'first_name,' 'last_name,' 'link,' 'username,' 'gender,' and 'locale'—this is described as 'public data' in what follows. More information can be requested of the user through specific permissions through the Facebook Open Graph API. Figures 2.1, 2.2, and 2.3 indicate the additional information an application developer can request from users through Facebook.

These additional permissions encompass more than 70 data fields beyond a user's basic public profile information. Given the increased reliance upon social media for personal expression and connections to others, these fields are intimately connected to the 'who' a person is in terms of characteristics and attributes, the way a person is identified, and the relationships she may have. Based on the data in these fields, an application can gather rather significant amounts of information that is available about its users.

Twitter's current REST (representational state transfer) API does not package the data that can be accessed by using their interface in the same way as Facebook. Rather, all the accessible data by applications can be retrieved

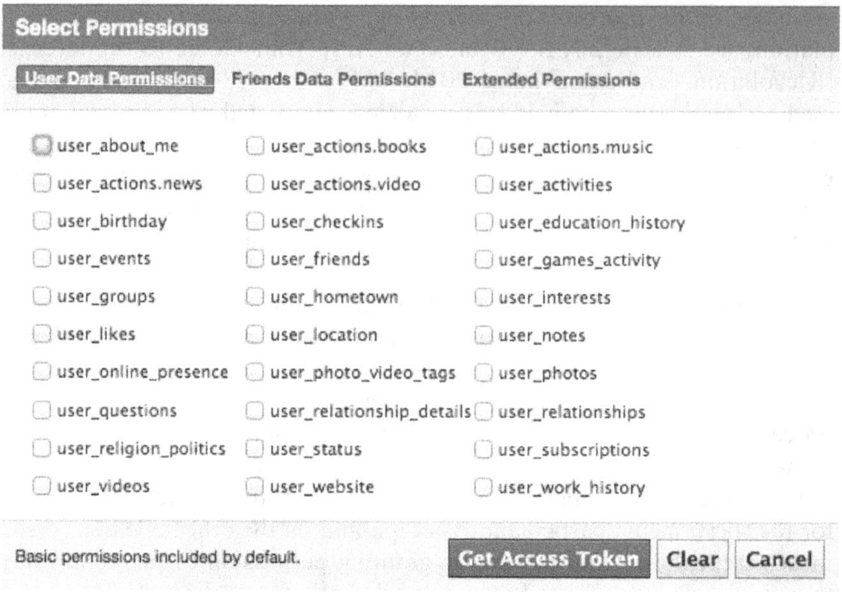

Select Permissions

User Data Permissions | Friends Data Permissions | Extended Permissions

user_about_me	user_actions.books	user_actions.music
user_actions.news	user_actions.video	user_activities
user_birthday	user_checkins	user_education_history
user_events	user_friends	user_games_activity
user_groups	user_hometown	user_interests
user_likes	user_location	user_notes
user_online_presence	user_photo_video_tags	user_photos
user_questions	user_relationship_details	user_relationships
user_religion_politics	user_status	user_subscriptions
user_videos	user_website	user_work_history

Basic permissions included by default. Get Access Token Clear Cancel

Figure 2.1 Data permissions for users

Source: publicly available developer interface form from Facebook

Select Permissions

User Data Permissions | Friends Data Permissions | Extended Permissions

friends_about_me	friends_actions.books	friends_actions.music
friends_actions.news	friends_actions.video	friends_activities
friends_birthday	friends_checkins	friends_education_history
friends_events	friends_games_activity	friends_groups
friends_hometown	friends_interests	friends_likes
friends_location	friends_notes	friends_online_presence
friends_photo_video_tags	friends_photos	friends_questions
friends_relationship_details	friends_relationships	friends_religion_politics
friends_status	friends_subscriptions	friends_videos
friends_website	friends_work_history	

Basic permissions included by default. Get Access Token Clear Cancel

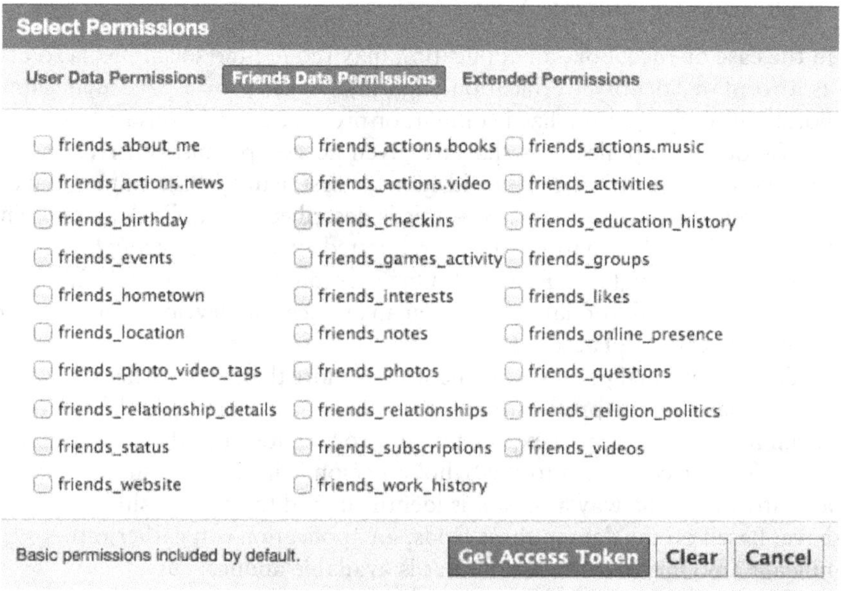

Figure 2.2 Data permissions regarding friends of users

Source: publicly available developer interface form from Facebook

Select Permissions

User Data Permissions | Friends Data Permissions | Extended Permissions

ads_management	ads_read	create_event
create_note	email	export_stream
manage_friendlists	manage_notifications	manage_pages
photo_upload	publish_actions	publish_checkins
publish_stream	read_friendlists	read_insights
read_mailbox	read_page_mailboxes	read_requests
read_stream	rsvp_event	share_item
sms	status_update	video_upload
xmpp_login		

Basic permissions included by default. Get Access Token | Clear | Cancel

Figure 2.3 Extended data permissions requested from users
Source: publicly available developer interface form from Facebook

or posted for the Twitter user based on data from the following categories, which contain some 80+ 'GET' or 'POST' commands: Timelines, Tweets, Search, Streaming, Direct Messages, Friends & Followers, Users, Suggested Users, Favorites, Lists, Saved Searches, Places & Geo, Trends, Spam Reporting, OAuth (Open Authorization), and Help. For instance, under the Friends & Followers category, the GET friends/list request can be used to return "a cursored collection of user objects for every user the specified user is following (otherwise known as their 'friends')" https://dev.twitter.com/docs/api/1.1/get/friends/list). That is, information on a limited number (currently 30) of a Twitter user's followers can be accessed by an application once that Twitter user has given permission to the application. Or using the POST statuses/update allows the application to "update the authenticating user's current status, also known as tweeting" (https://dev.twitter.com/docs/api/1.1/post/statuses/update). This includes the possibility of geolocating the user if geolocation tags are enabled. For the application developer, the process of being able to obtain permissions for all of the 'GET' resources or 'POST' possibilities (though there is a substantial amount of overlap for these) appears through a rather simple read/write developer request screen shown in Figure 2.4.

What is readily visible in Figure 2.4 is the requirement that access tokens need to be renegotiated if in fact there is a change in the permission requests. However, if there are no changes to permission requests, once granted, acceptance on the part of the user is given in perpetuity. One of the biggest

Application Management
Application Name
Test OAuth
Details Settings API Keys Permissions
What type of access does your application need?
Read more about our Application Permission Model.
Read only
Read and Write
Read, Write and Access direct messages
Note:
Changes to the application permission model will only reflect in access tokens obtained after the permission model change is saved. You will need to re-negotiate existing access tokens to alter the permission level associated with each of your application's users.
Update settings

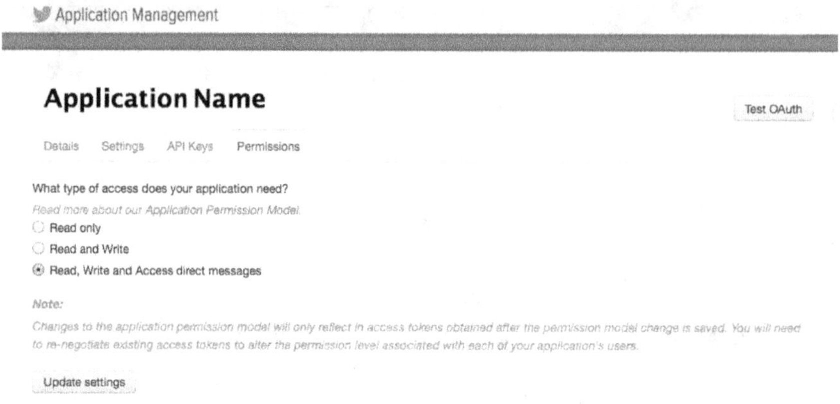

Figure 2.4 Data permissions for Twitter

Source: publicly available developer application manager interface form from Twitter

issues for Twitter appears to be the ability of an application to read, write, or delete direct messages—those that are seen only by the user. This is the focus of the application permissions model that is hyperlinked in Figure 2.4. It seems that public tweets (or followers and retweets) are far less a concern than those messages that are not made public by default. However, as much of what happens with Twitter is done on and through a public forum, the API focuses on allowing an application to quickly and easily access this more public data.

This is a rather significant difference in the two APIs. Twitter's API for the most part acts to collate significant pieces of publicly available data about a user as well as offer a form of user identification and authentication (largely by relying on OAuth or Open Authorization protocols). It also allows an application to 'tweet' for the user, but this is connected to the 'buttons' on websites or applications that say 'tweet this' in connection with a news article, achievement in a game, recent purchase through a webshop, and so forth. Facebook's API offers identity verification as well but also allows applications access to data that is not public—that goes beyond the user's public profile and that is arguably more robust in terms of indicating social connections more directly. Both of these resources allow the application to gain continual access to a 'profile,' updating the data that is produced in the everyday use and interactions with the social media.

SOCIAL MEDIA PARTICIPANT PERMISSIONS

The above description and figures are indicative of how Facebook and Twitter (differently) organize and standardize access to activities done within their social media platforms. These categories are made available for application developers, who then can choose which features of the API they wish to include for their API. This is the basis for knowledge about personal profiles, statuses, connections, and the relevant activities of people who participate on Facebook and Twitter. Though several of these items are oriented to more qualitative descriptions than easily quantifiable data (for instance Facebook's categories of 'about me,' 'interests,' 'religion_politics'), many of these are oriented toward pre-formulated responses that appear once a person begins to fill these out in their profile (that they can choose to use or not). Likewise, the GET statuses function for Twitter is likewise qualitatively oriented, but the GET statues/retweets and GET friends/id can be compiled and used for more quantitative and systematic purposes. The details about 'who' a person is, how they are connected to others and what they deem worthy of 'sharing' can be quite significant here.

However, a brief examination of the application requests of several major international corporations reveals that a number of these do not request too many additional permissions from Facebook, with the exception of email addresses and birthdates. The open possibilities for Twitter as read/write/access permissions are, however, often present, but these are again connected to the more public data that is central for Twitter and seem to be rarely used. This may shift or change, but at present Figures 2.5, 2.6, and 2.7 indicate the process by which applications ask permissions from users to use their data. Figure 2.5 indicates a minimal request for data from Facebook, and Figure 2.6 shows a substantial request from the application for Facebook data (the black square in each figure is where the user's profile picture is inserted):

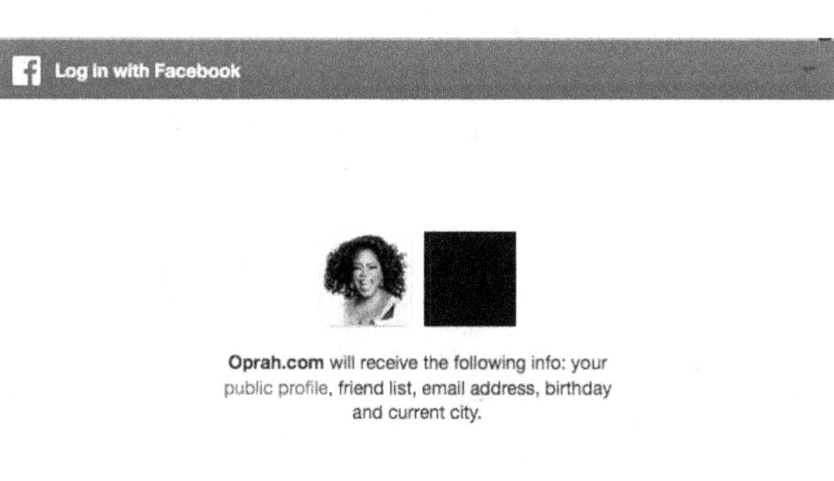

Figure 2.5 User permission request on Facebook from Oprah.com

Source: publicly available user authorisation form from Facebook

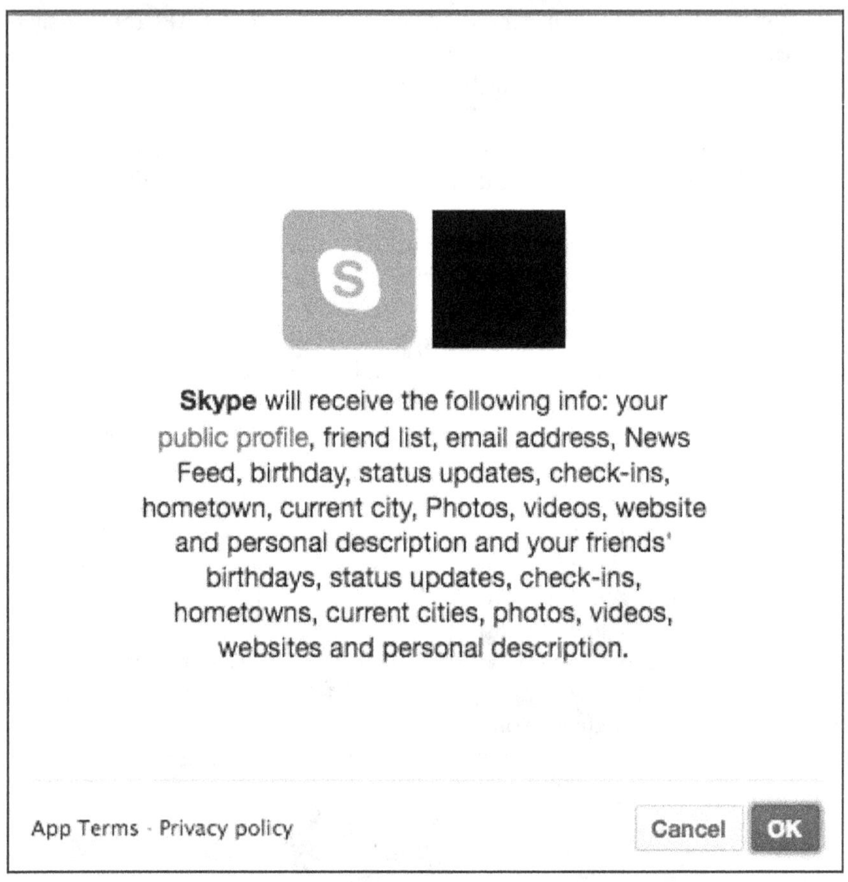

Skype will receive the following info: your public profile, friend list, email address, News Feed, birthday, status updates, check-ins, hometown, current city, Photos, videos, website and personal description and your friends' birthdays, status updates, check-ins, hometowns, current cities, photos, videos, websites and personal description.
App Terms · Privacy policy
Cancel
OK

Figure 2.6 User permission request on Facebook from Skype
Source: publicly available user authorisation form from Facebook

Facebook actually notes that "the more permissions an app requests, the less likely it is that people will use Facebook to log into your app" (see https://developers.facebook.com/docs/facebook-login/permissions). However, clicking on the public profile hyperlink indicates that part of this permission is to give a somewhat extensive set of data, including your "name, profile picture, age range, gender, language, country and other public info." Again, the preceding two figures only appear when a user chooses to 'connect with Facebook' or 'sign in with Facebook' on the website or the application, and the 'OK button' approves the process by which these applications (or sites) gain initial and then subsequent access to personal and personalized information, data, and features. This is the moment at which the data transfer following what is set out by Facebook's Open Graph API is begun and continues until the terms, conditions, or permissions requested change or until the user changes his or her password.

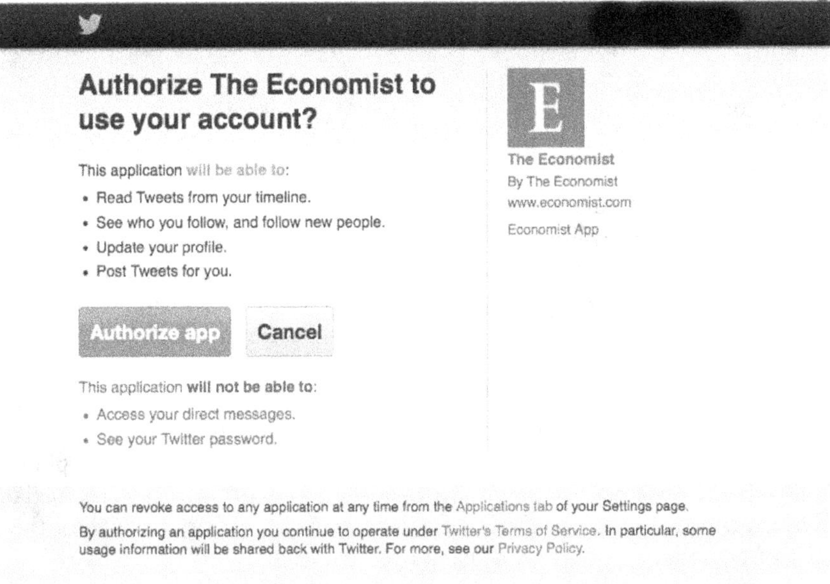

Figure 2.7 User permission request on Twitter from *The Economist*
Source: publicly available user authorisation form from Twitter

A similar process happens in the use of applications for Twitter. While Figure 2.4 indicates the process on the application developer's side for Twitter, Figure 2.7 indicates the authorization request made of Twitter users. This gives permission to a particular site to access certain pieces of Twitter data so the user may continue to use the site. Beyond accessing basic information from Twitter such as the name and 'handle' of the user, the application is further able to update consumer profiles, learn whom the user follows and is followed by, and even post information (tweets) for that user from their site (for example, products purchased or articles recommended).

This permission process indicates very specifically where a Twitter user can find the applications for which he or she has given access and specifies what an application can do. The most significant difference between permission requests for Twitter and Facebook is the indication that the Twitter application may post on a user's behalf. Facebook's Open Graph API focuses on the information that external applications can receive rather than their ability to post information for the user. Twitter, however, with its largely publicly available data, has combined a simplified collection of this data by an application with permission for that application to mediate particular posts for the user. Facebook's approach to this is different, relying on separate processes known as 'social plugins' to post on behalf of the user, most notably the like and the share buttons.

With the basic information of a user available in their 'public profile,' and presuming an on-going use of and/or interaction with these particular applications, both these APIs facilitate an extensive collection of personal data. This collection may be a bit myopic in nature, relying on a fragmentary set of 'identity attributes' that make up the participant profile, but for the purposes of evaluating and analysing use patterns and engagement, this data can become quite significant. Of course, while Facebook and Twitter might be the most prolific social media offering APIs with which application developers are most likely to interface, other social media and services like LinkedIn, Yahoo, Google, and Microsoft Live alongside Tumblr (owned by Yahoo), Pinterest, and Instagram (owned by Facebook) also provide these services. All of these set particular parameters around which social media participants and their lives can be made 'known' and traceable. Further, these figures are only indications of web-based processes, but applications are predominantly found in connection with mobile devices, namely phones and tablets. As numerous applications connect with and rely upon data derived through both Facebook and Twitter APIs, the significance of these bits of personal attributes that have been translated into specific attributes and actions on social media only escalates, particularly in terms of its relation to 'markets.'

Given the availability and frequent use of social media, seeing APIs as market devices allows us to understand how applications connect to the inner workings of social media and its users in order to gain significant information about these users. Precisely how this connects with contemporary understandings of identity is the focus of the next section.

APIs AND CONCEPTIONS OF IDENTITY

The request and permissions processes indicated earlier show how categories of data—predefined by social media—become available to external applications for both the production and consumption of user data. This is predicated on APIs. They determine the access of applications to that data. This data is representative of the lives of social media participants, who use the platform to communicate and relate to others. They both indicate to others 'who' they are and are perceived in certain ways by the 'connections' the social media platform has provided for them. In the earlier text, the descriptions of requests and permissions are focused on a social media participant's *profile*, while the more theoretical concerns in the descriptions preceding this were focused on conceptions of *identity*. In large measure, the two terms are used interchangeably in common discussions, but here it is important to see the profile as a digital collection of attributes and a means of producing and 'consuming' identity. As such, social media are in this sense identity intensive environments, with profiles as the means for both the production of identity (or identities) and their consumption.

There have been more than two decades' worth of work examining the relationship between technology and the production and consumption of identity, particularly in an online environment (see Turkle, 1995; Zhao et al., 2008; Trottier in this volume). This has largely been focused on the participants—their experiences and practices—rather than on the processes of how they are identified. Identity, as has been argued, is a central concern in contemporary life. Zygmunt Bauman suggests that identity is experienced as the new problematic—that is, *it* is what we are all focused on in part because the contemporary world is unable to present or legislate the world as cohesive, continuous, and consistent (Bauman, 2000; see also Elliott, 2007). While it is not clear that this cohesive, continuous, and consistent world ever genuinely existed (see Latour, 1991), Bauman's sociological perspective aligns with others that suggest that we are no longer 'given' an identity by the (social) world(s) that surrounds us; rather, identity is predicated on symbolic constructions based on the choices we make or are made for us (see Giddens, 1991). Increasingly, these symbolic constructions can be seen in terms of associations made present in social media profiles that have in turn become more accessible through APIs.

Interactional and relational conceptions of identity, drawn from works such as those from symbolic interactionists like Charles Horton Cooley and George Herbert Mead and dramaturgists such as Erving Goffman,[1] have largely ignored the role of technologies more substantively in their ability to determine or direct identity, particularly in relation to social media. There are some exceptions, as for instance Katherine Walker draws directly upon Goffman's work to describe identity production through the Internet (2000), and Zhao and colleagues do so similarly in relation to early Facebook use (2008). Even in these exceptions, technology is largely seen as a tool in the identity-construction process. That the interactional basis for the development of identity can occur in conjunction with technology was something Anthony Giddens suggested to some degree long before the advent of the Internet. He noted that with the "development of mass communication, particularly electronic communication, the interpenetration of self-development and social systems . . . becomes ever more pronounced" (1991, 4). It is this interpenetration that becomes evident in the use of APIs, as these technologies allow for desirable applications to continually retrieve and produce personal data for the user—thus they are about both the development of self and the (social) systems in which this occurs.

This interpenetration has also been readily seen in very early texts about the Internet. Sherry Turkle's descriptions in *Life on the Screen: Identity in the Age of the Internet* (1995) explores the relationship between new information and communication technologies (ICTs) and their effects upon and production of personal identity. The point of her work was to uncover "the story of constructing identity in the culture of simulation" that in her terms was seen as "evidence of fundamental shifts in the way we create and experience human identity" (ibid., 10). However, her work was focussed on the early days of the Internet, specifically interactions that occurred within multi-user domains (MUDs)—online role-playing games in which text on the screen was used to choose and describe characters (avatars), actions, and environments. It was limited in scope and focused on a limited number of persons who participated in these communities. With the expansion of social media and its pervasiveness in everyday life, the construction of identity and its experience through and with technology are no longer clearly limited within contexts of 'simulation.' Rather, the technological foray of early Internet users in producing and consuming 'identities' through social media profiles has become an almost universal experience.

The entirety of these approaches to identity and technology stands largely in contrast to ascribed notions of identity, namely the means by which persons are given an 'identity' in terms of identification documents and the development of identity-management systems. The process of the identification of citizens, for instance through technologies of identity cards, has elsewhere been more explicitly seen as a form of surveillance (see Lyon, 2009). Without delving into the sometimes conflicting and sometimes complementary ways in which identity in the form of personal subjectivity and sense of self intersects with identity in the form of identification by external structures and technologies (see, for instance, Jenkins, 2008), it is sufficient to say that APIs connect with both notions of identity through participant profiles. They are increasingly *the* way in which 'identity' is both provided for and produced on a daily basis. APIs give access to social media as an 'identity provider,' structuring this identity-provision process on the basis of a singular notion of identity (see van Dijck, 2013). They also give access to prescribed lists of ongoing activities and associations in the form of uniform fields of data. Yet the 'provision' of identity and the changing identity attributes found within social media profiles are also contingent and relational—they stem from voluntary practices and connections chosen by users. These profiles are based on an accumulation of everyday choices and experiences that have been made digitally accessible.

APIs render readable the active production of identity on a day-to-day basis as it is increasingly intermingled with consumption (see Slater, 1997; Bauman, 2005; Lury, 2011) or perhaps further, the notion of 'prosumption' (Beer and Burrows, 2010; Ritzer and Jurgenson, 2010). This production of personal identity can be seen to take place in the consumption choices people make (or not) in order that they may "construct, maintain, interpret, negotiate [and] display who they are to be or be seen as" (Slater, 1997, 84). These choices have become more visible through social media profiles as their ever-extending relevance and availability within everyday life has grown. 'Consumption' in this sense should be seen more broadly in terms of daily practices or use rather than simply 'purchases' (see Shove et al., 2007). As such, it includes the significant amount of content *produced* by participants within social media (which is what has given rise to the 'prosumption' neologism), even as this is guided and directed by the structures and everyday practices that make up these media (see Madrigal, 2013). Prosumption here, should be seen as a 'sensitizing concept' intended to reiterate the observation that people are actively involved in the production of media content (Beer and Burrows, 2013, 3). This is the point at which technology, consumption, and identity become increasingly intertwined.

Social media are predicated on content that is 'prosumed' every day in increasingly large amounts—personal information, status updates, connections, pictures and videos, notes, shared links, and so on. The mixed set of content, often significantly guided by social media that attempt to 'get out of the way' and allow participants to produce and receive this content (see Madrigal, 2013), becomes relevant for a variety of purposes. Making this content available, editable, measurable, and quantifiable through and from social media is what APIs allow. They are important for understanding and conceptualizing the fluctuating collection of attributes indicated to others *and* those characteristics attributed to and expected of us by others within social media profiles. In consumption terms, "the anthropology of consumption has . . . clearly shown classifying products, positioning them and evaluating them inevitably leads to the classification of the people attached to those goods" (Callon, Méadel and Rabeharisoa, 2002, 212). By extending this to more proactive forms of consumption, what gets 'done' with social media is both a production and classification of participants and their content. Social media profiles are entities in which 'identity' is both produced and provided, and APIs stipulate and enable access to these identities.

STABILIZING DIGITAL RELATIONS

Given the understandings of identity noted earlier, from its provision to its production through social media profiles, what precisely is it that social media APIs can be seen to 'do' in terms of identity? And what is it that these identities do to APIs? APIs are very much about 'identities' in use. They can be seen to make more accessible the socio-technical productions of identity in many facets. First, APIs both show and reinforce how applications have become a central part of people's everyday practices with technology and their increased reliance on social media. Second, they reiterate the self-referential but also contingent processes that are a part of the expression of identity by producing both flexible and persistent categories and classifications that connect with personal profiles. Finally, these social media APIs have made accessible data profiles indicative of the flexible and mutable identities provided for and produced in relation to social media.

The Shift to Applications

Over the past several years, we have seen the transformation of the Internet into interconnected and (mostly) smoothly functioning sets of software rather than through the traditional 'window' of a browser. These softwares are applications that make use of a variety of resources and are integrated into multiple technological devices, from smartphones to tablets to laptop computers. They are part of the increasingly 'customizable' range of devices that rely more on applications and less on browsers to access information or perform certain functions for the user (see Khalaf, 2013). In the case of social media, the data made available through the APIs of Facebook and Twitter provide a significant resource for a variety of purposes, from tracking activities to conversing with friends or acquaintances to meeting someone new to playing a game and numerous other possibilities.

It is this shift to applications that is significant for identity. Following Anthony Giddens's understanding that in terms of developing our identity (or self more specifically), "we have no choice but to choose" (1991, 81), and given the proliferation of portable devices that can access the Internet, applications provide a variety of possibilities to enact the "routine practices" that are part of a "lifestyle" (ibid.). These lifestyles are very much a part of the 'choices' people are making in everyday life, and myriads of choice become expressible and embedded in bits of technology. Applications connect the users of these technologies into a socio-technical configuration of practices, people and information that they deem important and, with increasingly directed advertising and marketing, the people and information deemed important for them.

The relationship of applications to social media is mixed. On the one hand, social media applications are themselves fairly robust technologies that attempt to serve a number of 'functions' for their participants. For instance, both Twitter and Facebook as applications and websites promote particular social connections that can include indications of location and messaging services, for which Facebook in particular has introduced its own stand-alone messaging application. On the other hand, a number of non-social media applications promote the connection with social media APIs like Twitter and Facebook as part of their identity verification processes and/or the promotion of social connections. Some of these applications are dependent upon or require a connection with social media. When connected, social media APIs allow for the collection and production of significant amounts of data by the social media participant. Taken together, the proliferation of softwares that interconnect specifically with social media APIs do not just indicate potential connections but the 'success' of these social media to be an increasingly ubiquitous part of people's lives.

Identity Expressions and Social Media

The second facet that indicates how APIs connect with socio-technical productions of identity is that these reiterate and produce certain types of 'relevant' categories and classifications. The choices for a short-term diversion in the form of a game or the 'pinning' of a recipe to what can be seen as a virtual scrapbook or the indication of romantic interest in a person based on a photo and profile, all of which are available through applications, reinforce particular attributes of the application user. As many of these either request or are based on connections with social media data, they draw upon and produce particular forms of data connected with the lifestyles of the social media participant. There is a dual process here—social media participants choose what might be relevant for themselves in the form of social connections, entertainment, activities, and their lifestyle—all the things they 'like' (see Gerlitz and Helmond, 2013)—even as these are being reinforced by those they are connected to by the algorithmic analyses of social media providers. They both refer to current self-perceptions and aspirations as well as being placed upon them from without.[2]

Social media provide reference points through which others, including applications, are able to classify and categorize participants. APIs form the basis by which this content of "circulating references" (see Latour, 1999; see also Beer and Burrows, 2013) within social media—that is data about the (selective) content of everyday life—moves from these proprietary systems to external applications. As such, APIs substantially contribute to and reinforce forms of digital identity that applications are able to retrieve, but they also allow the freedom of social media participants to shift and change. Participants are free to change or emphasize particular associations and relationships, to follow new people and like different status updates even as these new choices are producing a 'new and improved' version of the participant's (altered/updated) identity. These decisions are then integrated into the social media platforms' algorithms, and different status updates or tweets (in the cases of Facebook and Twitter) become more readily visible and promoted. APIs standardize access to certain social media practices and categories of information that participants willingly choose to associate themselves but do not define these further—participants are encouraged to 'fill in the spaces' (see Madrigal, 2013). The data they produce creates selective biographies of participants in the first instance, but the permissions given by social media participants further allow applications to access, modify, and build upon these biographies in ways that are seen as relevant to the participant, even as he or she may pursue new experiences, lifestyles, relationships, or associations.

Market Devices That Make Changing Identities Accessible

It isn't just that social media APIs reinforce the use of applications and provide ways to express or classify the identities of participants—they also make a contingent and relational notion of identity 'workable' on a continual basis. Though the majority of social media are built on proprietary technologies, the development of APIs allows interoperable access to information from these media by different external systems. This is enabled in the first place at the moment in which a social media participant accepts the conditions at a singular point—the 'clicking' of the 'log-in' or 'authorize' button. This click sets in motion the potential for information to be both obtained from and produced for social media. In most normal circumstances, the authorization obtained for the transfer of data remains in perpetuity, though this may be requested at each update of the application.

Social media APIs provide a way for applications to measure and monitor the everyday practices of social media participants by outside organizations. Though the data made available by these APIs is rarely requested in full, the selection of categories of data made available by the likes of Facebook and Twitter, amongst others, provide a selective and partial 'understanding' of 'who' a social media participant is on an on-going basis. In terms of identity, this is not something simply voluntary or something simply classifiable and imposed, but rather an identity that is shaped in relation to both voluntary choices and categorical assumptions or analyses. Shifts to different activities, locations, friendships, and other affiliations are not only possible and anticipated, but these are easily made traceable through the data provided. This not only serves to stabilize relationships with identity as an ongoing production but allows these identity profiles to move beyond the parameters of immediate interaction. As the permissions noted above, a number of these application request the authority to act on a user's behalf specifically in relation to the social media. API interactions (or calls) now number in the billions per day for larger social media companies (such as Facebook, Twitter, and Google), and there are others moving in this direction (Microsoft, LinkedIn).[3] To be clear, these API calls are not being initiated every time by social media participants. Rather, applications are seeking and posting information in an automated fashion. Arguably the sheer number of these calls can be seen to stabilize conversations with consumers by making them more or less constant. This strengthens the durability of consumer audiences, limiting the liabilities inherent in the "irrational consumption behaviours of individual actors" (Bauman, 2001, 17).

In the process, social media APIs can be seen to render the complexities of changing digital identity accessible and stabilize access to this information. The significance in the use of social media APIs in their various forms is that these are distinct means through which observations and/or on-going 'conversations' are made embedded into technologies. This is of particular interest to marketing companies (see Pridmore, 2013) as well as the social media companies themselves, particularly as they 'tweak' their participant interfaces, and should not be underestimated. Through the acceptance process set out by APIs, applications connect social media participants with a variety of resources and provide services on the basis of standardized sets of dynamic information. They are a vital part of how a number of different elements connect—they draw together identity, technology, marketing, and consumption into a unified market device.

CONCLUSIONS

As social media play an ever more important role in people's daily routines and practices, they have become a significant aspect in the development of personal understandings and presentations of identity. The consumption (or perhaps 'prosumption') of social media has begun to change how identity is 'made to happen' in everyday life. The unseen role of APIs allowing for the collection of rich personal data as well as the modification and alteration of digital profiles suggests that identity remains active beyond the intermittent interactions, categorizations, and profiles found within digital social media. There are of course numerous concerns on the part of participants regarding their own profiles (see Trottier, Chapter 3, this volume), but overall the use of social media is largely seen as voluntary, as are the choices to use applications that connect with social media data.

However, there are some significant issues that arise in the 'one-click' process presented by application programming interfaces. First, this raises concerns about a continual 'care for the self' in a Foucauldian vein (Foucault, 1988; see also Elliott, 2007). There are expectations of a continual engagement built into social media and into applications that can access these media. What is interesting is the degree to which applications are able to act on the behalf of others in posting 'status updates' and 'tweets' in the social media cases presented here. The acceptance process makes evident the blurred boundaries among social media, its participants, softwares and hardwares, and the expressions of personal identity.

Second, although there is flexibility in content, APIs dictate the types of data that become accessible in terms of its own categorization. They reinforce particular norms and limit the complexity of identity by dividing it into certain attributes and associations its platform is dependent upon. This is of course necessary to stabilize the production and consumption of 'identity,' yet in this way it seems that APIs can increasingly dominate the process by minimizing opportunities for participants, particularly in decisions involving the connections of applications with social media.

Finally, the acceptance process for applications enacts a form of visibility that is less than reciprocal, as the complicated protocols and processes of APIs are not seen or, by and large, understood by participants on social media (see Bodle, 2011). There is relatively little understanding of what data are both available and not in relation to application access. What is clear is that both marketers and social media platforms are increasingly leveraging these tools even as consumers increasingly rely on their convenience. Social media may facilitate participants in the production of personal identity—producing relevant profiles about themselves—but the accessibility of these profiles through APIs makes visible images and activities which individually may not be of consequence or value, but in combination with others it, allows patterns to become visible or associations (even non-obvious ones) to be connected. These are critical ethical and social concerns given the ubiquity of social media.

This chapter has begun to show that although both social media and applications have become significant technologies in the contemporary world, it is the connections between them and their users in the relatively obscure and unseen APIs that are of significance. These have substantial implications for how 'identities' are being both produced and consumed through digital profiles, as APIs are now important parts of the socio-technical configuration of identity in the contemporary world. This is particularly true in relation to the use of social media APIs. To begin to understand transitions in identity, we must begin to understand and examine the underlying protocols and processes that invisibly direct and are directed by the relations between everyday practices and the technologies that are an increasing part of them.

NOTES

1. The work of Cooley, Mead, and Goffman, amongst others, focuses on conceptions of the self. In large measure the distinctions between the notion of 'self' and that of 'identity' overlap significantly, but this discrepancy has raised several critiques as to the usefulness of the concept of identity (see Brubaker and Cooper, 2000).
2. This can be seen in terms of governmentality, which would require further discussion and analysis (see Beckett, 2012).
3. Details and statistics on API usage rates are available at www.programmableweb.com/ or at www.slideshare.net/mashups/web-ap-is.

REFERENCES

3SCALE. (2011) "What Is an API? Your Guide to the Internet Business (R)evolution." www.3scale.net/wp-content/uploads/2012/06/What-is-an-API-1.0.pdf.

AKRICH, M. (1992) The De-scription of Technical Objects. In Bijker, W. E. & Law, J. (eds.) *Shaping Technology/Building Society—Studies in Sociotechnical Change*. Cambridge (MA): The MIT Press, 205–224.

ANONYMOUS. (2014) "API Vs Protocol." Accessed May 15. http://c2.com/cgi/wiki?ApiVsProtocol.

ARAUJO, L., KJELLBERG, H., & SPENCER, R. (2008) Market Practices and Forms: Introduction to the Special Issue. *Marketing Theory*, 8(1). p. 5–14.

BAJDE, D. (2013) Consumer Culture Theory (re)visits Actor-Network Theory: Flattening Consumption Studies. *Marketing Theory*, 13(2). p. 227–242.

BAUMAN, Z. (2000) *Liquid Modernity*. Cambridge (UK): Polity Press.

———. (2001) Consuming Life. *Journal of Consumer Culture*, 1(1). p. 9–29.

———. (2005) *Liquid Life*. Cambridge (UK): Polity.

BECKETT, A. (2012). Governing the consumer: technologies of consumption. *Consumption Markets & Culture*, 15(1), 1–18.

BEER, D., & BURROWS, R. (2010) Consumption, Prosumption and Participatory Web Cultures: An Introduction. *Journal of Consumer Culture*, 10(1). p. 3–12.

———. (2013) Popular Culture, Digital Archives and the New Social Life of Data. *Theory, Culture & Society*. (April) p. 47–71.

BODLE, R. (2011) Regimes of Sharing. *Information, Communication & Society*, 14(3). p. 320–337.

BRUBAKER, R., & COOPER, F. (2000). Beyond "identity". *Theory and society*, 29(1), 1–47.

CALLON, M., MÉADEL, C. & RABEHARISOA, R. (2002) The Economy of Qualities. *Economy and Society*, 31(2). p. 194–217.

DIX, A. (2011) Living in a World of Data. In *Proceedings of the ACM SIGACCESS Conference on Computers and Accessibility (ASSETS '11)*. New York, NY.

ELLIOTT, A. (2007) *Concepts of the Self: Second Edition*. Cambridge (UK): Polity Press.

FOUCAULT, M. (1988) *The History of Sexuality, Vol. 3: The Care of the Self*. New York: Random House LLC.

GERLITZ, C., & HELMOND, A. (2013) The Like Economy: Social Buttons and the Data-Intensive Web. *New Media & Society*, 15(8). p. 1348–1365.

GIDDENS, A. (1991) *Modernity and Self-Identity: Self and Society in the Late Modern Age*. Stanford (CA): Stanford University Press.

JENKINS, R. (2008) *Social Identity*. New York: Routledge.

JUNG, G. & LEE, B. (2010) Analysis on Social Network Adoption According to the Change of Network Topology: The Impact of 'Open API' to Adoption of Facebook. *In Proceedings of the 12th International Conference on Electronic Commerce: Roadmap for the Future of Electronic Business*. p. 23–32.

LATOUR, B. (1991) *We Have Never Been Modern*. Cambridge (MA): Harvard University Press.

———. (1999) *Pandora's Hope: Essays on the Reality of Science Studies*. Cambridge (MA): Harvard University Press.

LURY, C. (2011) *Consumer Culture: Consumer Culture (Revised and Updated)*. Rutgers (NJ): Rutgers University Press.

LYON, D. (2009) *Identifying Citizens: ID Cards as Surveillance*. Cambridge (UK): Polity.

MADRIGAL, A. (2013) How Facebook Designs the 'Perfect Empty Vessel' for Your Mind. *The Atlantic*. [Online] Available at www.theatlantic.com/technology/archive/2013/05/how-facebook-designs-the-perfect-empty-vessel-for-your-mind/275426/. Accessed 12 July 2014.

MILLER, D. (1987) *Material Culture and Mass Consumption*. New York: Blackwell.

MUNIESA, F., MILLO, Y. & CALLON, M. (2007) An Introduction to Market Devices. *The Sociological Review*, 55. p. 1–12.

PRIDMORE, J. (2013) Collaborative Surveillance: Configuring Contemporary Marketing Practice. In Ball, K., & Snider, L. (eds) *The Surveillance Industrial Complex: A Political Economy of Surveillance*. New York: Routledge. p. 107–121.

RITZER, G. & JURGENSON, N. (2010) Production, Consumption, Prosumption: The Nature of Capitalism in the Age of the Digital 'Prosumer.' *Journal of Consumer Culture*, 10(1). p. 13–36.

SHOVE, E., et. al. (2007) *The Design of Everyday Life*. Oxford: Berg.

SLATER, D. (1997) *Consumer Culture and Modernity*. Cambridge (UK): Polity Press.

TURKLE, S. (1995) *Life on the Screen*. New York: Simon & Schuster.

VAN DIJCK, J. (2013) 'You Have One Identity': Performing the Self on Facebook and LinkedIn. *Media, Culture & Society*, 35(2). p. 199–215.

WALKER, K. (2000) 'It's Difficult to Hide It': The Presentation of Self on Internet Home Pages. *Qualitative Sociology*, 23(1). p. 99–120.

ZHAO, S., GRASMUCK, S. & MARTIN, J. (2008) Identity Construction on Facebook: Digital Empowerment in Anchored Relationships. *Computers in Human Behavior*, 24(5). p. 1816–1836.

3 Caring for the Virtual Self on Social Media

Managing Visibility on Facebook

Daniel Trottier

INTRODUCTION

This chapter considers the production, sharing, and gathering of personal information in a culturally and historically situated context, namely, university students who used Facebook during its expansion in the late noughties. In adopting Facebook as a platform for interpersonal communication, relations with peers are recast in terms of visibility and exposure. These users grew comfortable sharing with their peers but at the same time were troubled by the cumulative exposure to those peers and others. Interpersonal social media usage—including submitting their own personal information and watching over what other users publish—rendered respondents visible to one another in a way that warranted a care of the virtual self (Whitson and Haggerty, 2008). This involved both self-scrutiny and watching over what peers upload, as this may reflect poorly on them. Yet even this care was complicated by social media's growth at the time and especially Facebook's cross-contextual information flows that further publicized information beyond respondents' expectations. For respondents, watching over their profiles and their peers was a necessary—but not sufficient—condition of self-care on social media.

In the years following its launch, Facebook began to mediate social life in a manner that some users recognized as neither fully private nor fully public. Unanticipated visibility and exposure on social media was—and still is—pervasive, insofar as it is a product of ubiquitous mobile technology and a rapidly growing user base. These developments require scholarly attention on the conditions surrounding peer visibility on sites like Facebook. This research asks: in a context where early users were coping with an increasingly publicized platform, what compelled these users to engage in sharing and collecting personal information on Facebook, how did they perceive these conditions of visibility, and how did they manage their online presence?

EARLY USERS TAKING CARE

Between October and December 2008, I conducted a series of semi-structured, in-depth interviews to consider how Facebook users coped with peer-to-peer surveillance. A convenience sample of thirty undergraduate students who use Facebook was selected for study. Participants were enrolled at the same mid-sized Canadian university. These students were selected from all faculties and were recruited through a series of posters on campus as well as notices sent by email to undergraduate mailing lists. Of the thirty students interviewed, twenty-three were women and seven were men. As women are both more likely to use social media in Canada (Dewing, 2010) and participate in research (Sax et al., 2003), this distribution was expected. Seven respondents were in the first year of their studies, eight were in their second year, five were in their third year, seven were in their fourth year, and three were in their fifth year. Twenty-six respondents were in the faculty of arts and sciences, three were in health sciences, and one student was in the faculty of education. This distribution is explained by the fact that the majority of the student population are enrolled in the faculty of arts and sciences. Twenty-seven respondents checked their Facebook account at least once a day. The three that did not perform daily checks instead received email notifications from Facebook. Interviews focused on a set of themes, including describing respondents' Facebook usage over time, the types of personal information made available to others and reasons for doing so, the types of personal information acquired from others through Facebook and reasons for doing so, and perceptions of information exchange on Facebook. When quoted, respondents are identified by their program, year of study, and gender. Interviews were recorded as MP3 audio files, manually transcribed, and coded based on interview questions as well as additional themes that emerged during the interviews.

The interviews occurred at a noteworthy moment in Facebook's growth. While the platform was still closely linked to university student life in North America, it had been available to non-students for approximately two years. These respondents reported using Facebook to socialize with peers on campus and abroad. However, they were also coming to terms with unwanted watchers, including parents and employers. Some considered a long-term presence on Facebook to be a growing concern for when they would enter the job market, pursue postgraduate studies, or raise children. They anticipated that their presence on Facebook could harm these plans.

In the years following these interviews, Facebook's population grew to more than one billion users, it experimented with several advertising schemes, and it is now openly acknowledged to be a source of evidence for police and other investigative agencies (Omand et al., 2012). Contemporary concerns that are linked to these developments include how personal information may be repurposed in ways that users neither anticipate nor endorse (cf. Trottier, 2011). The focus of this chapter predates these developments, yet these respondents were coming to terms with unanticipated forms of visibility on Facebook. To be sure, Facebook has changed extensively in the years following these interviews. Its interface processes and displays personal details differently, and a comparatively vast and heterogeneous user base engages in a broader range of practices. However, a basic distinction remains between information that is visible to all users and information that is meant for a sub-set of users. Knowing and maintaining this distinction likely endures as an element of care for the virtual self on Facebook.

Respondents described their presence on Facebook as a matter of being both the subject and the agent of targeted scrutiny. In this context, Facebook stood as an exemplar of social media. Respondents used it to maintain profiles, upload photographs, and make personal information available to their peers. Facebook shared some features with other social media, such as the pervasive construction of an online presence populated by personal information. Yet this presence transcended any specific context, and this characteristic has become more evident in the years following this study. Thus, sharing personal details with specific peers was not the extent of the visibility it offers active users. The fact that invisible and unexpected audiences (boyd, 2008) can also access this information is a risk of social media use that has grown along with its user population.

Respondent adoption of social media was a form of visibility wherein some everyday interactions more closely resembled surveillance. Surveillance refers to the covert, sustained, and targeted collection of information of an individual or group of individuals (Lyon, 2001). Respondents were aware of this condition, with one respondent noting that through "examples that happen all the time, you realize like how much some people could be watching everything you say" (Artsci2F). Surveillance is a broader phenomenon than data collection. It typically relies on asymmetrical relations of visibility and power and is typically practiced in order to further these relations. It is a prevailing organizational logic of late modernity. Facebook, for example, organizes relations between individuals. Not only are interpersonal social ties mediated on an organizational platform, but interpersonal activity becomes asynchronous. Users watch over each other's profiles, which may take precedence over directly watching each other. Other kinds of surveillance take place through Facebook (Trottier, 2011), but peer relations also become more surveillant in nature.

Facebook can potentially be used as a surveillance tool, for example, by an individual who stalks a targeted user by monitoring their activity on this platform. However, a lot of interpersonal activity on this platform does not strictly fit this description. User activity on Facebook ranges from willingly publicizing details to attempts to obtain private details from another user without their awareness or consent. However, respondents note that risk of the latter shapes their relations for users and their practices on the site. One respondent posted a link to politically inflammatory content on her profile. Upon discovering that this reflected poorly on her, she stated, "there are things that—it's better just to sort of take care of it [by keeping it] private overall. And it's good to stay sort of apolitical on Facebook" (Artsci4W). Thus, the consequences of visibility on Facebook may contribute to self-monitoring and a dampening of political speech within this medium. This particular response anticipated the risks of unwanted data collection and exposure linked with the subsequent expansion of the Facebook platform, as well as other platforms.

Respondents occasionally experienced interpersonal (or peer) surveillance as a violation but also came to regard it as a pervasive condition of social media, suggesting a further normalization of surveillance practices (Murakami Wood and Webster, 2009). The intervisibility (Brighenti, 2010) these individuals exhibit and exploit is a prevalent feature of contemporary sociality. Peer surveillance is also mutual on social media, as users are able to watch and be watched. Earlier research on user-led surveillance practices noted that the possibility for users to watch others as well as make themselves visible adds an empowering dimension to their use of digital media (Koskela, 2004; Albrecthslund, 2008). Yet on Facebook, intentional visibility cannot be disassociated from unanticipated exposure. One function "creeps" into another, and information "leaks" to new contexts (Lyon, 2001).

In the context of peer surveillance, Andrejevic describes a media culture that compels individuals to watch over untrustworthy peers (2005). Paradoxically, an increased reliance on platforms like Facebook for peer surveillance furthers the risk of exposure and the need to be vigilant. As social media are intimately tied to both identity and communication, they shape how we are perceived and how respondents interact with others. The risk of unwanted exposure and other social harm necessitate a care of the virtual self, "whereby citizens are encouraged, enticed and occasionally compelled into bringing components of their fractured and dispersed data double into regular patterns of contact, scrutiny and management: (Whitson and Haggerty, 2008, 574).

New risks emerge as a result of offloading social processes online. Whitson and Haggerty identify initiatives by the financial, law enforcement, and government sectors to compel individuals to mitigate the risk of identity fraud. Their prescriptions amount to a generalized project whereby "data management practices" are located at "the forefront of personal projects of responsibilized risk management" (ibid., 587). Whereas identity fraud primarily concerns the individual's financial well-being, personal reputation is at stake on Facebook. That such self-care would emerge on social media is not surprising, as Foucault notes that self-care constitutes "an entire activity of speaking and writing in which the work of oneself on oneself and communication with others were linked together" (1988, 51). Thus, self-care as an individual project is both devoted to and expressed through social ties. This care is manifest through the monitoring and more general control over information flows, a feature that is congruent with the extent to which care and control intersect in individual and institutional surveillance practices (Lyon, 2001). Respondents are sorting out responsible use among themselves, yet this is an occasionally contradictory project.

Peer monitoring on social media is a product of the domestication of media technology. Domestication literature (e.g. Silverstone and Haddon,

1996) recognizes technology as a lived experience and anticipates a qualitative focus on respondent reception of social media for peer surveillance. Domestication addresses how information and communication technologies are integrated into everyday life, with a focus on the tensions that emerge in consequence. The tensions between familiar and unexpected conditions (ibid.) are observable on a comparatively novel and dynamic platform where interpersonal relations are mediated. As she was discovering how Facebook would aggregate user activity—including her own—and display it on the platform's welcoming page, one respondent noted that she was "freaked out" (Educ1W). Coming to terms with how Facebook displayed personal information, she noted "all of a sudden, you can see what other people see. It's like you're there and you know that when other people log in, that's what they see and it just brings it all full circle and it's like 'Wow, Facebook's creepy'" (ibid.). Social media reconfigure familiar relations through unfamiliar and often unwanted kinds of exposure as a result of its accumulation of personal information and social ties. Also, following Whitson and Haggerty, reputations on social and digital media are understood by users as an individual responsibility, while in practice these exceed individual control.

The following sections are arranged thematically in order to chart respondents' exposure to, use of, and familiarity with Facebook. The first section explores how as a result of peer pressure and convenience, joining Facebook became a de facto decision. The next section addresses how respondents came to realize that visibility was central to their interpersonal use of Facebook. They described these practices through terms like "creeping" and "stalking," which are described in the third section. The fourth section considers how these experiences lead to a reconsideration of privacy and publicity. The fifth section considers how respondents developed a set of tactics to manage more problematic forms of exposure. The sixth section addresses how respondents regarded other users as being responsible for caring for their own virtual selves but also acknowledged the difficulties involved in this task.

TIES THAT BIND: PEER PRESSURE AND CONVENIENCE

Many respondents felt compelled to join Facebook due to peer pressure, either from new friends at university or high school classmates. On occasion peer pressure went beyond recommendation or prescription. Some respondents had friends who constructed profiles on their behalf and then transferred control of this nascent profile to them. In more extreme cases, non-users discovered Facebook contained photos and other content about them. This perplexed respondents, who were not familiar with the kinds of visibility in which they were implicated:

> I was like, "How can pictures of me be on the Internet?" They would show me and they'd show a picture of me with other people and

> they'd show comments that other people had made and, like, "How are people making comments on this photo of me and I don't even know it's there? I should be involved in this. I should know what's going on."
>
> (Artsci2W)

This respondent realized they already had a presence on Facebook, even if they never intended to join the site. This presence was only manageable by becoming a Facebook user. Respondents joined Facebook as a result of their peers' influence, and they decided to maintain a presence because of its social convenience. Facebook was often used for on-campus coordination, like announcing one's presence in the library or requesting class notes. In other cases, it was used for a more spectacular kind of visibility, such as uploading photographs from a recent vacation. Facebook was a mix of memorable events coupled with mundane details, and respondents recognized it as a resource for sociality. By allowing respondents to upload content for no explicit audience, Facebook enabled a visibility between users that extended beyond what they would typically know about each other. This provided peers with "a general feeling of how your life is going" (Artsci3W). As submitting personal information was a more pervasive activity, Facebook produced a visibility akin to a 'general feeling' of individuals. This marked the familiar side of visibility on domestic technologies (Silverstone and Haddon, 1996), as Facebook was mundane and consensual and could be integrated into peer relations.

Some respondents actively disliked Facebook, going so far as to deactivate their profiles. These respondents invariably returned to Facebook, though their absence only strengthened their criticism of the site. Their return to a service they disliked was fuelled by the perceived need to stay online. Respondents equate being off of Facebook with being cut off from peers and social events. Nobody directly prevented them from leaving, but they noted clear costs associated with abstention:

> It's my damn friends, man. Like, there's Homecoming and there's a bunch of people coming up to Homecoming and [for] a lot of my friends, Facebook is the only reliable way to get a hold of them. Which is annoying. It's really annoying. Because I don't really want to be on it and I probably—like, after university's done, I probably won't be. But I don't know, right now it's just—it's almost too convenient not to have it.
>
> (Artsci4M)

Staying on Facebook was seen as "too convenient," and leaving it was too costly in terms of the loss of connectivity with peers (cf. Chang and Chen, 2008). Thus, respondents chose to join and maintain a presence because of social ties with friends, even if they have a negative opinion about the platform itself. To be sure, this peer connectivity is presented as a desirable feature. However, this connectivity—the manner in which Facebook diffuses information—is also a source of unwanted exposure for respondents.

FACEBOOK PRESENCE AS EXPOSURE

Respondents presented Facebook as a vast and accessible resource for personal information. In describing their visibility on this platform, they reported feeling as though they were being watched by others. In addition to former and current romantic partners, respondents were concerned with parental scrutiny. Parental access to profiles led to a convergence between social contexts respondents wanted to avoid (boyd, 2008). Facebook was seen to provide a distorted representation of the person. One respondent described how Facebook misrepresented him to his father:

> My dad is on Facebook. He knows what I'm up to. He knows the shenanigans that happen. But at the same time, he doesn't see that I put in like twenty hours a week at the library along with fifteen hours a week of classes. He doesn't see that I'm working every weekend on essays and stuff. He sees the guy holding the red plastic beer cup.
>
> (Artsci1W)

The above user makes reference to several social contexts in which he is engaged and notes that Facebook provides a selective account of these contexts. We may presume that the photographs of "shenanigans" are shared among his university peers and that this is a less problematic exchange for him. However, this becomes unwanted exposure when this content—and only this content—is made accessible to his father.

Peer monitoring on Facebook is also mutual, as watching and being watched both feature prominently. Respondents turned to Facebook to discover more about people who were of interest to their romantic lives. This is justified by the availability of relevant information on profiles, including sexual orientation, relationship status, the kind of relation the user wishes to pursue, and conversation topics. Respondents described their own exposure as a distinct concern from watching their peers. They held different standards between what they wanted to expose about themselves and what they wanted to find out about others. Yet when considering their own visibility, their ability to access their peers' personal information was the most accessible yardstick:

> I find it kind of weird that I have such insight into her life and I can, like, basically judge her, like I don't know, it's really weird to me. That's why I don't really use it that much, because I feel like all these people can do the same thing.
>
> (Artsci4W)

Peer visibility led respondents to guard their own information. Knowing they were being watched and knowing the extent to which they could watch others compelled respondents to monitor their online presence for content they believed others would find objectionable. This kind of self-scrutiny triggered the strategies for impression management detailed later in this chapter.

"CREEPING" AND "STALKING" ON FACEBOOK

Two terms associated with peer surveillance on Facebook warrant exploration: 'stalking' and 'creeping.' Both describe problematic ways of getting information on Facebook. In the interviews, creeping was seen as a milder version of stalking, which in turn was meant to reflect more negatively on the respondent. Creeping was a more involved and targeted way of using Facebook, though respondents treated this as a matter of circumstance: "It's all a matter of degree. I mean, if you were looking to assign either Facebook stalking or Facebook creeping to one person's activities, I'd think you would have to do it on a case-by-case basis" (Health3M). Creeping involves perusing content: a few pages of wall posts or a photo album. It is also presented as function using the site in the way it was intended, which in consequence amounts to a prolonged scrutiny of other users' information. Creeping can also be brought on due to boredom or simply because content on a user's news feed—the content that first greets people when they sign on—caught their attention.

> I guess most people would define the stalking one as more, like, actively searching, but I guess creeping would be if you're just bored and you're just looking at people's profiles and you don't have an active interest or motive to look at it.
>
> (Artsci4W)

The fact that creeping is fuelled by a lack of purposive motivation (i.e. boredom) and consists of viewing readily available information suggests that this behaviour is anticipated and reinforced by the way Facebook is configured. By "looking at people's profiles" in the absence of an "active interest," the respondent who engages in creeping is making use of the way Facebook renders personal details visible to its user base.

Stalking resembles creeping, although it is more purposive and "a little bit more aggressive" (Artsci4W). If a user consistently returned to a particular user's profile, this would be framed in terms of stalking. As Facebook stalking is not restricted to those who have been apprehended and prosecuted as stalkers, respondents suggested the site facilitates this kind of behaviour from its users. Much as Shirky (2008) claims emergent media lower the threshold on group activity, social media facilitate peer monitoring by virtue of how they organize interpersonal exchanges.

Terms like 'creeping' and 'stalking' imply some forms of exposure on Facebook are more troubling than others. Yet in general, respondents grew accustomed to this range of visibility, illustrating a tension between accepted and unwanted kinds of exposure on social media. One respondent stated having his personal information accessible to a network of peers had consequences he was only beginning to realize and accept:

> I've had like a few people phone me and I'd say, "How'd you get my phone number?" "Oh, yeah I got it from Facebook, sorry." "Okay, yeah, no that's totally fine." Because I put it up there, right? I put it up there for a reason.
>
> (Artsci2M)

After he had uploaded personal details, including phone numbers, to his profile, other people were able to use his information in ways that he did not anticipate initially. Such experiences provided respondents with a general impression of their visibility on Facebook. These incidents lead to greater self-scrutiny and management of their presence but also a level of comfort with their exposure. Visibility between users ranges from casually discovering what a close friend did over the weekend to the targeted and prolonged monitoring of strangers. This range of practices is unique in comparison to earlier forms of online digital media, as they emerge seamlessly from a localized everyday context. For this reason, many respondents suspected Facebook was designed specifically for activities like 'stalking' and 'creeping.' As a domesticated media technology, Facebook itself creeps from the familiar to the objectionable.

MAKING SENSE OF A PRIVATE/PUBLIC DISTINCTION

In its simplest terms, privacy is a value that is endangered by this exposure on social media. Scholars and respondents both approach social media surveillance by way of privacy, yet these sites underscore the complexity of understanding and maintaining privacy (Nippert-Eng, 2010). Other research on digital youth suggests youth reconsider while actively managing their privacy on social media (boyd, 2008; West, Lewis and Currie, 2009). These users were experienced in maintaining a degree of privacy from parents prior to social media, and these experiences inform their use of sites like Facebook. Yet they do not simply hide information from some peers; they actively share it with others. In doing so, they maintain a trade-off between ensuring privacy and achieving public exposure when placing their personal content on Facebook (Tufekci, 2008; boyd and Hargittai, 2010).

Respondents made reference to the terms 'private' and 'public' when discussing Facebook. Not only was a public/private binary insufficient, but they framed Facebook as a catalyst to reconsider these values. Facebook represented a kind of blurring of private and public, at least as generally understood in North America prior to the advent of social media. In addition, the term 'personal' crosscut these discussions, such that personal information appeared in public spaces, private spaces, or both. Facebook was a public presence where respondents are ostensibly comfortable sharing personal details with friends they have wilfully chosen. Some respondents, especially those in their first year of studies, drew parallels between their exposure on Facebook and the kind of publicity sought by reality TV stars. Clearly one of the key motivations for using Facebook was to share specific information with a somewhat amorphous (though occasionally specific) audience.

> It's pretty much all about attention, as far as pictures; taking pictures, things like that—because everyone can see that. (. . .) It's almost as if we're in a world where we watch a lot of reality TV and there's [reality] TV shows like *The Hills* and things like that, Facebook is our own little form of entertainment where we can get a glimpse of everyone's life.
>
> (Artsci3M)

Other respondents approached Facebook publicity with trepidation, making comparisons to other types of exposure to underscore the difficulty of adjusting to the service. One respondent likened the circulation of photos on Facebook as if they "had a photo album at my house and somebody came and copied it and then put it in their photo album" (Artsci4M). Another claimed the wall was modelled after the whiteboard on students' doors in residence halls, making it a kind of public space. Respondents also drew comparisons between putting content on Facebook and being visible outdoors. However, the implications of this imagery were not unanimous. While some believed being outside legitimated scrutiny, others still held expectations against unwanted forms of exposure.

Privacy violations mattered to respondents, notably when their personal information leaked in unanticipated or undesirable ways. One respondent who described Facebook as private referred to its extensive privacy controls yet also acknowledged a public element insofar as the site is open to all:

> I'd say it's private in the sense that like your own profile is like, your own profile and you can control what's on it because even if somebody writes on your wall, you can make it invisible kind of thing. So, it's totally private because you can have as much information as you want or as little information as you want, but then it's public in the sense that anyone can use it.
>
> (Health1W)

Most respondents contemplated their privacy and publicity simultaneously. One respondent referred to Facebook as "a completely public expression of private and personal matters" (Artsci4W). This statement suggests a paradox of values that governed respondents' use of Facebook. Following default settings, respondents placed their personal information in a context that was more public than desired. The fact that this was a deliberate and wilful act perplexed respondents:

> It's supposed to be personal information but Facebook makes it very public and you're supposed to be, I guess, with every post you make, keeping in mind the fact that everyone can see this and that this is a public sphere for, I guess, private communication.
>
> (Artsci4W)

In suggesting that a typical user ought to "keep in mind" the extent to which personal details on Facebook are public, this respondent was coming to terms with potential exposure on this platform.

MANAGING ONLINE PRESENCES

Although social media like Facebook offer new opportunities for public exposure, respondents had a range of tactics at their disposal to manage their presence. Caring for the virtual self (Whitson and Haggerty, 2008) involved restricting information flows and exceeded the range of privacy features offered by Facebook. In general, respondents made extensive use of privacy settings. They did this to restrict information from a general public but also for more targeted purposes like hiding a particular photo album from specific individuals. The majority of respondents were familiar with privacy settings. Others found them confusing but maintained a commitment to mastering these settings. Based on prior experiences, respondents periodically returned to their settings to ensure they were still in order. Upon joining his school's academic network, one respondent noticed his personal information had leaked to a degree he did not anticipate. Following this incident, he appraised his privacy settings "every so often (. . .) to make sure that only my friends can see my profile" (Artsci3M). One respondent said she set her privacy such that other users could not seek her out. In effect, she had to initiate contact with others.

Another tactic employed by respondents was to maintain dynamic and contextual privacy settings. Many respondents stated their intention to revise their settings, with one respondent doing this mid-interview. Respondents augmented their privacy during job searches, such that potential employers could not locate their personal content. One person went so far as to cancel his Facebook account temporarily in recognition of how his position as a political leader could be compromised by his online presence:

> I cancelled Facebook for a little while; it was for quite a long period of time. It was because I was vice-president of the [youth political group].

> (. . .) I had that leadership position too and, that's when I realized that you know, this is my personal life but, it's publicly . . . like my public personal life, that could reflect negatively on the [youth political group].
>
> (Artsci1M)

Other respondents logged onto their friends' accounts to see the extent to which they were visible. By looking at their presence from another user's perspective, they had a better sense of how their presence was perceived. Facebook later integrated this feature into their privacy settings, an acknowledgment that peer visibility matters to respondents.

Respondents also cared for their virtual selves by choosing not to upload certain information. This self-censorship is described along common-sense lines, as respondents simply did not share content that they believed would harm their reputation:

> Anything I put out there on the Internet—if I'm afraid of it ever coming back to haunt me, I won't put it out there. And I consciously make that decision for every piece of information that I put out. So I'm not really worried about stalking or creeping because anything out there on me is kind of what I've already put out.
>
> (Artsci3W)

> Anything that you wouldn't want your parents to know isn't something that should be on the Internet.
>
> (Artsci4W)

Respondents cared for their virtual selves by omitting or removing damaging content. Parents and stalkers were invoked as potential watchers and thus as justification for self-care through self-censorship. The latter included not uploading information but also not behaving in a way that could be photographed or otherwise documented:

> For me to be caught on photo doing something stupid, I had to be doing something stupid in the first place. And if I avoid that, which I have been hit or miss about in the past, then it's a non-issue. They can't post photos of me that didn't happen.
>
> (Health3M)

Many respondents monitored the content their friends posted about them. These respondents objected to some wall posts and photos authored by friends, deleted these posts, and scrutinized their friends. In extreme cases respondents also pruned their social network by removing users from their friend lists who posted problematic content on their profiles. Following Foucault (1988), care for the virtual self on social media was manifest as a combination of reflection on risk and visibility, as well as routine activities performed in order to manage that exposure. Yet some respondents also suggested they could not know the full extent of their virtual self on social media and that their efforts to manage their reputation were insufficient.

RESPONSIBILITY AND FUTILITY

Respondents felt responsible for their exposure on social media and extended this sense of responsibility to others. In the event of privacy violations or other unwanted consequences, respondents believed other users only had themselves to blame. This suggests a perceived locus of control by respondents when users upload information to Facebook: "you can exercise so much control over what's visible, it's boggling to me, honestly. If I didn't want people to see my profile, I'd make it private, and that would be that" (Health3M). Because of this perceived sense of agency, respondents had little sympathy for users who encountered trouble with exposure. Respondents claimed that by uploading information onto their profiles, users were "inviting people to look into their life" (Artsci3M). Such users were seen as deliberately uploading information about themselves in a public setting and then coping with consequences they presumably should have anticipated. Respondents did treat their own creeping and stalking of others as problematic, but self-judgement was tempered by the perception that other users are responsible for the care of their virtual selves. As a result, they justified their lateral surveillance of others by citing the other user's decision to upload this information or their failure to use more stringent privacy settings: "If I'm looking at it, I feel like if she has it public, then I can just look at it and I don't feel bad" (Artsci4W).

Respondents felt responsible for managing their online visibility, all while acknowledging the challenges associated with this duty. Attempts to manage privacy are often case based; that is, to stop specific information from circulating in a particular context. Many respondents believed information would still leak beyond an intended audience. The sheer volume of information as well as social ties complicates an online presence. Respondents claimed simply having information on a profile, whether public or private, left users open to considerable risk because of the growing number of individuals who would have access to that information: "I guess we all tend to forget is that what we put on Facebook isn't personal or private in any means because of the hundreds and sometimes thousands of people that you allow to see your profile" (Artsci4W). This respondent compared this unexpected exposure to the 'reply all' button on email interfaces, where users accidentally send a message meant for one person to an entire community. Respondents also described the non-friend friend (a Facebook friend who is a stranger in other social contexts) as a potential vulnerability:

> I think just the people who you kind of add, maybe two or three years ago, who you've kind of forgotten about. They're still on your friends

> list but you may not actually be friends with them in real life and you may not see them ever or talk to them ever, but you still have access to their profile and they still have access to yours.
>
> (Artsci4W)

The quantity of seemingly trusted friends prevented respondents from managing their entire audience. Even when respondents placed the locus of control—and blame—on individual users, they acknowledged Facebook was primarily a public domain, and attempts to limit exposure were futile. Social media are thus presented as domestic technologies through which personal information leaked in unanticipated directions. Respondents were aware that proper conduct on Facebook is based on a contradiction: Individual users are expected to be vigilant, but this vigilance will not offset all potential risk. For these respondents, safe use of social media was necessary but not sufficient to prevent unwanted exposure to peers and strangers.

The above suggests an acknowledgement of partial futility: If information is uploaded, it may leak into unanticipated contexts. Indeed, this condition has likely become more pronounced as Facebook's user population continued to grow and as more institutions began to treat the site as a source of information. Respondents viewed the consequences of Facebook exposure as a concern, because the platform took on a greater presence in various social contexts:

> Like, Facebook is so new, like, we don't know what kind of social implications it's going to have. And it's becoming such a momentous force that I don't think, like, it's like people jumped on board before they knew where it was going.
>
> (Artsci4M)

As this exposure was rooted in the everyday use of social media, the corresponding self-care was embedded in mundane practices like un-tagging photos and choosing not to upload damaging content. These risks were tied to information flows between previously distinct contexts, and respondents used privacy settings extensively to ensure these leaks were kept to a minimum. However, some respondents were overwhelmed by Facebook's opportunities for public exposure and cited this as a reason to not be diligent:

> I'm pretty sure all my private information is already long gone. There's no sense of privacy in this modern world and because everything I do is basically online these days, I feel like there's little or no safety and, therefore, I don't need to curb what I'm doing on Facebook.
>
> (Artsci4W)

This respondent was ambivalent about her comfort with Facebook. She grew accustomed to being visible, but this was in response to the overwhelming exposure on the site. She actively participated in her visibility, but this was not necessarily the kind of social media she wanted. From her perspective, care for the virtual self was understood though—and overshadowed by—a perception that her control of her personal information had already been compromised.

CONCLUSION

At the time of data collection, respondents were developing a growing familiarity with interpersonal visibility on Facebook. However, this familiarity was mixed with uncertainties and tensions. Respondents joined at the behest of their friends and provided personal information to Facebook as a way to communicate with these friends. The kind of visibility required from Facebook was thus borne out of everyday practice, with respondents maintaining relations with their colleagues. In order to maintain social ties with peers, they willingly supplied information about themselves to this platform, making it suitable for interpersonal scrutiny. An ever-growing friendship network led to unanticipated risks, but a sense of agency and responsibility was placed on users themselves despite this complexity. Tensions between individual control and greater complexity on social media, much like tensions between private life and public exposure, are indicative of the further growth and domestication of social media (Silverstone and Haddon, 1996). As a central feature of their everyday life, respondents framed social media exposure as less of a violation and more of a condition that they need to manage. Visibility and exposure on Facebook were normalized and were not limited to any specific instance but were instead framed as a pervasive condition of social life on social media.

Respondents expressed some ambivalence in their responses. They grew accustomed to Facebook visibility, yet its effects remained chilling. These developments complicated efforts to manage their online presence. Respondents felt responsible for their presence but were aware that managing this presence was beyond their control. They perceived online reputation as being a personal responsibility, even while acknowledging that caring for the virtual self by way of vigilant self-scrutiny is not enough. They were aware different audiences and social contexts intersect on the site, but they still constructed a visible profile for close friends. This is emblematic of interpersonal visibility on Facebook: An online presence is built from mundane contributions by users and their friends. Respondents join because their peers are online and build a presence to remain visible to these friends. No single act seems risky or malicious. However, when taken together over time, they contribute to exposure that may lead to social harm. The risk of unwanted visibility and social harm becomes especially salient at a time when Facebook's user population is sharply increasing, with a consequential increase of contributors to any user's visibility, audiences of that visibility, and social contexts in which that visibility will have consequences. A photograph that was uploaded when there were a million Facebook users becomes all the more important when its potential audience exceeds one billion users.

This chapter has focused exclusively on interpersonal visibility and monitoring on social media. Respondents expressed their concerns on this topic in terms of their relations with friends, family, and other known individuals. They were generally concerned with situated and immediate forms of surveillance. Respondents wanted to maintain boundaries that separated different social contexts. From their perspective, these concerns eclipsed other kinds of scrutiny conducted through Facebook. Subsequent research should consider these other kinds of social media monitoring. As law enforcement branches, marketers, employers, and governments take a continued interest in sites like Facebook, the visibility produced by interpersonal social media surveillance will undoubtedly augment the scope and capacity of other kinds of social media surveillance. This research is also limited to digital youth in a university environment. While this provides specific context for user concerns, subsequent research should focus on how other populations are coping with social media platforms and their conditions of intervisibility.

REFERENCES

ALBRECHTSLUND, A. (2008) Online Social Networking as Participatory Surveillance. *First Monday*, 13(3). Accessed August 16, 2011. http://firstmonday.org/htbin/cgiwrap/bin/ojs/index.php/fm/article/view/2142/1949

ANDREJEVIC, M. (2005) The Work of Watching One Another: Lateral Surveillance, Risk, and Governance. *Surveillance & Society*, 2(4). p. 479–497.

BOYD, D. (2008) Facebook's Privacy Trainwreck: Exposure, Invasion, and Social Convergence. *Convergence: The International Journal of Research into New Media Technologies*, 14(1). p. 13–20.

BOYD, D. & HARGITTAI, E. (2010) Facebook Privacy Settings: Who Cares? *First Monday*, 15(8). Accessed August 16, 2011. http://firstmonday.org/htbin/cgiwrap/bin/ojs/index.php/fm/article/view/3086/2589

BRIGHENTI, A.M. (2010) *Visibility in Social Theory and Social Research*. Hampshire: Palgrave Macmillan.

CHANG, H. & CHEN, S.W. (2008) The Impact of Customer Interface Quality, Satisfaction and Switching Costs on E-Loyalty: Internet Experience as a Moderator. *Computers in Human Behavior*, 24. p. 2927–2944.

DEWING, M. (2010) Social Media: 2. Who Uses Them? *Parliamentary Information and Research Service*. Accessed March 4, 2012. www.parl.gc.ca/Content/LOP/ResearchPublications/2010-05-e.htm

FOUCAULT, M. (1988) *The History of Sexuality, Vol. 3: The Care of the Self*. New York: Vintage.

KOSKELA, H. (2004) Webcams, TV Shows and Mobile Phones: Empowering Exhibitionism. *Surveillance & Society*, 2(2/3). p. 199–215.

LYON, D. (2001) *Surveillance Society: Monitoring Everyday Life*. Buckingham (UK): Open University Press.

MURAKAMI WOOD, D. & WEBSTER, C.W. (2009) Living in Surveillance Societies: The Normalisation of Surveillance in Europe and the Threat of Britain's Bad Example. *Journal of Contemporary European Research*, 5(2). p. 259–273.

NIPPERT-ENG, C. (2010) *Islands of Privacy*. Chicago (IL): University of Chicago Press.
OMAND, D., BARTLETT, J. & MILLER, C. (2012) Introducing Social Media Intelligence (SOCMINT). *Intelligence and National Security*, 27(6). p. 801–823.
SAX, L. J., GILMARTIN, S. K. & BRYANT, A. N. (2003) Assessing Response Rates and Nonresponse Bias in Web and Paper Surveys. *Research in Higher Education*, 44(4). p. 409–432.
SHIRKY, C. (2008) *Here Comes Everybody: The Power of Organizing Without Organizations*. New York (NY): The Penguin Press.
SILVERSTONE, R. & HADDON, L. (1996) Design and the Domestication of Information and Communication Technologies: Technical Change and Everyday Life. In Silverstone, R. & Mansell, M. (eds.) *Communication by Design: The Politics of Information and, Communication Technologies*. Oxford: Oxford University Press, p. 44–74.
TROTTIER, D. (2011) A Research Agenda for Social Media Surveillance. *Fast Capitalism*, 8(1). Accessed March 4, 2012. www.uta.edu/huma/agger/fastcapitalism/8_1/trottier8_1.html
TUFEKCI, Z. (2008) Grooming, Gossip, Facebook and MySpace: What Can We Learn About These Sites From Those Who Won't Assimilate? *Information, Communication, and Society*, 11(4). p. 544–564.
WEST, A., LEWIS, J. & CURRIE, J. (2009) Students' Facebook 'Friends': Public and Private Spheres. *Journal of Youth Studies*, 12(6). p. 615–627.
WHITSON, J. & HAGGERTY, K. (2008) Identity Theft and the Care of the Virtual Self. *Economy and Society*, 37(4). p. 572–594.

4 Shaping Children's Consumer Identity Within Contemporary Dutch Market(ing) Practices

Isolde Sprenkels and Irma van der Ploeg

INTRODUCTION

Contemporary marketing communication and research practices are increasingly designed with children's digital technology use and online activities in mind. Often as part of a cross-media approach, market practitioners[1] employ such digital means in order to connect with children. The online presence they establish for corporations and brands includes banner advertisements, different forms of gamevertising, and branded social networking profiles, viral video advertisements, brand presence within online virtual worlds, and websites aimed at children, related for instance to food, beverage, and toy brands or television programmes. Such presence offers ways to meet corporate goals such as building brand awareness and stimulating product purchase. It also enables corporations to monitor children and collect valuable information about them, turning children's online playgrounds into sites for detailed surveillance (Chung and Grimes, 2005; Steeves, 2007). As Kathryn C. Montgomery and Jeff Chester claim,

> "the interactive nature of digital technologies makes it possible for market research to be woven in the content of new media, offering marketers the opportunity to remain in constant contact with teens and creating a feedback system for the refinement of marketing techniques" (Montgomery and Chester, 2009, S19).

This co-shaping of contemporary marketing communication and research is central to this chapter. We will unfold ways in which the 'Dutch kids' market' and children's identities as consumers are constituted within a configuration of such practices by re-describing them in order to disclose some of the socio-material mechanisms at work. For this re-description, a *practice-based approach* to markets and marketing is used (Araujo, 2007; Kjellberg and Helgesson, 2007), which draws from the works of Bruno Latour and Michel Callon. Inspired by Latour's first rule of method, that we should "study science in action and not ready-made science or technology" (Latour, 1987), Hans Kjellberg and Claes-Frederik Helgesson claim that it is impossible to define a list of properties that are typical of markets and that therefore markets should be studied in the making (Kjellberg and Helgesson, 2007). Markets are not fixed entities to be found or discovered, and as 'social-theory-inspired' perspectives on identity claim, neither are identities[2] (Van der Ploeg, 2007; Van Zoonen, 2013). A practice-based approach suggests that market practices contribute to the continuous constitution of markets and consumer identities; they have a "*performative*[3] role in helping to create the phenomena they purportedly describe" (Araujo, 2007, 211).

In this chapter, we adopt the model Kjellberg and Helgesson introduce, which presents markets as continuously realized, as the ongoing results of three strongly interlinked types of practices: *representational practices*, which serve to portray markets and how they work; *exchange practices*, which serve to realize economic exchange of goods and services or transactions; and *normalizing practices*, which serve to establish rules and norms concerning market behaviour, how a market should work (2007). Interestingly, they use the concept of *translation*, the way something spreads and transforms across time and space (Callon, 1986; Latour, 1987), as a way to address how the three practices are entangled as they are linked through chains of translations, which themselves are brought about by those practices. It is these links that are considered to be central to the process through which market practices constitute markets and consumer identities, and we closely follow these links within the two sections of this chapter.

In the first section, I describe two representational market practices using a selection of quotes from semi-structured interviews with market practitioners and presentations held at the annual Dutch conference on kids and youth marketing.[4] Market practitioners constantly seek representational conceptions of children in order to tune their marketing communication strategies with these conceptions and optimize certain results. By employing such practices serving to depict markets (Kjellberg and Helgesson, 2007), they seek what they call 'insights' in matters such as children's development, behaviour, interests, preferences, consumption habits, brand experiences, media use, or leisure activities. Or, as Daniel Thomas Cook explains, they seek to 'know' children (2004, 2011). In order to 'accurately' conceptualize children, market practitioners appear to build upon academic theories on children's (cognitive) (consumer) development and conduct their own market research in which children's life worlds are studied and translated into 'insights' and models representing children's abilities, interests, 'needs, and wants.' These two practices help market practitioners characterize and categorize children, dividing them up in to smaller and more specific 'manageable' groups or segments. We use Geoffrey Bowker and Susan Lee Star's work on categories and knowledge production (1999), together with John Law's work on the performativity of (social) research methods (2009; Law et al., 2011), to describe ways in which these two representational practices depict Dutch children and the Dutch kids' market. Such an approach challenges the basic assumption that there are child consumers 'out there' in an existing and clearly defined 'kids' market' which can be described with specific characteristics (Harrison and Kjellberg, 2010) and helps illustrate instead that they are constituted within these very same practices employed to 'get to know them.'

In the second section, we provide a case study of market exchange practices. We describe how two commercial online environments for children are designed in such a way that they attempt to meet particular corporate goals, ranging from stimulating brand awareness and building a 'personal relationship' between brand and child to the stimulation of product purchase and consumption and collecting personally identifiable information. We demonstrate that their design is informed by both representational practices. Building on what we have seen market practitioners do as they characterize and categorize children, we follow the ways in which that obtained 'knowledge' or those 'insights' are materialized, translated, and inscribed (Akrich, 1992; Bowker and Star, 1999; Oudshoorn et al., 2004) into these two contemporary (digital) marketing communication strategies. Inspired by Madeleine Akrich's concept of *script* (1992), we argue that representational practices are translated into age-specific scripts, which are attributing and delegating specific competencies, actions, and responsibilities to children and are present within or translated into exchange and normalising practices, the latter establishing particular norms, rules, and codes concerning the Dutch kids' market. We demonstrate that developmental psychology–inspired insights and the ones retrieved from market research practices help design exchange practices in such a way that they enable marketers to reach particular corporate goals. We further reveal that both insights are used to legitimize exchange practices as well as representational practices themselves, which, as we argue, holds some serious misapprehensions.

DEPICTING 'CHILD CONSUMERS'

Market practitioners claim that the 'kids' market' is a difficult and even a volatile one to fully understand (Buckingham, 2007). These practitioners continuously seek representational conceptions of children, 'knowledge' about their presumed abilities, interests, 'needs, and wants,' in order to tune their marketing communication with these 'insights.' These are based on ways in which they translate (cognitive) developmental theory into various age-based classification models and on particular market research strategies, employed to study and translate children's life worlds into valuable 'insights.'

Age-Based Categories

Gender, and many other variables such as ethnicity or socio-economic status, can be used to divide children up into 'target' groups, but market practitioners first and foremost divide children up by age. Many of the practitioners we interviewed and who presented at the conference appear to base their categorizations on (cognitive) developmental psychology.[5] Their practices rely heavily on developmental stages, relating to children's presumed cognitive abilities. Such a take can be traced back to the seminal work of developmental psychologist Jean Piaget (1954), who understood childhood as a patterned, predictable sequence of stages (Cook, 2004). Various practitioners presenting at the conference on kids and youth marketing talked about the need to focus on child development from a variety of academic disciplines. Even though they seemed to lump them all together, their work reveals similarities with developmental-stage models. The following paragraphs demonstrate ways in which they have translated and transformed such models into their own age-based classification models.

Vic,[6] the commercial director of a Belgian (television) entertainment company popular in the Netherlands, explains in the following quote that at his company, they classify children based on developmental stages and subsequently consider how they need to act upon them. Their classification helps answer questions about how to design their marketing communication strategies and what types of products and merchandising they need to manufacture for these age-group categories:

> The target group between 0 and 15 does not exist . . . There are clear developmental stages, we conducted research together with [a research agency] . . . 2–3 year olds focus on themselves . . . copy others . . . develop eye hand coordination, 4–5 year olds are more explorative . . . 6–8 year olds fantasize and understand more complex stories . . . 9–12 year olds peer pressure is important . . . how do you aim for that as a brand, show individual children or groups in our commercials? 13–15 is more analytical . . .
>
> What types of merchandising do you have to make for which age-category, what types of toys do you have to make for which age-category?
>
> (Presentation 4, ECX, 2012)

This quote illustrates that for Vic, 'the kids' market' is not a homogeneous group of children but consists of separated age-group categories. These categories are created together by market actors such as Vic, the Belgian (television) entertainment company, and the marketing communication research agency.

Although Vic talks about 'clear' developmental stages, other presenters at the conference spoke of slightly different age groups and mentioned slightly different abilities and interests to go with these stages. A couple of weeks after the conference, we conducted an interview with Cherie, the owner of a kids and youth communication research agency. Cherie responded to Vic's conference presentation, and claimed, "We later went up to [(television) Entertainment Company] and said that they were wrong, that they had added two years to every category" (Interview 8, YCRA-3, 2012).

Cherie is working on a model "for the whole development of children" herself. During her presentation at the conference, she explained this model.

She suggests that between 4 and 6, children are in a magical phase in which the difference between fantasy and reality is still blurry. Between 7 and 9 they are in a more realistic phase in which they develop friendships, and peer influence is increased. And between 10 and 12, which she calls 'tweens,' a tension is experienced between becoming an adult and being a child[7] (Presentation 7, YCRA-3, 2012). Cherie claims that the entertainment company added 2 years to every category, but after doing the maths, her claim doesn't seem to match the differences that can be distinguished between the two age-based classification models of Vic and Cherie. Her remark, being precise in demarcating age ranges, illustrates a literal and very strict application of stages, while Piaget, for instance, actually stressed the succession of stages and not exact age-ranges (Ville and Tartas, 2010).

There were also market practitioners who expressed experiencing difficulties relating to children's abilities and interests within a particular category. As Deniz, owner of a kids and online digital production agency, mentions:

> Some kids' marketers use the phrase 'tweens' to refer to the category of 10–14 year olds. But there are problems with this category: children up to 12 years of age stick to what they know. But when they are 12 years and over, they go and look for new things.
>
> (Interview 10, DPA, 2011)

Deniz explains that there are problems with the 'tween' category itself, as according to her own experience, children between 10 and 12 years of age and children between 12 and 14 years of age differ strongly. This, according to Deniz's understanding, would lead to 'problems' when market practitioners want to target this tween category, as they will fail to speak to all children within this category due to the strong differences between them. The existence of another tween age-range—Cherie, for instance, referred to 10- to 12-year-olds as 'tweens'—confirms the varieties in age range, indicating a lack of consensus between practitioners.

Other practitioners point at differences between age-category concepts among distinct disciplines and argue that classification models and their categories change over time. Mischa, a senior researcher with a kids and youth communication research agency, explains:

> Tweens is a marketing concept I think because in psychology we call the 10–14 year olds early adolescence . . . When I started working in the kids' market back in the nineties, we approached the 6–12 year olds as one group. . . . Then, there was a switch, children getting older younger.
>
> (Interview 7, YCRA-2, 2012)

Before working as a researcher with agencies in this field, Mischa conducted scientific research at a university. Both her knowledge of developmental psychology and her experiences as a market practitioner inform her comments. According to Mischa, in the 1990s, 'tween' was a non-existent category. Such a category is constituted into being, as Natalie Coulter found in her work on the discursive construction of the tween girl market (2009).

Mischa connects the rise of the tween category with the phenomenon of "children getting older younger." For market practitioners this is better known as KAGOY: Kids Are Getting Older Younger. Sociologist Juliet Schor refers to this phenomenon as 'age compression' and explains that market practitioners offer products originally designed for older children and target them to younger ones (2005). David Buckingham states that children are "constantly calibrating themselves in terms of age: other social institutions, most obviously the school, help to define what it means to be a child of a particular age" (2007. 20). But in practice, they often perceive or act out on it in far more complicated ways (ibid.). Indeed, as mentioned, sometimes they aspire to consume things that appear to be targeted to older children, but on the other hand, for some older children, products and services targeted at younger children are appealing, too. This is illustrated by the following quote from Joss and Esra, brand managers at a toy company:

> Our target group is girls between 6–10, though we see younger girls getting interested in brands for older girls, and children over 10 still like the brand as well, perhaps not the dolls, but other merchandise.
>
> (Presentation 9, TC, 2012)

This longing to be slightly older is what market practitioners employ by inscribing it in their practices, their design of products, merchandising, shops,[8] and marketing communication. They serve their commercial interests when they speak of KAGOY, as they will make more money when their target market for products and services used by adolescents, which are often more expensive, becomes larger. Making younger children aspire to those products and services as well increases profit (Schor, 2005).

Interestingly, in one way, market practitioners are inspired by (cognitive) developmental theory, conceptualising children's development in a linear way with predetermined stable sets of age stages. But in another way, they seem to let go of such rigid, structured, universalistic ideas on child development, leaving room for change and variation, as for instance the quote from Mischa shows. As demonstrated, market practitioners have slightly different ideas on the matter. Some of them come up with their own categories, different realities so to say, which is a continuous effort to construct and stabilize their 'stages.' This indicates that categories are contestable constructions, they are contingent, could have been, or are different according to numerous actors and within diverse settings; they travel from theory to various practices or models or systems. Just as Geoffrey Bowker and Susan Lee Star have shown with their work, classification systems organize and are organized in work practice (1999). They are "a set of boxes (metaphorical or literal) into which things can be put to then do some kind of work—bureaucratic or knowledge production" (Bowker and Star, 1999, 10).

Empowering 'Child Consumers'

Market practitioners' 'insights' on children come not only from (self-made) models of child development. These 'insights,' this 'knowledge' about children's abilities and interests, also come from other representational practices, such as their market research and communication concept-developing practices. There is a large variety of research methods employed in order to depict children's life worlds. Schor mentions organizing consumer panels, test panels, the use of surveys, questionnaires, and focus groups, as well as conducting interviews and ethnographically oriented observations—ranging from playgrounds to bedrooms—hiring children as company consultants, and using eye movement tracking and neuro-imaging technology (2005). With the rise of the Internet and its World Wide Web, new methods emerged; Internet market research and data mining techniques are increasingly employed within children's online playgrounds, like the online environments described in below, covertly collecting various types of information about children (Chung and Grimes, 2005).

Cofounder of kids and youth communication research agency 4, Jules, explains how she envisions traditional and new research methods to co-exist and hints at involving youth directly in research:

> Traditional research methods will stay, but I think it will be both. I think it would be great to say to a particular focus group: download this app and keep track of the following things this week and you will receive a new push message every day when we have a new assignment . . . I think youth would enjoy it very much . . . they like to cooperate with our research because we focus on them, on what they think . . . we often say to them that they are really helping us and that we are very happy with that.
>
> (Interview 9, YCRA-4, 2012)

In line with Cook's descriptions of a rise in 'taking the child's perspective' in the work of marketing scholars and market practitioners (2004) and the increased attention in interdisciplinary childhood studies since the 1980s for children's subjectivity and agency and involving them as participants in research (Qvorttrup et al., 2011), calls for the 'right' of children to 'have a voice' have also increased in the field of market research (Todd, 2010). Children are engaged more directly in market research and communication concept-developing practices, using notions such as 'giving children a voice,' 'give them influence,' 'involve them,' and 'start a conversation.' This empowerment language contributes to market practitioners' discursive legitimization of their practices.

One of the ways in which market practitioners tend to 'give children a voice' is through what is referred to as 'co-creation.' The website of kids and youth communication research agency 4 addresses potential clients of their agency and explains their ambition of involving youth in their practices:

> Do you want to involve youth in your organization, then ask them what you want to know from them! Do you have a vision, an idea, a plan; present it to youth. Start a conversation with them, organize a creative session, have them talk to each other, brainstorm. What form you use does not matter, as long as you involve them. Because what could be more fun than creating value together, and while talking, exploring and brainstorming, going from 'them' to 'us'!
>
> (YCRA-4)

This invitation or advice illustrates situating children discursively as the 'other,' or 'them,' about whom market practitioners want to find out as much as possible. Natalie Coulter might describe this in terms of the colonization of young people as markets (2012),[9] but it also demonstrates the assumption of 'joining forces'; of turning 'them' into an 'us,' a 'co,' creating marketing communication, products, and services together. Who is helping whom here remains unclear.

Pascal, senior advisor at kids and youth communication research agency 1, stresses the value of co-creation:

> I think your relationship with your target group is very important for making really good choices . . . co-creation is the core of our thinking . . . it allows us to have children design in ways that really 'fit' them, and by which implicitly you can analyse a lot of research data . . . having a child [involved in] design is a way to find out what the core behind that topic is for a child . . . co-creation is helpful to get to the real perception of things.
>
> (Interview 6, YCRA-1, 2012)

According to Pascal, co-creation is a good way to get to 'the real perception of things,' to 'discover' the core of what children are like and what they consider to be important, interesting, or desirable. It also offers important research data along the way. However, following John Law and his work on the performativity of methods (2009), there is no such thing as 'discovering' and gaining a 'real perception' of something 'out there,' some sort of essence of children's abilities, interests, 'needs, and wants.' Instead, these are produced or enacted within these very practices employed to 'get to know them.'[10] While conceptualising and categorising children, market practitioners construct various identities of their target group. These are constituted into being by re-describing them in their own terms and acting upon them.

"Good Work and Good Business Go Hand in Glove"

Market practitioners research the abilities, interests, 'needs, and wants' of youth through representational practices in order to take these into account in marketing communication strategy design. At the same time, it is a way to legitimize these practices: Practitioners argue to do 'good work' because they meet children's 'needs and desires.' Amy Henry explained having a similar experience. According to her, US industry leaders claim that "good work [meaning ethical[11]] and good business go hand in glove"; they argue "that the same process that allows them to create effective advertising also ensures that the advertising is ethical and that age-appropriate advertising is both clearer and more appealing to children" (2005, 11).

Meeting children's 'needs and desires' for market practitioners means that their marketing communication, products, and services 'add value' to children's lives. As Pascal, working at kids and youth communication research agency 1, clearly explained:

> Though it is not that I would say that selling candy doesn't have any value . . . value is not a judgement about a product, about content, nor about the services of a client, it is about the desires and needs of youth.
> (Interview 6, YCRA-1, 2012)

'Having value' is important for market practitioners' professional ethics, which is based on normalizing practices, on establishing rules and norms on how they should act. Jules mentioned:

> When it comes to commercial clients . . . This means that if I help them, the world for youth becomes a little bit better, as it means less annoying advertising . . . more fit to their needs . . . Of course, it is still selling to youth, but we can't change that any more . . . and youth want those products too, they want those phones.
> (Interview 9, YCRA-4, 2012)

Jules explains that she can make the world for youth a bit better when she succeeds in developing marketing communication that fits the 'needs' of youth. At the same time, she distances herself from her industry when she claims to be able to develop less annoying advertising, implying that there are others who do not succeed in meeting youth's needs.[12] She expresses her ambivalence with her industry also in another way, saying it is still selling to youth, while condoning it at the same time by claiming that it can't be changed anymore and that it is what youth want.

In the next section, we use a case study analysis of two exchange practices, of two commercial online environments for children, to demonstrate that both depicting representational practices are translated and inscribed into the design of these online environments in order to serve economic as well as moral purposes.

TRANSLATING AND INSCRIBING 'INSIGHTS'

In this section, we will first describe how two advergame environments for children are designed in such a way that they meet particular corporate goals, ranging from stimulating brand awareness and building a 'personal relationship' between brand and child to the stimulation of product purchase and consumption and collecting personally identifiable information. This is followed by a description of ways in which market practitioners deal with ethical criticism by employing representational market practices in a particular way.

Achieving Corporate Goals

Many children play online casual or mini-games. These short, 'free,' and easy-to-learn games have friendly designs with bright colours and fun tasks to perform and are developed to entertain, to educate, or to deliver a particular commercial message. This case focuses on the latter, 'advertisement as game,' often referred to as 'advergame.' Within this chapter, advergames, or more broadly, advergame environments, are considered to be online environments owned by brands, consisting of elements such as casual or mini-games specifically developed around a particular product or brand.[13]

OLA Ice Age and Max Adventures

In 2007, OLA and Nickelodeon organized a multi-channel campaign together, which involved branded competition days in swimming pools in order to enlarge OLA's market share and to generate a healthy image for a product which normally isn't associated with a healthy lifestyle. Among other things, OLA provided their ice cream wrappers with stamps called 'heartbeats,' which could be saved for the inflatable water fun products used at the competition days. Nickelodeon reported on these days during one of their best-viewed shows named *SuperNick*, and a special OLA Water Games website was built with information about the competition.

For their successor campaign, OLA and Nickelodeon decided to build on the positive experiences they had with the popular gaming section on this website (Goeij and Kwantes, 2009). In the process of coming up with a concept for their new campaign in 2009 to enlarge OLA's market share and to familiarize children with OLA's assortment, they decided to invite children over to brainstorm with them about their associations with ice cream (Houben, 2009). Generating 'insights' through such sessions with children can be considered a form of 'co-creation,' a representational market practice. These 'insights,' in turn, were translated into an exchange practice, the specifically designed advergame environment OLA Ice Age,[14] which was placed at the centre of their multichannel campaign. The leading role for the OLA Ice Age campaign was taken by a cartoon character: OLA ice cream inventor 'Professor Freeze,'[15] who lives in an ice cave, where he turns children's dreams into ice cream by using his ice cream machine.

The campaign was followed by the Max Adventures campaign in 2011, which is developed in order to create brand awareness for the Dutch OLA sub-brand for children called Max Adventures, to generate a healthy image by promoting an active lifestyle (Colak and Helmons, 2013). Central to this campaign are an animation series starring lion king Max and his fellow adventurers,[16] programmed at the Nickelodeon television channel, and a Max Adventures advergame environment in which reruns of this animation series can be watched and where Max related casual or mini-games can be played.[17]

Building a Relationship

The parents' section on OLA Ice Age claims that Professor Freeze is "taking children on an adventure and guides them through the games and activities on the website" (OLAIJstijd, 2010). In their brochure informing potential advertisers, they explain that Nickelodeon is like a crazy mentor, taking children on an adventure within a secure and trusted environment and bringing them back home safely afterwards (MTV Networks, 2009). Both Professor Freeze and lion Max, characters representing the OLA brand, are presented as mentor or role models, someone to trust. Inviting children to engage in a trust relationship, building a personal relationship with them, is a strategy used in marketing targeted at children. Or, as Valerie Steeves states, children are encouraged to consider brands "as role models for the child to emulate, in effect embedding the product right into a child's identity" (Steeves, 2006).

When he's not on vacation, Professor Freeze drives around in his ice cream van to copy children's dreams at night. Back at his ice cave, he turns these dreams into ice cream by using his ice cream machine. When one enters the website, an animation is showing Professor Freeze packing his bags, announcing that he is going on a vacation and needs an assistant to operate the ice machine. Professor Freeze promises that when a child has earned all badges in the ice cave, he or she can become the assistant that Professor Freeze is looking for. On the Max Adventures website, children are not ascribed such a role in order to connect with them, but they are invited to choose either lion Max or his friend lioness Leena as their avatar when playing the games.[18] Pretending to be either Max or Leena offers children the opportunity to identify with these characters, their characteristics, and their place in the story line.

Raising Brand Awareness

Within the ice cave, there are several games to play, wallpapers and ringtones to download, quizzes to enter, pictures to upload, and videos to watch.

These videos contain the OLA Ice Age commercial aired on Nickelodeon and a realistic video about how ice cream is actually made, wrapped, and transported to stores. Children are also encouraged to play with actual OLA products in the ice cave, and most games and quizzes are related to existing ice creams in OLA's assortment. These features enable children at a later point in time, for instance in a store, to identify the brand and its products (Grimes and Shade, 2005). On the Max Adventures website, the connection with ice cream or OLA is not made that explicit. Only after watching an episode of the animation series *Max Adventures* is it mentioned that the series is offered by OLA. But Max Adventures is a sub-brand for OLA, and children recognize the character and his name in many places, they see him on television, on the Nickelodeon website, and the Max Adventures website, and recognize him in stores on things like ice cream wrappers and boxes.

OLA Ice Age contains multiple game levels and public displays of high scores, and new games are added on a regular basis. This prolongs contact time with the brand continuously (Moore, 2004) and happens on the Max Adventures website as well, contributing to this brand awareness. High scores are shown, and multiple game levels are built into the games. New games are displayed but inaccessible, which triggers children to go back to the website regularly to see whether the new games are made available. As they progress within these games, children can earn coins and buy accessories, collect dinosaurs, and develop their status from 'adventurer' to 'master' to 'hero' and finally to 'legend,' which stimulates their return to the advergame environment as well.

Spreading the Brand 'Virally'

Receiving many unique website visitors and possible new customers is also important to the brand, and there are several ways to make that happen. One of the many features of OLA Ice Age is decorating 'one's own room' by choosing particular colours for the elements in it. It is one of the first things a child is invited to do. A picture of this 'room' can be sent to friends, which allows OLA, represented by Professor Freeze, to invite other children to the OLA Ice Age website. This is a form of viral marketing in which children are encouraged to share their experience and communicate with others about OLA. Friends receive a message such as "Do you want to decorate your own room in the OLA Ice Age cave and play cool games? Go to . . ." Sharing one's gaming experience with others also offers the possibility to collect personally identifiable information such as email addresses (Gurău, 2008).

The first competition related to Max Adventures was a dance competition. Market practitioners from OLA and Nickelodeon based the idea of this competition on the claims or 'insights' that children like to dance, want to become famous, and want 'priceless prizes' (Colak and Helmons, 2013). They inscribed these insights into the Max Adventures campaign. Children were invited to mimic a pre-choreographed Max or Leena dance and to upload it to the Max Adventures website and to Twitter, Facebook, its Dutch equivalent Hyves, and a special YouTube channel. The 'priceless prize' was dancing a part in the video clip of a Dutch junior song contest idol. Sharing this video with friends and family created a viral effect for OLA and its sub-brand Max Adventures, which triggered many more children to participate in the competition and to visit the Max Adventures website (ibid.).

Encourage Product Purchase

Other competitions related to OLA Ice Age were designing one's ultimate fantasy ice cream using the ice cream machine and an arts and crafts competition for which children are asked to draw or glue together their own ice cream, take a picture of it, and upload it to the website. Both competitions offer 'insights' into children's ice cream preferences. Also, a competition was organized for which children were encouraged to buy a popsicle containing a code on its stick, required to enter the competition. Such direct encouragement to purchase products is also a common strategy in advergames (Moore, 2004). Currently there is no active competition on the Dutch Max Adventures website. But the Australian website, for instance, named Paddle Pop adventures,[19] shows a competition called 'lick a prize'; the popsicles contain codes which can be collected and are rewarded with prizes ranging from bikes to family vacations to the US.

As the above illustrates, advergame environments such as OLA Ice Age and Max Adventures are designed in such a way that they offer a brand the opportunity to reach a range of corporate goals. Advergame research also shows how some of these games include product-related polls or quizzes, offering valuable information for market research on children's habits and preferences (Moore, 2004; Grimes, 2008). As in OLA Ice Age and Max Adventures, these environments may also encourage players to register and share their gaming experience with friends or family as we have shown, thus enabling the collection of personally identifiable information (Gurău, 2008). Combined with possibilities these digital technologies offer for the analysis of in-game-behaviour and activities, marketers are able to construct detailed consumer profiles based on the aggregation of behavioural with demographic data (Chung and Grimes, 2005; Grimes, 2008). Therefore, advergame environments can be described as Schull's "electronic surveillance devices" (2005), as they enable tracking children's activities and whereabouts both within the game as well as their physical location through IP addresses. This illustrates that they are not only market exchange practices informed by representational practices, they can also be considered representational practices themselves, crossing market practice boundaries.[20]

Notably, the OLA website contains no clear statement of its marketing purposes to either children or their parents. The 'parents' section' on the website states that the goal is to "entertain children, stimulate their imagination and discover the world behind OLA ice cream" and "Ice cream is not to be sold on the website, as it is only a fun world for children" (OLAIJstijd, 2010). However, beyond a fun world for children or one that inspires children to be adventurous and exercise more, as claimed on the Max Adventures website, commercial ends are served with advergame environments designed this way.

Agnes Nairn and Haiming Hang criticize disguising the purpose of advergames as a marketing communication strategy (2012). For instance, they found that Miniclip—an internationally oriented game site for children—advises companies who want to place an advergame or another form of gamevertising on their website as follows: "Don't use your brand name too much. Subtle brand messages can get the message across better than in your face logos. The key point is that the player enjoys the game" (ibid., 10). Similarly, game advertising expert David Edery states in a presentation on the general field of gamevertising that "the whole point is to eliminate recognition" (2009) of the advertisement. With advergame environments such as OLA Ice Age and Max Adventures, play and fun tend to be put all up front[21] while remaining silent on processes, activities, and intentions in the background, rendering any market practice described in this chapter invisible. To children it seems indeed "just a fun world," as play and fun are probably the first and only associations they have with these environments.

According to the current critical academic and societal debate[22] regarding advergame environments, children are most vulnerable because they are still developing the competencies to understand techniques of persuasion and are not yet capable of defending themselves and thinking critically. Market practitioners tend to deal with this critique regarding the ethics of digital forms of marketing communication such as advergame environments in different ways. Their defence has its roots in the representational market practices discussed in this chapter.

Deflecting Moral Criticism

Academic, societal, and business attempts to evaluate digital forms of marketing communication with children such as OLA Ice Age and Max Adventures from an ethical or moral point of view are rooted in a history of studying and questioning the 'fairness' of more traditional forms of advertising. It dealt with children's cognitive abilities to recognize advertising and develop a critical understanding of its mechanisms. The main points made in this body of work, as Sonia Livingstone explains, merge "a philosophical question about ethics (is it fair to persuade those who are unaware of such efforts?) with an empirical question about influence (who is particularly susceptible to persuasive messages?)" (Livingstone, 2009, 170). It is usually based on certain presumed cognitive abilities of children, or lack thereof. Underlying this and frequently referred to is the age-stage evolution model of children's cognitive development from developmental cognitive psychology (Nairn and Fine, 2008), which is translated into models of consumer socialization (Roedder-John, 1999). This posits several developmental 'milestones' (Lunt and Livingstone, 2012, 147), the first of which is reached when a child is around 3 years old. This is the moment when a child is considered to be somewhat capable of distinguishing advertising from programming. The moment a child can understand the selling and persuasive intent behind an advertisement and can distinguish it from information, usually at around 8 years old, is considered to be the second milestone.[23] A third and final 'milestone' is reached somewhere around age 12, when a child is presumed to have acquired the ability to critically reflect on, weigh, and refuse an advertisement. It is not until children have reached this latter stage that targeting advertising to them is considered to be 'fair' (Nairn and Hang, 2012).

Given this, the primary way in which market practitioners deflect moral criticism, claiming their market practices to be ethical, is to argue that they take children's (cognitive) developmental abilities into account. They base their market exchange practices and normalising practices such as their codes of conduct on children's cognitive psychological development and associated interests. But, as we claim in what follows, they appear to do so selectively.

For instance, the academic discourse on children and advertising and the age-stage model of consumer socialization has evolved. In this academic discourse, it is argued that several difficulties exist when using the model as an ethical yardstick for assessing the 'fairness' of advertising to children. Following the argument, it is generally taken for granted that "those whose literacy is lower are assumed to be more susceptible to effects"[24] and that "an increase in media or advertising literacy is assumed to reduce susceptibility to media effects" (Livingstone and Helsper, 2006, 564). But Sonia Livingstone and Ellen Helsper found little empirical evidence for this claim. They argue that although teenagers are presumed to be more 'media literate,' that does not mean that they are less influenced by advertising than younger children are. They conclude that "different processes of persuasion are effective at different ages, precisely because literacy levels vary by age" (ibid.). Which means that younger children, being less media literate, are merely persuaded differently than teenagers are. Younger children tend to be persuaded by superficial or peripheral features of advertising such as jingles and colourful and funny images, whereas teenagers tend to be persuaded by, for instance, strong arguments and references to peer-group approval (ibid.).[25]

Another problem with this claim on literacy levels and susceptibility, which has already led certain academics to reject such a model, has to do with contemporary marketing communication formats such as OLA Ice Age and Max Adventures. Livingstone concludes that the age-stage evolution model of children's cognitive abilities no longer fits the diversity of the 21st-century media environment (2009). She claims that the idea of 'milestones' related to age is not convincing, "both because there is no universal relation between understanding and age, and because persuasion occurs, in one way or another, across the range" (Livingstone, 2009, 172). In saying this, she follows Agnes Nairn and psychologist Cordelia Fine, who doubt the possibility of establishing any 'magical age' at which children are supposed to understand and resist persuasion, as contemporary formats often intentionally bypass children's explicit persuasion knowledge and instead persuade implicitly (2008). They tend to be more covert, as the brand and its corporate goals are integrated into non-commercial contexts. This challenges not only younger and older children's cognitive defences but those of teenagers and even adults as well (Moore, 2004; Fielder et al., 2007; Nairn and Fine, 2008). It indicates that vulnerability depends on both an individual's cognitive social resources and the (social or mediated) environment (Livingstone, 2009). Focusing exclusively on cognitive abilities implies a specific view of technology, considering it to be inherently neutral. We have argued elsewhere that the 'fairness issue' can be considered as something that is a function of the set of socio-material relations in which children's options, choices, and chances to resist are also shaped by the marketing communication tactics and formats themselves (Sprenkels and van der Ploeg, 2014).

The specific characteristics of contemporary marketing communication touch on some of the issues with market practitioners' codes of conduct. They argue that they have translated the abovementioned developmental milestones into normalising practices, into their codes of conduct based on self-regulation. One example is the Dutch Advertising Code[26] and its special section on children and advertising,[27] which proposes to help children differentiate content as it prescribes that the distinction between editorial content and advertising targeting children—defined as a person being 12 or younger—should always be made recognizable. For instance, television commercials are preferably clustered, and banner and pop-up advertisements on the internet should be labelled with the word 'advertisement.' However, as mentioned, the age-stage model of consumer socialization is problematic, and when it comes to contemporary formats such as advergame environments, the code is not followed because the distinction is not made explicit in any way at all (Fielder et al., 2007). Not only do such 'seamless environments' (Moore, 2004) fail to follow the code, this form of self-regulation advocates a strategy that runs exactly counter to what advergames tend to be about, namely presenting advertisements, and all related market practices running in the background, as game.

As suggested earlier, market practitioners translate academic theories on children's cognitive development into various age-based classification models. They come up with a variety of age categories in practice, refining and reducing them to smaller and smaller age groups. It is a continuous effort to construct and stabilize these 'stages,' which they constitute into being by re-describing them in their own terms. We have demonstrated that such categories or market segments are contestable constructions, they are contingent, different according to different actors and within different settings. Market practitioners consider their work to be ethical, as they claim to follow children's developmental needs, which they presume to be clear cut, out there, which as shown, they are not.

The secondary way in which market practitioners consider their market practices to be ethical relates to their claim that they take children's 'needs and wants' into account by giving them a voice, *empowering* them, including them, using representational practices such as co-creation. But we have illustrated in the previous sections that those practices tend to be performative, too, producing what they seek to describe. There appears to be an assumption that it is perfectly legitimate to target children as long as this is based on and provides 'what children want and need,' as if the latter can be considered to be a moral right. Thus, the more market practitioners attempt to know what children think, want, and need, the better they will be able to provide this, and hence, the less reprehensible it is to use sophisticated marketing strategies aimed at children. But as illustrated earlier in this chapter, the 'knowledge' about children required for this, the 'listening' to their 'needs and wants,' comes from their own marketing communication and research focussed on children from the very market practices in need of legitimization. We argue that contemporary marketers' constitution of children's preferences and identities as consumers are actually socio-technical enactments enabled by the market practices and research techniques under discussion and described in this chapter. Using children's identities as competent and desiring consumers as legitimization of these same practices is circular.

CONCLUSION

This chapter portrayed a configuration of contemporary market practices, characterizing and categorizing, monitoring and targeting Dutch children in a digitising society. It illustrated the performativity of such socio-material practices and discussed market professionals' self-produced legitimizations based on their presumed 'insights' or 'knowledge' of children. It demonstrated ways in which the Dutch 'kids' market' and children's identities as consumers are constituted within this configuration, that they are not pre-existing entities, but that they are continuously enacted into being. What became clear was that the 'insights' gained from the representational market practices are not only translated and inscribed into market exchange practices, such as the commercial online environments or advergames discussed, in order to meet corporate goals. They also contribute to the legitimization of both exchange practices and representational practices themselves. But the outcomes of market practitioners' representational practices are contingent and performative; they partly constitute these abilities, interests, and 'needs and wants' themselves. In other words, within the configuration of market practices, children are enacted as full-fledged competent consumers, a notion that is subsequently invoked to legitimize the very practices involved in its production.

The practice-based approach as well as the semiotic approach to user–technology relations used in this chapter, with notions such as performativity, enactment, translation, inscription, representational, exchange, and normalizing practices, can contribute to the current social and academic debate concerning contemporary (digital) marketing communication targeting children. Contrary to most views on the matter, it allows us to take a broad perspective on the various market practices involved, how they are entangled and translated, and what it is that these practices and their connections do. It also allows us to take the various digital means themselves, used by both children and market practitioners in a digitising society, into account. These digital means are not to be considered neutral; for instance, advergames play an active role in shaping these market practices, children's consumer identities, and children's commercial literacy (see also the chapter by Sprenkels and Wyatt in this volume), and conversely, they are actively shaped by market practices and children's new media use themselves.

NOTES

1. Daniel Thomas Cook defines the term 'market practitioners' as "marketers, researchers, designers, manufacturers, and other market actors" (2011, 258).
2. Following social and constructivist studies of science and technology (STS), more particularly actor-network theory (ANT) (Callon, 1986; Latour, 1987, 1991; Akrich, 1992), identity can be considered to be *enacted* within sociomaterial arrangements, by and through relations between both human and non-human actors, shaping and defining each other and constituting networks.
3. As explained by MacKenzie and colleagues (2007), the notion of performativity has its origins in the work of philosopher J. L. Austin on speech acts, utterances that bring a state of affairs into being such as 'I apologize.' Later on, the notion has been taken up and broadened by the social sciences, humanities, and science studies.
4. '*Trends in kids en jongerenmarketing*' in Dutch, currently the only major Dutch conference in this field.
5. Sociologist Juliet Schor explained having a similar experience when talking to market practitioners about their research methods; they appeared to rely on a common psychological model of the child, seeing children steadily developing into adulthood (2005).
6. The names of interviewees and conference speakers in this chapter are fictitious.
7. Interestingly, Cherie refers to this phase as 'no longer being a child.' This probably stems from children's often-heard statement to consider certain things to be 'childish.' But it is re-used and translated in such a way that it benefits market practitioners' 'kids getting older younger' claim discussed later.
8. For instance, in his work on the rise of the children's clothing industry, Cook explained that younger children needed to pass through the older children's area in a shop (2004).
9. Coulter applies Homi Bhabha's reading of colonialism to the colonizing of young people as markets in need of 'discovery.' She uses Bhabha's "regime of truth" (Bhabha, 2001; in Coulter, 2012), in "which the colonizer controls the colonized through finding out everything about the colonized and using this

knowledge to construct an identity of the colonized in a unified and coherent way" (Coulter, 2012, 151).

10. Similarly, Eva Heiskanen has conducted research on the performative nature of consumer research depicting 'the green consumer' (2005), and Catherine Grandclément and Gérard Gaglio have studied the performance aspect of focus group–based market research (2011).
11. By most industry leaders defined as "advertising that is age-appropriate, socially sensitive, and honest in its portrayal of the advertised product" (Henry, 2005, 11).
12. Amy Henry, who wrote a report on marketers targeting children and their perspectives on 'good work' and US industry leaders' discomfort with the label 'kids' marketer,' also found that when it comes to professional ethics, marketers stressed that they did not engage in unethical work themselves but expressed their concern that others might do so (2005).
13. Advergames are considered to be a particular form of gamevertising, with gamevertising in general being the promotional or advertising possibilities before, within, or after an often already existing console, PC, or Internet game (Hufen, 2010).
14. In Dutch: OLA IJstijd. The website www.olaijstijd.nl is no longer in use.
15. 'Professor De Vries' in Dutch, which is a very common name in the Netherlands.
16. In many other countries such as South Africa, Indonesia, India, New Zealand, and Australia, Max is known as the Paddle Pop Lion. Similar campaigns run in those countries. Paddle Pop is, just like Max Adventures is for OLA, a sub-brand for Streets, the Australian equivalent of OLA. It originates from a particular Australian ice cream type developed in the 1950s. The ice cream wrapper contained a cartoon character which was known as the Paddle Pop lion.
17. www.max-adventures.com/nl-nl/
18. Lion Max has many fellow adventurers besides lioness Leena, as well as several enemies, all playing active roles in the series. On the website all the characters of the latest story 'Dino Terra' are described. The website shows two previous series as well: Kombatei and Begins. They are all divided up in 8 to 10 episodes with a duration of 10 to 24 minutes.
19. See endnote 16.
20. Marketing professor Agnes Nairn and market research company director Barbie Clarke stress a line between market research, which according to them does not seek to alter opinion, and marketing, which according to them does seek to alter opinion (2012). This chapter clearly argues that such clear distinctions are difficult to uphold.
21. According to Cook, market practitioners tailor messages and design products, packages, websites, campaigns, and advertisements in such a way that they appeal to children, designing it to be fun, playful, entertaining (2011).
22. For instance, there is some debate regarding marketing communication targeting children in the Netherlands. In reports from consumer organizations (Foodwatch, 2013), governmental institutions (Autoriteit Consument en Markt, 2013), and child and media knowledge centres (Mijn Kind Online, 2008), various practices are being criticized.
23. Although, as David Buckingham explains, some studies suggest that this understanding is not necessarily used. He claims differences in these estimations are a consequence of research method (Buckingham, 2009).
24. Advertising effects can be intended by advertisers, such as brand awareness and buying intent, and non-intended, such as materialism and family conflicts (Valkenburg, 2002, 140). In this chapter we call intended effects by advertisers 'goals.'

25. Here Livingstone and Helsper are inspired by Petty and Cacioppo's elaboration likelihood model of persuasion, which distinguishes two routes of persuasion, a central one and the peripheral one.
26. Nederlandse Reclame Code
27. For another example, the Dutch Advertising Code for Foods—Reclamecode voor Voedingsmiddelen—forbidding targeting of children under 7 years of age with (commercial) food advertisements and stressing the abstention in targeting children between 7 and 12 years of age, view (Sprenkels, forthcoming). It offers a close analysis of Unilever's principles for responsible food and beverage marketing and their motivation of their practices related to OLA Ice Age and Max Adventures.

REFERENCES

AKRICH, M. (1992) The De-scription of Technical Objects. In Bijker, W.E. & Law, J. (eds.) *Shaping Technology/Building Society—Studies in Sociotechnical Change.* Cambridge (MA): MIT Press, 205–224.

ARAUJO, L. (2007) Markets, Market-Making and Marketing. *Marketing Theory*, 7(3). p. 211–226.

AUTORITEIT CONSUMENT EN MARKT. (2013). *Marktscan naar online games.* Den Haag: Mediawijzer.

BHABHA, H. (2001) The Other Question: Stereotype, Discrimination and the Discourse of Colonialism. In Seidman, S. & Alexander J.C. (Eds.), *The New Social Theory Reader: Contemporary Debates.* New York: Routledge, 388–402.

BOWKER, G.C. & STAR, S.L. (1999) *Sorting Things Out. Classification and Its Consequences.* Cambridge (MA): MIT Press.

BUCKINGHAM, D. (2007) Selling Childhood? Children and Consumer Culture. *Journal of Children and Media*, 1(1). p. 15–24.

BUCKINGHAM, D. (2009) Beyond the Competent Consumer: The Role of Media Literacy in the Making of Regulatory Policy on Children and Food Advertising in the UK. *International Journal of Cultural Policy*, 15(2). p. 217–230.

CALLON, M. (1986) Some Elements of a Sociology of Translation: Domestication of the Scallops and the Fishermen of St Brieuc Bay. In Law, J. (ed.), *Power, Action and Belief: A New Sociology of Knowledge?* London: Routledge, 196–223.

CHUNG, G. & GRIMES, S.M. (2005) Data Mining the Kids: Surveillance and Market Research Strategies in Children's Online Games. *Canadian Journal of Communication*, 30, p. 527–548.

COLAK, E. & HELMONS H. (2013) OLA Max Adventures. Presentation at Branded Content Event, January 31, 2013. Retrieved from http://brandedcontentevent.nl/, accessed July 23, 2013.

COOK, D.T. (2004) *The Commodification of Childhood. The Children's Clothing Industry and the Rise of the Child Consumer.* Durham and London: Duke University Press.

COOK, D.T. (2011) Commercial Epistemologies of Childhood. "Fun" and the Leveraging of Children's Subjectivities and Desires. In Zwick D. & Cayla, J. (eds.), *Inside Marketing: Practices, Ideologies, Devices.* Oxford: Oxford University Press, 257–268.

COULTER, N. (2009) *Tweening the Girl: The Crystallization of the Tween Market 1980–1996.* PhD dissertation, Simon Fraser University.

COULTER, N. (2012) From Toddlers to Teens: The Colonization of Childhood the Disney Way. *Jeunesse: Young People, Texts, Cultures*, 4(1). p. 146–158.

EDERY, D. (2009) *Rethinking the Impact and the Potential of Brands in Games*. Presentation at Brands and Games 2009. The game advertising network event. March 10, 2009.

FIELDER, A., GARDNER, W., NAIRN, A. & PITT, J. (2007) *Fair Game? Assessing Commercial Activity on Children's Favourite Websites and Online Environments*. London: Report National Consumer Council and Childnet International.

FOODWATCH. (2013). *Kindermarketing: Onverantwoord en Ongereguleerd*. Retrieved from www.foodwatch.nl, accessed December 3, 2013.

GOEIJ, M. DE and KWANTES, E. (2009) *Nickelodeon and OLA. Hoe betrek je kids écht bij je merk?* Presentation at Brands and Games 2009. The game advertising network event. March 10, 2009. Retrieved from www.nlgd.nl/fog/pdf/bag09/BG8.pdf, accessed June 10, 2010.

GRANDCLÉMENT, C. & GAGLIO, G. (2011) Convoking the Consumer in Person: The Focus Group Effect. In Zwick, D and Cayla, J. (eds.), *Inside Marketing: Practices, Ideologies, Devices*. Oxford: Oxford University Press, 87–115.

GRIMES, S.M. (2008) Kid's Ad Play: Regulating Children's Advergames in the Converging Media Context. *International Journal of Communications Law and Policy*, (12). p. 161–178.

GRIMES, S.M. & SHADE, L.R. (2005). Neopian Economics of Play: Children's Cyberpets and Online Communities as Immersive Advertising in NeoPets.com. *International Journal of Media and Cultural Politics*, 1(2). p. 181–198.

GURĂU, C. (2008 The Influence of Advergames on Players' Behaviour : An Experimental Study. *Electronic Markets*, 18(2). p. 106–116.

HARRISON, D. & KJELLBERG, H. (2010) Segmenting a Market in the Making: Industrial Market Segmentation as Construction. *Industrial Marketing Management*, 39(5). p. 784–792.

HEISKANEN, E. (2005) The Performative Nature of Consumer Research: Consumers' Environmental Awareness as an Example. *Journal of Consumer Policy*, *28*, 179–201.

HENRY, A. (2005) *Marketing to Children: Industry Insiders' Perspectives on Good Work* (p. 1–33). Harvard University, Good Work Project Report Series, Number 40.

HOUBEN, J. (2009) *OLA IJstijd Kids campagne 2009*. Presentation at Kids Insights Day, October 21, 2009. Retrieved from: http://media.mtvnetworks.nl/kidsday/kidsdayjoosthouben.pdf, accessed June 1, 2010.

HUFEN, B. (2010) *Laat met je merk spelen. Games als marketingmiddel*. Amsterdam: Kluwer.

KJELLBERG, H. & HELGESSON, C.F. (2007) On the Nature of Markets and Their Practices. *Marketing Theory*, 7(2). p. 137–162.

LATOUR, B. (1987) *Science in Action. How to Follow Scientists and Engineers Through Society*. Cambridge (MA): Harvard University Press.

LATOUR, B. (1991) Technology Is Society Made Durable. In Law, J. (ed.), *A Sociology of Monsters: Essays on Power, Technology and Domination*. New York: Routledge, 103–131.

LAW, J. (2009) Seeing Like a Survey. *Cultural Sociology*, 3(2). p. 239–256.

LAW, J., RUPPERT, E. & SAVAGE, M. (2011) *The Double Social Life of Methods*. CRESC Working Paper Series. Working Paper No. 95.

LIVINGSTONE, S. (2009) Debating Children's Susceptibility to Persuasion—Where Does Fairness Come In? A Commentary on the Nairn and Fine Versus Ambler Debate. *International Journal of Advertising*, 28(1). p. 170–174.

LIVINGSTONE, S. & HELSPER, E.J. (2006) Does Advertising Literacy Mediate the Effects of Advertising on Children? A Critical Examination of Two Linked Research Literatures in Relation to Obesity and Food Choice. *Journal of Communication*, 56(3). p. 560–584.

LUNT, P. & LIVINGSTONE, S. (2012) *Media Regulation. Governance and the Interests of Citizens and Consumers*. London: Sage Publications.

MACKENZIE, D., MUNIESA, F. & SIU, L. (2007) Introduction. In MacKenzie, D., Muniesa, F. & Siu, L. (eds.), *Do Economists Make Markets? On the Performativity of Economics*. Princeton: Princeton University Press, 1–19.

MIJNKINDONLINE. (2008) *Gratis! (maar niet heus)—dossier over digitale reclame voor kinderen*.

MONTGOMERY, K.C. & CHESTER, J. (2009) Interactive Food and Beverage Marketing: Targeting Adolescents in the Digital Age. *Journal of Adolescent Health*, 45. p. S18–S29.

MOORE, E.S. (2004) Children and the Changing World of Advertising. *Journal of Business Ethics*, 52(2). p. 161–167.

MTV NETWORKS. (2009). Adverteren bij MTV Networks in 2010. Available at: www.mtvnetworks.nl/index.php?list/5, accessed 12.06.2010.

NAIRN, A. & CLARKE, B. (2012) Researching Children: Are We Getting It Right? A Discussion of Ethics. *International Journal of Market Research*, *54*(2): 177–198.

NAIRN, A. & FINE, C. (2008). Who's Messing With My Mind? The Implications of Dual-Process Models for the Ethics of Advertising to Children. *International Journal of Advertising*, 27(3). p. 447–470.

NAIRN, A. & HANG, H. (2012) *Advergames: "It's not an advert—it says play!": A review of research*. Retrieved from Family & Parenting Institute, p. 1–22 http://www.bath.ac.uk/management/news_events/pdf/advergames-report-december 2012.pdf

OLAIJstijd (2010) Informatie voor ouders. Online at: www.olaijstijd.nl/ijstijd/info_ouders.html, accessed 15.06.2010.

OUDSHOORN, N., ROMMES, E. & STIENSTRA, M. (2004) Configuring the User as Everybody: Gender and Design Cultures in Information and Communication Technologies. *Science, Technology, and Human Values*, 29(1). p. 30–63.

PIAGET, J. (1954) *The Construction of Reality in the Child*. (M. Cook, Trans.). New York: Routledge.

PLOEG, I. VAN DER. (2007) *Social and Ethical Aspects of Digital Identities, Towards a Value Sensitive Identity Management*. European Research Council Starting Grant research proposal.

QVORTRUP, J., CORSARO, W.A. & HONIG, M.S. (2011) Introduction: Why Social Studies of Childhood? In Qvortrup, J., Corsaro, W.A. & Honig, M.-S. (eds.), *The Palgrave Handbook of Childhood Studies*. Basingstoke (UK): Palgrave Macmillan, 21–33.

ROEDDER-JOHN, D. (1999) Consumer Socialization of Children: A Retrospective Look at Twenty-Five Years of Research. *Journal of Consumer Research*, 26(3). p. 183–213.

SCHOR, J.B. (2005) *Born to Buy*. New York: Scribner.

SCHULL, N.D. (2005) Digital Gambling: The Coincidence of Desire and Design. *The ANNALS of the American Academy of Political and Social Science*, 597(1). p. 65–81.

SPRENKELS, I. & PLOEG, I. VAN DER (2014) Follow the Children! Advergames and the Enactment of Children's Consumer Identity. In van der Hof, S., van den Berg, B. & Schermer, B. (eds.), *Minding Minors Wandering the Web—Regulating Online Child Safety*. The Hague: TMC Asser Press/Springer Press. p. 173–188.

STEEVES, V. (2006) It's Not Child's Play: The Online Invasion of Children's Privacy. *University of Ottawa Law and Technology Journal*, 3(1). p. 169–188.

STEEVES, V. (2007) The Watched Child: Surveillance in Three Online Playgrounds. In *International Conference on the Rights of the Child*. Montreal: Wilson Lafleur, 119–140.

TODD, S. (2010) The Ethics of Marketing to Children. In Marshall, D. (ed.), *Understanding Children as Consumers*. London: Sage, 221–238.
VALKENBURG, P. (2002) *Beeldschermkinderen. Theorieën over kind en media*. Amsterdam: Boom.
VILLE, V.-I. DE LA & TARTAS, V. (2010) Developing as Consumers. In Marshall, D. (ed.), *Understanding Children as Consumers*. London: Sage, 23–40.
ZOONEN, L. VAN. (2013) From Identity to Identification: Fixating the Fragmented Self. *Media, Culture & Society*, 35(1). p. 44–51.

Part II

Growing Up

Children and Guardians

5 Risk Identities
Constructing Actionable Problems in Dutch Youth

Karolina La Fors-Owczynik and Govert Valkenburg

INTRODUCTION

Dutch child-care policy has become increasingly focused on making the lives of children 'transparent.' This is accomplished by connecting multiple digital databases and aggregating data about children and the persons to which they are connected. This is to give the most 'complete picture' possible of children who may be at some sort of risk. This is believed to increase the success rates of interventions made in the lives of these children (Keymolen and Prins, 2011, 21). The (potential) problems these systems are to address include abuse and negligence within families, educational problems including dropping out of school, and petty criminal behaviour such as shoplifting, nuisance, and vandalism.

In this chapter, we explore developments in 'completing the picture' of children through the use and development of youth-care–related databases. First, we argue, these systems are not just a matter of installing the right software and operating it appropriately. Rather, it requires a lot of work to make the systems work and literally make them match a rather complex and ambiguous world. Second, while this work is intended to make the risks visible, it also inevitably obscures some of the realities it tries to represent, which in turn entails that some of the risks are 'constructed' rather than merely 'represented.' Finally, we observe that the whole logic of the system is such that it tends to expand: If it fails in some sense, the response is typically to install more risk assessments, to implement more risk indicators, and to start the risk identification processes earlier in a child's life.

It is perhaps not that surprising that a comprehensive approach to youth risks includes the establishment of the most complete possible set of information from a variety of professionals, as this increases the likelihood that a risk or future wrong is identified in time. One of the explicit aims of national youth-care policies is that 'no child should go unseen' (Inspectie Jeugdzorg, 2008).[1] However, we will show that the ever-increasing demand for information on a child does not always work out the way it was intended, for example when stigmatization arguably occurs (Dutch Youth Institute, reported by NOS, 2010).

Risk and prevention are not simple concepts. On the contrary, in this context they refer to complex arrangements of children, professionals, institutions, personal records, data technologies, legal statuses, communication protocols, and professional routines. Within the Netherlands, youth care is organized across medical, educational, and law-enforcement institutions. In practice, this means risks are identified and shared among various youth healthcare organisations, police departments, schools, judicial institutions such as the Child Protection Council and the Youth Care Bureau, municipalities, emergency departments of hospitals, social workers, housing companies, sport clubs, and a variety of other organizations involved with youth. We show that some problems occurring in child care are in fact owing to the heterogeneity across parties.

We will discuss three database systems currently used in the Netherlands. First, we discuss the Digital Youth Healthcare Registry (DYHR, or Digitaal Jeugdgezondheidszorgdossier in Dutch). It is designed for the registration of healthcare information on children between 0 and 19 years. Second, we discuss the Reference Index for High Risk Youth (RI, or Verwijsindex Risicojongeren in Dutch). The RI is a large-scale risk-signalling system that connects various digital systems, youth-care organizations, and professionals by providing digital exchange of risk signals about children and youngsters aged between 0 and 23 years in the Netherlands. Finally, we discuss ProKid SI 12- (pronounced 'ProKid SI twelve-minus,' henceforth ProKid). This is a tool for risk assessment on children aged between 0 and 12 years, used nationwide by the police. In ProKid, colour codes are assigned to children, reflecting various levels of estimated risk.

At face value, it appears as if 'risks' are simply identified and then communicated through particular networks and relationships. On the one hand, 'risks' indeed appear in the form of simple indicators such as classifications, signals, and colour codes. These forms make risks 'actionable.' On the other hand, the indicators consolidate extensive assessments. When indicators arrive at a new location, they are in turn interpreted and re-imbued with a potentially different meaning, instigating different interventions. This occurs because of divergent backgrounds of professional knowledge, routines, codes of conduct, and anything else on which professional practices may just differ. As we continue to argue, the work done to deal with risks is successful in some ways and perilous in others.

RISK ASSESSMENT SYSTEMS FOR YOUTH IN THE NETHERLANDS

Following Dutch youth policy, both youth care and law enforcement have increasingly become geared towards prevention: problems are to be solved proactively before they become real. 'Risks' and their identification serve to make problems actionable before they actually occur. Indeed, wordings such as "making risks visible" or "making the child transparent"[2] often appear in youth policy. This eagerness for making visible the potential problems of children is reflected by mottos from professional reports: "to establish a comprehensive approach to children" (Berkeley and Van Uden, 2009), "to create a complete view of children," and "no child should go unseen" (Inspectie Jeugdzorg, 2008). Identifying those who might be responsible for future crimes provides the rationale of many prevention practices. As one professional explains:

> The goal initiating ProKid was to ensure that police officers in the field work more efficiently. What you see with the police is that normally they respond to an incident. Only when something happens, the police are called, and then they arrive to start an investigation. [. . .] The idea was that you want to know the 5% of people that are responsible for 60% of all crime incidents. If you know them, you can focus on the 5% of children who may actually come in contact with the police.
>
> (ProKid professional, city A)

This 'making visible' of children's problems serves a two-tier purpose: First, it facilitates the identification and classification of the 'abnormal,' and second, by consequence, it makes these abnormalities actionable or at least presents the indispensable object for action. This practice is justified by the assumption that intervention will be more effective if it takes place earlier. This entails a need for early identification of risks. Thus, early risk assessments on youth are considered essential resources for professionals.

Emphasis on prevention is also evident in other areas of youth care, such as for example youth healthcare (Gorissen, 2002; Mathar and Jansen, 2010). The availability of interconnected risk identification systems also facilitated police corps and social workers to increasingly carry out proactive actions and prevent harms not suffered and crimes not committed yet by youth (Min. van Veiligheid en Justitie, 2012). At the same time, youth healthcare professionals increasingly take up tasks that shift from counselling and support towards the prevention and control of youth and the crimes they potentially commit (Frissen, Karré and Van der Steen, 2011). This preventive approach to youth care and the according arrangements of organizations have received wide acclaim in professional policy discourse. The consensus seems to be that the results are good and investments justified (ACTIZ, 2012).

Digital Youth Healthcare Registry

In the Netherlands, children aged between 0 and 19 are screened periodically through consultations with healthcare professionals. These occur at specialized youth healthcare offices for children from 0 to 4 years and by school doctors for children from 5 to 19. The Digital Youth Healthcare

Registry (DYHR) is a healthcare database used for the registration of children's psychological, social, and cognitive data. Use of the DYHR by school doctors and advice centres became mandatory as of 2010.

In the DYHR, a child's record is kept as a basic data set (BDS). In addition to generic medical data (weight, height, visual and auditive capacity, etc.), the BDS contains indicators that could be regarded as risk indicators. Most prominent among these is the list of "invasive events" that was part of the 2011 version of the BDS (Nederlands Centrum Jeugdgezondheid, 2011). This includes suspected physical abuse, serious illness of the parents, parental divorce, alcohol abuse by the parents, and teenage pregnancy. Notably, as this list was found to be too much of a straightjacket, it was replaced by a 'free text field' in the subsequent version (Nederlands Centrum Jeugdgezondheid, 2011, 2013). Although the text field now allows for less specified ('free') descriptions of risk, it remains a significant indicator for risk. Also, while the 'freedom' to report increases, it is still only a freedom to report risks, which entails that the possibilities for a child to become risk profiled grow.

Reference Index for High-Risk Youth

The Reference Index for High-risk Youth (RI) is a comprehensive risk-signalling system that connects a variety of digital systems. It enables youth-care organizations and professionals to digitally exchange risk signals on children and young adults aged 0 to 23 years. It is an infrastructure rather than a single system. Each time a risk is identified and entered into a local system, this identification is automatically forwarded to the national RI. The aforementioned DYHR as well as other youth healthcare practices in general are connected to the RI (Rijksoverheid, 2005; Rouvoet, 2007), and it has been operational since 2010.

The RI facilitates the communication of alerts regarding children among professionals. The transmitted risk signals represent potential harms. The risk signals only consist of risk flags and are not automatically supplied with explanatory information or any other content of the children's files. The only information accompanying the risk flag is the name of the professional who issues it, the name of the organization the professional works for, and the name of the child the signal is related to (Nouwt and Hogendorp, 2010). The concealment of more substantial information was demanded by the Dutch Medical Association (Dutch: KNMG, Koninklijke Nederlandse Maatschappij tot Bevordering der Geneeskunst), as the RI would otherwise have posed too much of a privacy and confidentiality encroachment.

ProKid SI 12-

ProKid SI 12- is a risk-categorization system for children between 0 and 12 years. The child's address serves as the primary key to the database. ProKid employs four colour codes to represent risks: white, yellow, orange, and red, respectively signifying a growing gradation of concern. White signifies that no risks have been identified as yet, yellow represents a possible development of risks, orange indicates that problems and even criminal behaviour have already occurred, and red symbolizes children who have repeatedly shown criminal behaviour or of whom multiple cases of suspicion have been recorded (Abraham, Buysse, Loef and Van Dijk, 2011). Following a pilot phase, the system has been in operation nation-wide by the Dutch police as of 2013 (Tweede Kamer, 2012).

The risk categories and their attributions are based on behavioural-scientific models and explicitly aimed at early detection of potential criminal behaviour of children. The attribution of colour codes is done automatically, by means of algorithms, on the basis of information in other large police databases. These include the Basic Facility for Law Enforcement (BFLE, or Basisvoorziening Handhaving in Dutch) as well as the Basic Facility for Forensic Investigation (BFFI, or Basisvoorziening Opsporing in Dutch). Information from ProKid is shared among youth-care partners if a ProKid manager decides that there is reason to do so.

DOING 'RISK' IN PRACTICE

Identifying and eliminating youth risks is complex work. Numerous professionals are involved, ranging from educational and social practitioners to healthcare workers and legal and police professionals. By definition, the knowledge one professional has of a child is always limited: not so much because they do their work poorly or because they have limited resources but because any profession has things on which it focuses and things on which it does not. A medical professional 'sees' different things than a police officer or a schoolteacher does.

In recognition of this partiality of knowledge, the information systems introduced are explicitly set up to meet the challenge of crossing boundaries between professions. The systems are intended to yield a more comprehensive view of the risks children are exposed to than any single profession could have by itself. This sharing of information is increasingly seen as an essential resource for a range of youth-care professionals in the execution of their daily preventive tasks (Radaradvies, 2011). The emphasis is adopted by many regulations that legally stimulate the deployment of digital risk profiles. The Public Health Act (Rijksoverheid, 2008) requires professionals to digitally register data including risks about children in DYHR. The Law on the Reference Index (Rijksoverheid, 2010) stimulates the aggregation of risk profiles on children by a variety of professionals involved in youth care.

However, it turns out that the sharing of information is not just a panacea to eliminate risks. Managing the information requires work of its own, and while often fruitful, this work is also at times difficult and frustrating.

One corollary of the fact that professions frame problems differently is that seemingly the same information might have different meanings and implications in different situations. In the doctor's office, a mother with a medical problem might be just that, but from a social-work perspective, more structural problems might be suspected. In choosing between these options, a healthcare professional may need more comprehensive information from other professionals, which may not be available through mere risk indicators.

Risk indicators are compact representations of risks. They may be shaped as, amongst others, categories, colour codes, or signals. While facilitating communication, indicators also consolidate comprehensive assessments, complex sets of information, and tacit professional knowledge. An indicator (at least partly) obscures the process of risk identification. This (at least partly) precludes their discussion and revision, and indicators become more fixed *de facto*. A perfect example is the use of colour codes in the ProKid system, which turn out to be both elegantly compact and sources of confusion (Willems and Van der Heijden, 2011, 3).

The practices in which individual professionals operate are more unruly than the ideal of comprehensive risk identification suggests. Among different institutions and professions, consensus is often lacking on what a risk exactly is. A youth healthcare professional, for instance, explained her frustration over this problem and how it troubles her ability to assess risks:

> You see the categories with a red checkmark, with certain families the screen is almost only red. You still need to read the record [underlying the checkmarks], and you can relatively quickly figure out what the problems are. But it is often difficult to fill in the risk assessment form, or to risk-score children, because there is no clear definition of risks. For instance, a 'sleeping problem' of a child can be just that, but it can also be a symptom of issues between the parents; or it can be caused by cultural elements that are just different between one family and another.
>
> (CB-nurse, city D)

While the meaning of the symbolic representation of the risk may remain unclear, its presence in a graphic material form seems to express a very clear urgency for action. Yet if professionals find themselves confronted with this urgency, they obviously want to be sure that they can tell a sleeping problem from parental tensions before proceeding to action. While an indicator is aimed to deliver 'actionability,' it also carries ambiguity. This ambiguity entails that different professionals may conclude to different 'optimal' solutions.

Within the RI, similar ambiguities occur in the presentation and interpretation of risks. One professional using the RI reports that it often remains unclear what others mean by particular risk signals. This is owing to the fact that the contents of children's records are not shared for privacy and confidentiality reasons.

> Professionals have a web-based system, which can send signals automatically. In addition, we have also some 'soap connections' [automated connections]. Risk signals can be sent directly to the RI, if professionals register a risk in their own files. But they only send signals, no content. We do not know what the risk signal is about.
>
> (RI manager, city B)

Finally, the very definitions of risks within the context of ProKid are themselves ambiguous. This is remarkable, as ProKid is based on standards that explicitly describe when a child needs to be scored with a white, yellow, orange, or red flag. For example, the orange code is to be attributed to children

> "who either have at least once been registered as suspects of a serious crime (such as animal abuse, arson, sexual offences, public violence or robbery) or more than once have been reported as missing. Furthermore, a child can also be profiled with an orange flag, if he/she has been reported as a suspect five times or more, or he/she it has been registered five times in relation to various incidents, or if he/she has been reported ten times or more as a victim or a witness" (Willems and Van der Heijden, 2011, 3).

This orange colour code thus represents a rather heterogeneous set of problems, the complexity and heterogeneity of which remain implicit. Within the orange class, the distinctions among perpetrators, victims, and witnesses vanish. Whereas the colour codes were intended to speed up the assessment of reports by offering a quick summary, the resulting ambiguity compels police officers to yet investigate the whole background of an issue.

On top of these direct identifications of risks—in the sense that professionals explicitly regard something as a risk and enter it into the system—risks are also constructed indirectly, through what could be called 'circumstantial evidence.' Such construction is particularly facilitated by systems that are connected to ProKid, such as the BFFI. The following quote shows how a risk identification emerges in or 'between' these systems. It is the result of observations made by a police officer at a crime scene which are not directly related to the crime but may be related to a child:

> [W]hen our officers are at an address, and find drugs, [. . .] this information becomes registered in BFLE. But if they find a baby bottle in the kitchen, and ask whether there is a baby; and the inhabitants of the house answer: 'No, the bottle belongs to my sister who comes here occasionally.' If the officer cannot find hard information about whether we need to seek care for the baby, or who exactly lives there, to what

> extent the person makes something up . . . and the officer has a bad feeling [about it], and wants to use the information [about the bottle], he can register it in BFFI. We, ProKid managers, can see that.
>
> (ProKid manager, city C)

This 'soft' information will eventually become relevant in risk assessments done by means of ProKid. It thus adds to the whole assemblage of early warnings and early risk identification, so as to further help prevention. This emergence of risk identification is exemplary for what happens when multiple institutions become involved: risk identifications propagate through systems, through which their genesis fades out of scope, and their content becomes more solidified.

Early detection and a comprehensive view hinge importantly on communication and the distribution of information.

> [The DYHR] helps you to create a better problem overview. You can provide better advice and guidance based on the information it contains. [. . .] Previously, we had a hand-written 'integral paper record' in which you needed to search for information manually. Now, you click on a section and it appears immediately before your eyes in a digital format. Extracting, sharing and analysing data from the digital dossier is much faster.
>
> (CB-nurse, city D)

Yet communication and distribution of risk assessments are not just that. They are mechanisms, mobilized to bring a variety of professionals together and promote communication among them. In the view of one RI manager, such promotion of communication and the matching of risk signals are beneficial to rendering multiple problems with children visible. The infrastructure brings those aggregated problems under the attention of professionals. As the RI manager explains:

> The number of [risk signal] matches increases over time. For us, this indicates that professionals increasingly contact each other over a child's case. In 2008, we had 30,000 signals and 2,277 matches. In 2009, we had 30,313 signals and 3,100 matches. Up until now [July 2010], we have had 30,081 signals and 3,500 matches. [. . .] The idea behind the system was to arrange a child's case as a point of connection between professionals. Thus, children with multiple problems would become visible earlier, [. . .] receive better help, in case they have multiple problems within a family. Such complexity needs to be addressed comprehensively, so that a child will not be 'ping-pong-ed' between professionals, each of them needing to start the child's assessment from scratch.
>
> (RI manager, city A)

However, this leaves untouched the fact that risk-related data potentially represent different issues for different professionals. For example, the police officer managing ProKid reported her difficulty in interpreting what the colour-coded risks symbolize. For example, concerning one incident, the police officer explained her hesitation in assessing the gravity of the incident and reducing it to a single risk indicator:

> The problem we encounter with ProKid is that we get our colour lists in Excel each week, but we also need to read all the reports and what a yellow or a red colour symbolizes. If there is a report about a child, who has set something on fire, we only know that it has set something on fire. We do not know whether it has set a newspaper on fire, or a whole school building, for instance. So, you have to read the reports to learn the severity of the crime. This is important for your risk analysis.
>
> (ProKid manager, city B)

It is not straightforward what kind of risk information is to be shared between the police and youth-care institutions. This is partly the consequence of the fact that policies to stimulate co-operation between law enforcement and youth care organizations are still developing. The following manager doubts the validity of the instruments in practice, even though they are 'scientifically founded.' He explains that it would be better to exchange information already if files of children are tagged with orange, yellow, and even white flags:

> If I see a child who has just a yellow or white coloured registration—and I know this does not yet qualify it for sending to the Youth Care Bureau—but the child's friend is 'red' in the system; then I bring this extra information into the case discussion within the Youth Care Bureau.
>
> (ProKid manager, city B)

The professional thus seeks his own way in dealing with colour codes and looks for ways to include information that would otherwise *not* fit into the system. Particularly, information from the social environment of the child is sought to be incorporated.

Numerous examples exist of when the smooth, digital sharing of information obscures rather than improves the view of professionals on children. For example, the distribution of erroneous information shows a perilous irreversibility:

> Everything I register goes instantly into the computer and can be monitored. [. . .] If someone has filled in something wrong, then I need to receive an email query whether I would take out the wrong information. Until then, [the wrong information] remains in the file.
>
> (CB-doctor, city A)

This quote indicates how risks are foregrounded and consolidated by digital mediation. On the one hand, the registration of data is distributed in such a way that it becomes instantly visible for professionals in different locations. This is supposed to be helpful for the early identification of risks. On the other hand, erasing these data from files becomes a highly work-intensive process. Erasure is not automated but involves extensive e-mail correspondence. This means that, in case of erroneous information, the rapid sharing adds confusion rather than clarity, as corrections are always delayed. As the information is predominantly about risks and the identification of those risks travels much faster than their possible correction, the system *de facto* favours the emergence of risks over their correction.

This is where the systems clearly show a non-neutrality between the negative realities of risks and potential positive realities that may be articulated to oppose them. They are designed to store not just any information but a particular selection of information. This entails that some information cannot be stored, even if a professional assesses the information as relevant and even if the data is seemingly neutral or innocent.

RISK PREVENTION BITING BACK

As we have discussed, the DYHR, RI, and ProKid systems all in some way manage risk identities of children. Also, each system connects multiple practices, providing channels among different professions. In this section, we discuss this identity management across professional boundaries as an 'ontological practice of selection' (Hacking, 1986, 1991; Bowker and Leigh Star, 1999; Law, 2008). Whether something counts as 'normal' or 'abnormal,' 'deviant,' 'at risk,' or 'as risk' always has consequences for the very world those attributed classes describe, which makes this 'description' also a performative affair. One intended consequence is that these classes offer a ground for preventive action. Yet not all consequences are intended or justified, and we will articulate some of the structural issues that carry unintended consequences.

The dominant idea informing the installation of the risk-assessment systems is that transparency, visibility, and comprehensiveness are key to prevention of youth problems (Van der Hof, Leenes and Fennell-van Esch, 2009; Keymolen and Prins, 2011). We approach this 'making visible' as an ontological affair, as risk identification also *transforms* the problems that are identified. For sure, there are serious and real problems among youth that merit intervention by social workers and other professionals. Clearly, these problems must first be identified, if possible before they actually emerge, before any intervention can be made. However, the shape in which these problems are articulated does not stand in a one-to-one, unequivocal relation to what actually happens in the life of the child. We show that the

DYHR, the RI, and ProKid do indeed identify real problems, but that they also transform these problems, represent them in non-neutral ways, and introduce ambiguities of their own.

To identify risks in children and make them actionable, risks are consolidated into indicators: items on which children are scored and which offer justification for a particular intervention to be made. On the one hand, such indicators are compact and practical: They reflect the severity of a situation and instigate interventions. On the other hand, these indicators conceal a lot. A percentage, a colour code or a 'yes/no' item hides the work through which a professional arrives at the indicator. This work includes professional interpretation and judgment, professional discretion, conversation with a range of other professionals, intuition, tacit knowledge, contextual knowledge, and so forth. The necessity of these non-formalized ingredients is recognized by official reports and guidelines (Inspectie Jeugdzorg, 2008), yet they are not reflected by the indicator itself. Even if formal standards are in place that specify how an indicator is to be scored, as with the colour codes, this formalized part of the assessment is never the whole story (for otherwise we would not need professionals but only administrative clerks or even computers to do the assessment).

In addition to identification, the systems are about communication and distribution of risk assessments. More specifically, communication is to take place between different practices of youth care, and these practices employ potentially incompatible approaches. This entails that the identified risks need to be presented in multiple ways, that they are mobilized for multiple programmes, that they are to fulfil multiple tasks, and that they will be imbued with different meanings across situations. Communication in this sense is not the transparent transport of information but complex work of translation across boundaries.

The use of indicators as tokens of complex judgments makes such communication possible in the first place. Indicators are 'mobile': they are compact and can be conveniently passed on to another professional. They are also 'immutable': as they are deeply rooted in the practices that establish them, it becomes hard or even impossible to deny or contest them. As 'immutable mobiles' (Latour, 1987), indicators are able to mobilize a wide range of actors by their alerting characteristic. At the same time, the compactness that allows their mobility entails a continuous need for reinterpretation and adjustment to local knowledge, traditions, codes of conducts, and objectives.

While crossing disciplinary boundaries, the aforementioned concealment enables indicators to help keep responsibilities in place. For example, even though intensive sharing of data between medical and non-medical youth-care professionals was pursued by connecting the DYHR and the RI, the Dutch Medical Association KNMG pled for strict limitations on the sharing of medical information. Obviously, the KNMG held paramount the privacy and confidentiality of patient data. The 'best interest' of the child should be the touchstone for whether medical data would be shared (KNMG, 2009). By reducing such complex information to single indicators, exchange of that information became possible in the first place.

Offering both 'transport' and 'seclusion' of information, risk indicators are perfect examples of what have been conceptualized as *boundary objects*: entities that are ambiguous and flexible enough to work in different contexts but also stable enough to meaningfully connect between those contexts (Star and Griesemer, 1989; Star, 2010). They deliver some of the promises for which the information systems were installed, namely the connection of different professional practices. At the same time, what they actually convey is not a simple representation of a pre-existing reality but a particular construction of that reality.

Once these indicators are established, they become harder to modify. To some extent, they start to live a life of their own, not least because the exact conditions under which they were established become invisible. While they are supposed to be representations of chances and possibilities for deviance, deviance also becomes more 'real': It 'exists' as representations presented by the systems. The reality of the issues in part consists of a certain irreversibility once an indicator has been assigned to a child. As one RI manager explains:

> The problem is that the Reference Index at the time of its introduction was presented as a 'Concern reporting system,' similar to the 'concern reports' police write. You know, it created among professionals an idea of quite a 'serious and heavy' system. Hence, professionals are often afraid of signalling anything in there, although in practice it is just an alerting system and only contains data from the municipality register. This fear to signal is a pity.
>
> (RI manager, city D)

We observed that professionals sometimes become hesitant to enter issues into the system, as they cannot oversee the effects their data input might bring about elsewhere. The same professional expresses her own fear of the potential consequences of risk profiles. Quite delicately, a few minutes later, she reports:

> [O]h while I am showing you this, I have almost put a risk flag on my own child, that is something I would absolutely not want as a mother.
>
> (RI manager, city D)

The 'making real' of risks through the establishment of indicators is not just in making a solid representation of what is already there. This 'solidification' is not neutral but prioritizes risks: Indeed, they are *risk* indicators, and a risk constitutes a negative frame and calls for action. The risk assessment system does not accommodate positive realities or anything else that could mitigate or oppose an observed risk. One professional explained her frustration at not being able to register that a child is doing well:

> Many professionals who have already been working for years within youth healthcare, notice for instance, that they cannot register signals in the system that reflect that things are going well for the child. I find it to be frustrating that I can only register negative things, only risks, and not that the kid is doing well. The system only allows you to record risks. For example, that the child is hyperactive. It is as if children can only have problems. If things are going well for the child, then I would like to register that, but I cannot.
>
> (CB nurse, city D)

The system is geared towards prevention, but it *de facto* disallows professionals to retract concerns if they think the measures would be too much or unnecessary.

Although solidifying risks is intended to ease professional communication across practices, certain translations of risks into technological software or scripts (Akrich, 1992) can be sources of frustration for professionals. A quote from an interview with a ProKid managing professional exemplifies this. For ProKid, changes of address are key. However, the system is not able to register two addresses with one child. This is potentially problematic:

> Address changes in the [ProKid] system are not connected to changes in the municipal registry.[3] When a police officer reports on an address, [the data] are checked automatically against the municipal registry. However, if parents divorce and move to two different addresses, and they arrange co-parenthood, the child is usually registered only at the mother's address. So, if a problem occurs at the father's address, ProKid unfortunately misses out on that.
>
> (ProKid manager, city B)

The inability to associate two or more addresses with a child is seen to hamper risk assessments. This is more than just a design flaw. It is a technological solidification of the social norm that children live with their married parents. Oddly, it opposes the tendency of risk assessments to extend into the broader social environment of children beyond their immediate family (see what follows).

PROLIFERATION OF RISK ASSESSMENT

The preoccupation with risks as actionable, negative realities parallels a proliferation of risk indicators. It is one thing that risk indicators are arranged in ways that they can be shared easily among different professionals. It is another thing that risk assessments and the communication of those risks seems to engender an ongoing expansion of the number of risk indicators.

This connects to what Van der Ploeg (2001) observes in the context of pre-natal care. She shows that pre-natal interventions are always susceptible to the critique that the intervention would have been more effective if it had been made earlier, when the problem was supposedly still smaller and easier to encapsulate. This instigates ever more intensive and earlier screening. Van der Ploeg describes this as the "logic of infinite regression." In the present case, a similar logic suggests that risks linked to children can be dealt with better if their registration is more comprehensive and indeed earlier.

We discuss three dimensions of this multiplication of risk indicators. First, practices of risk assessment increasingly include the family of the child explicitly in the registration of risks. Second, a similar development is visible regarding the broader social environment of the child. Third, as suggested, there is an assumption that earlier identification of risks leads to their being better manageable. In conclusion, these three developments culminate in the growth of the number of indicators.

Extending the View Onto the Family

The attention paid to a child's family in youth-care practices continues to increase and to be integrated formally in the system. A police officer working with ProKid, for instance, emphasizes the influence of parents on their children. As changes of the parents' relationships may have serious consequences for a child, according to him, these should be part of a child's risk assessment. The following example illustrates how a risk profile of a new family member may affect a child's colour code in ProKid:[4]

> Many times you see, the mother is divorced and has a child, and the child gets a report. The child is reported as hyperactive. Then, later the mother starts a new relationship with a man, who moves in at the same address. If the mother's new boyfriend, for instance, already has a police record, or has been involved in domestic violence, this creates a high risk factor for the child. The child lives at one address with this man. Therefore, the yellow colour of the address [in the child's record] will turn into orange [. . .] Another example is when the mother has been caught with shoplifting, and then she explains that she did the shop lifting because of her severe circumstances, e.g.: 'otherwise I am not able to feed and take care of my child.' This also constitutes a risk factor.
>
> (ProKid manager, city B)

Beyond criminal concerns, the profiling of parents also plays a central part during risk assessments in youth healthcare practices. Screening the health conditions of parents constitutes a significant part of health screening processes for children. In the use of the DYHR, the social and financial statuses of parents increasingly receive attention from professionals, and they are taken into account when assessing the health risks children may be exposed to:

> You need to know of possible healthcare risks; whether the parents, for instance, have a [social or financial] problem. Moreover, if the parents have problems, the broader picture needs to be looked at, and not only the child. It is possible that you have already noted down issues in the DMO protocol.[5] For example, the parents might be unemployed, have high debts, or the child has been taken out of the family home, etc. These issues [. . .] importantly influence the child's development.
>
> (CB nurse, city D)

In some youth healthcare practices, even the extended-familial relations are considered essential for an adequate risk assessment. A professional using the DYHR shares her frustration at not being able to properly assess a child's risk profile, as assessment of the broader social environment of the child was not possible with the digital system at the time. This complicated her work, as here knowledge remained incomplete. She could not see a child's relation to its stepfather, stepmother or to its grandparents. She argues that familial relations should be made more visible:

> You actually need a structural description of the family. I mean all those relatives with which the child interacts daily. So far, only the biological father and mother are registered in the [DYHR] record, but not the stepfather, stepmother, stepbrothers and stepsisters. Or, if the child often stays with grandpa or grandma, then the grandparents need to be registered in the dossier, too. But the system does not allow for such registration, unfortunately. Nowadays, there are a lot of divorces. We should also make those family relations visible, I think.
>
> (CB nurse, city D)

In contrast to this, the RI contains a novel 'family functionality.' This functionality increases the number of family members that can be made relevant in a risk profile of a child. It also increases the number of youth-care professionals that are connected to the RI. In particular, it ropes in professionals who are not focusing on the child but on older (even adult) brothers or sisters and on parents.

Expansion Into the Broader Social Environment

Another dimension of proliferation is the increasing attention paid to the social environment of the child within practices connected to

ProKid. Even the behaviour of neighbours can be relevant to a child's assessment:

> Suppose there was a fight between neighbours. [. . .] Then, I know that the children of the neighbours have probably been involved in that fight, too. The police come and make a report. Then, in ProKid, I see that a child from one address fought with a child from the neighbouring address. I can then check back in time, and see that these children's fathers also fought, two years ago. I can then connect these things, and that is the analysis I do.
>
> (ProKid manager, city B)

This shows how multiple profiles, including the profile of the neighbour or the father, are drawn together in a ProKid-based analysis. From these combined risk profiles, risk factors to which the child is exposed are identified and registered more sophisticatedly in the child's ProKid record.

In addition to familial and social relations, ProKid even brings forward a child's relations to animals. ProKid incorporates behavioural-scientific research findings holding that the way children interact with animals is indicative of the risks a child might pose to society in the future:

> We also have another, somewhat strange risk factor in our list: animal abuse. If a child abuses an animal at an early age, then, according to the scientific findings of Radboud University of Nijmegen, that child has a higher inclination for sexual abuse at a later age. We relied on scientific explanation to include such a category into the system.
>
> (Police officer responsible for ProKid project, city B)

Also the child's friends' risk profiles are made part of risk assessments. Links between friends' risk profiles increase the weight attributed to those profiles:

> If I see a child who has a 'yellow' or 'white' colour code, and although officially the case is 'not yet worth' being sent to the Youth Care Bureau (YCB),[6] but if a friend of that child is 'red' in the system, then I share this extra information [about the 'yellow' or 'white' colour-coded child] during the case discussion within YCB.
>
> (ProKid manager, city B)

These examples demonstrate that the proliferation in social space is becoming visible as a redefinition of social roles. Children who are diagnosed as being 'at risk' are increasingly also treated themselves 'as risk': Behavioural-scientific evidence suggests that children who are exposed to risks run a greater chance of becoming perpetrators themselves. While this is taken as a reason for additional care, and not, say, for pre-emptive punishment, it is indicative of the logic of ever-earlier and more comprehensive detection. What is more, indicators attributed to persons surrounding the child not only offer more risk indicators against which a child is to be assessed but also intensify the preventative monitoring of persons who are seen to fall within the social space of a child.

Extension in Time

The third dimension of this proliferation of risk assessment concerns time. One example is provided by the installation of so-called 'pre-signals' into the Reference Index. These are flags that can be added to a child's record in the local Reference Index. If such a flag is set, on any new information added about the child by a different youth care agency, an automatic email is sent to the institution that originally set the flag. Differently, a 'real' match leads to an email being sent to *all* those institutions that have signalled a risk about the same child in the reference index. These pre-signals are not forwarded to the National Reference Index; neither are they 'matched' by any automatic process. Pre-signals provide opportunities for early warning, legitimated by the consequences of the pre-signal being comparably limited. However, they remain part of socio-technical assessments and stimulate earlier evaluations and consequently interventions. Likewise, the aforementioned advancement of colour codes based on indirect risks can be seen as a proliferation into time: issues surface earlier, and this is thought to improve prevention.

Proliferation in time concerns not only the past but also the future. The RI distinguishes between 'active' and 'passive' risk signals. The active state of a signal refers to the period a risk signal can be automatically matched:

> Each signal has an expiration date. [. . .] For instance a police signal remains for 3 months, a signal from an educational institution for 6, signals of other organizations generally remain for 12 months, and we keep BYC signals for 24 months in RI. Signals can be matched only during these periods. [. . .] According to the new Youth Care Act, after a signal becomes passive, it remains visible for another 5 years on the web-site. Afterwards, it must be deleted.
>
> (RI manager, city C)

Despite technical restrictions, such as the absence of automated matching, the 'passive state' in practice produces an extension of the time a signal remains actionable for professionals. Within this period, a 'passive' signal keeps presenting a negative reality that should be mended:

> This passive signalling allows for another professional to use the source of the passive signal, in order to acquire information from the professional about the child.
>
> (RI manager, city D)

The constructions of pre-signals and 'passive' signals in the RI and the colour-code classifications of risks in ProKid epitomize the proliferation of risks in time. Risk indicators accompany a child on a longer time span in practice, thus offering a longer window of opportunity for preventive intervention.

Ever More Indicators

Taken together, these developments lead to a growth in the number of risk indicators. In addition, difficulties of communication across various professions are often attributed to a certain incompleteness in the available information on a child (Inspectie Jeugdzorg, 2008). This incompleteness instigates the addition of ever more risk indicators, which are thought to be more usable in different contexts if these indicators are more diverse and comprehensive. If risk assessments work imperfectly in one context or another, the response has been to add more indicators so as to increase the likelihood that they contain information that is meaningful in a particular context. Certainly, professionals working with these systems are not necessarily uncritical or naïve about such additions. Quite the contrary, the removal of the fixed list of invasive events from the BDS described earlier reflects a critical stance, as does the recognition that building systems are a matter of trial and error.

The mere growth of the number of indicators perpetuates and amplifies problems we have observed so far. Opacity and ambiguity are more likely to cause problems if there are more indicators to materialize them. Similarly, the increasing number of indicators combined with their 'permanence' increases the chances for a child to become and remain qualified as being either 'at risk' or 'as a risk.' Also, the increasing number of connections among risk factors, colour codes, risk signals, and risk profiles and their surrounding practices increases the chance that combinations of those indicators produce a 'hit.' As Van der Hof (2010) argues, while the DYHR eases the circulation of information, the resulting escalation of information itself poses new difficulties for professionals, as the most problematic cases become more troublesome to sort out. What is more, 'less serious' issues increasingly raise alerts, because the large number of indicators makes the system in a way too sensitive.

All the issues described are the consequence of a sincere pursuit of good care for children. New risk indicators often result from new scientific evidence and the recognition of real flaws in care practices. However, practices of youth care and the digital systems through which they operate entail a proliferation that brings severe problems of their own.

CONCLUSION: IT'S HARD NOT TO BE AT RISK

Modes for identifying and preventing risks in youth care in the Netherlands are being reconfigured in unprecedented manners. Prevention is performed by a growing range of youth-care and law enforcement organizations, systems, and professionals. The problems they face include various forms of child abuse, anti-social behaviour, and medical problems. Attempts to solve these problems occur through the use of comprehensive digital means and the enrolment of ever more socio-technical practices of youth care, as well as an extension of what is thought to be relevant. Involved practices currently include the police, healthcare professionals, social workers, municipality administrators, educational institutions, and debt-counselling services.

Underlying all these developments is the sincere aim of improving the protection of children. First, this aim is translated in a need for ever more information and improved sharing of information and translated into digital technology. Second, this need for information is transformed into a pursuit of 'making children transparent,' or to create a 'comprehensive picture' of the child. Third, as we have shown, this picture is subject to the dynamics that spawns risk assessments in various ways described.

In this study, the practices of youth care seem to be built on the presumption that risks are pre-existing and real and can be made more actionable by making them visible. While we do not deny the *existence per se* of such risks, our analysis shows that in practice a very *specific reality* of risks is constructed. Risk indicators proliferate, propagating ambiguities and interpretational problems. Making risks 'real' and existent in the form of technologically mediated indicators also transforms chances of deviance into real expectations. Particularly, the gradual transformation from a child 'at risk' towards a child 'as risk' is to be understood as a consequence of this proliferation.

This study suggests that the mentioned practices of youth care 'produce' risks in two ways. The first refers to the construction of risks as risk indicators. This construction is key to making risks actionable and for initiating prevention. The second sense raises more concern. The dynamics of consolidating risks into indicators and of the proliferation of those indicators simply raises chances for a child to become subject to a regime of care or raised attention. In many cases, this will be justified; however, in other cases it is problematic.

These 'false positives' are recognized, but accepted as a 'cost' of the system. The spokesman of an umbrella organization[7] for Dutch youth-care agencies responds to recent findings that 10% of all suspicions of child abuse reported to the Advice and Reporting Centre Child Abuse (ARCC, in Dutch: Advies en Meldpunt Kindermishandeling, AMK)—a sub-organization within Bureau Youth Care—were false.

> JOURNALIST: The Dutch Youth Institute argued today in the daily newspaper 'Trouw'[8] that families feel stigmatized, if they are falsely accused [of child abuse]. Do you recognize this?
>
> SPOKESMAN: Yes. If for a small circle of professionals risks remain known about a child, and if parents return to the GP, they know

> that a suspicion had been registered and investigations took place. We argue, however, that this price we must pay for the remaining 90%. That is more than 14000 children per year in The Netherlands where investigations happen correctly. In these cases, it proves to be crucial that investigations happen. So this [10% false suspicion] is a consequence that we cannot entirely prevent.
>
> (NOS, 2010)

Despite this acceptance, our analysis has shown that such negative side effects are contingent upon particular technological choices, such as the reduction of complex observations to simple indicators. Side effects include false positives, the impossibility of indicating that a child is doing well, and emerging ambiguities of risk indicators that entail misunderstandings between care practices. Solutions for these effects may not be in finding better technological solutions, nor would we argue for an abolition of risk assessments as if they were only bad. Rather, improvement could be sought in reconsidering *how* risks are made present and whether technological, professional, and organizational elements could be arranged differently, such that they present those risks in ways that invite reflexivity and awareness of the side effects showcased in this chapter.

NOTES

1. This chapter contains numerous phrases that we translated from Dutch to English. We take full responsibility for the translations and choose not to point this out throughout the entire text. Only with proper names, we add the Dutch original when possible.
2. The paradoxical point that transparency strictly refers to a particular kind of 'invisibility' will not be elaborated further here.
3. In the Netherlands, municipalities maintain central registries of addresses of all their inhabitants.
4. One assumption underlying ProKid is that incidents with persons living at the child's address constitute a risk factor for the child. Therefore, they are to be reported.
5. The DMO protocol is a standard, early signaling/warning instrument used within Dutch youth healthcare practices in order to assess children aged 0 to 4 years (Hielkema, de Winter, de Meer and Reijneveld, 2008).
6. According to the ProKid instructions, each case with a 'red' or 'orange' colour code needs to be forwarded directly to Bureau Youth Care.
7. www.mogroep.nl/
8. www.trouw.nl/tr/nl/4492/Nederland/article/detail/1087513/2010/02/09/Een-op-tien-meldingen-kindermishandeling-vals.dhtml

REFERENCES

ABRAHAM, M. et al. (2011) *Pilot ProKid Signaleeringsinstrument 12- Geevalueerd*. Den Haag: WODC.

ACTIZ. (2012) Flyer: *Preventie door Jeugdgezondheidszorg Loont*. Utrecht: ACTIZ.

AKRICH, M. (1992) The De-Scription of Technical Objects. In Bijker, W. & Law, J. (eds.), *Shaping Technology/Building Society: Studies in Sociotechnical Change*. Cambridge (MA): MIT Press, 205–224.

BERKELEY, E. & VAN UDEN, A. (2009) *Risicojongeren: Een Bundeling van Inzichten uit Onderzoek, Beleid en Praktijk over een Effectieve Aanpak*. Den Haag: Nicis Instituut.

BOWKER, G.C. & STAR, S.L. (1999) *Sorting Things Out: Classification and Its Consequences*. Cambridge (US), London (UK): MIT Press.

FRISSEN, M., KARRÉ, P.M. & VAN DER STEEN, M. (2011) *Zorg door de Staat: Gevolgen van Gemeentelijke Keuzes in de JGZ*. Utrecht: ACTIZ.

GORISSEN, W. (2002) *Kennis als Hulpbron: Het Gebruik van Wetenschappelijk Kennis bij Beleidsvorming in de Jeugdgezondheidszorg voor 4–19 Jarigen*. PhD Thesis. Utrecht: University of Utrecht.

HACKING, I. (1986) Making-up People. In Heller, T. & Wellbery, E.D. (eds.), *Reconstructing Individualism, Autonomy, Individuality and the Self in Western Thought*. Stanford CA: Stanford University Press, 222–236.

HACKING, I. (1991) The Making and Molding of Child Abuse. *Critical Inquiry*, 17(2). p. 253–288.

HIELKEMA, M. et al. (2008) *Effectiviteit van Vroegsignalering binnen het Programma Samen Starten*. ZonMw Project Website. Available from: www.zonmw.nl/nl/projecten/project-detail/effectiviteit-van-vroegsignalering-binnen-het-programma-samen-starten/samenvatting [Accessed 21–09–2013]

INSPECTIE JEUGDZORG. (2008) *Jaarverslag 2007*. Utrecht: Inspectie Jeugdzorg.

KEYMOLEN, E. & PRINS, C. (2011) Jeugdzorg via Systemen. De Verwijsindex Risicojongeren als Spin in een Digitaal Vangnet. In Broeders, D., Cuijpers, C.M. & Prins, J.E.J. (eds.), *De Staat van Informatie*. Amsterdam/Den Haag: Amsterdam University Press/WRR, 293–348.

KNMG. (2009) *EKD Niet Te Breed Toegangelijk Maken*. Web News Item. Available from: http://knmg.artsennet.nl/Nieuws/Nieuwsarchief/Nieuwsbericht-1/KNMG-Elektronisch-Kinddossier-niet-te-breed-toegankelijk-maken.htm. [Accessed 23–03–2014]

LATOUR, B. (1987) *Science in Action: How To Follow Scientists and Engineers through Society*. Cambridge (MA): Harvard University Press.

LAW, J. (2008) On Sociology and STS. *The Sociological Review*, 56(4). p. 623–649.

MATHAR, T. & JANSEN, Y. (2010) (eds.), *Health Promotion and Prevention Programmes in Practice: How Patients' Health Practices are Rationalised, Reconceptualised and Reorganised*. Bielefeld: Transcript Verlag.

MINISTER VAN VEILIGHEID EN JUSTITIE. (2012) *Rechtstaat en Rechtsorde*. Brief van de Minister van Veiligheid en Justitie aan de Voorzitter van de Tweede Kamer. Den Haag, 29 juni 2012, kst-29279–147.

NEDERLANDS CENTRUM JEUGDGEZONDHEID. (2011) *Inhoud voorstel 127*. Available from: www.ncj.nl. [Accessed 18–12–2012]

NEDERLANDS CENTRUM JEUGDGEZONDHEID. (2013) *Basisdataset Jeugdgezondheidszorg Versie .3.2.1*. Available from: www.ncj.nl/informatisering-jgz/basisdataset. [Accessed 03–10–2013]

NOS. (2010) *Veel Onterechte Meldingen over Kindermishandeling*. Web News Item. Available from: http://nos.nl/audio/135462-veel-onterechte-meldingen-over-kindermishandeling.html. [Accessed 21–03–2013]

NOUWT, S. & HOGENDORP, J. (2010) Landelijke Verwijsindex Risicojongeren Ingevoerd. *Medisch Contact*, 2010(31–32). p. 1560.

RADARADVIES. (2011) *Preventief Risicosignaleringsinstrument Jongeren en Overlast*. Brochure. Available from: www.radaradvies.nl/producten/preventief_risicosignaleringsinstrument_jongeren_en_overlast/521. [Accessed 21–03–2013]

RIJKSOVERHEID. (2005) *Wet op de Jeugdzorg*. Available from: http://wetten.overheid.nl/BWBR0016637. [Accessed 25–04–2012]

RIJKSOVERHEID. (2008) *Wet Publieke Gezondheid*. Available from: http://wetten.overheid.nl/BWBR0024705. [Accessed 12–04–2012]

RIJKSOVERHEID. (2010) *Wet Verwijsindex risicojongeren van kracht op 1 augustus 2010*. National Government Press Release 09–07–2010. Available from: www.rijksoverheid.nl/documenten-en-publicaties/persberichten/2010/07/09/wet-verwijsindex-risicojongeren-van-kracht-op-1-augustus-2010.html. [Accessed 15–03–2012]

ROUVOET, A. (2007) *Alle kansen voor alle kinderen. Beleidsprogramma Jeugd en Gezin 2007–2011*. Policy Document. Den Haag: Ministry for Youth and Family.

STAR, S.L. (2010) This Is Not a Boundary Object: Reflections on the Origin of a Concept. *Science, Technology & Human Values*, 35(5). p. 601–617.

STAR, S.L. & GRIESEMER, R.J. (1989) Institutional Ecology, 'Translations' and Boundary Objects: Amateurs and Professionals in Berkeley's Museum of Vertebrate Zoology, 1907–39. *Social Studies of Science*, 19(3). p. 387–420.

TWEEDE KAMER DER STATEN GENERAAL. (2012) *Vaststelling van de Begrotingsstaten van het Ministerie van Veiligheid en Justitie (VI) voor het Jaar 2013*. Den Haag: Tweede Kamer der Staten General.

VAN DER HOF, S. (2010) Het Elektronisch Kinddossier: Kansen en Kantekeningen. In Munnichs, G., Schuijff, M. & M. Besters (eds.), *Databases: Over ICT-beloftes, Informatiehonger en Digitale Autonomie*. Den Haag: Rathenau Istituut, 54–62.

VAN DER HOF, S., LEENES, R. & FENNELL-VAN ESCH, S. (2009) *Framing Citizens' Identities: The Construction of Personal Identities in New Modes of Government in the Netherlands. Research on Personal Identification and Identity Management in New Modes of Government*. NWO, Network of Networks Programme, Tilburg: TILT, Tilburg University.

VAN DER PLOEG, I. (2001) *Prosthetic Bodies: The Construction of the Fetus and the Couple as Patients in Reproductive Technologies*. Dordrecht: Kluwer Academic Publishers.

WILLEMS, M. & VAN DER HEIJDEN, M. (2011) *Provinciale Pilot Vroegsignalering risicojeugd*. Available from: www.nogveiligerhuis.nl/UserFiles/File/thema_jeugd/.pdf. [Accessed 21–03–2013]

6 Swimming in the Fishbowl

Young People, Identity, and Surveillance in Networked Spaces

Valerie Steeves

This chapter draws on the findings of Media Smart's Young Canadians in a Wired World research project in order to examine young people's experiences with identity and surveillance in networked spaces.[1] Canada is an interesting example to examine, because the Canadian government was the first in the world to connect all its schools to the Internet in 1999 and, within a decade, home access to networked technologies approached universality (CRTC, 2010). Since that time, Canadian youth have continued to be early adopters of various networked communications technologies, the most recent example being social media. The statistics on Facebook use are illustrative of this trend; Canada has the largest *per capita* participation on Facebook in the world (Oliveira, 2012) and 95% of 17-year-old Canadians have a Facebook account (Steeves, 2014). As such, Canadian youth are among the most wired in the world and have fully integrated networked technologies into their schooling and social lives.

From as early as 2000, the young Canadians we spoke with were using the technologies of the day—primarily chat rooms and instant messaging—to try on new identities and connect with friends. Our research participants also celebrated the privacy they found online; they believed themselves to be outside the gaze of their parents and teachers and accordingly embraced the Internet as a safe place to explore and experiment (Media Awareness Network, 2001). As new technologies emerged over the next 10 years, other researchers reported similar findings. Chat rooms (Mendoza, 2007), instant messaging (Steeves, 2005), personal home pages and blogs (Stern, 2004), cell phones (Ito, 2005), and social networking sites (boyd, 2007; Livingstone, 2008; Shade, 2008) were each, in turn, appropriated by children and reconstituted as socio-technical spaces; children used these spaces to connect with peers and engage in a reflexive project of constructing the self, away from the watchful eyes of adults.

When we returned to the field in 2012 to 2013, the children we interviewed reported that they continue to use the latest networked technologies, including social media, smartphones, networked MP3 players, tablets, and gaming platforms to experiment with their identities and connect with their friends. However, the online spaces they now frequent are structured by pervasive monitoring, particularly from peers, parents, family members, teachers, and school administrators, and the various forms of surveillance they encounter online pose challenges for them when it comes to using the technology for identity play.

This chapter discusses the ramifications of our findings, in three sections. First, I explore the types of visibility and lateral surveillance our participants experienced with peers and the kinds of strategies they relied on to manage their online personas. Second, I examine the dual face of parental surveillance as care and control and the complex negotiations that the children and parents we talked to undertook with respect to both access to and use of online media. Third, I turn to the panoptic surveillance our participants experienced at school and explore their perceptions of the impact of this surveillance on their ability to use networked technologies to enhance their learning.

PEERS, LATERAL SURVEILLANCE, AND IDENTITY-MANAGEMENT STRATEGIES

As noted, our participants in 2012 to 2013[2] enjoyed the ways in which networked communications enable a playful engagement and experimentation with different ways of being online. For example, our 11- and 12-year-old participants searched for information to learn more about things they would encounter in the future, like high school and jobs, and saw this as a safe way to 'rehearse' the roles they would play as teens and adults. Our teenaged participants relied heavily on various media to express themselves, communicate with friends, explore their interests, keep in touch with family, and generally figure out who they wanted to be when they grew up.

A large part of the appeal of networked technologies for all age groups was the visibility they provide. A number of researchers (Peter, Valkenburg and Fluckiger, 2009; Phillips, 2009; Shade, 2011; Draper, 2012) suggest that, by monitoring how others respond to their online personas, young people are able to evaluate their various identity performances. This allows them to co-produce their subjectivity through their interaction with others who mirror back their performances for them to see (Mead, 1934; Goffman, 1959). From this perspective, their online identities are fluid (Giddens, 1991) and tied to an ongoing project of "writing the self into being" (boyd, 2007).

The concept of lateral surveillance (Andrejevic, 2005), in which peers monitor peers and are monitored in turn, is a particularly important element of this kind of reflexive identity construction and performance, especially for our teenaged participants. Ninety-five percent of the 17-year-olds we surveyed had a Facebook account, and 72% read or posted on friends' social network sites at least once a day or once a week. Thirty-nine percent of all survey respondents indicated that they slept with their cell phone next to them in case they received messages during the night. The teenagers we interviewed saw this as a way to monitor the 'drama' that unfolded when they were not at school, and indicated that they used their networked devices to keep an eye on peers throughout the day and night.

Much of this lateral surveillance was playful in nature. Our participants knowingly slipped in and out of the online gaze to play jokes on each other and enjoy themselves. Pranking—setting online traps for someone or misdirecting them to a joke site—was a common activity,[3] especially among boys. Although pranking was "just for fun" (Steeves, 2012a, 28), it was also a way of acquiring and demonstrating the skills they needed to distinguish between 'real' and 'fake' online representations. Another form of playing with the gaze was to impersonate a friend by using his or her login and then posting comments under his or her name.[4] Our interview participants indicated that this typically involved in-jokes or poking fun at each other and was a regular—though sometimes trying—part of their online interactions with their friends.

However, lateral surveillance also exacerbated the consequences of a failed performance (e.g. a picture in which they appeared foolish or did not look their best, or a sext—a sexually explicit text message—that was forwarded to others within the teen's peer network) because failed performances could be seen, copied, and forwarded across a range of technological platforms used by their peer group. In other words, although being seen online was part of the fun, being seen badly was a significant risk. Our participants accordingly developed a number of strategies in order to minimize this risk.

In this regard, decisions about what photographs of themselves to post were particularly important. Our qualitative participants told us that they put a great deal of care and attention into selecting these images—as one 15- to 17-year-old girl put it,

> I just don't take stupid pictures that I know could ruin my reputation, or something.
>
> (ibid., 33)

Of our survey respondents, 91% reported that they used privacy settings to block someone from seeing the photos they post, and most of the persons blocked were known to the respondents. Of the people being blocked, 31% were friends, 20% were people they had stopped being friends with, and 20% were people they knew but with whom they were not friends.

They also closely monitored their peers' sites to see how they were being portrayed by them. Forty-five percent of our survey respondents indicated that they had asked someone to delete something that person had posted about them because they did not want someone else—especially friends (21%)—to see it. The young people we interviewed told us they routinely 'de-tagged' photos of themselves so they could retain control over the distribution of their image. Accordingly, this lateral surveillance enabled them to see how they were being portrayed and to take proactive steps to protect their online image. As one 15- to 17-year-old boy said,

> I don't want . . . myself to be in someone else's phone or computer . . . Or, like, other people showing other people, being like, "look at this!'"
>
> (ibid., 32)

Our interview participants also relied on friends to help them manage their online personas. It was generally understood that friends do not post embarrassing or compromising photos of friends online. Moreover, if someone did post an embarrassing photo or say something mean about someone, that person's friends were expected to go online and restore his or her reputation. For example, 11- to 12-year-old Emma told us that an acquaintance had posted an unflattering picture of her on Facebook, and people were making mean comments about her appearance. She texted her friends, who immediately went to the site and posted comments like, "'no, Emma looks cool, she's awesome, she's so brave' and stuff, and [Emma] was like, 'I love you guys'" (ibid., 32). Although lateral surveillance exacerbated the impact of the mean comments because they were seen by so many people, it also alerted Emma to the attack and enabled Emma's friends to repair her online reputation by visibly coming to her defence.

Interestingly, our participants proactively purged particularly candid or bad photographs of themselves before they could be posted online in order to keep these images away from the lateral surveillance of their peers. Although they routinely allowed friends to take photos of them when they were goofing around, they would later go into their friends' phones or cameras to delete them. As Emma and Taylor explain:

> EMMA: Cause . . . if there's a picture of my goofing off, like making a funny face, you don't want everyone to see that, it's between you and your friends.
>
> TAYLOR: Yeah, other people, other people probably all make fun of you, and then that'll stay around for a while because that's happened before.
>
> EMMA: Yeah, only your friends understand why you're doing it . . .
>
> TAYLOR: Yeah, and then everyone else, like, sees it and then they're kind of like, "oh, why are you doing this?"
>
> (ibid., 32)

Failure to allow someone access to a device so he or she could delete a photo placed a strain on the friendship. A number of our participants told us that, in those circumstances, it was acceptable to break into the person's phone or social media account without his or her permission to delete the photo. If they were unsuccessful and the person posted the photo or made negative comments about them online, the friendship was at an end.

In this sense, lateral surveillance was a form of self-protection; by routinely monitoring what photos of them were held by others, they were able to intervene when necessary to prevent the distribution of unwanted images. On the other hand, possession and non-distribution of a potentially embarrassing photo was seen as a sign of close friendship. For example, during one 15- to 17-year-old qualitative group session, Bridget started teasing her best friend Maddy about a particularly embarrassing photo of Maddy she had on her phone:

> BRIDGET: [Giggling] Look at the picture that I have of you. [Laughter from everyone even though Bridget only showed it to Maddy]
>
> ALICIA: But it's not like something I wouldn't send to somebody, I wouldn't post pictures that I have of people . . .
>
> MADDY: Oh, it's nothing dirty. [Laughter] It's just a lot of makeup with . . . facial hair . . .
>
> BRIDGET: I wouldn't post it on Facebook, I'm not like that.
>
> FACILITATOR: By keeping it on your phone you've got it, but it's not as public as Facebook?
>
> MADDY: Yeah.
>
> (ibid., 33)

Keeping something off social network sites and away from the lateral surveillance of peers was therefore a way of signalling closeness and trustworthiness.

Lateral surveillance among peers accordingly played a variety of functions. It provided access to an audience for the purposes of identity construction, in the Meadian sense, and opened up spaces for fun and playful teasing. Although it magnified the potential consequences of a failed performance, it also enabled our participants to monitor how they were represented by others and respond in ways that allowed them to publicly repair their reputations. It further served to demarcate intimacy when images shared with trusted friends were kept out of the surveillant gaze and stored 'privately' on media such as mobile phones.

PARENTS AND THE COMPLICATIONS OF SURVEILLANCE AS CARE AND CONTROL

Parental monitoring was one of the most common forms of surveillance our participants discussed. However, both the parents and young people we talked to were ambivalent about it and entered into complex negotiations around access to and use of online services, social media accounts, and cell phones.

From the parents' perspective, online monitoring was a form of care. Almost all of them expressed concerns over the possibility that their child could be hurt online,[5] and most required full password access to their child's various accounts so they could keep an eye on him or her to keep him or her safe. Although the nature of online risks was ill defined and parents could not point to specific harms, they felt that they were forced to monitor their children to protect them from stalkers and other ill-intentioned strangers.

However, the parents who did this also worried that it would negatively affect their relationship with their child, because monitoring could potentially signal that they did not trust their child to act appropriately. As Rooney notes, a child learns how to enter into trusting relationships with others by relying on "the good will of others . . . such as parents, caregivers, friends and strangers in a variety of ways to care for and protect them" (Rooney, 2010, 346). Having opportunities "to trust and be trusted" are an integral part of learning "how to be with others in a way that supports [children's] capacity to live and live in a meaningful way." Accordingly, children need to learn to "trust with good judgment," actively negotiating situations in which they can rely on others and situations in which distrust may be an appropriate response to some potential harm (Steeves, 2012a, 347). She concludes:

> Where there is a climate of fear about public spaces, it is possible to see how parental fears might lead to a tendency to use tighter mechanisms of control . . . However, such an approach, particularly where it is an overreaction to the risks involved, makes it difficult for children to negotiate an appropriate, realistic and constructive balance between trust and risk . . . and as a result the opportunities for a child to negotiate terms of freedom or to subvert the controls that are placed on them rapidly diminish.
>
> (ibid., 350)

Interestingly, our 11- to 12-year-old survey respondents were much more comfortable with parental monitoring than were their older counterparts and accepted it as a form of care. However our qualitative participants told us that much of this comfort was rooted in the fact that they found posting personal information on social media sites or talking with strangers 'boring.' As one girl summarized,

> Wilhelmina: *Ben normalement nous, à notre âge, on a pas vraiment besoin de . . . ben y'a des filles au secondaire qui ils ont besoin mais comme moi admettons j'ai comme cinq amis*—Well normally, us, at our age, we don't really need to [use social media] . . . there are high school girls who need to but me, I admit, I have like five friends.
>
> (ibid., 16)

This is consistent with Livingstone's (2009) observation that younger children construct their online identities through display, as opposed to adolescents, who construct their identities through their social connectedness to others. Surveillance was accordingly more acceptable to our younger participants[6] because they were not yet predisposed to break away from their identity within the family and begin to explore who they were in connection to peers.

Nonetheless, all our participants indicated that they took steps (e.g. using privacy settings to limit what parents could see or clearing histories on shared computers) to avoid parental monitoring. Our teenaged participants were highly adept at using technical controls to evade 'lectures.' One 15- to 17-year-old girl's comment that, "My mom keeps on [posting] me, 'You're on Facebook! Get off! Do your homework!' And I'm like . . . de-friend" (17), was met with both commiseration and a flurry of stories about evading the parental gaze online. Even many of our youngest survey respondents felt that parents should not force their children to friend them on social media sites (56%) or read their texts (44%)[7] and took steps to avoid being watched. Sharing their passwords was one thing; having their parents constantly looking over their shoulders was another. This is in keeping with Valentine's (2004) observation that young people make their own decisions about risk and disrupt the kinds of controls parents put in place to protect them from risk.

But concerns about online privacy from parents were particularly acute for our teenaged participants. Communication with friends was a central part of their lives, and they enjoyed the way networked tools gave them a deep sense of connection with their friends (Licoppe, 2004; Shade, 2011). They also articulated a strong need for autonomy from parents so they could better explore the "public–private boundaries of the self" (Peter, Valkenburg and Fluckiger, 2009, 85) and be free to experiment in ways that were difficult in offline contexts (Livingstone, 2009, 91). They felt that constant connection to parents also made it difficult for them to accomplish the central tasks of adolescence to

> renegotiate their familial relationships . . . seek to define themselves within a peer group . . . [and] venture out into the world without parental supervision.
>
> (Draper, 2012, 223)

As one 13- to 14-year-old in Toronto put it,

> There should be a point where parents will just like, leave you alone and not have to know every single thing about you. Like I get, the protection side, but they don't need to know every single thing about you.
>
> (Steeves, 2012a, 18)

Because of this, our teenaged participants were much more likely to seek out private online spaces in which to interact with their peers. They articulated a clear need for privacy and explicitly linked it to their need for autonomy and independence, drawing on Samarajiva's notion of privacy as "the capacity to implicitly or explicitly negotiate boundary conditions of social relations" (Samarajiva, quoted in Livingstone, 2009, 110). However, many parents of teens told us they had to increase their level of vigilance as their child entered adolescence because this age group was more likely to do or say something inappropriate online. Moreover, they worried that the impact of such a misstep would be magnified because so many people would be able to see it. They therefore recruited other family members, such as older siblings or cousins, to monitor their child online and report back to them, creating a hybrid form of surveillance that was both hierarchical and lateral.

Although all our parent participants were uncomfortable with this level of scrutiny, almost all of them felt they had little choice because surveillance was perceived to be a necessary tool to protect their children from their own poor judgment. This exchange was typical:

> Who was it that said you had spies out there? I have nieces [who] will write to [my daughter], even call me to say, "uh, tell her to change . . . her wall, her status, or whatever," so that's good.
>
> (Steeves, 2012a, 14)

Others spoke of the need to read every text, every social media posting, and every email to make sure their child was not in a position to make a mistake. Accordingly, just when teenagers were asking for more freedom from the parental gaze—precisely so they could make their own mistakes—many parents were increasing the level of online monitoring in order to shut down any possibility of their child behaving poorly. Parental surveillance accordingly moved from monitoring for protective care of a child at risk of harm from ill-intentioned others to monitoring for behavioural control of a child that was a source of risk himself or herself.

From our teenaged participants' perspective, this kind of surveillance created a great deal of conflict and interfered with their family relationships. As one 15- to 17-year-old said,

> "I blocked my little brother, he's like a little spy for my mother" (18). And, after cousins of one of our 13 to 14-year-old participants 'snitched' on her, she told us, "the same night I go and delete them . . . then [my mom] gets mad, she's like 'don't delete your family members.' I'm like, well, tell them to stop stalking me."
>
> (18)

Interestingly, it was also not in keeping with the kinds of monitoring they experienced in offline situations. Whereas parents were comfortable with their child's judgment in general, they were much more concerned about their child's actions when networked technologies were involved. The teenagers we interviewed found this confusing, because online (and surveilled) actions were perceived by parents to be more dangerous than offline (and unsurveilled) actions. One 13- to 14-year-old girl summarized:

> My mom trusts me enough to, like, actually bring a guy home, like one of my guy-friends home? But she doesn't trust me enough to like, have him up on Facebook, which kind of makes me depressed.
>
> (19)

They told us that this kind of surveillance made it more difficult for them to express themselves online and explore their various roles as friend, romantic partner, and emerging adult because online performances for their peer audience would often unintentionally become visible to their family audience. This meant they were often held to account for comments that were taken out of context or seen as more dangerous because they were made online or by text. This in turn disrupted their "ability to disclose private information in appropriate ways and settings" (Peter, Valkenburg and Fluckiger, 2009, 83), both with their peers and with their family members.

Rooney's work on trust is particularly relevant here. She argues that young people must not only learn to trust others; they must also learn how to be

> "trusted *by* others to be responsible, to take control and do things in ways that extend their skills and competencies" so they can develop into "competent, confident and active human agent[s]."
>
> (2010, 344, emphasis added)

From this perspective, surveillance as control teaches children the wrong lessons: family members who monitor you for your own protection do not trust you to make the right decisions and are not to be trusted because they exaggerate risks and interpret actions out of context.

At the same time, our participants were empathetic to their parents' concerns and acknowledged that parents were only trying to protect them from harm. Moreover, all age groups of survey respondents indicated that parents were a helpful resource for solving problems. Younger children tended to see parents as a first response—three quarters of 10-year-olds indicated they would ask their parents for help first if someone was mean or cruel to them online—but more than one quarter (27%) of 15- to 17-year-olds continued to rely on parents if self-help strategies (including ignoring the problem, confronting the person who said it face to face, and asking friends for help) were unsuccessful. The presence of parental rules about online activities (as opposed to parental monitoring) also appears to have a protective effect for all age groups; survey respondents who reported that they had house rules against risky online behaviour were statistically less likely to participate in that behaviour.

Interestingly, our teen participants who were not monitored were also the ones who were the most likely to willingly share aspects of their online lives with their parents and to go to them for help. Trust for them was mutual—their parents trusted them to behave appropriately, and they trusted their parents not to over-react (Steeves, 2012a, 19).

Kerr, Stattin, and Trost (1999) report that this kind of voluntary disclosure increases trust for parents as well as for children. The more a child is able to express feelings and talk about problems with a parent, the more the child trusts the parent. Conversely, the more a child spontaneously reveals about his or her daily life to a parent, the more the parent trusts the child. Surveillance as control, on the other hand, diminishes measures of trust and, interestingly, also correlates with higher, not lower, rates of anti-social behaviour (Stattin and Kerr, 2002). So although parental surveillance may be well intentioned, it does not provide a "realistic form of protection" (Rooney, 2010, 351) for the child. It also may reduce the opportunities for the child to explore other independent identities with a sense of competence and confidence (Steeves, 2012a, 351).

One story in particular illustrates the importance of adult support as a child begins to explore the world outside the home and competently navigate new identities. A 13- to 14-year-old boy told us that he was being 'stalked' online by a 13-year-old girl who wanted to be his girlfriend. After she posted a comment on his Facebook wall that "btw, I'm not a virgin," he was subjected to cruel comments and uncomfortable teasing from his friends. He did not know what to do, so he showed the posts to his mother. His fear was that she would take the matter out of his hands and, in fact, she immediately wanted to intervene. However, he articulated his concerns about exacerbating an already uncomfortable situation, and they negotiated an appropriate strategy that met his need for protection in a way that also respected his need for independence. He removed the comments from his wall, and the teasing stopped (ibid., 20).

This boy's problem was not resolved by parental surveillance—in fact, the mother only knew of the situation because the boy told her about it. It was resolved by dialogue structured by mutual trust and a willingness on the part of the parent to provide the child the opportunity to solve his own problem, with her guidance. This illustrates that the negotiations between parents and children around technologies are complex and multifaceted and implicate broader concerns about the competing needs to allow a child freedom and exert control over the child.

SCHOOLS, PANOPTIC SURVEILLANCE, AND A LOSS OF PRIVACY

Monitoring at school was pervasive and often posed problems for the young people we interviewed as they sought to complete their schoolwork. Not only was certain content blocked, but their online communications with peers were closely scrutinized, and they were held to account for interactions they interpreted among themselves as harmless. Moreover, they were given little to no opportunity to explain themselves if one of the technical controls indicated they had done something they were not allowed to do.

Our participants were most vituperative about this kind of panoptic control. They both actively resisted it (e.g. sharing technical fixes to get around filters) and questioned the school's need to police their every word, to make sure they did not 'swear' or say something 'inappropriate.' From their perspective, the school should give them access to networked technologies without placing them under surveillance and, instead, rely on teachers to help them learn how to use them. One 13- to 14-year-old explained:

> But then, again, we're supposed to write every day everywhere else, except for school. What's the big deal if we do exactly what we do at home, at school? . . . Teachers should be allowed to read what we write, and if it's inappropriate, they can make us take it down, but they shouldn't just block us out from it, that is our own right.
>
> (Steeves, 2012a, 21)

Interestingly, the key informant teachers we spoke to agreed. From their perspective, school filters, acceptable use policies, and keystroke loggers made it incredibly difficult to productively use networked technologies in the classroom because they decreased learning opportunities and restricted the teachers' ability to teach. As one teacher from Ontario noted,

> For me it would be so much easier if it were just unblocked and the Board trusted the teachers to show the kids how to actually use this material. That's how I'd prefer to teach.
>
> (Steeves, 2012b, 12)

This form of panoptic surveillance also took away the teachable moments in which teachers could help students learn to act as good digital citizens. A teacher from Western Canada put it this way:

> It's not like all of a sudden you hit 18, and now you can have autonomy. I mean, children do not learn to make good choices by being told what to do and follow instructions. And, unfortunately, they have to be given the opportunity to make bad choices as often as good choices. And they need adults to be the saving, caring allies that we need to be to help them make [good choices], to learn from their mistakes.
>
> (12)

A teacher from Eastern Canada suggested that surveillance can interfere with the privacy of the classroom and make it more difficult to create a safe, confidential learning environment:

> When the conversation was intended to provoke intellectual curiosity and you're expected to take intellectual risks and really share and

> expose your thoughts about a particular text or event, to have that trust, that collaboration, that safe learning environment sort of ruined from access to technology or a recording device or posting online, I don't know if you could overcome that to build [the] kind of classroom [where students feel safe to experiment].

A teacher from Northern Canada agreed. He told us students

> need to trust you in order to take risks . . . being able to answer questions and know that if I get a wrong answer, that's okay, they won't laugh or make fun of me. That's risk taking for some students. That's a big risk.

Interestingly, both the young people and the teachers we talked to indicated that the panoptic surveillance they both experienced in school was the most difficult to negotiate, because they had very little control over the gaze or input into how their actions were interpreted by the school administrators that monitored the use of the system.

CONCLUSION

Our research findings suggest that the young people and adults we talked to have a complex relationship with networked technologies and continually negotiate the degree of monitoring young people are subjected to in the socio-technical spaces they inhabit. Young people are attracted to networked spaces because of the visibility they provide, but the monitoring they experience in these spaces makes it difficult for them to draw lines between their various audiences and attain the level of privacy they desire. That lack of privacy also detracts from their ability to enter into relationships of trust—particularly with parents, teachers, and other family members but also with friends—which in turn complicates their attempts to meet the developmental objective of individuating and 'growing up.'

Moreover, young people's experiences of monitoring involve different kinds of surveillant relationships, each of which offers different opportunities for freedom and control. Lateral surveillance among peers is highly nuanced, both opening up opportunities to reflexively perform a variety of social roles and potentially magnifying the consequences of failed performances. Self-representations are accordingly carefully crafted on and through social networks, and young people rely upon friendships within these networks to help them manage how they are perceived and understood, particularly in these contexts.

Negotiations between young people and parents are particularly complex, as parents seek to balance surveillance as care with surveillance as control. This balance becomes more challenging when children enter adolescence—when young people seek a greater degree of privacy from parents so they can explore their identity outside the family. However, this is also when many parents feel they should increase the level of monitoring to ensure that their children do not engage in relationships or practices that they see as inappropriate or dangerous. Again, failed performances are seen as more problematic because they take place on networked media and can be reproduced and distributed widely. In addition, the ubiquity of being watched through social networks by a variety of audiences makes it more difficult for a teen to craft a specific persona for peers within that social network without disrupting the expectations of family members. This difficulty is magnified when parents see these behaviours on social networks as particularly risky.

Monitoring in school most closely aligns to the panoptic conception of surveillance, and young people participate in a number of strategies to resist this kind of watching. Interestingly, both the young people and the teachers we spoke to lament the ways in which panoptic surveillance invades the privacy of the classroom and detracts from the relationships of trust that are at the heart of learning.

NOTES

1. The Young Canadians in a Wired World project began in 2000–2001 when we interviewed parents and children and surveyed approximately 5,500 Canadian students aged 10 to 17 to examine children's use and perceptions of the Internet. In 2004 to 2005, we conducted a similar study, broadening the technology to other forms of networked communications, including cell phones and gaming platforms. In 2012 to 2013, we again returned to the field but added a series of interviews with teachers to get a better understanding of the impact of the full range of networked technologies in the classroom. This chapter draws on the most recent data from 2012 to 2013, which includes the results of interviews with 10 key informant teachers and 12 qualitative group sessions (four each in Calgary, Toronto, and Ottawa) with a total of 66 young people aged 11 to 17 and 21 parents of children and youth aged 11 to 17, and a quantitative survey of 5,436 children and youth aged 10 to 17 from across the country. For a full report of each phase of YCWW, see http://mediasmarts.ca/research-policy.
2. All information about and quotes from our 2012 to 2013 qualitative research are taken from Steeves, 2012a. The survey results are taken from Steeves, 2014.
3. Twenty percent of our survey respondents reported pranking online at least once a day or once a week, and 28% reported pranking over a cell phone (Tables 8, 9).
4. Although only 20% of 11-year-old survey respondents reported that they did this, the proportion rose to 50% by age 17.
5. Vandoninck, d'Haenens, and Roe (2013) report similar concerns among European parents, independent of socio-economic status.

6. Seventy-nine percent of children aged 10 agreed with the statement that parents should keep track of their children online all the time, compared to only 23% of 17-year-old respondents.
7. The percentages increase with age, to 77% of 17-year-olds and 83% of 17-year-olds respectively.

REFERENCES

ANDREJEVIC, M. (2005) The Work of Watching One Another: Lateral Surveillance, Risk and Governance. *Surveillance & Society,* 2(4). p. 479–497.

BOYD, D. (2007) Why Youth (Heart) Social Network Sites: The Role of Networked Publics in Teenage Social Life. In Buckingham, D. (Ed.), *Youth, Identity, and Digital Media*. Cambridge (MA): MIT Press, 119–142.

CANADIAN RADIO-TELEVISION AND TELECOMMUNICATIONS COMMISSION. (2010) Communications Monitoring Report, July 2010. www.crtc.gc.ca/eng/publications/reports/policymonitoring/2010/cmr2010.pdf, accessed 22–09–2013.

DRAPER, N. (2012) Is Your Teen At Risk? Discourses of Adolescent Sexting in the United States. *Journal of Children and Media,* 6(2). p. 221–236.

GIDDENS, A. (1991) *Modernity and Self-Identity*. Cambridge: Polity Press.

GOFFMAN, E. (1959) *The Presentation of the Self*. New York: Basic Books, Inc.

ITO, M. (2005) Mobile Phones, Japanese Youth, and the Re-placement of Social Contact. *Computer Supported Cooperative Work, 31*. p. 131–148.

KERR, M., STATTIN, H. & TROST, K. (1999) To Know You Is to Trust You: Parents' Trust Is Rooted in Child Disclosure of Information. *Journal of Adolescence,* 22. p. 737–752.

LICOPPE, C. (2004) 'Connected' Presence: The Emergence of a New Repertoire for Managing Social Relationships in a Changing Communication Technoscape. *Environment and Planning D: Society and Space,* 22. p. 135–156.

LIVINGSTONE, S. (2009) *Children and the Internet*. Cambridge (UK): Polity Press.

———. (2008) Taking Risky Opportunities in Youthful Content Creation: Teenagers' Use of Social Networking Sites for Intimacy, Privacy and Self-expression. *New Media and Society*, 10(3). p. 393–411.

MEAD, G.H. (1934) *Mind, Self, and Society from the Standpoint of a Social Behaviorist*. C.W. Morris (Ed.). Chicago: University of Chicago Press.

MEDIA AWARENESS NETWORK. (2001) *Young Canadians in a Wired World: The Students' View*. Ottawa: Media Awareness Network. http://mediasmarts.ca/research-policy. Accessed 22–08–2013.

MENDOZA, K. (2007) *"WATZ UR NAM?": Adolescent Girls, Chat Rooms, and Interpersonal Authenticity*. Media Education Lab. www.mediaeducationlab. Accessed 22–08–2013.

OLIVEIRA, M. (2012, Feb 29). Canada's 'Most Socially Networked' Title Slipping Away. *Globe and Mail*. www.theglobeandmail.com/technology/digital-culture/social-web/canadas-most-socially-networked-title-slipping-away/article550205/. Accessed 29–02–2012

PETER, J., VALKENBURG, P. & FLUCKIGER, C. (2009) Adolescents and Social Network Sites: Identity, Friendships and Privacy. In Livingstone, S. & Haddon, L. (Eds.), *<Kids Online>: Opportunities and Risks for Children*. Bristol: The Policy Press, 83–94.

PHILLIPS, D. (2009) Ubiquitous Computing, Spatiaility, and the Construction of Identity: Directions for Policy Reponses. In Kerr, I., Steeves, V. & Lucock, C.

(Eds.), *Lessons from the Identity Trail: Anonymity, Privacy and Identity in a Networked Society*. New York: Oxford University Press, 303–318.

ROONEY, T. (2010) Trusting Children: How Do Surveillance Technologies Alter a Child's Experience of Trust, Risk and Responsibility? *Surveillance and Society*, 7(4). p. 344–355.

SHADE, L. R. (2008) Internet Social Networking in Young Women's Everyday Lives: Some Insights from Focus Groups. *Our Schools, Our Selves*. p. 65–73.

———. (2011) Surveilling the Girl via the Third and Networked Screen. In Kearney, M. C. (Ed.), *Mediated Girlhoods: New Explorations of Girls' Media Culture*. New York: Peter Lang, 261–276.

STATTIN, H. & KERR, M. (2002) Parental Monitoring: A Reinterpretation. *Child Development*, 71(4). p. 1072–1085.

STEEVES, V. (2005) *Young Canadians in a Wired World—Phase II Trends and Recommendations*. Ottawa: Media Awareness Network. http://mediasmarts.ca/research-policy. Accessed 19–08–2013.

———. (2012a) *Young Canadians in a Wired World, Phase III: Talking to Youth and Parents about Life Online*. Ottawa: Media Smarts. http://mediasmarts.ca/research-policy. Accessed 19–08–2013.

———. (2012b) *Young Canadians in a Wired World—Phase III Teachers' Perspectives*. Ottawa: Media Smarts. http://mediasmarts.ca/research-policy. Accessed 19–08–2013.

———. (2014) *Young Canadians in a Wired World, Phase III: Student Survey*. Ottawa: Media Smarts. http://mediasmarts.ca/research-policy. Accessed 19–08–2013.

STERN, S. R. (2004) Expressions of Identity Online: Prominent Features and Gender Differences in Adolescents' World Wide Web Pages. *Journal of Broadcasting & Electronic Media*, 48(2). p. 218–243.

VANDONINCK, S., D'HAENENS, L. & ROE, K. (2013) Online Risks. *Journal of Children and Media*, 7(1). p. 60–78.

7 Makers of Media Wisdom
Translating and Guarding Media Wisdom in the Netherlands

Isolde Sprenkels and Sally Wyatt

INTRODUCTION

Children in the Netherlands and elsewhere spend ever more time online using various new media devices and applications to help them with their homework, to play games, and to communicate with friends and family. As Van der Ploeg and Pridmore discuss in the Introduction to this volume, digitization and automation processes pervade nearly all social, political, cultural, and economic domains in advanced industrialized societies, affecting people in their various roles as citizens, consumers, and workers. Children, as future workers, proto-consumers, and citizens-in-the-making, are a particular focus of attention. On-going public debates about children's use of new media can be divided between those who draw upon discourses of 'celebration' and those who draw upon discourses of 'concern' (Drotner, 2011). Kirsten Drotner explains that in the celebratory discourse, children are perceived as media savvy, as pioneering experts, as digital natives, while discourses of concern focus on the content-, contact-, and conduct-related dangers possibly posed by new media (ibid.; see also Livingstone, 2009, and Hasebrink et al., 2008). This distinction opposes an optimistic image of children and their relationship with new media technology with a more pessimistic and fearful image of the role new media technologies play in children's lives. Both views contain a dualistic picture of children as being either media savvy or vulnerable (Buckingham, 2011) and a dualistic view of new media technology posing either opportunities or risks (Livingstone, 2009). Either way, whether describing savvy or vulnerable children and portraying technologies as offering opportunities or risks, it is increasingly seen as necessary to educate children about the possibilities of new media. In these contexts, new media is either seen as a medium for creative self-expression, public participation, and cultural heritage or as a means of encountering harmful or offensive content and people (Lunt and Livingstone, 2012). This suggests another dualism, one that includes advocates for empowerment versus those with a more protectionist take on media education (Hobbs, 2011).

While the need for education in itself may be undisputed, these opposing positions make it less clear which approach should be used and how 'responsibility' should be distributed amongst all those involved, including parents, teachers, and librarians as well as those more removed from children's daily lives, such as policy makers, private corporations, and the various non-governmental organizations (NGOs) developing digital material aimed at children. There are also many terms circulating that attempt to capture the knowledge and skills assisting people to use, interpret, and produce media. These terms are a part of a range of educational activities. Terms in circulation include not only 'media literacy' (European Commission), but also 'media and information literacy' (UNESCO), 'digital literacy,' 'information literacy,' and the concept of 'media wisdom.' Dutch policy makers now favour this latter term. However, these terms are not neutral. As Sonia Livingstone says, "how media literacy is defined has consequences for the framing of the debate, the research agenda and policy initiatives" (2004, 3).

In this chapter, we trace how 'media wisdom' took root in the Dutch policy context.[1] Our analysis draws upon insights from the interdisciplinary field of science and technology studies (STS), moving beyond technological determinist views of technology (Wyatt, 2008a), and essentialist views of either technology or of users' identities (Oudshoorn and Pinch, 2005; Wyatt, 2008b). We prefer to emphasize that people—adults and children alike—engage with new media technologies in many different ways. Without denying the enormous power of contemporary digital technologies, we also recognize their contingency, flexibility, and multiplicity of everyday (Internet) use and users (Wyatt, 2005). In particular, we make use of the concept of 'boundary object' in order to understand how terms like 'media literacy' and 'media wisdom' are able to engage and mobilize social actors across disparate areas. We suggest that the concept of media wisdom functions as a boundary object (Star and Griesemer, 1989; Star, 2010) in the way it bridges boundaries between different sectors and the organizations and representatives operating within them. They all have different viewpoints on media wisdom deriving from the sectors in which they operate and their concomitant priorities and target groups. As a concept, 'media wisdom' is simultaneously flexible and robust, adapting to different viewpoints and retaining a common identity across diverse sectors, organizations, and their representatives. As we will show later in this chapter, the concept of 'media wisdom' meant different things to the Dutch Council for Culture who introduced the term than to the Dutch Cabinet adopting it a few years later. But it is also translated many more times and in many more ways. As Susan Leigh Star and James Griesemer suggest, boundary objects are "weakly structured in common use, and become strongly structured in individual site use . . . they have different meanings in different social worlds but their structure is common enough to more than one world to make them recognizable, a means of translation" (1989, 393).

In the next section, we provide some of the pre-history, outlining earlier European and international definitions of the various terms mentioned in the preceding paragraph. The following section outlines how 'media wisdom' emerged, starting in an advisory report to the government in 2005 and becoming more official in a Cabinet report in 2008. Next, we focus on how this concept was translated in practice, leading to a proliferation of initiatives across sectors, all claiming to be implementing 'media wisdom.' The following section explains how this initial flowering was pruned back or became operationalized in a more narrow interpretation of the term, contributing to the institutionalization of media wisdom into education. We observe that media wisdom is sought as a quality to be developed in new media users themselves, specifically in children, but such a view fails to take into account that users and technology are constituted in relation to one another, which means media wisdom is also facilitated or hindered by and reliant on the design of new media. In the Conclusion, we reflect on what this process has taught us about how concepts and definitions serve to enrol different types of actors and distribute responsibility across all of them.

BACKGROUND: MEDIA EDUCATION AND LITERACY

Media education is generally considered to provide the means of implementing the aspirations of media literacy (Lunt and Livingstone, 2012). Both have been studied, debated, and defined in various domains and disciplines for decades. Although debate continues on how best to define media literacy and what it means for educational practices, there seems to be some agreement on a conceptual level. An oft-quoted definition formulated during the National Leadership Conference on Media Literacy held in the United States in 1992 defined media literacy as "the ability to access, analyse, evaluate, and communicate messages in a variety of forms" (Aufderheide, 1993). Most definitions within academic and policy discourse contain similar elements, relating to people's knowledge and skills, aiding them to use, interpret, and produce media.

There are two prominent approaches within debates about media education. The first, a protectionist approach, advocates "an intervention designed to counter the negative effects of mass media and popular culture" (Hobbs, 2011, 423), by some described as a "pedagogic equivalent of a tetanus shot" (Bazalgette, 1997, 72). In other words, the approach emphasizes inoculating children against the 'damaging effects' of media by lecturing about media's negative influences, manipulated messages, and so on. It is thinking and acting for children, who are generally perceived as passive and vulnerable media consumers. The second approach is supported by empowerment advocates, which aims to teach children to think and act for themselves, generally perceiving them as competent social actors. These empowerment advocates take account of what children already know about media instead of laying out what they ought to know (Buckingham, 2011). Not only do they strongly promote a critical analysis of media, but they also recommend teaching "children to use the technical tools of self-expression, all the better to participate in modern society" (Lunt and Livingstone, 2012, 118), as the media afford "an expressive, cultural, and participatory opportunity which brings significant benefits to those who are able to 'read' its codes and conventions and to use its tools and technologies" (ibid., 119). We argue that in the approach of empowerment advocates, both educators as well as new media technology can be considered to be 'empowering.' By this we mean that it is about empowering youth, teaching them to think critically for themselves regarding the opportunities and risks new media possibly pose, as well as the empowering affordances of new media technologies. Within this empowerment approach, children sometimes are discursively positioned as pioneers, digital natives leading the way into the future (Helsper and Enyon, 2010; Lunt and Livingstone, 2012), considering them as naturally autonomous and competent—as spontaneously 'media literate' (Buckingham, 2011). David Buckingham warns that adopting such a view can provide a useful alibi for avoiding the obligation to care for children in this matter (ibid.).

Media literacy has long received attention on international policy agendas. On a global level, UNESCO (United Nations Educational Scientific and Cultural Organization) stresses the need to provide citizens with competences (knowledge, skills, and attitudes) necessary to engage with traditional media and new technologies.[2] It has published several documents related to the topic (UNESCO, 1982, 2005, 2007) using the terms 'media education' and 'information literacy.' Since 2011, UNESCO uses 'media and information literacy' (MIL) as a composite concept (Wilson et al., 2011). "MIL brings together Information Literacy and Media Literacy, along with Information and Communication Technology, and Digital Literacy, as a new literary construct that helps empower people, communities and nations to participate in and contribute to global knowledge societies" (UNESCO, 2013, 17). Later in the same document, it explains the benefits of MIL as it "empowers citizens to access, retrieve, understand, evaluate and use, to create as well as share information and media content in all formats, using various tools, in a critical, ethical and effective way, in order to participate and engage in personal, professional and societal activities" (UNESCO, 2013, 29). Elsewhere, it states that MIL can be considered to be a way to "expand civic education movement that incorporates teachers as principal agents of change" (Wilson et al., 2011, 11). Its strategy includes initiatives such as a curriculum for teachers (Wilson et al., 2011), guidelines for policies and strategies (Grizzle et al., 2013), and setting up a university network to stimulate research that can inform policies.[3]

On a European Union level, 'media literacy' is not only considered to be important for active citizenship, participation, inclusion, and social cohesion, but it is also considered to be crucial for the establishment of a competitive knowledge-based economy, in which digital media and the Internet in particular are emphasized (European Commission, 2007, 2009; European Parliament, 2008). 'Media literacy' entered the European policy stage when it came to be considered essential in meeting the goals of the *2000 Lisbon Strategy* (European Commission 2007, 2009; European Parliament, 2008), and its connection with economic interests became even more important in the *Europe 2020 Strategy for Smart, Sustainable, and Inclusive Growth* (European Commission, 2010a) and one of its initiatives, *A Digital Agenda for Europe* (European Commission, 2010b). Enhancing 'media literacy' or 'digital literacy' as the Commission chooses to use in the *Digital Agenda*, is deemed necessary, as "Europe is suffering from a growing professional ICT skills shortage and a digital-literacy deficit. These failings are excluding many citizens from the digital society and economy and are holding back the large multiplier effect of ICT-take up to productivity growth" (European Commission, 2010b, 6). The EU definition of media literacy focuses on "the ability to access the media, to understand and critically evaluate different aspects of the media and media content and to create communications in a variety of contexts" (European Commission, 2007, 2009). In order to develop this definition, a public consultation among industry, media organizations, education institutions, regulators, and citizen and consumer organizations was held, and a Media Literacy Expert Group meeting was organized in which academics and media professionals contributed.

Apart from describing a duality in media literacy education, the preceding paragraphs briefly illustrate two points. First, the understandings of 'media literacy' differ between key actors, for instance between UNESCO and the EU. UNESCO focuses on civic education and participation, and the EU highlights employability and economic growth. In this chapter, we demonstrate that this also happens on a more local level. Second, various actors adopt different terms such as 'media literacy,' 'media education,' 'digital literacy,' and 'information literacy,' which carry different meanings and connotations. This influences the foci of the 'media literacy' policy agendas and practices.

In this chapter, we refrain from assigning *a priori* definitions to 'media wisdom' or 'media literacy.' Instead, we look at how they were created and put on the policy agendas as solutions to deal with a variety of potential problems such as civic, social, and economic disadvantage and exclusion, which, in turn, may occur due to developments in media technology, and processes of digitization and globalization. Therefore, we argue, it is important to explore and follow the concepts of 'media literacy' and 'media wisdom' while keeping in mind that they are an outcome of relations, of choices, practices, an interplay between negotiating actors, and not something stable with a fixed meaning across time and place. Inspired by Bruno Latour's first rule of method, that we should study science in action and not ready-made science or technology (Latour, 1987), we trace 'media wisdom' 'in the making', in action as it emerged in Dutch policy and practice.

We follow it and trace the ways in which the various meanings and connotations shape the 'media wisdom' debate and various 'media wisdom' practices, enrolling different types of social actors and distributing responsibility across them.

FROM MEDIA EDUCATION TO MEDIA WISDOM

As described, in the early years of the 21st century, there were already several terms in circulation, aimed at capturing and addressing the problems faced by children in learning to use and in using advanced digital technologies. Nonetheless, in its advisory report to the Dutch government in 2005 titled *Media Wisdom: The Development of New Citizenship* (Raad voor Cultuur, 2005), the Dutch Council for Culture (Raad voor Cultuur: RvC) decided not to use either 'media education' or 'media literacy' but to use 'media wisdom' instead. According to the RvC, media education in the Netherlands had been passive, defensive, and narrowly focused on youth and formal education. It wanted to move away from such a protectionist approach. The RvC claimed that Dutch society is saturated with media and that citizens have to be(come) 'media wise' in order to be able to participate in various domains, ranging from healthcare, leisure, and the labour market to politics, education, and commerce. It defined 'media wisdom' as: "The whole of knowledge, skills, and mentality by which citizens can consciously, critically and actively move within a complex, dynamic and fundamentally mediated world" (Raad voor Cultuur, 2005, 2). It further stressed that the purpose of 'media wisdom' is not just dealing with media as such but participating in wider societal processes (Raad voor Cultuur, 2005). 'Media wisdom,' the RvC argued, would provide a much broader perspective than media education. The RvC noted that citizens were dealing with various technological and societal developments, contributing to new forms and practices of citizenship. It described a move from a welfare state to a society in which the government increasingly calls upon citizens' self-reliance in various areas for which they need to use digital media. In light of such developments, citizens need "tools and expertise to shape this responsibility in a satisfying way for themselves and society" (Raad voor Cultuur, 2005, 3). They needed to be able to participate in the societal process so that social exclusion and the emergence of a 'digital divide' would be prevented, related to differences in media use and skills. In other words, citizens needed to be 'media wise' in order to fit this 'new citizenship.'

The RvC stressed that the government has a duty of care for enhancing such media wisdom in citizens. It did not propose to make media wisdom obligatory in formal education, but it did suggest that it should be considered part of a school's citizenship education and of the curricula for training teachers. It also recommended that schools could hire media coaches to promote the coherence of media wisdom within educational programmes, to guide other staff members, and to initiate media projects. The RvC emphasized that media wisdom should not only be part of formal education but also of the tasks and practices of public media, cultural organizations, and public libraries. Prior to this point, initiatives had been made within all these sectors, but there was no shared policy.

The RvC considered it "of great importance to concentrate on enlarging media competences, or rather: media wisdom of citizens" (Raad voor Cultuur, 2005, 13), emphasizing the competences and skills needed for media wisdom. The definition provided by the RvC makes this clear: "media wisdom is the whole of knowledge, skills and mentality by which citizens can consciously, critically and actively move within a complex, variable and fundamentally mediated world" (Raad voor Cultuur, 2005, 18). Knowledge includes that which is "needed to interpret media messages, the awareness that media content is constructed, the ability to detect which interests or value systems are steering them" (Raad voor Cultuur, 2005, 19). Skills include "the ability to watch, being able to choose, and to control buttons" (Raad voor Cultuur, 2005, 20), so that one could not only consume but also produce media content. Mentality has to do with "citizens' awareness of the way they use media, and the effect that has on themselves and others" (Raad voor Cultuur, 2005, 2).

Most media literacy definitions contain similar items relating to people's knowledge and skills, helping them use, interpret, and produce media. Mentality, on the contrary, is a more specifically Dutch element. The most striking difference in this RvC document is the use of 'wisdom,' *wijsheid* in Dutch, instead of the more widespread *geletterdheid*, the usual translation of 'literacy.' The RvC justifies its choice in a single sentence, which reads, "the more commonly used *media geletterdheid* is more suitable, but not preferred by the RvC due to its linguistic associations" (Raad voor Cultuur, 2005, 18), arising from the analogy with print literacy, namely the ability to read, write, or produce text. The RvC deliberately chose the term 'wisdom,' which it felt was broader than literacy. 'Wisdom' carries connotations with various philosophical and religious perspectives dating back to ancient classical and biblical times, namely "the ability to use your knowledge and experience to make good decisions and judgements" (Cambridge Dictionaries online). This matches the perspective of the RvC on media wisdom as an on-going process that citizens continue to develop, in contrast to a more binary take on literacy in which one can or cannot read and write at a basic level. Literacy is taught in school from an early age, provided for by the government, through the right to education (United Nations, 1948). This is not the case for media wisdom, which, we argue, carries a different connotation in relation to responsibility. Through the education system, the government is primarily responsible for teaching literacy but not for developing lifelong media wisdom. As will become clear in the following pages, media wisdom has not been made compulsory in education. This worries Terry, editor-in-chief of one of the first Dutch websites on parenting and editor-in-chief at a knowledge centre for youth and (digital) media, focusing on schools, parents, and the media industry. She claims:

> So now we have a situation that at the Ministry of Education it is said "yes it is important that citizens are made media wise and that it happens in school," but that's it. We are the only country in Europe that does not have the obligation to include media wisdom in its curriculum.

Terry worries about this. She compares media wisdom education with teaching children how to read and write, and raises concerns about the emergence of an illiterate citizenry and all the concomitant consequences:

> I don't think we would accept it if children finished primary education from one school knowing how to read and write, and finished at another school not knowing how . . . In fact, this is the new illiteracy which we are creating, what we allow to happen, people have no idea.

Even though the RvC chose 'wisdom' and not the Dutch equivalent *geletterdheid*, Terry associates media wisdom with print literacy on the level of knowledge and power differences, connecting it with societal disadvantage and exclusion.

The Dutch government did follow up on some of the recommendations of the RvC advisory report. In a response to the RvC's advice, the Minister of Education, Culture and Science acknowledged the importance of media wisdom, arguing that a mediated society leads to different relationships between media and citizens, government and citizens, and citizens and business (Hoeven, 2006). The minister advocated cooperation and knowledge exchange within networks and organizations already dealing with media wisdom in one way or another. After the report, numerous initiatives concerning media wisdom were undertaken, including the development of courses and teaching material and the organization of workshops. However, the minister criticized this proliferation of initiatives for its lack of coherence. To address this, the ministry organized a conference together with the RvC in 2006 in order to search for "the meaning and impact of the media wisdom concept which is difficult to grasp" (Ministerie OCW, 2006, 1). It became clear, perhaps for the first time, that there were some difficulties with the concept, that it carried many connotations, meanings, interpretations, and practices. The conference "had people from various sectors and disciplines discuss the topic at different levels of abstraction in contact with each other" (ibid.).

The Dutch Cabinet published its vision on media wisdom, called *Mediawijsheid*, three years after the RvC's report (Plasterk and Routvoet, 2008). It cites the RvC's broad definition in one of its footnotes, but the notion of 'media wisdom' had changed. In the introduction, the cabinet states that it wants to foster safe and responsible media use by equipping citizens to take advantage of the opportunities new media are said to offer and to deal with the risks they are assumed to pose and to stimulate a safe media environment, using self-regulation and a system of complaints for parents and other carers. Immediately following this, it states that the focus of media wisdom is no longer on all citizens but on youth, their social environment, their media use, and positive and negative media effects. The target group for media wisdom initiatives was narrowed down, and the goals had changed. In addressing media wisdom, the cabinet took up the RvC's concept but translated it in such a manner that the meaning of the concept changed, as did the target group, government policy, and implicated actors. In other words, a new configuration emerged of practices, policies, social actors in which media wisdom is enacted into being. Youth and their wider social environment including parents, teachers, and other carers became top priority. Media wisdom became connected to media effects and the ways in which parents, other carers, and media producers play a part in guiding children's media use. In a way these actors were turned into guardians of media wisdom. The government itself also carried out a protectionist-oriented policy, for instance through its involvement in public broadcasting, providing support for media self-regulation and rules and regulations to protect (young) media users.[4] It also stimulated research on the topic and supported media users in critical and conscious media use. The latter would become a task of the media wisdom expertise centre the cabinet suggested starting, which had as a goal to bring together various media wisdom initiatives mainly focusing on supporting youth, parents and other carers. According to the cabinet, the mission of the media wisdom expertise centre was to strengthen media wisdom within society through first focusing on youth, parents, carers, and teachers in order to empower youth, to help them use media wisely and actively.

In this section, we have outlined how the concept of 'media wisdom' emerged in the Dutch policy landscape, how it changed from being a broad concept capturing a lifelong process of learning to something aimed primarily at empowering young people by those responsible for their development and education, as well as protecting them by particular provisions and regulations. In the next section, we turn to the many organizations that took up the concept in myriad ways, focussing on its empowering connotations, giving examples from different sectors.

MAKERS OF MEDIA WISDOM

As mentioned in the previous section, one of the initiatives of the Dutch government was to establish a media wisdom expertise centre bringing together the variety of existing initiatives related to media wisdom. Funded by the Ministry of Education, Culture and Science, this networking organization, named *Mediawijzer.net*, Media Wiser in English, started in 2008 in order to strengthen media wisdom in society, with a primary focus on youth between 2 and 18 years of age and their carers and teachers.

Mason, a colleague of Terry, and director of the knowledge centre on youth and (digital) media, mentions that "*Mediawijzer.net* has been initiated to prevent fragmentation. I have the idea that fragmentation has grown." He connects this fragmentation with not making media wisdom obligatory within the formal education system:

> *Mediawijzer.net* is not to blame for that, they do a terrific job, they also connected many people together, strengthening the network. A regulation to stimulate projects has led to many beautiful initiatives. But the theme is not being concretized by the government, it is not a compulsory section of education, so the market can do with it as it likes.

Mediawijzer.net relates to the intention to make citizens more media wise using these initiatives. It considers itself to be "an active and diverse network with one shared interest: making The Netherlands media wise" (Mediawijzer.net, 2013a). *Mediawijzer.net* describes itself as "[a] network of makers of media wisdom" (ibid.). As will be seen in this section, the fragmentation of *Mediawijzer.net* and the broad variety and struggle for conceptual unity and understanding also "makes media wisdom." In other words, media wisdom is continuously shaped in a variety of ways, eventually moving towards standardizing and institutionalizing it.

Mediawijzer.net connects a variety of organizations concerned with media wisdom, promoting cooperation and synergy between them (Kwartiermakersgroep, 2008). Its mission is formulated as follows: "The expertise centre *Mediawijzer.net* connects, strengthens, and inspires initiatives and organizations around media wisdom" (Mediawijzer.net, 2010a). It functions as a platform for knowledge sharing, conducting research, organizing events and campaigns, and advising local and central government.

Mediawijzer.net has a programme council. Five organizations form the core of the centre: the Netherlands Institute for Sound and Vision (NIBG) preserving audio-visual heritage, *Kennisnet*, a public expertise centre for ICT in education, the Institute for Public Libraries Sector (SIOB), the public broadcasting company (NTR), and the Electronic Commerce—or information society—Platform (ECP-EPN). Each has a specific role. NIBG is the national meeting point or 'clubhouse' and responsible for communication. Networking meetings are held there, and visitors of the NIBG can test their media wisdom skills in a specially equipped pavilion. SIOB provides local counters or 'houses of media wisdom' for citizens and is formally responsible for libraries. NTR is responsible for communication in general and for broadcasters and media, and ECP-EPN coordinates research. *Kennisnet* is responsible for online environments and for the website of *Mediwijzer.net*, which disseminates news and information on media wisdom and provides information about the activities and services of the network partners, or "makers of media wisdom" (Mediawijzer.net, 2013a). The five organizations represent different sectors, including culture, media, education, and business, each of which already has a strong knowledge base for media wisdom. Media wisdom means something slightly different in each of these sectors and the organizations and representatives operating within them. To SIOB and its representatives, media wisdom might be related to developing information (-seeking) skills, while NIBG and NTR focus on the manipulation of images, and *Kennisnet* might support initiatives concerning digital bullying or setting up rules concerning smartphone use in schools.

Since its start in 2008, more than 900 network partners (Mediawijzer.net, 2014) are part of *Mediawijzer.net*, and this keeps increasing. "This network should form a representative reflection of the breadth of the media wisdom concept in combination with its target groups" (Mediawijzer.net, 2010b, 28). Anyone can take part, and the variety of organizations is enormous: primary, secondary, and tertiary education, research organizations, independent researchers, companies engaged in consultancy and coaching in education and IT, charitable organizations, media companies, communication bureaus, libraries, cultural organizations including museums, and drama and art workshop organizers, youth care, youth work. The number of initiatives are manifold, yet their link with media wisdom is sometimes tenuous. For example, there is a reference to 'autism training' in the list. Following the link, it turns out to be a 'mind academy,' offering 'neuro-linguistic programming training.' Terry comments on this pluralism:

> It is meant to be diverse, but now it is so diverse that you don't know, actually all different possible takes on media wisdom are represented, no choice is made, no structure, no selection . . . Anyone can become a member now, every month a list of twenty new partners join. Eventually it is about reading and writing, so after a while everybody has joined.

We argue that in this way, media wisdom functions as a boundary object (Star and Griesemer, 1989; Star, 2010). It bridges boundaries, not only among the five organizations that form the core of the centre and the sectors they represent but also among the 900 networking partners, the RvC, the Dutch Cabinet, and many other actors, such as the news media reporting on media wisdom–related topics. The term 'media wisdom' retains its identity among all of these organizations and their representatives, being recognizable to all. At the same time, it is adaptable in such a way that everyone involved can fill in their own meanings relating to their own practices, priorities, and target groups. A continuous movement back and forth between the two forms of the boundary object, between the weakly structured and the well-structured aspects of media wisdom, takes place (Star, 2010). As Star explains, over time, people try to control this movement, which will be demonstrated in the next section.

MOVING FROM MEDIA WISDOM TOWARDS MEDIA EDUCATION

According to *Mediawijzer.net*, the abstract way in which the RvC defined media wisdom facilitated the proliferation of initiatives and meanings put forward by different social actors (Madiawijzer.net, 2011a). By providing a financial incentive, *Mediawijzer.net* invited its networking partners to provide clarity on the concept of media wisdom, to establish its elements and the measurable competences a person needs to be media wise (Wiebenga et al., 2011).

Meten van mediawijsheid (Measuring Media Wisdom) is the report written by six of the partners which received funding from *Mediawijzer.net*. They used the RvC definition of media wisdom as a starting point and promised to 'operationalize' it in order to support parties that would subsequently measure it. They formulated a definition of media wisdom, explicitly in terms of competences, considering it to be "a collection of competences a person needs to master in order to be media wise" (Wiebenga et al., 2011, 28). They translated the broad RvC definition of media wisdom into a model containing 14 competences. A person who masters all these competences is considered to be media wise, offering "an essential vehicle for self-reliant citizenship and full participation in the media society" (Mediawijzer.net, 2011a, 3). *Mediawijzer.net* argues that a model offers the possibility to order the proliferation of media wisdom initiatives in a new way. "With projects, workshops, websites and educational material it is now possible to determine to which competences they contribute" (Mediawijzer.net, 2011a, 8). We argue that it not only aids in ordering, but it also serves to standardize the media wisdom concept and its practices by focusing on particular competences. The definition of media wisdom provided by *Mediawijzer.net* from that moment on is "the set of competences which everyone needs, to participate actively and consciously to the media society" (Mediawijzer.net, 2013b).

In 2012, a slightly different competence model was developed, consisting of 10 competences instead of 14, divided into four groups: use, understanding, communication, and strategy. The 10 competences are: awareness of the growing influence of media on society, understanding how media are made, understanding how the media colour reality, using equipment software and applications, orientation within media environments, finding and processing information, creating content, participating in social networks, reflecting on own media usage, and achieving objectives through media. All 10 competences can be achieved on a level from zero to four and cover the three elements as provided for by the RvC, namely knowledge, skills, and attitude. "The model forms an invitation to teachers and professionals (media coaches, librarians, researchers) to apply it in their daily practice" (Gillebaard et al., 2013). "It forms a handle in developing media wisdom products and services, making the offer of media wisdom initiatives more insightful, and helps shaping (simple) measurement instruments" (website Mediawijzer[5]). It should be used as "[a] starting point for media wisdom initiatives" (Mediawijzer.net, 2012).

The point here is not the exact details of the 10 competences but rather the overall effort to create a model with a set of measurable standards and indicators. According to boundary object theory, "over time, people (often administrators or regulatory agencies) try to control the tacking back-and-forth, and especially, to standardize and make equivalent the ill-structured and well-structured aspects of the particular boundary object" (Star, 2010, 613). Star mentions that people try to control this constant moving between the ill-structured and the well-structured form of the boundary object and that at a certain point, the movement between the two forms scales up or becomes standardized. From that point, boundary objects begin to move and change into infrastructure, into (methodological) standards. We have described a 'tacking back and forth' between the ill- and well-structured forms of media wisdom. With the development of a competence model, a methodological standard was developed, changing media wisdom from a loose, broad set of definitions into a standard for all network partners to use when developing their products, services, and activities. All network partners need to connect with this model and these competences and comply with their further development in order for projects, websites, workshops, and educational material to be transparent about the competences to which they can contribute and develop (Mediawijzer.net, 2011a). Here *Mediawijzer.net* establishes itself as an obligatory passage point (Callon, 1986),[6] strengthening its position by standardizing media wisdom and enabling its operationalization. In the remainder of this section, we demonstrate how this contributes to the institutionalization of media wisdom in schools.

Mediawijzer.net stimulates the integration of media wisdom in educational curricula, either as a separate course or integrated in existing courses (Mediawijzer.net, 2010b). It explains that this is difficult, as it is not considered a compulsory subject in formal education, but that a way into education is through influencing educational publishers, schools, and teachers. And as described earlier, a way into the schools is through the network partners who are stimulated to use the competence model in developing their initiatives, which in turn may be deployed by individual schools for their media projects. *Mediawijzer.net* does not develop services for media users but stimulates its network partners to do so. For instance, it provides funding to its network partners to develop media wisdom projects which contribute to the stimulation of media wisdom through an annual incentive round providing funding for agreed themes. Each year several projects receive funding based on an annual topic, goal, problem, or set of spearheads. *Mediawijzer.net* explains that projects in this first period were mainly focusing on an "operational level: practical guides, lessons, policies, and descriptions of media wisdom" (Mediawijzer.net, 2011b). From 2012, the themes of the incentives focus on more strategic support, integrating media wisdom into education.

The 2013 incentive requests the network to develop solutions for three topics (Mediawijzer.net, 2013b). The first request is to develop a 'learning tool bank media wisdom'[7] for students in primary education to be used by teachers. The second is a learning tool bank for people undergoing teacher training. The third is a learning tool bank for teachers to keep them up to date. There is already media wisdom material for primary education, but according to *Mediawijzer.net*, it is hard to find and difficult to use, because it is not clear what media wisdom competences are developed, whether they relate to the school's curriculum or to the core goals for primary education established by the Dutch government, whether it matches students' needs at a particular age, and there are no exams (Mediawijzer.net, 2013b). In teacher training, not much formal attention is yet paid to media wisdom; rather, those learning to be teachers need to develop their own skills and learn how to teach media wisdom to children (ibid.). Finally, teachers in primary education want to be kept up to date and continuously develop their competences and skills. According to *Mediawijzer.net*, the learning tool bank could offer this to them (ibid.). *Mediawijzer.net* has also developed a step-plan to integrate or "embed media wisdom structurally in primary education."[8] It offers its network partners such as libraries, museums, publishers, cultural organizations, and companies an approach to make their products and services visible for primary education and suggests possible activities to reach target groups, such as teachers, school boards, and the school environment including parents and libraries. Most of its advice connects with *Mediawijzer.net* initiatives, for instance participating in the incentive funding and using the competence model in developing products.[9]

As the foregoing indicates, media wisdom is treated as a matter of education—developing competences. *Mediawijzer.net* attempts to have this incorporated into formal education. This time an empowering approach is followed, contrary to the previous protectionist approach from which the Dutch Council for Culture advised its government to distance itself. Sonia Livingstone argues that even if media literacy would be taught in schools, there would still be difficulties in providing media literacy for all. She starts by sketching the difficulties relating to continuous technological change and a need for lifelong learning. Contrary to print literacy, education at a young age does not last a lifetime; therefore, she also discusses ways to reach adults and some of the difficulties in doing so. But the biggest challenge she distinguishes in establishing media literacy for all is not a practical one; it is "a fundamental point of definition, or to be precise, of mutual definition. Media design and media literacy can be considered as reverse sides of the same coin" (2011, 33). She argues that "difficulties experienced by citizens are being framed as media literacy tasks when an alternative description would point to failures of design, provision or regulation" (ibid.). She argues that "the task of acquiring media literacy is unnecessarily burdened by the insufficient design, planning and provision of media services and providers" (2011, 32).

In support of this argument regarding failures of provision or regulation, we claim that a strong focus on media wisdom in children, empowering or enabling children in a variety of ways, teaching them to think and act for themselves risks losing sight on protectionist measures, thinking and acting for children, by for instance regulating media and children's media use through legal, social, and technical measures. For a long time, there has been a debate in the Netherlands among media wisdom practitioners whether children should be protected or empowered ('*weerbaar maken*'). Justine Pardoen, affiliated with one of the first Dutch websites on parenting as well as a knowledge centre for youth and (digital) media, said in an online column:

> I have changed my mind: as caretakers it is our duty to protect children from being exposed to harmful material. And we cannot do that by solely empowering them. We can quarrel about what exactly is harmful, but protection has become very important, as well as proper guidance.[10]

Pardoen previously supported an empowerment perspective but changed her mind due to developments such as the increase in domestic Internet access, as well as an increase in the amount of extreme violence, harassment, and pornography available online. She now supports technological means for regulating children's Internet use, for example, by installing web filter software. She argues that choosing between protection and empowerment is not necessary, as one can do both. We would argue that the one implies the other, which Pardoen implicitly recognizes when she states that we can't protect children solely by empowering them, which means empowerment can also be considered as a form of protection.

In addition, we argue that a tension arising with media wisdom comes from its strong reliance on the individual skills and competences of a generalized media user. Insights from the interdisciplinary field of science and technology studies (STS) help us understand the limits of relying on individual skills and competences. Not only are the multiplicity of uses or situated use (Bakardjieva, 2005; Wyatt, 2005; Wyatt et al., 2005) and the multiplicity of users not adequately considered (Wyatt, 2005), nor are the character of new media technology itself and the economic context in which it is produced.

Users and technology are constituted in relation to one another; focusing on one cannot be done without also considering the other. As Leah Lievrouw claims, "technologies and people alike would be thought of as interrelated nodes in constantly changing sociotechnical networks, which constitute the forms and uses of technology differently in different times and places for different groups" (2006, 250). Similarly, Bakardjieva and Gaden explain that "technologies come to life in the hands of human operators, practitioners who are situated in a much wider and richer network of relations and experiences than a single technology, no matter how totalizing, is able to encompass" (Bakardjieva and Gaden, 2011, 410). In other words, the everyday practice or use of technology is complex, and so is the variety of users. In media wisdom policy making and practices, new media usage is set as a 'norm.' Those who do not use new media or do not use it 'wisely' are believed to face risks such as socio-economic exclusion. But users of new media technology are not a homogeneous group. For instance, the focus of media wisdom policy makers is often on the 'have nots,' or 'illiterates' and does not take into account the 'want nots,' who may have good reasons for rejecting or resisting some new media forms (Wyatt, 2005).

In the documents we have analyzed, new media technology remains black boxed, and is considered to be neutral, static and homogeneous. Together with Livingstone (2009, 2011), we argue that media wisdom is also shaped by new media, in the sense that it is facilitated or hindered by and reliant on the design of new media. Livingstone argues that "media literacy is also medium-dependent, a co-production of the interactive engagement between technology and user" (2004, 12). She has shown, for example, that the design of Internet environments, can actually shape and limit media literacy (2009). 'Failing' to engage in such an environment is not just caused by a lack of competences or skills on the part of a user but by the legibility of the medium. This means one should also consider media technologies themselves and the ways in which they allow a user to 'read' an environment. In some cases, for instance with particular forms of marketing communication such as advertising disguised in games, the ability to detect the economic interests underlying such environments is prohibited by their design (Sprenkels and Van der Ploeg, 2014). Livingstone refers to the work of Steve Woolgar and the notion of 'technology as text.'[11] Woolgar's use of the metaphor of 'machine as text' is part of a semiotic approach to user-technology relations. It was introduced by actor-network theory scholars who have "extended semiotics—the study of how meanings are built—from signs to things" (Oudshoorn and Pinch, 2005, 7). Or, as Peter Lunt and Sonia Livingstone claim,

> technologies are also text, and the institutional purposes and culture, organizational norms and structures, and communicative design and intent are all embedded in the very construction of the interface, as is also an implicit conception of the user—what they know, don't know, can and cannot do, take for granted or need to learn. The more impenetrable, opaque or ill-designed the text or interface . . . the more users will struggle.
>
> (Lunt and Livingstone, 2012, 135)

CONCLUSION: CONTEXTUALISING MEDIA WISDOM

In contemporary society, various technological and societal developments contribute to calls for a media-literate citizenry. In this chapter, we have traced how media wisdom as a concept, goal, practice and identity in the sense of 'being media wise' took root in the Dutch policy context. We demonstrated how it was translated by the Dutch Cabinet, narrowing down the target group and changing the goals set by the Dutch Council for Culture, focusing on youth, their social environment, media use, and positive and negative media effects. We briefly discussed a dualistic picture of children (vulnerable vs. savvy), a dualistic picture of new media technology (risks vs. opportunity), and a dualistic picture of media (literacy) education (protectionist vs. empowerment). While all these perspectives are present within the media wisdom landscape, it is generally the empowering affordances of technology as well as empowering children to use media wisely and actively that are foregrounded in Dutch policy initiatives regarding this topic.

We described how media wisdom was translated many times and in several ways. This allowed configurations of practices, policies, goals, and social actors to emerge, which indicated that it is not a stable, natural, and neutral concept, but instead media wisdom is highly contingent. We have argued that it is an outcome of relations, of the various choices, practices, and policies, made by the social actors involved in its continuous constitution. We suggest that while the recent Dutch scene has been characterised by a successful mobilization of many actors around media wisdom as a boundary object, it has been less successful in providing for long-term education and training needs.

In addition, we have claimed that its various meanings, connotations, and practices, provided by the social actors involved, and its contingent fluid character shape the 'media wisdom' debate, policy, and practices. We have demonstrated that media wisdom is adaptable, with various social actors across many sectors each adopting their own meanings and practices, but media wisdom is nonetheless common enough to bridge boundaries between them, recognizable to all organizations and representatives. What they share is a focus on developing the skills and competences of media users. We have shown how the connotations of the term 'wisdom' contributed to the distribution of responsibility for stimulating media wisdom across numerous actors instead of leaving it with the government and formal education sector, as is the case with more traditional literacy. We traced how one party establishes itself as an obligatory passage point, controlling the move between the common identity of media wisdom and its more adaptable side, by standardizing media wisdom through the development of a specific model. This model served to order media wisdom initiatives and standardize the concept and its practices, first by focusing on competences set within the model, for all to use, in order to institutionalize it, across organizations and in formal education. And second, with this distributed responsibility, several actors are left out of the picture, including the technology itself and its contingency, flexibility, and the multiplicity of its use and users, and technology designers are similarly neglected.

In the Dutch situation described in this chapter, we observed that media wisdom is mainly sought as a quality to be developed in new media users themselves, specifically in children, with media technology considered as neutral, static, and homogeneous. We, however, have argued that media wisdom is also shaped by new media, in the sense that new media technologies are never neutral, always changing and heterogeneous. Thus media wisdom can be facilitated or hindered by the design of new media. Media wisdom policies and practices need to take into account the full range of relationships between technology and users, children as well as adults—in other words, the network of relations between all of the human and non-human actors involved, as responsibility for media wisdom can be sought in all of them.

NOTES

1. The chapter draws on a selection of national and international policy documents, academic studies on 'media literacy' originating from various disciplines, and professional and popular literature focusing on developments in technology, business, and education in relation to youth. The latter tend to inspire many actors dealing with media wisdom. Semi-structured, face-to-face interviews were conducted between January and June 2012 with five representatives from five different Dutch media literacy initiatives, focusing on their background, goals, work methods, teaching and research materials. In addition, the annual networking event for media wisdom representatives was attended in May 2012. All interviewees have been given pseudonyms. Interviews were conducted in Dutch and translated by Sprenkels. This is discussed more fully within Sprenkels's PhD thesis (forthcoming).
2. www.unesco.org/new/en/communication-and-information/media-development/media-literacy, visited March 26, 2014.
3. www.unesco.org/new/en/communication-and-information/media-development/media-literacy/mil-university-network/, visited March 26, 2014.
4. Although the Dutch government tends to be reluctant in its actions (Valkenburg, 2005), it is stimulated by article 17 of the Convention on the Rights of the Child on access to information and mass media to initiate action regarding harmful media content. Section e reads: "State Parties shall encourage the development of appropriate guidelines for the protection of the child from information and material injurious to his or her well-being, bearing in mind the provisions of articles 13 and 18" (United Nations, 1989). Important actors in this matter are the Ministries of Education, Culture and Science; Health, Welfare and Sport; and Security and Justice; the Dutch Media Authority; the Netherlands Institute for the Classification of Audio-Visual Media; the Pan-European Game Information age rating system; and the Advertising Code Committee (Nikken, 2013).
5. www.mediawijzer.net/competentiemodel-voor-mediawijsheid-gepresenteerd, visited March 26 2014.
6. Similar to the case of the scallop researchers in Callon's much-cited paper, *Mediawijzer.net* imposes itself and its take on media wisdom on other actors such as its network partners. It defines the identities and interests of other actors that are consistent with its own interests and establishes itself as an obligatory passage point through which the other actors must pass, rendering itself indispensable. The actors are persuaded to identify with their roles and start speaking on behalf of *Mediawijzer.net*, thus further strengthening its position.

7. 'leermiddelenbank mediawijsheid'
8. *Mediawijzer.net* brochure, year of publication unknown, available at www.mediawijzer.net/wp-content/uploads/2013/05/PO-Stappenplan.pdf, visited April 15 2014.
9. *Mediawijzer.net* also wants to initiate initiatives to integrate media wisdom in secondary education (Evers, 2013). The Royal Netherlands Academy of Arts and Sciences also wants to do so, as suggested in its report on digital literacy (KNAW, 2013). However, contrary to *Mediawijzer.net*, it wants schools to offer separate courses in 'information and communication' for younger students and 'informatics' for older students instead of integrating digital literacy in existing courses. This digital literacy should focus on 'basic knowledge,' 'use,' and 'behaviour.'
10. www.katholiekgezin.nl/index.php?option=com_content&task=view&id=89&Itemid=110, visited May 8 2014.
11. According to Nelly Oudshoorn and Trevor Pinch, Woolgar "suggested that how users 'read' machines is constrained because the design and the production of machines entails a process of configuring the user" (Oudshoorn and Pinch, 2005, 8).

REFERENCES

AUFDERHEIDE, P. (1993) *Media Literacy: A Report of the National Leadership Conference on Media Literacy*. Aspen: Aspen Institute.

BAKARDJIEVA, M. (2005) *Internet Society. The Internet in Everyday Life*. London: Sage Publications.

BAKARDJIEVA, M. & GADEN, G. (2011) Web 2.0 Technologies of the Self. *Philosophy & Technology*, 25(3). p. 399–413.

BAZALGETTE, C. (1997) An Agenda for the Second Phase of Media Literacy Development. In Kubey, R. (Ed.), *Media Literacy in the Information Age: Current Perspectives, Information and Behavior (Vol. 6)*. New Brunswick: Transaction Publishers, 69–78.

BUCKINGHAM, D. (2011) Studying Children's Media Cultures: A New Agenda for Cultural Studies. In van den Bergh, B. & van den Bulck, J. (Eds.), *Children and Media: Multidisciplinary Approaches*. Apeldoorn: Garant/Centrum voor Bevolkings- en Gezinsstudie, 49–66.

CALLON, M. (1986) Some Elements of a Sociology of Translation: Domestication of the Scallops and the Fishermen of St Brieuc Bay. In Law, J. (Ed.), *Power, Action and Belief: A New Sociology of Knowledge?* London: Routledge, 196–223.

DROTNER, K. (2011) Children and Digital Media: Online, On Site, On the Go. In Qvortrup, J., Corsaro, W. A. & Honig, M.-S. (Eds.), *The Palgrave Handbook of Childhood Studies*. London: Palgrave Macmillan, 360–374.

EUROPEAN COMMISSION. (2007) *Communication from the Commission to the European Parliament, the Council, the European Economic and Social Committee of the Regions. A European approach to media literacy in the digital environment*. COM(2007) 833 final. Brussels.

———. (2009) *Commission Recommendation on Media Literacy in the Digital Environment for a More Competitive Audio-visual and Content Industry and an Inclusive Knowledge Society*. C(2009) 6464 final. Brussels.

———. (2010a) *Communication from the Commission. Europe 2020. A Strategy for Smart, Sustainable and Inclusive Growth*. COM(2010) 2020. Brussels.

———. (2010b) *Communication from the Commission to the European Parliament, the Council, the European Economic and Social Committee and the Committee of the Regions. A Digital Agenda for Europe*. COM(2010) 245 final. Brussels.

EUROPEAN PARLIAMENT. (2008) *Report on Media Literacy in a Digital World.* (2008/2129(INI). Brussels.

EVERS, F. (2013) Mediawijsheid Structureel Inbedden in Gehele Curriculum. Retrieved April 02, 2014, from www.kennisnet.nl/themas/mediawijsheid/mediawijsheid-structureel-inbedden-in-gehele-curriculum/

GILLEBAARD, H. et al. (2013) *Kennispositie van Mediawijsheid Competenties: Inventarisatie Onderzoek 2005—Heden.* Utrecht: Nextvalue Research & Dialogic.

GRIZZLE, A. et al. (2013) *Media and Information Literacy. Policy and Strategy Guidelines.* Paris: UNESCO.

HASEBRINK, U. et al. (2008) *Comparing Children's Online Opportunities and Risks across Europe: Cross-national Comparisons for EU Kids Online.* London: EU Kids Online.

HELSPER, E.J. & ENYON, R. (2010) Digital Natives: Where Is the Evidence? *British Educational Research Journal*, 36(3). p. 503–520.

HOBBS, R. (2011) The State of Media Literacy: A Response to Potter. *Journal of Broadcasting & Electronic Media*, 55(3). p. 419–430.

HOEVEN, M.J.A. VAN DER. (2006) *Brief aan de Tweede Kamer over Mediawijsheid: Burgerschap in de Informatiemaatschappij.* Den Haag: Ministerie van OCW.

KNAW. (2011) *Digitale Geletterdheid in het Voortgezet Onderwijs. Vaardigheden en Attitudes voor de 21ste Eeuw.* Amsterdam: Koninklijke Nederlandse Academie van Wetenschappen.

KWARTIERMAKERSGROEP MEDIAWIJSHEID. (2008) Programma Mediawijsheid. De Inrichting van een Expertisecentrum voor Mediawijsheid. Den Haag: Ministerie van OCW

LATOUR, B. (1987) *Science in Action. How to Follow Scientists and Engineers through Society.* Cambridge (MA): Harvard University Press.

LIEVROUW, L.A. (2006) New Media Design and Development: Diffusion of Innovations v Social Shaping of Technology. In Lievrouw, L.A. & Livingstone, S. (Eds.), *The Handbook of New Media. Social Shaping and Social consequences of ICTs. Updated Student Edition.* London: Sage, 246–265.

LIVINGSTONE, S. (2004) Media Literacy and the Challenge of New Information and Communication Technologies. *The Communication Review*, 1(7). p. 3–14.

———. (2009) *Children and the Internet. Great Expectations, Challenging Realities.* Cambridge: Polity Press.

———. (2011) Media Literacy for All? On the Intellectual and Political Challenges of Implementing Media Literacy Policy. In Livingstone, S. (Eds.), *Media Literacy: Ambitions, Policies and Measures.* Brussels: COST (European Cooperation in Science and Technology, 31–35.

LUNT, P. & LIVINGSTONE, S. (2012) Media Literacy. In Lunt, P. & Livingstone, S. (Eds.), *Media Regulation. Governance and the Interests of Citizens and Consumers.* London: Sage, 117–142.

MEDIAWIJZER.NET. (2010a) *Meerjarenplan 2011 t/m 2014.*

———. (2010b) Jaarplan 2011.

———. (2011a) *Helderheid over Mediawijsheid. De Betekenis van "Meten van Mediawijsheid" voor het Netwerk.*

———. (2011b) Stimuleringsregeling 2012.

———. (2012) Competentiemodel: 10 Mediawijsheidcompetenties.

———. (2013a) Mediawijzer.net: Expertisecentrum voor Mediawijsheid.

———. (2013b) Stimuleringsregeling 2013.

———. (2014) Partners Mediawijzer.net Februari 2014.

MINISTERIE van OCW. (2006) *Mediawijsheid, Leven in de Gemedialiseerde Samenleving.* Den Haag: Ministerie Onderwijs Cultuur en Wetenschap.

NIKKEN, P. (2013) *Media-risico's voor Kinderen. Een Verkenning.* Utrecht: Nederlands Jeugdinstituut.

OUDSHOORN, N. & PINCH, T. (2005) Introduction: How Users and Non-Users matter. In Oudshoorn, N. & Pinch, T. (Eds.), *How Users Matter. The Co-construction of Users and Technology*. Cambridge (MA): MIT Press, 1–28.

PLASTERK, R. & ROUVOET, A. (2008) *Kabinetsvisie Mediawijsheid*. Den Haag: Ministerie van OCW.

RAAD VOOR CULTUUR (2005) *Mediawijsheid. De Ontwikkeling van Nieuw Burgerschap*., Den Haag: Raad voor Cultuur.

SPRENKELS, I. & PLOEG, I. VAN DER (2014) Follow the Children! Advergames and the Enactment of Children's Consumer Identity. In van der Hof, S., van den Berg, B. & Schermer, B. (Eds.), *Minding Minors Wandering the Web: Regulating Online Child Safety*. The Hague: Asser Press, 173–190.

STAR, S.L. (2010) This Is Not a Boundary Object: Reflections on the Origin of a Concept. *Science, Technology & Human Values*, 35(5). p. 601–617.

STAR, S.L. & GRIESEMER, J.R. (1989) Institutional Ecology, 'Translations' and Boundary Objects: Amateurs and Professionals in Berkeley's Museum of Vertebrate Zoology, 1907–39. *Social Studies of Science*, 19(3). p. 387–420.

UNITED NATIONS. (1948) *United Nations Universal Declaration of Human Rights 1948*.

———. (1989) *Convention on the Rights of the Child*.

UNESCO. (1982) *Grunwald Declaration on Media Education*. Grunwald, Germany.

———. (2005) *Beacons of the Information Society: The Alexandra Proclamation on Information Literacy and Lifelong Learning*. Alexandria, Egypt: UNESCO.

———. (2007) *Paris Agenda or 12 Recommendations for Media Education*. Paris, France: UNESCO.

———. (2013) *Global Media and Information Literacy Assessment Framework: Country Readiness and Competencies*. Paris, France: UNESCO.

VALKENBURG, P. (2005) *Schadelijke Media en Weerbare Jeugd: Een Beleidsvisie 2005–2010*. Amsterdam: Amsterdam School of Communications Research.

WIEBENGA, F. et al. (2011) *Meten van Mediawijsheid. Een Studie naar een Raamwerk, Meetmiddelen en Toepassing Hiervan*. Amsterdam: Mediawijzer.net.

WILSON, C. et al. (2011) *Media and Information Literacy. Curriculum for Teachers*. Paris, France: UNESCO.

WYATT, S. (2005) Non-Users Also Matter: The Construction of Users and Non-Users of the Internet. In Oudshoorn, N. & Pinch, T. (Eds.), *How Users Matter. The Co-construction of Users and Technology*. Cambridge (MA): The MIT Press, 67–80.

———. (2008a) Technological Determinism Is Dead; Long Live Technological Determinism. In Hackett, E., Amsterdamska, O., Lynch, M. & Wajcman, J. (Eds.), *The Handbook of Science & Technology Studies*. Cambridge (MA): MIT Press, 165–180.

———. (2008b) Feminism, Technology and the Information Society. Learning from the Past, Imagining the Future. *Information, Communication & Society*, 11(1). p. 111–130.

WYATT, S. et al. (2005) The Digital Divide, Health Information and Everyday Life. *New Media & Society*, 7(2). p. 199–218.

Part III

(Mis)Behaving

Suspects and Deviants

8 Data Mining 'Problem Youth'

Looking Closer But Not Seeing Better

Francisca Grommé

INTRODUCTION

In 2011, the Dutch municipality of Burgcity conducted a pilot study about data mining. It aimed to find out whether this statistical technique could be used to improve its understanding of 'problem youth,' loosely defined by the city as youth below 23 years of age who are likely to commit minor offences such as vandalism, littering, or shop theft.[1] In particular, it aimed to learn whether a combination of municipal data, police data, and commercial data about consumption could lead to new insights for youth crime policy.

Especially salient in this pilot study was the policy makers' use of the metaphor of 'zooming in.' The policy makers expected data mining to provide knowledge that was local, particular, and timely. This understanding of data mining is not unique to Burgcity. Indeed, proponents of data mining promise increased detail and granularity. As was stated in a project plan, data mining techniques would generate "local theories" that "the general theories of social science" cannot provide.

Vision metaphors are never innocent, however, as Donna Haraway has famously argued (1991). The metaphor of zooming draws on the imagery of a mechanical lens, which reveals more detail about an object. The resulting 'close-ups' are assumed to have a high truth status because of their implied precision. In this chapter, I am interested in how digital data are put to use according to a rationale of zooming in to profile problem youth. Profiles can be understood as identities that are ascribed to youth and used as bases for government intervention (Pridmore, Chapter 2, this volume).

I aim to challenge zooming as an underlying principle in data mining practices and scholarly and professional accounts. I do so because sticking to this metaphor risks mobilization of data mining in an argument for the acquisition of ever more personal data. Namely, if a technology by itself can provide ever more detailed representations of youth, all it needs are more or better data. Furthermore, the metaphor obscures the normativities that are part of the practice of data mining. With this I mean that it diverts attention from the 'goods' and 'bads' that come into play when 'detailed knowledge' is produced.

My questions are how zooming in was done in the Burgcity data mining pilot and what norms were embedded in and produced through these practices. I attend to the bodies of knowledge, discursive practices, and artefacts that were part of zooming in. Adopting a material-semiotic approach, I focus on the heterogeneous relations that bring objects, such as problem youth, into being (Mol, 2002; M'charek, 2013). From this approach, it follows that by zooming in, one does not simply see the same thing in more detail. Instead, the practices of zooming in bring new objects into being (Strathern, 2005). I draw on Charles Goodwin's work to describe data miners' practices as 'situated improvisation' (1995, 1996).

This chapter is based on fieldwork that I conducted before, during, and after the Burgcity pilot for a period of 18 months. I focus on the interactive sessions at the core of the pilot, in which policy makers and corporate experts analysed the data. We will follow the participants through various attempts to zoom in. First, from zooming in to the level of the sub-city district, we learn about two modes of situated improvisation the participants engaged in: evocation and comparison. Second, from zooming in to the level of the neighbourhood, we learn from the trouble that the participants ran into: they could not zoom in any further without losing sight of the problem youth. This part if the pilot draws out the regimes of evidence that are part of zooming in.

Attending to the practicalities of zooming in also allows us to learn that it is normative work. I show that results needed to be made relevant as surprises; that the 'lens' focused on the neighbourhood as a source for truth; that city youth were constituted as a norm; that detail is produced by the application of general categories; and that zooming in includes making judgements about good knowledge for government. These normativities suggest that taking seriously the metaphors by which technologies are brought into practice might be a good starting point to change the terms by which digital identities are produced.

ZOOMING IN AS SITUATED IMPROVISATION

Mining for Local Knowledge

Ever more digital data are available for analysis. People produce increasing amounts of data through activities as simple as browsing on the Internet and using a chip card on public transport. This development is joined by a growing capacity to search and analyse these data. Data mining is a statistical technique often used for the analysis of big datasets. It is commonly referred to as "the automatic or semi-automatic process of discovering patterns in data" (Witten, Eibe, and Hall, 2011, 5) or "the application of specific algorithms for extracting patterns" (Fayyad, Piatetsky-Shapiro, and Smyth, 1996, 39). In everyday usage, it can refer to both software and analytical skills.

Data mining is argued to challenge traditional science, because, in contrast with statistical techniques such as regression analysis, the software allows the analyst to search for relations in the data without defining hypotheses and limiting the number of variables in advance (Witten, Eibe, and Hall, 2011; Hildebrandt, 2008). Instead, an algorithm is applied to automatically find co-occurrences in a large dataset that can comprise thousands of variables.[2] Industry therefore advertises data mining as 'digging' into the data to find 'nuggets of gold' (yet other metaphors).

It needs to be noted that although data mining provides analysts with new possibilities, it is often practiced as a combination of old and new statistical techniques. In the application studied in this chapter, for instance, conventional geodemographic marketing techniques are combined with data-mining algorithms.[3] Furthermore, in practice, patterns are often not found automatically but rely on the expert's insight to choose variables (Ang and Goh, 2013) Following boyd and Crawford, it therefore seems appropriate to approach data mining not as a "higher form of intelligence and knowledge that can generate insights that were previously impossible," but as a mythology as well as a technological development (2012, 663).

In policy practice, data mining is most often used to create profiles: sets of correlations that can be used to identify or represent individuals or groups (Hildebrandt, 2008, 19). It is applied in a variety of policy domains, such as anti-terrorism programs, programs against tax evasion, welfare policy and, as this chapter describes, local crime policy. In these cases, the promise of data mining is specificity: More data and diverse data sources generate a closer view. Policy makers are seldom interested in general patterns, policy ethnographies show (Yanow, 2002; Choy, 2005). They are in search of particularities, and commercial data mining is brought in for this purpose. This is also reflected in the marketing analytics industry, which has specialized in the provision of ever more locally specific knowledge (Phillips and Curry, 2003).

Empirical scholarly work on the use of data mining and large datasets by (local) policy agencies mainly describes the limitations of data mining. It is argued that digital data do not necessarily lead to descriptions of individuals and groups that are more precise. In Gary T. Marx's words, users of this technology "see hazily (but not darkly) through the lens" (2005, 339). A fundamental reason is that profiles give very little information about individuals and small groups of people because they aggregate data. The characteristics of the profile may therefore not be applicable to all the individuals it represents (Curry, 2004; also see Custers, 2004). It is also argued that the data do not represent individuals correctly because government datasets are often incomplete or simply wrong (Pleace, 2007). Moreover, not all types of large datasets are valuable or reliable. This is the case for some social media data, such as statements on Twitter (boyd and Crawford, 2012). In acquiring data, furthermore, local governments are limited by privacy restrictions. An example is the use of police data. Last, the possibilities of acquiring commercial datasets are often limited for financial reasons and because companies are not always allowed or willing to share them (Pleace, 2007; boyd and Crawford, 2012).

Localized and Embodied Visions

These considerations put data mining into perspective. The reason I raise them here, however, is because they bring to mind a similar issue in anthropology. In *Partial Connections* (2005), Marilyn Strathern identifies the problem that there never seems to be sufficient data to adequately describe social life. Whenever one looks closer or from another angle, there still does not seem to be enough data. One would expect complexity to decrease when a smaller part of society is examined; instead, there always seems to be something new to discover. The similarity between these two practices—data mining and anthropological observation—is that they are both based on the premise that seeing better requires more or better data.

Strathern takes issue with the idea that there are an infinite number of perspectives, each requiring more data. She argues that all perspectives exist as "localized, embodied visions" (40). These visions do not present different versions of reality but enact the object in different, partially connected ways (also see Mol, 2002). To change perspective, therefore, does not amount to seeing part of a whole. For zooming in, this means that one does not see a part of the same object in more detail. When scientists, professional analysts, policy makers, or others zoom in, they bring an object into being.

This is a relevant distinction because it avoids the notion that technologies by themselves reveal the characteristics of populations that exist independently of the practices by which they are mapped (M'charek, 2005; Ruppert, 2011). This notion of technology is problematic in academic discourse because it feeds into the idea that lack of data or analytical power obstructs perfect close visions. It therefore fails to question data mining in terms other than those of an information problem. I suggest examining how zooming in is done in practice in order to overcome this limitation.

Situated Improvisations

To be sure, to insist on a critical attitude towards metaphors of vision is not new.[4] Donna Haraway is especially known for her contribution to this project. In *Situated Knowledges* (1991), she argues that, with contemporary visualizing technologies, "Vision in this technological feast becomes unregulated gluttony; all perspective gives way to infinitely mobile vision, which no longer seems just mythically about the god-trick of seeing everything from nowhere, but to have put the myth into ordinary practice" (189). Claims for scientific objectivity are based on a 'view from nowhere,' thus creating a science that is detached and totalizing. What is needed, Haraway argues, is a commitment to situated knowledges: knowledges that are understood as local, embodied, and partial.

Inspired by this body of work, Christopher Gad and Peter Lauritsen (2009) suggest that social scientists with an interest in surveillance practices such as digital identification should study them as situated phenomena. To observe something, actors in the field of surveillance need to draw together bodies of knowledge, artefacts, and human actors at a certain place and time. Surveilled objects thus achieve their status in terms of the relations between heterogeneous entities (M'charek, 2013).

I use this notion of situatedness to study zooming in as a metaphor comparable to Haraway's vision metaphor of 'seeing everything from nowhere.' Goodwin's work about situated improvisations (1995) provides a point of departure for understanding how the participants of the Burgcity pilot zoomed in on youth. Goodwin coined the term to describe how an object of knowledge emerges through the interplay of screens, common knowledge, lay theories, everyday artefacts, and professional repertoires (606). Importantly, with improvisation I do not refer to random actions but to actions that are informed by bodies of knowledge, artefacts, and emerging priorities at a certain place and time.

Following Goodwin, I will attend to talk and gestures by which the relations between these heterogeneous entities were achieved. For instance, Goodwin describes how marine biologists highlighted the information presented to them on a screen by pointing at it with a pencil or by making comments such as "that nice feature again" (262). In his work on archaeology, he shows that some of the talk makes some results more relevant than others; it sets out the conditions of relevance (1996). Furthermore, from Goodwin's analysis of the Rodney King trial, we learn that some actors may use the status of their profession to influence enquiries. This is what he refers to as professional privilege (1996).

DATA MINING PROBLEM YOUTH: A PILOT STUDY

Marketing Intelligence Methods

Burgcity is a medium sized Dutch city of about 200,000 inhabitants. The pilot study took place at the Department of Community safety, which employed 16 persons at the time I was present. Data Inc. is a data analyst company employing no more than 10 persons. It had mainly accepted assignments from the Dutch police force and corporations in the Netherlands. Data Inc. provided the software, collected and cleaned the data, and performed the analyses.

The case description and the case study that follow are based on observations of the pilot meetings, the city's policy makers' everyday routines, and interviews. As the reader might suspect, Burgcity and Data Inc. are fictitious names, as are the names of all other organizations, places, and persons mentioned in this chapter (with the exception of the international corporation that delivered the commercial data used in this pilot: Experian). I agreed to anonymity because confidential information regarding suspects, their backgrounds, and crime-control practices often passed my eyes on the Burgcity work floor. I also agreed because I felt a responsibility to protect the livelihood of my informants. I believe this is an especially sensitive issue because both the company and the city were involved in an experimental activity, making themselves vulnerable as they treaded uncertain ground.[5]

The pilot study's aim, as stated in Data Inc.'s project proposal, was to develop "more efficient and effective approaches"[6] to non-criminal nuisance and minor criminal offences committed by youth. The use of the Experian dataset, which contains 'lifestyle data,' was advertised as the pilot's main innovative feature. 'Marketing intelligence methods' were to lead to new insights into problem youth, their life worlds, and their motivations. If one knows that the "most troublesome youth" wear Nikes, a new approach in policy might be to involve Nike stores in a campaign against vandalism, one of the project's initiators argued in a 2010 presentation.

The Experian lifestyle dataset incorporates about 1,500 variables on basic information about household income and age; interests and activities, such as membership to a sports club; and media usage, such as Internet usage and newspaper subscriptions. These variables also include pre-set profiles, referred to as Mosaic groups, such as 'free spirits,' 'mini machos,' or 'digital families.' The data come from sources such as property or telephone registrations and surveys. Experian datasets are sold for marketing purposes, to develop strategies for the collection of bills and debts, and to manage financial risk.

These data were combined with police data about suspects and offences and with municipality data including variables such as age, income, and school attendance. A remark about the police dataset is in order here. It contains records about individuals suspected of one or more offences. Even if police investigation has pointed out that an individual was not involved in an incident, he or she remains registered. For the purposes of the pilot, young suspects were used as an approximation of problem youth, which raises the obvious issue of whether these data can really help Burgcity learn about the group it is interested in.

Data mining was expected to help the city understand problems more "thoroughly and quickly," understand patterns that characterize problem youth at neighbourhood level, identify the groups that need attention, and identify and influence causal relations. Thus, it would allow the city's policy makers to "zoom in" on local youth and generate "local theories" (Interview, former CEO Data Inc., November 12, 2010). In policy maker Anna's words, it could be another method to "reach out" to Burgcity's inhabitants (Interview, September 5, 2011).[7]

Pilot Results

Prior to the pilot, Burgcity's Department of Community Safety had already considered data mining to improve the city's 'information position.' As the department's information specialist put it, "data mining is definitely going to happen in Burgcity, there is no doubt about it. The head of our department asks me how data mining is coming along every week" (Interview, April 21, 2011). So when the department head was asked by an innovation platform to participate in the pilot, he consented. The funding was supplied by a grant from the Dutch Ministry of Internal Affairs.

The innovation platform chose to focus on problem youth, which was and still is a hot topic in Dutch crime policy. Next, it was up to Burgcity to select a case study. It chose its newest and demographically youngest city district, Molendistrict, as a case study. Molendistrict has about 40,000 inhabitants. The district seemed to suit the purposes of the pilot because one third of Burgcity's youth lives here, and nuisances in the area are of considerable concern for the city's staff at the Department of Community Safety.

Data Inc. insisted that the policy makers' input was crucial to assess which results were of value for Molendistrict. Three of Burgcity's civil servants were involved in the pilot: Mieke, Anna, and Liesbet. Mieke is the department's information specialist, Anna the department's specialist on youth, and Liesbet the district manager of Molendistrict. The group would ideally explore the possibilities of the software together to learn what insights could be gained by using it. Data Inc. suggested taking an "iterative approach," whereby Burgcity's policy makers would formulate questions, find answers, and "learn how to ask better questions" (Fieldwork notes, February 28, 2011).[8]

Next to preparatory and strategic meetings, the city's civil servants and Juriaan, Data Inc.'s analyst, met four times for interactive sessions in Burgcity's city hall. During these sessions, Juriaan operated a laptop and the city employees faced him. Everybody in the small meeting rooms could see the computer interface on an LCD screen. During the meetings, a question for analysis would be formulated by the policy makers or by Juriaan. Juriaan would then attempt to answer the question, showing the results on the screen.

Three types of results were generated. First, frequency tables presented counts, for example, of the number of suspects living in each neighbourhood. Second, profile analysis was used to compare two or more populations. The resulting table displayed the variables for which significant differences between the populations were found. Third, the data mining system was used to generate 'hotspot' maps: clusters of offences committed in a certain location on the map.

The pilot did not result in a set of stable and generally acknowledged conclusions about problem youth and youth crime policy. Data Inc. did present a number of conclusions in the final report, amongst others about the types of neighbourhoods that have a relatively high risk of youth delinquency, such as neighbourhoods in which household income varies strongly (Data Inc. 2012, internal document). In the end, however, the report stated that it could not characterize problem youth using the lifestyle data due to privacy restrictions (on which I will elaborate later in the chapter).

In what follows, I describe how zooming in was done and what bodies of knowledge and objects informed the efforts to obtain a closer view. I attempt to understand how, once the results had been presented on the screen, a close view of youth "emerged through the interplay between a domain of scrutiny (. . .) [and] a set of discursive practices (. . .), being deployed with a specific activity" (Goodwin, 1996, 606). Two themes that regularly returned in the sessions are presented to the reader: the place of residence of youth that commit offences in Molendistrict and the use of lifestyle data to characterize youth that commit offences. I have chosen to elaborate on these themes because they were discussed most frequently and thoroughly during the sessions and therefore are the most instructive about the practice of zooming in. For each of these themes, I focus on the participation of one of the policy makers.

ZOOMING IN FROM CITY TO DISTRICT

Surprise

The first story is about Liesbet's question for the technology. It demonstrates the particularities of zooming in from the city to the district level.[9] Liesbet is the district manager for Molendistrict. It is her job to facilitate communication between the central city and Molendistrict's local politicians, interest groups, and case workers. As she puts it, she defends the district's interests at city level. Of all the participants in the pilot, she visits the district most frequently. This is what data mining should answer for Liesbet:

> Where in Molendistrict do the young people who commit offences live? And how can useful policies be developed for youth who commit offences in Molendistrict but live in other districts?
>
> (Data Inc., internal document, June 18, 2010)

These questions require zooming in. It is necessary to look closer, she explains, because, although she is familiar with the area and its inhabitants, it is difficult to learn about the causes of youth crime. Statistics, she argues, often obscure local circumstances because they aggregate data. Furthermore, because the neighbourhood is relatively new (construction started in the early 1980s), she feels that the social networks that should theoretically help her stay informed do not yet exist.

To find the answer to Liesbet's question, Juriaan starts out by producing a frequency table about Molendistrict. A frequency table is a basic list that presents the number of occurrences in a query.

> Liesbet, Mieke and Anna take a good look at the results presented on the LCD screen. It shows a list of numbers: the number of young suspects in Molendistrict, broken down by neighbourhood. "Neighbourhood H, this surprises me," Liesbet says. "Neighbourhood K makes sense because it has a shopping mall. But neighbourhood H is only a small residential area."
>
> Anna asks her to show neighbourhood H on the map on the wall. Liesbet points at it: "There it is, the park is also part of it, nowadays." "Is there a sports park nearby?" Anna wonders. This is not the case, but Liesbet notes that there is a swimming pool in the area.
>
> Anna has another suggestion: perhaps these are conflicts between neighbours? "No, not in neighbourhood H," Liesbet replies, "this is not a neighbourhood known for fights between neighbours." Next, Liesbet wants to know more about neighbourhood H: "This is making me curious, what types of offences were committed here?"
>
> (Fieldwork notes, April 7, 2011)[10]

This tells us that not all results count. A result counts when it is *surprising*, as in the case of neighbourhood H. Surprise, in Goodwin's terms, is a condition of relevance for data mining. A close view is a view that is revealing. It provides a look under the surface.

Evoking

The group returns to the question of problem youth's place of residence at the end of the meeting. This time they take a different approach. To learn more about the questions that neighbourhood H raises, they need to know more about the registered suspects. Therefore, Juriaan creates a frequency table that shows information about the suspects for offences committed in Molendistrict. This table is different from the previous one because it does not present youth living in Molendistrict but youth that have committed an offence there.

> Many of the young suspects come from other districts, Liesbet notes. She points at the map: "Neighbourhood G, this is quite far away, it is in another district." But "distance is not so important to youth," she adds. Juriaan agrees: "Youth have a large radius of activity." They look a little longer at the list. "These are neighbourhoods with a lot of social housing," Liesbet notes. "Indeed, one of these neighbourhoods is a weak neighbourhood," Juriaan adds.
>
> (Fieldwork notes, April 7, 2011)

So youth travel from other places to Molendistrict. They might come from neighbourhoods in other districts with fewer facilities, the group adds, and when they come to Molendistrict, they cause a nuisance.

This is the type of account that was often generated in this pilot: propositions, statements, descriptions, and explanations that loosely hang together. An important part of producing an account of Molendistrict's suspects is 'evocation'; the data need to come to life and make sense, to be made 'tellable' (see also Curry, 2004; Ziewitz, 2011). This first of all required maps. During the same session described in the first fragment, Anna asks Liesbet to show neighbourhood H on the paper map on the wall. Almost every meeting room has one of these maps. They are large, about one and a half meters by one meter, and detailed. They show the borders of the districts and neighbourhoods as designated by the Dutch central government (National Statistics Netherlands or *CBS*).

The map displays what the screen does not: the borders between neighbourhoods, the distances between the neighbourhoods, and a detailed street plan. The data mining software can plot the results on a digital map, but this is an oblique map: It does not show borders and specificities. The detailed paper map helps Liesbet locate the neighbourhood and tie it to her previous experiences: For instance, neighbourhood H is not known for conflicts between neighbourhoods. Maps also help to fill in the particulars of the neighbourhood. They show whether there is a park nearby, or a shopping mall. Furthermore, they show distances, revealing that youth travel. So pointing at a map is part of bringing the data to life.

The second, and related, part of making the data come to life is to tie the results to policy theories, categories, and local knowledge. This might be policy's equivalent of what Mariana Valverde refers to as administrative knowledge in legal practices: "in-between knowledge" used by officials that is neither scientific nor lay (Valverde, 2003, 20). When they talk through these policy theories, categories, and local knowledges, the results on the screen are pieced together. For instance, neither the frequency tables nor the maps give information about social housing, yet the policy officers apply this characteristic to the area on the map. Subsequently, they apply the notion that neighbourhoods with social housing are poorer, and poorer neighbourhoods are more troublesome. Juriaan's additional remark about 'weak neighbourhoods,' moreover, pieces the account together. He refers to the 40 neighbourhoods the national government has pointed out as the most problematic in the country in 2007 (also known as *Vogelaarwijken*).

My point here is not that the city's knowledge base is not 'scientific' enough. Policy practitioners need at hand knowledge to do their jobs. Rather, I argue that this mode of improvisation shows that producing such accounts under the banner of more granularity introduces more general categories. In this example, moreover, a neighbourhood category invokes judgments about youth behaviour.

This is also relevant for the outcome of these sessions: namely, that youth who commit offences in Molendistrict are not from Molendistrict but from other, 'bad' neighbourhoods. This outcome was partly informed by local politics. At the time of the pilot, Liesbet was involved in a discussion about the construction of new facilities in Molendistrict, such as practice rooms and bars. The dominant notion was that more facilities would help reduce complaints about youth behaviour, as youth could engage in more activities. Liesbet reasoned that facilities might in fact cause more complaints because problem youth would come from other places to use them.

Comparing

At the next meeting, the group returns to the theme of the Molendistrict suspects. The question is how neighbourhoods within Molendistrict differ. Juriaan performs a 'profile analysis'—a comparison between young suspects living in Molendistrict neighbourhoods with all inhabitants of the district. He states:

> Now we see that of all persons we are looking at, all 772 [registered suspects aged 23 and younger], 5.3 per cent lives in neighbourhood K. Of all Molendistrict inhabitants, 3.4 per cent lives in neighbourhood K. This is a difference, but not dramatically so. The difference in percentage is 1.9.
> (Fieldwork notes, April 26, 2011)

Not everything counts as a surprise. From Juriaan's quote, we learn that surprise also comes with difference. Neighbourhood youth need to be distinguished from district youth.

Comparison is another mode of situated improvisation, next to evocation. In order to zoom in, one needs to find a difference. This is built into Data Inc.'s software as 'profile analysis.' As with evocation, however, the results on the screen do not make sense by themselves. This is an instance in which the pilot's participants aimed to zoom in from city to district:

> Juriaan is asked to compare young suspects living in Molendistrict with suspects living in the city as a whole. First, the results on the screen show that 17% of the Molendistrict group is suspected of vandalism, against 11% in the city.
>
>> "So it must be the case that city youth commit different types of offences, whereas Molendistrict youth mostly commit vandalism," Liesbet argues.
>
> Next, Juriaan turns to the absolute numbers. He shows that there were about 7,000 young suspects in Burgcity in 2007–2010, of which about 600 suspects live in Molendistrict. Juriaan asks Liesbet for the total number of inhabitants. Liesbet answers that 40,000 people live in the district, compared to 200,000 in the city.

> "So the city is only five times as big, while the number of suspects is about ten times larger." This means that, relatively, Molendistrict youth are not that bad, Juriaan concludes.
>
> (Fieldwork notes, April 7, 2011)

The issue of size is central in this fragment, and Liesbet's knowledge of the numbers is basic but crucial. In this case, comparison serves to estimate the size of the problem of Molendistrict youth delinquency. Interestingly, the group concludes that the problem of youth delinquency is relatively small.

At other times, a paper map was used to compare. Liesbet was not always sure of the neighbourhoods' sizes in terms of numbers of inhabitants, but a map could be used to estimate the geographical size. In the one meeting in which no maps were present, Anna got up, walked to the whiteboard, and drew a map for Juriaan. She did so to demonstrate to Juriaan the relatively large size of a neighbourhood compared to the district as a whole.

The two modes of improvisation, evocation and comparison, indicate that the results on the screen did not establish close views on their own. Part of the work of zooming in only started when the results had appeared on the screen. It was done by applying professional and everyday knowledges and reading paper maps. Problem youth, therefore, was by no means an identity established by algorithms alone.

Zooming in, moreover, was normative work. First, the use of maps in this section draws attention to a, perhaps obvious, characteristic of this practice: the idea of formal neighbourhoods as units for policy. Consequently, the nature of magnification is geographical; it focuses on a magnification of neighbourhood processes. This is telling, as income or educational levels could have also served as focal points for zooming in. Instead, the project group focused on the physical and spatial characteristics of the neighbourhood, such as facilities.

Neighbourhoods are taken to be the determining factor in many urban processes, and the neighbourhood is central in policy practice in the Netherlands as a whole, as exemplified by national programs that focus on 'weak neighbourhoods.' This focus on the neighbourhood derives from an era of social science in which it was also a marker of social class. As David Phillips and Michael R. Curry note, it brings into practice the notion that "you are where you live" (2003, 143). The latter was especially true for the Burgcity policy makers, as they were not only looking for pragmatic information to sell products, but they wanted "deeper information" to "get close to youth" (Interview, November 15, 2010).

Second, through comparison, the entity representing the 'whole' is constituted as the norm. So when Molendistrict youth are compared to city youth, the city is the norm. In this case, Molendistrict's deviation from the norm was positive: The problem of youth delinquency was, comparatively speaking, small.

ZOOMING IN TO NEIGHBOURHOODS

Lifestyle Analysis: A Discovery

For Anna, the city's policy specialist on youth, results at district level are not specific enough. She wants to know what characterizes problem youth in specific neighbourhoods. This closer view of problem youth, however, was never established in the pilot study. In fact, Data Inc. finally suggested zooming out in order to zoom in.

Anna participated in the meetings as the city's project's manager. Her main concern was to find out whether the software could be of added value to policy. Her point of departure was 'the funnel model' (Interview, July 18, 2011; Burgcity 2012, internal document). According to this model, 20% of all youth is in the lower end of the funnel's cone; these youth are at risk of committing an offence. The 4% in the tip of the cone is out of the police's and government's reach. Anna's aim was to find proactive approaches for this 4%.

To this end, Anna contributes the following question to the pilot study: What types of problem youth can be found in the neighbourhoods in terms of combinations of characteristics and behaviour? (Data Inc., June 18, 2010, internal document). This question is to be answered with the lifestyle data. During the meetings, Anna poses her question with some humour: "Do girls that read *Tina* [a Dutch teen magazine] set fire to litterbins more often?" On April 26, 2011, the group finally discovers something:

> Partly joking, Anna introduces what has been her main question for the past few meetings:
>
> > "Which offences do girls that read *Tina* commit? Or, in other words, can we find a relation between offences and the Mosaic [Experian] data?" When Juriaan does not reply straight away, she rephrases the question: "So can you say that people who own a Jaguar or whose parents own a Jaguar are guilty of different offences than youth whose parents drive a Mini?"
>
> Juriaan's first step in generating an answer to this question is to find the characteristics that distinguish young suspects in Molendistrict from all inhabitants of Burgcity. He presents a long list of characteristics that differentiate these youth on the LCD screen. We only see the characteristics for which the difference is statistically significant. Strong correlations with high values are shown at the top of the list; weak correlations are at the bottom. Among the latter are the Experian lifestyle variables. Anna and her colleagues had been waiting for Juriaan to use the lifestyle

data, so quite excitedly they ask him to scroll down. Suddenly Anna exclaims:

> The sport darts! Yes, so the pilot is a success!
>
> (Fieldwork notes, April 26, 2011)

Anna finds what she is looking for: an association between lifestyle and youth crime and nuisance. To be sure, she does not believe this relation to be causal. In fact, the nature of the relationship is not relevant to her. But if it would be possible to find a 'segment' of Molendistrict problem youth that could be located in a darts club, that reads *Tina*, or whose fathers drive Jaguars, she would know how to reach them (Interview, November 15, 2010).

In the meeting, Anna continues to discuss how these findings could be used to inform policy. She reasons that, on the basis of these and similar patterns on the neighbourhood level, one could initiate a marketing campaign. One could address darts associations, for instance, to reduce vandalism. Anna does not expect this approach to lead to drastic reductions of vandalism rates; however, if offences would decrease from 100 to 80 incidents, this would be a satisfactory result. "We can ask a marketing intern whether this is a useful tool for a communicative government," Anna concludes. (Fieldwork notes, April 26, 2011)

How Surprise Disappeared

Anna's discovery did not make it to the end report. When I asked Juriaan about it shortly after the pilot group's last meeting, he did not remember the finding. In fact, Juriaan had discarded it soon after its discovery, arguing that there were simply not enough young suspects living in the individual Molendistrict neighbourhoods to perform such an analysis.

There was an additional problem. The police had not granted the project group access to the names and individual addresses of the young suspects due to privacy restrictions. This was a problem, because the lifestyle information needed to be related to the suspects on the basis of residential address, while the police had only provided information about the neighbourhoods these youth live in. The lifestyle data therefore also needed to be aggregated to neighbourhood level.[11] Accordingly, a correlation between darts and registered suspects only meant that a number of people played darts in the suspects' neighbourhood; it did not mean that the suspects actually played darts themselves.

Anna was disappointed. Not only were the results statistically significant, but in a previous meeting, one of Juriaan's Data Inc. colleagues had argued that even if a difference in terms of lifestyle data was found on the basis of only 4 suspects in one neighbourhood and 10 in another, this could be an interesting lead for a policy maker. Even though the numbers are small, the difference between 4 and 10 is telling, so this analyst argued.

There were two ways in which using small numbers as a basis for policy were discussed. The first of these comes from the world of marketing. As Juriaan explained:

> Well, in marketing, it's like this . . . When you are flyering, for instance, it is about making very small differences. So if you start a campaign that leads to a difference [in sales] of one per cent in one neighbourhood and 0.7 per cent in the other . . . you could say this is insignificant but it actually is a very good result.
>
> (Fieldwork notes, February 28, 2011)

Marketing had inspired Anna to think about lifestyles in the first place. To Juriaan she responded, "It is the same for us, really. I mean, even if one person is prevented from becoming a suspect or a criminal, this would be a welcome result." In terms of the darts club example, even if just one person matched the darts profile, this could be interesting.

The second way in which the use of small numbers as evidence for policy was discussed comes from policing. In detective practices, a difference between 4 and 10 provides a 'lead.' It means that one has a starting point for investigation. For instance, if the profile for pickpocketing is a tennis player that reads glossy magazines, a detective can start investigating tennis clubs.

At work here are 'professional regimes of evidence' (Kahn, 2013): professional standards for the type of evidence acceptable as a basis for intervention. In this case, the regime of evidence for policy had not yet crystallized. Juriaan, in his role as analytical expert, had final decision-making power over the acceptability of the regimes of evidence that were applied. In other words, he had the professional privilege (Goodwin, 1996) to decide on this, as he stated in the final pilot project meeting:

> BART: So what about interventions, as in the *Tina* example?
> JURIAAN: Well, if we are talking about a neighbourhood of 300–800 people, and maximum five per cent are registered suspects, should one start a campaign?
>
> (Fieldwork notes, September 26, 2011)

The question was put forward by Bart, a member of the innovation platform that supported the pilot. In response to Juriaan's question, Bart, Anna, Liesbet, and Mieke all shook their heads.

Crime, Juriaan argued, is too serious a topic to flyer for if one can only expect the numbers to range from 10 to 20 persons. Moreover, they could not even be certain about the actual relation between the young suspects and the lifestyle data, as explained. Juriaan furthermore rejected the detective logic; in the case of the Burgcity pilot, the results were not reliable enough to justify a visit to the darts club (Interview April 13, 2012).

Zooming Out

In the final meeting, Juriaan and his senior colleague Frank argued that lifestyle analysis was not a feasible option. Nevertheless, Frank suggested changing to a "helicopter perspective." He advised acquiring data about young suspects in other cities. Youth from similar neighbourhoods in different cities, in terms of income similarities, for instance, could be grouped together and compared to other types of neighbourhoods. More variety between neighbourhoods and larger numbers would benefit the analysis and lead to statistically significant results: "to uncover the real processes on a micro level, one needs more material for comparison" (Fieldwork notes, September 26, 2011). Once a pattern was found for a general type of neighbourhood, it could be applied to Molendistrict neighbourhoods. It follows that to zoom in, they would first need to 'zoom out.'

The reasoning here seems surprisingly similar to what Data Inc. and Burgcity's policy makers had earlier referred to as 'general social science.' With this, they referred to national statistics and criminological theory, as well as knowledge of a more universal kind (not specifically tailored to the neighbourhood). This was the type of knowledge that "should inform policy," Frank argued.

Data Inc. seemed to have decided that the regime of evidence suitable for policy should be based on large numbers and statistical significance. Ironically, this was exactly the type of analysis that Data Inc. had promised to avoid at the outset of the pilot when it proposed formulating 'local theories.' Anna therefore argued against Data Inc.'s new suggestion, claiming that this type of analysis lacks specificity. For instance, it overlooked the fact that Molendistrict does not have sufficient facilities for youth between 12 and 18 years of age. With that, the pilot meetings came to an end, and Data Inc. commenced writing the end report.

PROBLEM YOUTH

At the outset of the chapter, I proposed that by zooming in with data mining one, does not obtain a more detailed view of the same object. Rather, zooming in brings a new object into being. In Burgcity, profiles of problem youth were never stabilized, that is, accepted by all participants and included in the end report as an outcome of the pilot study. Yet we observed several tentative profiles in this case study. In the first instance of zooming in described in this chapter, for example, problem youth were evoked with crime statistics and physical and spatial neighbourhood characteristics, such as the presence of swimming pools. Later on, we learned how problem youth came into being by assembling more general categories and aggregates, such as weak neighbourhoods and city youth. When Data Inc. suggested zooming out, problem youth were related to youth in similar neighbourhoods in other cities; they became part of a national trend.

A particularly contentious issue is how corporate data and methods affect government policies. The ways in which corporations categorize and differentiate in order to increase profits may be at par with egalitarianism and the provision of social justice as principles of government (Gandy, 2007). I will further elaborate on the profiles of problem youth that were created in Burgcity with this issue in mind. First, I discuss the use of pre-set Experian lifestyle profiles. Next, I discuss the profiles in terms of their regimes of evidence.

The Experian lifestyle profiles played an important role in this case study. The application of consumer profiles was expected to reveal a more personalized and closer view of youth. Problem youths would be consumers, to be identified by their media usage or their parents' cars. Yet the profiles did not always seem to easily fit into a crime-control environment, as is illustrated by the following fieldwork fragment. A local police officer attended part of an interactive meeting at Anna's invitation. She suggested how the Experian categories might be used:

> POLICE OFFICER: Well, I think you can learn from this [the Experian data]. Those "quiet radio listeners" will be very annoyed by kids playing soccer outside, and they will surely call the city or the police and say: "I can't hear the radio because of the noise."
>
> LIESBET: I think you should see this as a marketing profile (. . .) It is a characteristic of the neighbourhood, where residents use the radio more often than the Internet.
>
> (Fieldwork notes April 26, 2013)

'Quiet radio listeners' refers to an Experian profile. Here it was used to learn about the types of people that file complaints with the police and the city about youth. The short dialogue illustrates how marketing profiles can be used to explain and predict behaviour. The profile's name invited connotations about a certain type of person: quiet and peaceful (see also Curry, 2004).

The fragment also indicates that practitioners do not necessarily accept the categories they are presented with. Liesbet argued that these profiles are tailored to marketing usage, not to understand other types of behaviour—let alone those of problem youth. Marketing variables and categories with less obvious titles, however, may be more easily integrated into government practice. In another meeting, for instance, Liesbet argued that persons in the category of "two times average income and self-employed" complain more often and insist that the government should solve their problem (Fieldwork notes, April 21, 2013).

With regard to the regimes of evidence that were applied, we learn two things about corporate intervention. The first is that Data Inc. approached problem youth as an information problem, thereby justifying the collection of more data (Schinkel, 2009). It argued for the collection of more data as it aspired to a universal truth value in the guise of large numbers and statistical significance.

Second, we should nevertheless be careful in assuming that marketing methods simply 'contaminate' government practices. With regard to the regime of evidence, Data Inc. decided that a more 'traditional' social science analysis on the basis of more cases would be more suitable for local government. It was therefore Data Inc. that reified the ethics of government intervention. In Data Inc.'s view, a local government cannot deal lightly with the issue of youth crime. Juriaan and Frank emphasized the city's responsibility for careful and effective action in the field of youth crime policy. Burgcity, in contrast, was rethinking its own role in marketing terms, as a 'communicative government.'

CONCLUSIONS

My interest in this chapter was in how a digital identity of problem youth was created according to the rationale of zooming in. When brought into practice, I argued, this metaphor suggests that digital representations of youth have a high truth status. It therefore justifies the collection of ever more data and the use of profiles. I set out to challenge zooming in as a data mining metaphor by showing how it was done in practice and by drawing out the norms that were embedded in and produced through this work.

The Burgcity case shows the limitations of the metaphor. It had one obvious limitation: there simply were not enough registered suspects in a neighbourhood to perform an analysis on. Yet this did not discourage the analysts; Data Inc. argued that simply more data were needed.

I demonstrated, moreover, that data mining is not a practice based solely on digital data. Far from a smooth and technical operation, data mining was a situated practice. I identified two modes of situated improvisation: evocation and comparison. These were conducted by the interplay of screens, professional knowledges, paper maps, local politics, and regimes of evidence. By relating these heterogeneous entities, one does not acquire a better view of a smaller part of the same object, but a new object of intervention is brought into being. In this case, problem youth shifted from relations between categories of administrative everyday knowledge and objects in the neighbourhood, such as swimming pools, to relations between youth from comparable neighbourhoods in different cities.

We learn about several normativities that were part of zooming in. First, results needed to be made relevant as surprises. Useful knowledge was unexpected knowledge. Yet the results could not be too unexpected because data mining results needed to be made tellable. Furthermore, surprise depended on difference: Local problem youth needed to be distinguished from the problem youth in the larger geographical area they are part of, such as a city or district. This requirement also produced a norm: Local problem youth is invariably constituted as a deviation and the city or the district as the norm.

Second, zooming in had a focus: Useful knowledge was knowledge at the level of the neighbourhood. This had a consequence for problem youth: They were taken to "be where they lived" (Curry, 2004). Because crime policy is focused on neighbourhoods in Burgcity, categories of good and bad neighbourhoods already existed. These labels were easily transferred to the young suspects living in them.

Third, as the previous remark also indicates: Zooming in depended on the application of more general categories and aggregated data. Problem youth identities only became more particular by assembling generalities. The categories and knowledges that were applied were normatively laden themselves: They told of good and bad neighbourhoods, and they were mobilized in relation to local policy discussions about facilities (as these might attract youth from 'weak neighbourhoods'). Furthermore, standardized profiles were introduced from the domain of marketing, thereby equating problem youth identities with consumer identities. In this pilot, however, these profiles did not stabilize. It also needs to be noted that the policy makers did not accept every standardized profile.

Fourth, establishing a closer look depended on decisions about what counts as good evidence for policy practice. Two regimes of evidence were introduced into Burgcity's policy practice: a detective regime and a marketing regime. The marketing regime was appealed most to because it related to the idea of local government as a 'communicative government.' Data Inc., however, decided that government intervention needs a more 'scientific basis.' Intervention on the basis of small numbers would not be effective or justifiable. In this case, a corporation reified what it thought of as the ethics of government intervention.

If anything, these findings point out that improving the use of data mining for a better view of problem youth involves not only decisions about which digital data to use and how much. Producing knowledge about problem youth that can inform a fair policy practice will include rethinking the issues discussed. At the very least, it involves rethinking the relation of policy knowledge to social science and the corporate sector.

To conclude, a range of metaphors circulates digital identification practices such as data mining. Aside from zooming in, actors use 'connecting the dots' (Amoore and De Goede, 2008), 'deep knowledge,' and 'obscured knowledge hidden in the data.' These metaphors, I suggest, help perform the seemingly endless analytical possibilities of these technologies. We need to attend to them as situated practices in order to change the terms by which digital identities are produced.

NOTES

1. My informants used 'problem youth' and 'at-risk youth' intertwiningly. To avoid confusion, I will only refer to 'problem youth.' Although I will henceforth use the term without quotation marks, I emphasize that it is by no means a natural category and that applying this category can negatively affect individuals and groups (see Bowker and Star, 1999). Some of my informants shared this view.
2. In Burgcity, Data Inc. applied a nearest-neighbour associative algorithm. This algorithm is understood to be suitable for a wide variety of practical applications because it allows for the analysis of databases with many missing values.
3. Some would argue that this is not 'real' data mining. In using the term 'data mining,' I adopt my informants' terminology.
4. Surveillance Studies has had its own issues with the Panopticon, a model for visual surveillance that Michel Foucault (1994 [1975]) adopted as a theoretical model (see for instance Lyon, 2006). In this chapter, I am less concerned with theoretical models in social science and more with knowledge practices.
5. For this reason, I have chosen not to include the full titles of the policy documents that I cite in the bibliography. Instead, I mention the document types in the text.
6. All fieldwork quotes have been translated from Dutch by the author.
7. The participants focused on finding patterns. They did not aim to introduce an automated signal.
8. This process is referred to as the CRISP-DSM method; see Custers (2004).
9. The levels my informants worked with are, from high to low: city, (sub-city) district, postal code, neighbourhood, sub-neighbourhood, postal code-6 (about 20 households), individual.
10. The interactive meetings could not be recorded due to the sensitive nature of the data. The quotations from these meetings are based on notes that were typed out within 48 hours of the meetings.
11. The original lifestyle data were aggregated to postal code-6 level, which means this dataset provided information about the average characteristics of about 20 persons.

REFERENCES

ANG, R.P. & GOH, D.H. (2013) Predictive Juvenile Offending: Comparing Different Data Mining Methods. *International Journal of Offender Therapy and Comparative Criminology*, 57(2). p. 191–207.

AMOORE, L. & DE GOEDE, M. (2008) Transactions After 9/11: The Banal Face of the Preemptive Strike. *Transactions of the Institute of British Geographers*, 33(2). p. 173–185.

BOWKER, G.C. & STAR S.L. (1999) *Sorting Things Out: Classification and Its Consequences*. London: MIT Press.

BOYD, D. & CRAWFORD, K. (2012) Critical Questions for Big Data. *Information, Communication & Society*, 15(5). p. 662–679.

CHOY, T.K. (2005) Articulated Knowledges: Environmental Forms After Universality's Demise. *American Anthropologist*, 107(1). p. 5–18.

CURRY, M.R. (2004) The Profiler's Question and the Treacherous Traveler: Narratives of Belonging in Commercial Aviation. *Surveillance and Society*, 1(4). p. 475–499.

CUSTERS, B. (2004) *The Power of Knowledge. Ethical, Legal, and Technical Aspects of Data Mining and Group Profiling in Epidemiology*. Nijmegen: Wolf Legal Publishers.

FAYYAD, U., PIATETSKY-SHAPIRO, G. & SMYTH, P. (1996) From Data Mining to Knowledge Discovery in Databases. *AI Magazine*, 17(3). p. 37–54.

FOUCAULT, M. (1977) *Discipline & Punish. The Birth of the Prison*. New York: Random House.

GAD, C. & LAURITSEN, P. (2009) Situated Surveillance: An Ethnographic Study of Fisheries Inspection in Denmark. *Surveillance and Society*, 7(1). p. 49–57.

GANDY, O.H. (2007) Data Mining and Surveillance in the post–9/11 Environment. In Hier, S.P. & Greenberg, J. (eds.) *The Surveillance Studies Reader*. Maidenhead (UK): McGraw-Hill, 147–157.

GOODWIN, C. (1995) Seeing in Depth. *Social Studies of Science*, 25(2). p. 237–274.

GOODWIN, C. (1996) Professional Vision. *American Anthropologist*, (3). p. 606–633.

HARAWAY, D. (1991) Situated Knowledges: The Science Question in Feminism and the Privilege of Partial Perspective. In Haraway, D. *Simians, Cyborgs, and Women. The Reinvention of Nature*. London: Free Association Books, 183–202.

HILDEBRANDT, M. (2008) Defining Profiling: A New Type of Knowledge? In Hildebrandt, M. & Gutwirth, S. (eds.) *Profiling the European Citizen: Cross-Disciplinary Perspectives*. Dordrecht: Springer, 17–46.

KAHN, J. (2013) *Race in a Bottle: Law, Commerce and the Production of Race*. Lecture June 24, 2013. University of Amsterdam.

LYON, D. (2006) *Theorizing Surveillance: The Panopticon and Beyond*. Devon (UK): Willan Publishing.

MARX, G.T. (2005) Seeing Hazily (but Not Darkly) Through the Lens: Some Recent Empirical Studies of Surveillance Technologies. *Law & Social Inquiry*, 30(2). p. 339–399.

M'CHAREK, A. (2005) *The Human Genome Diversity Project. An Ethnography of Scientific Practice*. Cambridge: Cambridge University Press.

M'CHAREK, A. (2013) Beyond Fact or Fiction: On the Materiality of Race in Practice. *Cultural Anthropology*, 28(3). p. 420–442.

MOL, A. (2002) *The Body Multiple: Ontology in Medical Practice*. Durham (NC) and London: Duke University Press.

PHILLIPS, D. & CURRY, M.R. (2003) Privacy and the Phenetic Urge: Geodemographics and the Changing Spatiality of Local Practice. In Lyon, D. (ed.) *Surveillance as Social Sorting. Privacy, Risk and Digital Discrimination*. London: Routledge, 31–56.

PLEACE, N. (2007) Workless People and Surveillant Mashups: Social Policy and Data Sharing in the UK. *Information, Communication & Society*, 10(6). p. 943–960.

RUPPERT, E. (2011) Population Objects: Interpassive Subjects. *Sociology*, 45(2). p. 218–233.

SCHINKEL, W. (2009) De Nieuwe Preventie. Actuariële Archiefsystemen en de Nieuwe Technologie van de Veiligheid. *Krisis*, (2). p. 1–21.

STRATHERN, M. (2005) *Partial Connections*. Updated Edition. Walnut Creek (CA): Altamira Press.

VALVERDE, M. (2003) *Law's Dream of a Common Knowledge*. Princeton, Princeton University Press, 2003.

WITTEN, I.H., EIBE, F. & HALL, M.A. (2011) *Data Mining: Practical Machine Learning Tools and Techniques*. Amsterdam: Morgan Kaufmann Publishers.

YANOW, D. (2002) *Constructing "Race" and "Ethnicity" in America: Category-Making in Public Policy and Administration*. Armonk (NY): M.E. Sharpe.

ZIEWITZ, M. (2011) *How to Think About an Algorithm: Notes from a Not-Quite Random Walk*. Draft paper, September 29. Available from http://ziewitz.org/papers/ziewitz_algorithm.pdf. [Accessed 10–01–2014]

9 Sorting (Out) Youth

Transformations in Police Practices of Classification and (Social Media) Monitoring of 'Youth Groups'

Vlad Niculescu-Dinca, Irma van der Ploeg, and Tsjalling Swierstra

INTRODUCTION

This chapter highlights a set of methodological and normative issues related to technological developments and policy transformations in contemporary policing. It draws from data in the Netherlands, where the prioritization of the issue of 'problematic youth groups' on the government agenda entailed a proactive crackdown approach to sort out the problems generated by these youth.[1]

The crackdown approach uses a classification method to categorize these groups into 'criminal,' 'nuisance,' 'annoying,' and 'acceptable' depending on the gravity of their offences (Bureau Beke, 2010). The so-called 'shortlisting method' uses questionnaires filled in by field officers, who periodically assess group composition, activities, and behaviour.[2] Using this classification, police map the activities of groups in the first three categories with geographic information systems in order to maintain a view on the phenomena.

In addition to geographic mapping, the proactive crackdown approach promotes early signalling and the exchange of information about groups and their members among the multiple partners involved in interventions (e.g. police, municipalities, public prosecutor, child protection agencies). The information used in these practices is gathered from multiple databases of partners, as well as from Internet/social media monitoring of these youth.

In 2013, the approach was evaluated as generally being on a good track (Van Montfoort, Office Alpha and Dutch Youth Institute, 2013). Yearly statistics of classified groups show a drop in numbers of all categories at national level since the government introduced the approach in 2010/early 2011 (Bureau Beke, 2013). Nevertheless, the approach is set to continue. It now promotes extra emphasis on 'quick and effective crackdown' on the less problematic 'annoying' and 'nuisance' groups to prevent them 'slipping down to the status of a criminal group' (Van Montfoort, Office Alpha and Dutch Youth Institute, 2013).

According to the shortlisting method, the phrase 'annoying youth groups' refers to youth that hang around the neighbourhood and are occasionally noisy or have incidental small arguments, which are usually finished quickly. At the same time, they form the largest category of 'problematic youth groups' (e.g. in 2012 they formed 731 out of all 976 shortlisted youth groups). Given that the crackdown approach is set to focus more on these much larger categories of groups, bigger numbers of youth enter the scope of proactive surveillance. As the monitoring and intervention processes are influenced by the way in which groups are classified and counted, this chapter asks how the police classify, map, and monitor cases of problematic youth groups and what normative issues emerge in these technologically mediated policing practices.

The chapter draws on ethnographic research performed throughout the year 2012 at a Dutch police station, which I name in this document Dutch Urban Police (DUP).[3] There I was granted access to interview and observe officers involved in mapping youth groups of concern with geographical information systems and in monitoring them with Internet/social media monitoring technologies (SMM). Additionally, the chapter analyses an interview with one of the main designers of a dedicated police solution for Internet and social media monitoring. The solution enables Dutch police forces to collect and analyse large amounts of Internet information in an automatic way. The following gives an illustration of these practices and technologies.

Proactive Policing at Work

Working in front of her computer screen, agent Anna is responsible for monitoring 'problematic youth groups' on the Internet and social media (i.e. Twitter, Facebook, etc.):

> "The main objective of Internet surveillance is being [there] before the criminal offense happens. You don't have to have criminal offenses to use the Internet as an information source," she tells me when I ask about her tasks.

In between describing her practices, she comments on the very method used by the police to shortlist groups:

> "We're thinking that maybe we are running behind [with the shortlisting method]: In some situations we are saying: 'we cannot find our youth on the street. The groups are not there anymore. How is that possible?' And then she quickly answers herself: "There is much more contact on the Internet. They play a Playstation game, all that kind of stuff, online. They play against each other from their own homes. And they also make more contacts [with other groups]. That's what I want to show: the groups are mixing . . ."

I would later find out (see below) that this insight is shared by other police forces. What seemed to be the view of one officer appears to be spread among more officers and more police forces with implications for their approach to the phenomenon.

For Officer Bart, the Internet strategist of the police force, not seeing the groups on the streets is not a reason to let them pass without surveillance but to put more effort into monitoring them on social media. Even if they are off the street, he thinks that they merely changed their way of setting up whatever they used to do:

> "That's what you get on the Internet. You do not see that many youths hanging out on the streets anymore. Normally [the problematic activity] was brewing: okay, they sit at the bench, talk, and then do it! And now there's nobody at the bench. But they're still making contact, trying to communicate [through social media]. And that's the different thing. Normally, we used to know the group by seeing them: okay, there they are. But now, where are they?"

I remembered Officer Bart's challenges when, later that year, I interviewed Officer Cees, from the Dutch National Police Services Agency. He is one of the main designers of a dedicated police solution for Internet/SMM. The solution aims to enable Dutch police forces (and other governmental agencies) to automatically gather, store, and analyse information from the Internet, including social media. He explains that the technology differs from other (commercial) solutions that monitor all social media activity:

> "You can't get a big net on the Internet, 24 hours a day . . . You will violate privacy; you will violate all legal restrictions. I strongly believe you shouldn't do that. It should always be case related."

He translates his views about how to account for 'privacy violation' by only enabling monitoring when it is related to *cases* (as opposed to monitoring all social media activity). These restrictions (such as who can access which features of the system, which information, how many times, etc.) are to be delegated to the monitoring technology. In his view, this is the way to avoid undesired consequences:

> "[The solution] lets user A only look at public Facebook profiles and lets user B, because he has a lot more possibilities from a legal point of view, get behind the front door of Facebook. This should always be clear: when does the technology decide to do that and how does the technology do that; otherwise it's very scary stuff!"

Together with the views of Anna, Bart, and others and with observations about officers working on cases of 'problematic youth groups,' I take a closer look at the hidden normativities of these technologically mediated policing practices.

First I provide a more elaborate context, giving an account of policing 'problematic youth groups' in the Netherlands and of the evaluation report of the crackdown approach. The next section outlines the analytical stance of the chapter. It shows the ways in which actor-network theory (Akrich and Latour, 1992; Bowker and Star, 1999; Law, 2009) is particularly relevant for understanding how youth group classifications, their statistics, problematic character, suspicious behaviour and the very notion of 'youth group' are constructed or performed within technologically mediated practices. The subsequent two sections analyse police practices promoted by the crackdown approach, illustrating the ways in which youth groups are classified, mapped, and monitored. The analysis shows that depending on how youth are defined as 'cases,' how they are performed as 'problematic,' and/or how they are categorized, wider or more restricted data gathering is legitimated. The last section links these analyses and discusses the pivotal role of the notion of 'case' and its normative implications for proactive surveillance. While the notion of case is traditionally associated to reactive policing and to aspects such as committed crime, case (re)definition, and case closing, the chapter shows that these features are significantly transformed when they are translated in software code and employed in proactive policing practices. In conclusion, the chapter argues that a particular alignment of technological, policy, and organizational factors engenders the translation of the issue of 'problematic youth groups' into an information problem, fostering automatic monitoring of a growing number of youth.

THE ISSUE OF 'PROBLEMATIC YOUTH GROUPS'

For decades, the issue of 'problematic youth groups' has been addressed by the police in the Netherlands. These youth have been a major source of irritation for many Dutch citizens due to their loud noise, street nuisance, graffiti, disrespectful and intimidating behaviour, and criminal activities. The terminology and definitions, however, changed over the years. Terms such as '*jeugdbendes*' or '*gangs*' were sometimes used but also avoided. When avoided, they were criticized for not capturing the variety of behaviour and for not being adequate for the Dutch situation, bringing too much reference to stereotypes of American gangs (Frank van Gemert, 2012). Over time, the issue of definitions had consequences for policies, influencing the view on the statistics and approach to the phenomenon. For instance, Spergel writes: "Definitions determine whether we have a large, small, or even no problem, whether more or fewer gangs and gang members exist, and which agencies will receive funds" (Spergel, 1990, 177, quoted in Frank van Gemert, 2012). In the past decade, the more neutral definition of 'problematic youth groups' has been adopted in official reports (Bureau Beke, 2009), and since 2009, all regional police forces in the Netherlands are required to centralize the statistics from their area.

The shortlisting method enables the police to have a more fine-grained characterization and classification of youth groups, depending on their street-related behaviour and activities.[4] Besides their type, groups are characterized by the location(s) where they are seen by patrolling officers (who usually give the group a name based on this location), composition (size, ethnicity, age range), daily activities, risky habits (alcohol and drug use), and recent criminal behaviour. This information is fed into forms by the officers on the beat. To shortlist a group, the method specifies that there must be repeated nuisance on the street, caused by more than two members, and the groups must be more than 'virtual groups, active on the Internet' (Bureau Beke, 2009, 18). New members or youth that are seen together with the group are registered as well upon encounters with the officers on the beat. Once sorted, the police begin registering their activities with geospatial technologies in order to maintain a view on the phenomenon.

Approaching 'Problematic Youth Groups'

Early in 2011, the Dutch Ministry of Security and Justice put the issue of 'problematic youth groups' high on the agenda. It was argued that they needed a dedicated focus with an intensified crackdown approach. The 'seven-step approach' (Bureau Beke, 2010) goes beyond mapping and classification to involve comprehensive interventions at group level but also at individual level. Depending on information on each group member and also on how a group is classified, cases are handled in particular ways and with specific partners. A broad set of partners from the criminal justice chain and child protection chain are involved (municipalities, public prosecutor, child protection agencies, and the police). For example, for the 'annoying' and 'nuisance' groups, the lead role in interventions is taken by municipalities and in cases of 'criminal' groups by the public prosecutor. Depending on the analysis and information gathered, a juvenile offender in a group may face supervision and social reintegration measures but also investigation, prosecution, trial, and sentence execution (Borst, 2013).

An important step in the approach is building a common understanding between the involved partners in order to get a clear view of the group composition, relations, and activities. Partners are required to consult and agree on which measures need to be taken in each case. To inform these decisions, they share information between them and use information brought forth by the police. The kind of information varies widely from details on street activity to the inner motives and hopes of youth. For example—as can be found in a police poster supporting practitioners with the implementation—officers need to '*get the most complete picture possible on the person*' guided by a wide range of questions such as: 'What motivates a person? What are his/her dreams/talents/competencies? Is X active on the Internet? Digital identity/profile? Does he/she have multiple identities on the Internet?, etc.' Partners are required to look at information from geographic information systems, police databases, partner databases, the Internet, and social media (Bureau Beke, 2010, 9). Therefore, dedicated police officers have been assigned also to the task of monitoring them on Internet and social media.

Evaluation Report of the Approach to 'Criminal Youth Groups'

At the beginning of 2013, a report commissioned by the Ministry of Security and Justice (Van Montfoort, Office Alpha and Dutch Youth Institute, 2013) evaluated the crackdown approach on criminal youth groups. It concludes that the multi-level approach is generally on a good track. Drawing from the annual statistics (Bureau Beke, 2013), it reports a decrease in the number of youth groups that were listed as problematic.

As Figure 9.1 indicates, the report shows a drop in the number of cases in all categories. Split by category, this is a drop from 92 to 59 'criminal' groups, from 327 to 186 'nuisance' groups, and from 1341 to 731 'annoying' groups. Despite the drop, the report recommends further measures to

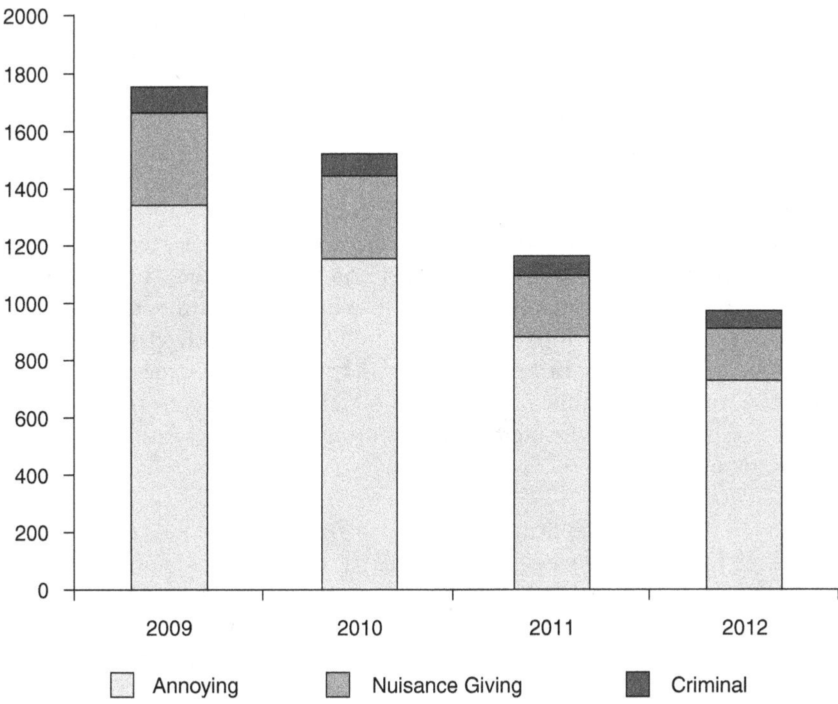

Figure 9.1 Evolution of problematic youth groups in the Netherlands by number and type

Source: Bureau Beke, 2013. Problematic youth groups in Netherlands, extent and nature in autumn 2012. Arnhem: Ministry of Security and Justice.

be taken concerning 'annoying' and 'nuisance' groups to prevent them from 'slipping down to the status of a criminal group' (Van Montfoort, Office Alpha and Dutch Youth Institute, 2013, 12), because 'criminal' groups are harder to dismantle than 'annoying' and 'nuisance' groups. These figures also show that the 'annoying' and 'nuisance' groups remain the largest categories at the national level. With group sizes varying widely between 10 and 100 members (Van Montfoort, Office Alpha and Dutch Youth Institute, 2013, 5), this is a total number ranging between 10,000 and 100,000 youth in these two categories in 2012.

The report also identifies challenges faced by the approach. It notes a lack of resources and personnel as a main challenge, affecting the capacity of the police to keep up with the dynamics of the phenomenon. Moreover, it notes the lack of a shared sense of urgency among the partners in prioritizing the approach, leading sometimes to late actions. The evaluation notes also that "a growth or drop in numbers of shortlisted problematic youth groups does not necessarily imply that the actual number of groups has grown or dropped" (Van Montfoort, Office Alpha and Dutch Youth Institute, 2013, 3). Analysing possible causes of inaccuracies, the report identifies the lack of expertise of police officers working with the shortlisting method or the "increased police attention [which] may, for example, well result in more groups being identified" (Van Montfoort, Office Alpha and Dutch Youth Institute, 2013).

Although the evaluation report raised many special points of attention, it did not have as a focus to evaluate the role of the technologies used in the approach: in the classification and geographical mapping; in the information-gathering process, in the Internet and social media monitoring process. Technologies are largely taken for granted or mentioned very briefly. For example, although the report notes possible inaccuracies in statistics, it does not account for the way in which these numbers are locally produced, how the groups that get counted are created, visualized, and classified in a category or another, and what role technologies play in this process. Another example is the way in which social media are mentioned (once), only as one of the factors contributing to the formation of criminal youth groups:

> In the forming, disappearing and transforming of criminal youth groups, three factors or processes seem to play a role: [. . .] (3) spread of 'gang culture' by (social) media.
>
> (Van Montfoort, Office Alpha and Dutch Youth Institute, 2013, 10)

Although the approach includes a step for information-gathering practices, including collection from Internet and social media, the evaluation addresses their role neither in generating statistics nor in the approach itself.

ANALYTICAL STANCE

Though a large body of policing literature seems to either take technologies for granted or render them as tools in the hands of police officers—that is, it helps them do their job quicker and better as for example in Chu (2001) and Williams and Williams (2008)—a growing number of studies have begun to pay attention to the more substantive roles technologies play in policing. These analyses began to look at technologies as more than just instrumental in relation to policing models, codes, and practices (Chan, 2001; Manning, 2008; De Pauw et al., 2011; Van Brakel and De Hert, 2011; Leman-Langlois, 2012) and sought to analyse the ways in which these technologies become active 'agents' in policing processes.

The idea that technologies are not merely neutral tools but actively mediate human action has been developed already for a few decades in science and technologies studies and in particular in actor-network theory (ANT; e.g. Callon, 1991; Akrich and Latour, 1992; Latour, 1994; Law and Mol, 2001). In analysing the agency of technological artefacts to the same extent as that of human beings, ANT aims to avoid reducing technologies to neutral tools or to clear-cut results of particular social practices without, at the same time, viewing them as a determinant of social relations (whether for better or worse). From an ANT perspective, actors, defined as entities that *do* things, should be conceived in relations with other actors, for it is in these networks of relations and associations that they are enacted in specific ways, becoming what they are and doing what they do.

Therefore, in order to understand the active role of technologies in policing and their outcomes, we need to look into these networks of actors and relations. This implies analysing the entities that emerge from these networks (e.g. classifications, suspicion, groups, etc.) and which are influenced by technology. It follows that normativity of technology would also have to be located within this interplay of (f)actors that constitute the socio-technical arrangements. For example, it means going beyond discursive claims about neutrality of technology to potentially disclose issues of normative relevance embedded in technology design or analysing laws, policies, and value statements and the way they are implemented in technology (e.g. the value of privacy translated and built in technologies).

A particular set of technologies not only pervading policing but penetrating a whole array of processes of human life are systems of classification. Sometimes explicit and mostly invisible, classifications are powerful artefacts ordering material and social realms alike (Bowker and Star, 1999, 4). We can feel their force instantly if we would try, for instance, to ignore the signposts at public toilets indicating male/female, at borders indicating types of passports, or at supermarkets indicating cash/PIN only, and so on. Already implicit in these examples is that classifications can be built into infrastructures and procedures. They often embody highly normative charge and shape people's identities (Bowker and Star, 1999, 4).

In order to understand how they are made and how they are often rendered invisible, an exploration of these bureaucratic and technological infrastructures is necessary (Bowker and Star, 1999, 5). The approach expands on Foucault's argument that an archaeological approach is necessary to dig up the origins and consequences of the categories with which our lives are imbued. In our case of policing technologies, I draw from this approach to analyse classification practices and technologies, entailing stronger or lighter monitoring and intervention.

Classifications not only organize modern life but also lie at the base of many statistics and surveys of various kinds. Things and people alike are often categorized and counted at the same time. Statistics based on various classifications also have normative consequences when taken up in policy making and translated into action as descriptions of reality. Building also on Foucault's practical archaeology, John Law (2009) argues for a performative understanding of social science methods. That is to say, rather than merely describing reality, the methods through which statistical knowledge is produced also *enact* these realities into being. Instead of only reporting on phenomena, the methods make them into 'realities.' For instance, in our case, the police are the ones filling in the forms that entail sorting youth groups into one category or another and, at the same time, they are the ones responsible for sorting out problematic behaviour. Their classifications and conceptualizations produce in a way the phenomena, while the aggregation of numbers about these classified entities performs them at that level.

PRACTICES OF CLASSIFICATION AND MAPPING

Therefore, this section looks more closely to these classification and mapping practices that precede monitoring. It illustrates the various translations occurring between 'groups hanging out on the street' and the entities they work with on their computer screens, which become the focus of policy making and intervention. The section draws from interviews and participant observation sessions with two officers—renamed Dirk and Erwin—in their daily routines.

In policing problematic youth groups, the Dutch Urban Police (DUP) use a geographic information system to map the incidents in their area. The system draws from data registered and stored in police databases. Amongst other possibilities, it allows the registration and visualisation of the groups and the individual members related to them, representing these groups with colour-coded icons that correspond with the gravity of their offences ('annoying' with grey, 'nuisance' with orange, and 'criminal' with red).

When asked about his tasks, officer Dirk explains how youth groups are represented in their systems and how this helps him get a clear view of the phenomenon.

> "So when I go to the group [Officer Dirk points to an icon on the screen], what it shows is the location, the last location known, that the officers

on the beat put in. I know that mostly they hang out there. [. . .] So the data they put in is shown here: the name of the group, the sort of group, whether they are criminal or annoying or nuisance."

Upon selecting a period of interest, the geographical information system (GIS) displays a map with icons representing events with listed groups. Each icon of a group can be clicked to open a list of members that were registered as belonging to that group at each particular encounter with the police. The maps can also display hotspots of various crimes, enabling analysts to form a picture of the phenomenon and potentially relate it to a group's activity.

> "After a while we also identified the group here [Officer Dirk points to an area on the map designating another department], in the neighbourhood of some bars and we saw a pattern of vandalism from here to here in the same time that they normally gathered here. So, by identifying the group here and here and knowing the timestamps, you could also identify them as the probable perpetrators of this vandalism trail . . . Without any analyses, we saw that it could probably be the group responsible for that trail."

Working in front of his screen when drafting his analysis, Officer Dirk needs to rely on the information put in by field officers, 'always bound to a location,' and on maps produced by the system. What he visualizes are the coded entities on his screen. Their mapping is contingent upon a set of factors that need to be aligned in order for the system to make these groups visible. This depends on officers on the beat, who translate whatever they see on the street into program fields; the officers need to have 'a group,' rendered as a stable entity; they need to translate the place they saw the group into the location marked in the system as the field designating the place they usually hang out. Highlighting this process shows how the phenomena in the street are translated into other, software-enabled entities visible on computer screens.

As it turns out, this process faces a set of challenges that give a good glimpse into the technologically mediated character of this work. The following quote is taken from a participant observation session with Officer Erwin, who needed to do an analysis of the situation of problematic youth groups in his area. He was about to issue a report showing a spike in 'nuisance,' based on generated statistics. After I questioned him on the probable reasons for the spike, Officer Erwin searched and read the database registrations to try to understand. He soon needed to discard the report after finding that many registrations were categorised as 'nuisance' when other codes were more fitting, designating lower offences:

> "It's good that we looked into that. Now we know. [. . .] They are all registered as '*melding overlast jeugd*' (youth nuisance). It's the same. You see? He went without a valid ticket [in public transportation].

> The problem with this kind of thing . . . I bet it's the same [the officer checks another set of registrations]. It's the same. So that's really a big issue there. So then in fact you could say: 'do we have a problem with "nuisance" here?' No, I don't think so. Because all the registrations are about the tickets, that they don't buy a ticket. I just want to check the other ones for 2011. This is another one: 'Young guy was sitting with his feet on the opposite chair.' Not allowed. So they have to find another incident number to put this in the system, because this is really screwing up the numbers like crazy. [. . .] So this really changes our view on nuisance. Same. [. . .] Oh my God. This means in fact that I can throw the whole analysis down the drain."

The quote does not merely highlight that there are challenges in working with police systems but illustrates how systems enact certain realities. In this case, the report showing a significant increase of 'nuisance' in that area classified 'people that go through the gate without a valid ticket' as 'nuisance,' which designates a higher level of criminality than would be appropriate for free riding. As Officer Erwin mentions, this proved to be a repeated classification problem and consequently a counting issue, which affected their view on the phenomenon, performing it in a category that entails the need for more intense monitoring.

These situations point out some of the contingencies involved in the socio-technical processes in the police, through which 'groups' are classified and mapped. Without inferring from this reduced set of examples that national statistics are affected, the section does remind us that what we count are software-enabled entities, prone to partiality and ambiguity (Gerson and Star, 1986). And it is these entities that lie at the basis of intervention and monitoring.

PRACTICES OF SOCIAL MEDIA MONITORING

In fact, the Internet monitoring procedure in the DUP force specifies that 'having a group' in the GIS is the starting point. Agent Anna, whom we met in the beginning of this chapter, explains the necessary condition to begin her monitoring tasks. She has to

> "always have the group, like this [she points to an icon of a group on the screen], always start with a group that's already in the system." Being practiced within a proactive approach, there is no need "to have criminal offenses, but use it as an information source."

'The group' defined as a case becomes an obligatory passage point in their working processes (Latour, 1987): necessary to begin monitoring but also sufficient, in the sense of legitimizing further data gathering.

While the monitoring of youth on social media has been made legal by the Ministry of Security and Justice, its legitimization builds on the idea that a form of displacement is at work. That is, an assumption is made that group members continue or increase their problematic behaviour as they spend time on the Internet and social media, even if they keep a low profile on the streets. The idea is known in policing as 'crime displacement' or—in informal police circles—as 'waterbed effect' or 'balloon effect.' This hypothesis implies that crime tends to shift or move, either upon police actions or due to changes in the societal structure, but remains the same in volume. The notion makes officers more prone to translate the absence of criminal activities into their shifting to other places, times, tactics, or types.[5] The quote of Officer Bart at the beginning of the chapter is indicative of the way in which the displacement hypothesis is sometimes taken up at an operative level. Not encountering a certain phenomenon (in this case youth hanging out at the street corner) leads the officer to use displacement for explaining the change. The quote performs youth groups as still 'out there' setting up their activities, which continue to be of a criminal nature. Thus the underlying assumption of this theorization of crime dynamics is that crime among these youth remains a constant. In this way, it becomes an argument to increase the distribution of resources towards monitoring these youth on social media.

Once engaging with this practice, officers look at individual group members to interpret various indicators specific to social media in order to infer suspect behaviour. For instance, in the following quote, Agent Anna reads several Twitter messages, pictures, and accounts leading one to the other. The situation is about a picture of a weapon held by a boy, who reportedly used the picture to threaten his girlfriend. The officer traced the picture through various social media accounts to find more pictures. Given their content, the police decided to bring the young boy to the station for questioning:

> "I follow one group on Twitter—and then there was this message about a boy being arrested for threatening his ex-girlfriend with a weapon. It was retweeted many times. [. . .] I found it looking into his followers on Twitter. And then somebody had this picture of a weapon [the officer points to a picture with a boy holding a gun]. I went to his Twitter and I found more pictures with weapons. So, on his account I found these pictures. I called the department and said 'Look what I found. We have to interrogate him again because of what I found here.' And we should confront him with that because he was this little boy crying and he's sorry and didn't know that it was wrong to have it. But if you take pictures like this, you're very well aware of that."
>
> Interviewer: So he's dangerous now?
>
> "Well, he's not dangerous, but . . . he deserves the attention, for sure."

This example shows how officers engaging in SMM not only monitor youth groups for street-related offences but assign suspicion to new kinds of behaviour or entities. Besides looking for the risky activities specified by the shortlisting methodology (e.g. graffiti, alcohol and drug use, street nuisance), officers now need to interpret pictures, social media relations, or status updates. Depending on the prior knowledge they may have, they infer suspect behaviour from new entities with their specific normativity: too-high numbers of 'followers' for the declared age, too many messages on a topic, the clothing in a profile picture, and so forth. This kind of behaviour is not necessarily problematic according to the shortlisting method, based on which the group was included for monitoring in the first place. Still, being related to a case legitimizes monitoring.

However, in this research, it became apparent that youth don't always continue their problematic behaviour. They also change their behaviour, and spending time on social media is part of this shift. They engage in gaming, picture sharing, sending messages, status updates, and chatting *instead* of spending time on the street. Even if these activities can also generate problematic behaviour, they are not necessarily suspect in the sense defined by the shortlisting methodology. This is also attested by Agent Anna:

> "Because they are not out on the streets—or less so—makes their way of interacting different."
>
> "[. . .] They are not criminal groups"
>
> "They put everything on here. 'Eating soup.' 'In a moment there will be the match,' they put it in there. 'Finished with internship.' This one's obviously sick, because he says: 'being sick is the most awful thing,' but then with a bad word, there it is. They say they buy things, so it gives me information about what they do."

This is also signalled by reports of other police forces:[6] According to a Dutch portal on youth and safety, the police in the city of Arnhem noticed a sharp drop in nuisance, and they link this with the increasing time spent by youth on social media and online gaming. These observations are also in line with several critiques of the crime displacement hypothesis. Multiple studies show that, upon successful prevention programs, displacement does not necessarily occur (Clarke and Weisburd, 1994; McLennan and Whitworth, 2008). Others, such as Barr and Pease (1990), argue that the notion is inadequate in the first place, as not all crime prevention results in crime being displaced. They propose the notion of 'deflection,' which encapsulates the idea that crime can also be prevented even if it may translate in other forms of crime.

Thus, the police shortlisting method needs to account more dynamically for changes in youth behaviour. Otherwise, once enacted as a problematic group, the youth have a hard time invalidating the conditions for which they were placed under monitoring, even when the reasons for which they were selected in the first place are not present anymore.

New Forms of Groups

Social media monitoring practices challenge not only the ways in which groups are assessed as problematic but the very police notion of youth group. As the quote from Agent Anna, in the very beginning of this chapter, suggests, police officers doing SMM begin challenging the shortlisting methodology. In the following quote, Agent Anna questions the size of a group, as registered in the system, and does that by checking its associated members on social media:

> "When they were in a group they usually stayed for a longer time, the changes were not that big. But now, if I check Twitter, for example, I look at the Keizerstraat group, 35 people are in [the system] as contacts of each other. I say: 'I do not believe that they are really contacts in the sense of friends.' So I will go and search for those 35 people on the Internet and see if I can find whether they are really having contact through the Internet and whether I can say, because of the messages they are sending, that they are friends. I dare to say that there are up to a maximum—and it's a real maximum—10 people of that group are really in contact with each other."

Besides the different group size, the following quotes illustrate that groups are not well defined and stable but mix and merge. Although the procedure needs to start from 'a group,' officers find connections with other shortlisted groups.

> "They often change more in the way they are constructed as a group."
>
> "[. . .] Then I saw the retweet and the retweet led me to him. And he is not part of that group but he belongs to a different group."
>
> "[. . .] I believe that this group is . . . [officer stops to explain] you have '*hinderlijk*' ('annoying') and overlast ('nuisance') . . . it's one of these two. The group I follow is called Koningstraat, that's this one [officer points to an icon on a screen]. And they are members of Hoogstraat."
>
> "[. . .] So the groups we had in the past, I think it's changing. And we cannot say in a short amount of time that this is that group, depending on that location. They are less location dependent and the loyalty is different because of the contact through the Internet."
>
> "[. . .] I think they are dissolving in a way that they are not that loyal to each other as they were when they were on the streets."

These quotes perform a much more fluid notion of group compared to the one produced by the shortlisting methodology, which treats the group as much more fixated through name, location, or category. These 'dissolving' relations of youth in online environments have been also highlighted by other analyses of surveillance of young people on the Internet (Steeves,

2012). These studies suggest that not only do Internet surveillance practices perform youth differently, but youth change their online behaviour over time, in part due to awareness of police monitoring.

In both situations, these new relations challenge the definition of groups and their classification. From the above quotes, we can see the easiness with which 'annoying' and 'nuisance' are interchanged by the officer. A big set of group identity attributes—as defined by the shortlisting method—are performed differently by social media monitoring practices. The size of the group, its composition, kinds of relations, their stability or their relation to location are enacted differently, indicating significant transformations of the police notion of group.

This has implications for the aggregated statistics that are based on these groups. More mingled relations may mean fewer groups. Thus, the under-representation of social media relations in the shortlisting method leaves room for misunderstandings when reading numbers in statistics. This is especially relevant for the higher number of cases of 'annoying' groups. As the evaluation report shows (Van Montfoort, Office Alpha and Dutch Youth Institute, 2013), they remain the largest but at the same time the least problematic category. Their characterization, according to the method, can easily encompass large numbers of youth that 'hang around the neighbourhood and are occasionally noisy or have incidental small arguments, which are usually finished quickly.' Their reinforced enactment as 'problematic' entails the need for their further monitoring. In its turn, this practice is gaining significant breadth and depth when amplified by the technological developments that afford increasing automation of this process.

AUTOMATING SMM

As mentioned by Officer Bart, the police engage with real-time monitoring afforded by the Internet and social media monitoring technologies. Depending on the task at hand, practitioners see them as powerful tools to automate the labour-intensive, time-consuming processes of information gathering. These solutions allow officers to program automatic alerts on certain events, crises, persons, or groups and to analyse the data even after it has been removed from the servers of the social media provider.

Officer Bart describes such a technological solution for social media monitoring that was purchased by their police force from a commercial vendor.[7] The solution is able to automatically monitor a broad set of social media providers, Internet forums, and websites:

> "It keeps everything. They [the social media monitoring provider] have 380.000 websites in the Netherlands. And that's a lot. For example, if there is an author that's very interesting, I want to make a search for everything the author said. [Or I can ask the program to] 'give me a signal whenever he's talking 'house party.'"

With such a large amount of Internet resources and power to automate the searching and analysis, the solution is interesting for the police. But the license to use it, Officer Bart explains, is expensive for their local police force, and it also poses a security problem, as they need to send their queries of interest outside the police domain, to the servers of the provider.

In part for these reasons, the Dutch police chose to develop an Internet/SMM solution themselves with similar functionality. Initially aiming for investigative purposes, the scope of the solution expanded to enable more generic research by a larger set of governmental agencies and police departments. The solution is set to allow gathering of information, storage, time stamping, retrieval for forensic research, and presentation of information in a Google-like interface. Nevertheless, as Officer Cees mentions, the same features that make this solution interesting for the police make it prone to trigger privacy infringements of various kinds, as also pointed out in several reports (Oerlemans and Koops, 2012; Bert-Jaap Koops et al., 2012).

In order to account for 'privacy violations,' Officer Cees explains that the solution is built with the idea of 'privacy by design' from the start.[8] That is, in his view, the system will be programmed such that it can be used only in relation to specific *cases*, and only by the officers that have the proper authorizations:

> "So if we get your personal information from your Facebook page and we have no case or there's no legal reason for us to keep this information, it should be gone after 24 hours. If it's not related to a case, we are not allowed to keep it [. . .] There's no restriction to getting it again the next day, reanalyse it and draw the same conclusion: we're not allowed to keep it and throw it away.
>
> "[. . .] As soon as you suspect that you want to investigate possible incidents related to bike gangs or whatever, you have a case and you have defined it as case, even if it's not related to picking up people and everything else. It's just mining information and analysing information related to a possible incident or whatever. So it's a case, it's always a case."

Thus, the practice and design of the notion of 'case' becomes a crucial factor regulating what information is legally stored and what's not. The way a case's scope is defined has far-reaching implications for the amount of data that can be gathered. This is because only data not related to a 'case' may qualify for deletion on a short-term basis (24 hours). The information that is gathered as part of a case ends up stored for longer periods, and potentially this is exposed to the scrutiny of officers.

To prevent the exposure of data to a wide range of officers, Officer Cees mentions that there are restrictions built into the design of the technology. Police officers are given specific regimes of use, depending on their 'legal profiles.' These are specifications that limit the system's affordances depending on each type of user:

> "Their legal profile decides whether they have all the widgets or just a few. So you can expect a policeman to have more legal possibilities than a tax investigator or somebody at a lower government."
>
> ". . . [The technology will] let user A only look at public Facebook profiles and user B, because he has a lot more possibilities from a legal point of view, get behind the front door of Facebook."

As pointed out by Akrich (1992), these quotes highlight that designers define anticipated users, endowing them with particular capabilities when *inscribing* predictions about the context of use. However, it may still be that actors define their own roles even though the technical artefact may *prescribe* certain imperatives or invite default patterns of action (Akrich and Latour, 1992). While 'privacy by design' may offer guidance with respect to information management, it remains abstract or silent in terms of what a user/police officer is able to define as a 'case.' When I asked the designer to give more examples of cases, these issues related to case design became clear:

> "Right now we're testing on the topic of the Olympics [. . .] to see what it's doing with all the information related to the Olympics. I can assure you that's a lot, even based on a few keywords. [. . .] All the information related to the Olympics is stored as a history. But it's always case related. We don't store all the information that is not related to it."
>
> Interviewer: "What if in the course of a case and its development, the boundaries of the case are changing because you acquire new insights?"
>
> "That's very flexible, because the investigators in control can always, at any moment in time, add new information or add new searches or add new source material of which they think: hey, we know something."

Thus a case's scope and its technological translation can be loosely defined. Larger or smaller amounts of information end up legally stored as part of a case at hand. This aspect is not regulated by design but by users and procedures. Police officers can define and redefine cases as small or as large as they need. While the notion of case is traditionally associated to reactive policing and to aspects such as committed crime, the case's scope, case (re) definition, and case closing, these features are significantly transformed or lose their ground when they are translated in software code and employed in proactive policing practices.

Having 'cases' as starting points for monitoring, these technological solutions are thus compatible with the practice and procedure of monitoring problematic youth groups. This is because shortlisted youth groups are already defined as cases in the crackdown approach. Each shortlisted group is analysed and prioritized, with some getting selected for closer monitoring, including on Internet and social media. As police departments are already interested to extend their technological solutions towards Internet and social media (i.e. they acquired and use commercial social media monitoring), the internally developed solution is an option for them.

Several points can now be brought together. SMM practices perform new forms of groups and new ways of inferring suspicion. The transformed practices may not require having 'a group' as a case for monitoring, as cases can be easily expanded, and each new suspect can be defined as a case ("*He deserves the attention, for sure*"). In a policy context which recommends '*getting the most complete picture possible on the person*' (police poster) and an organizational context lacking resources (as analysed in the evaluation report), automated solutions predispose the police to delegate more 'cases' to be monitored with automated technologies. Even if surveillance is announced to be only case based, as opposed to monitoring all social media activity, this does not limit the expansion of their number or loose definitions.

This section highlights the pivotal nature of the notion of 'case' in proactive surveillance practices. This includes their scope (what belongs to a 'case,' how and who expands it), their lifecycle (how is it redefined, when is it closed), and their translation in technological implementation.

CONCLUSION

This chapter analysed practices and technologies involved in policing 'problematic youth groups.' In line with the evaluation report presented in the first section (Van Montfoort, Office Alpha and Dutch Youth Institute, 2013), it showed how classifications and aggregated statistics on shortlisted youth groups do not simply mirror the dynamics of the phenomenon. That is, a variation in the number of groups reported by the shortlisting method may not necessarily mean that there are in fact fewer or more groups from a certain category. Rather, technologies and practices play an active role in the ways in which youth groups are performed as 'problematic' and classified in one category or another. As it was illustrated, practices of classification produce the entities that are counted. This insight not only points towards difficulties in the method but proves relevant for the amount of resources allocated to monitoring.

Proactive policies promote enhancing information exchange and early signalling on the larger sets of 'annoying' and 'nuisance' groups (Van Montfoort, Office Alpha and Dutch Youth Institute, 2013). Against the background of a broad adoption of social media by youth, the police tend to use the notion of 'crime displacement' to explain why they see fewer groups on the street and why they are still justified to monitor their Internet behaviour in order to '*get the most complete picture possible on a person.*'

Once engaging with SMM, officers encounter new youth relations and new forms of groups. At the same time, they define new indicators for suspicion. What a suspect situation, person, or behaviour is depends on metrics and features specific to social media: how many followers for the declared age, the clothing in a picture, and so on. Even if these are unaccounted for in the shortlisting method that was used to select a group in the first place, they predispose the police to find more cases and thus reinforce incentives for monitoring.

The chapter shows how these issues are exacerbated with new technological developments for social media monitoring. These developments promise to partially automate monitoring and reduce labour-intensive police processes. At the same time, the police aim to account for criticism of social media surveillance when employing these solutions. In order to account for 'privacy violation' of social media users, police designers delegate their views of privacy protection towards technology design. The monitoring solution is used only on 'cases' that require it, as opposed to monitoring all social media activity, and this is to be regulated by technology. However, 'problematic youth groups' are already defined as cases. This quickly expands the scope and depth of their monitoring and easily integrates into organizational procedures and technological designs.

The analysis of this arrangement shows the ways in which 'cases' legitimize proactive surveillance. The norms shaping this arrangement are not only to be found in legal provisions and policy documents but are also hidden in the details of software design and use contexts. Therefore, despite restrictions built into design, particular alignments of technological, organizational, and policy factors predispose increased automated monitoring and data gathering. These factors together engender a translation of the issue of 'problematic youth groups' into an information problem, fostering automatic (social media) monitoring of a growing number of youth.

ACKNOWLEDGMENTS

The research leading to these results has received funding from the European Research Council under the European Union's Seven Framework Programme (FP7 2007–2013)/Grant. No. 201853. Besides the support of the DigIDeas project, the author wants to thank Irma van der Ploeg, Jason Pridmore, Govert Valkenburg, Annelies Falk, Karolina La Fors, and Isolde Sprenkels (the members of the Digideas project) and Tsjalling Swierstra for their useful comments on previous versions of this chapter. Moreover, the author wants to especially thank the police staff, municipality officials, and technology developers for their generous collaboration.

NOTES

1. 'Problematic youth groups' is a term used in Dutch policy making to designate groups of youth (considered between 12 and 25 years of age) that have been associated with street nuisance and criminality and have been flagged by police and other governmental agencies for closer monitoring and intervention.

2. The method has been developed by the police in collaboration with Bureau Beke, a Dutch consultancy bureau specialising in providing advice for policies on crime and safety issues.
3. To protect the confidentiality of interviewees and of youth registered in police systems, their names have been anonymised in this study. Officers were renamed alphabetically (Anna, Bart, Cees, Dirk, and Erwin). This measure was also taken with respect to the name of the visited police forces, with the exception of the Dutch national police force, which is one for the whole country.
4. According to the shortlisting method, 'annoying youth groups' refers to groups that are seen to hang around the neighbourhood and are occasionally noisy or have incidental small arguments, which are usually finished quickly. Some of the members engage in mild violence and property crime. 'Nuisance youth groups' are groups with somewhat more pronounced, provocative behaviour (e.g. insulting bystanders). They may vandalize things more regularly and may not shy away from violence. They engage in minor crime and make an effort to ensure they do not get caught. The last category, 'criminal youth groups,' contains youth who (at least in part) have committed more serious crimes (e.g. burglary, robbery, pimping). They often come into contact with the police and are not afraid to use force. They usually commit crimes not just for status but also for financial gain.
5. Crime displacement has been classified into five types: 'temporal,' meaning that the intended crime is committed at a different time; 'spatial,' referring to the intended crime being committed in other places; 'tactical,' which implies the commitment of the same crime but in a different way; 'target,' which is about a different target then the one originally planned; and finally 'type' displacement, referring to another kind of crime from that initially intended. Simon Hakim and George F. Rengert, *Crime Spillover* (Beverly Hills, CA: Sage, 1981).
6. www.wegwijzerjeugdenveiligheid.nl/nieuws/2012/050912_jeugd-gaat-liever-gamen-dan-hangen
7. Coosto is a Dutch-based social media monitoring company whose solutions enable "monitor[ing of] social media, including Twitter, blogs, forums and Hyves. More than 380,000 sources are visited daily and indexed. Coosto gives rapidly a clear answer to the questions: who, what, where and when? The results of Coosto are always available" (Coosto website, 2013).
8. Privacy by Design is a framework which advances the view that privacy cannot be assured solely by compliance with legislation and regulatory frameworks. Privacy and data protection need to be embedded throughout the entire life cycle of technologies, from the early design stage to their deployment, use, and ultimate disposal. Ann Cavoukian, "Privacy by design: The 7 foundational principles" (Canada Information and Privacy Commissioner of Ontario, 2009); European Commission, "COM 609, A comprehensive approach on personal data protection in the European Union" (European Commission, 2010).

REFERENCES

AKRICH, M. (1992) The De-scription of Technical Objects. In Bijker, W. E. & Law, J. (eds.) *Shaping Technology/Building Society—Studies in Sociotechnical Change*. Cambridge (MA): The MIT Press, 205–224.

AKRICH, M. & LATOUR, B. (1992) A Summary of a Convenient Vocabulary for the Semiotics of Human and Nonhuman Assemblies. In Bijker, W. E. & Law, J. (eds.) *Shaping Technology/Building Society: Studies in Sociotechnical Change*. Cambridge (MA): MIT Press, 259–264.

BARR, R. & PEASE, K. (1990) Crime Placement, Displacement, and Deflection. *Crime & Justice*, 12. p. 277–318.

BORST, W. L. (2013) Privacy by Design on the Crossroads of Chains, Lessons from the Chain of Criminal Justice in the Netherlands. *Journal of Chain-computerisation, Information Exchange for Chain Co-operation*, 4(5). p. 3–10.

BOWKER, G. C. & STAR, S. L. (1999) *Sorting Things Out: Classification and Its Consequences*. Cambridge (MA): MIT Press.

VAN BRAKEL, R. & DE HERT, P. (2011) Policing, Surveillance and Law in a Pre-Crime Society, Understanding the Consequences of Technology Based Policing. In De Pauw, E., Ponsaers, P., Vijver, K. V. der & Deelman Piet (eds.) *Technology-Led Policing*. Antwerpen: Maklu Cahiers Politiestudies, 163–192.

BUREAU BEKE. (2009) *Shortlist Methodology in Seven Steps*. Arnhem: Bureau Beke.

BUREAU BEKE. (2010) *Approach to Problematic Youth Groups, Guidelines for Municipalities*. The Hague: Ministerie van Binnenlandse Zaken en Koninkrijksrelaties.

BUREAU BEKE. (2013) *Problematic Youth Groups in Netherlands, Extent and Nature in Autumn 2012*. The Hague: Ministerie van Veiligheid en Justitie.

CALLON, M. (1991) Techno-Economic Networks and Irreversibility. In Law, J. (ed.) *A Sociology of Monsters: Essays on Power, Technology and Domination*. London: Routledge, 134–164.

CAVOUKIAN, A. (2009) *Privacy by Design: The 7 Foundational Principles*. Ontario: Information and Privacy Commissioner of Ontario.

CHAN, J.B.L. (2001) The Technology Game: How Information Technology Is Transforming Police Practice. *Journal of Criminal Justice*, 1. p. 139–159.

CHU, J. (2001) *Law Enforcement Information Technology: A Managerial, Operational and Practical Guide*. New York: CRC Press LLC.

CLARKE, R. V. & WEISBURD, D. (1994) Diffusion of Crime Control Benefits: Observations on the Reverse of Displacement. *Crime Prevention Studies*, 3(2). p. 165–178.

EUROPEAN COMMISSION. (2010) *A Comprehensive Approach on Personal Data Protection in the European Union*. COM(2010)609 final.

VAN GEMERT, F. (2012) Five Decades of Defining Gangs in the Netherlands: The Eurogang Paradox in Practice. In: Esbensen, F. A. & Maxson, C. L. (eds.) *Youth Gangs in International Perspective: Results from the Eurogang Program of Research*. Dordrecht: Springer. p. 69–83.

GERSON, E. M. & STAR, S. L. (1986) Analyzing Due Process in the Workplace. *ACM Transactions on Information Systems*, 4(3). Special Issue: Selected Papers from the Conference on Office Information Systems.

HAKIM, S. & RENGERT, G. F. (1981) *Crime Spillover*. Beverly Hills (CA): Sage.

KOOPS, B., et al. (2012) *Juridische Scan Openbrononderzoek. Een Analyse Op Hoofdlijnen Van De Juridische Aspecten Van De Irn/Icolumbo-Infrastructuur En Hdief-Tools*. Tilburg: Tilburg University, TILT—Centrum voor Recht, Technologie en Samenleving.

LATOUR, B. (1987) *Science in Action*. Cambridge (MA): Harvard University Press.

LATOUR, B. (1994) On Technological Mediation: Philosophy, Sociology, Genealogy. *Common knowledge*, 3(2). p. 29–64.

LAW, J. (2009) Seeing Like a Survey. *Cultural Sociology*, 3(2). p. 239–256.

LAW, J. & MOL, A. (2001) Situating Technoscience: An Inquiry into Spatialities. *Environment and Planning D: Society and Space*, 19(5). p. 609–621.

LEMAN-LANGLOIS, S. (ed.) (2012) *Technocrime, Policing, and Surveillance*. Abingdon, Oxon, New York: Routledge.

MANNING, P. (2008) *The Technology of Policing: Crime Mapping, Information Technology, and the Rationality of Crime Control*. New York and London: New York University Press.

MCLENNAN, D. & WHITWORTH, A. (2008) *Displacement of Crime or Diffusion of Benefit: Evidence from the New Deal for Communities Programme*. London: Communities and Local Government Press.

VAN MONTFOORT, OFFICE ALPHA, AND DUTCH YOUTH INSTITUTE. (2013) *Evaluation of the Approach to Criminal Youth Groups*. The Hague: Ministry of Security and Justice.

OERLEMANS, J. & KOOPS, B. (2012) Surveilleren En Opsporen in Een Internetomgeving. *Justitiële verkenningen*, 38(5). p. 35–49.

DE PAUW, E., et al. (eds.). (2011) Technology-Led Policing. *Journal of Police Studies*, 2011–3(20). p. 1–32.

SPERGEL, I.A. (1990). Youth gangs: Continuity and Change. In M. Tonry and N. Morris (eds.) *Crime and Justice: A Review of Research*, vol. 12, Chicago, IL: University of Chicago, pp. 171–275.

STEEVES, V. (2012) Hide and Seek: Surveillance of Young People on the Internet. In Lyon, D., Haggerty, K. & Ball, K. (eds.) *The International Handbook of Surveillance Studies*. New York: Routledge, p. 352–359

WILLIAMS, V. & WILLIAMS, B. (2008) Technology Applications: Tools for Law Enforcement. In Ruiz, J. & Hummer, D. (eds.) *Handbook of Police Administration*. London, New York: Taylor & Francis, 224–258.

10 Identifying the Perpetrator

An Ethnographic Study of CCTV in Police Work in Denmark

Peter Lauritsen

INTRODUCTION

Within the last two decades closed-circuit television (CCTV) has become an integral part of police work in Denmark. It is used to solve a range of crimes from murder to shoplifting and has made the police develop new ways of thinking and acquire new competencies. Thus new practices revolving around the use of CCTV have come into being. When police officers arrive at a crime scene, they instantly look for surveillance cameras to see if the incident could have been filmed. With approximately 500,000 surveillance cameras in the country there is a fair chance that this is in fact the case (SecurityUser no. 5, 2013). At the police station the footage is handed over to technical experts who are employed by the police and know how to retrieve and handle the information. If some of the pictures are useful they are included in the further investigation of the incident, and sometimes the footage is used in court as a way of presenting what happened before, during, and after the crime was committed or as a direct means of identification.

This chapter focuses on the actual use of CCTV footage in crime investigation. This is an interesting area of study because the use of CCTV in police work is supported by a strong claim that the technology will make police work much more effective (Lauritsen, 2011). The basic and often-stated argument is that more crimes will be solved at a low cost because of the cameras. The article treats this claim as a folk theory (Rip, 2006). Like other folk theories the theory of CCTV effectiveness is characterized by two important aspects: (1) It lacks empirical support but (2) still serves as an engine for future action. Thus many important decisions and debates in Denmark rest on the theory of the effectiveness of CCTV, and it has become increasingly difficult for privacy advocates and other concerned citizens to have their voices heard. If crime can be fought with CCTV, why not use it?

The aim of the chapter is to use an ethnographic study to critically engage in a discussion of the effectiveness of CCTV in police work. Although it cannot be concluded that CCTV is never effective, the result is nevertheless a weakening of the folk theory. Or rather it is a more nuanced theory that points to CCTV as a valuable tool in police work but also shows how it often takes skills and hard work to make CCTV productive.

Theoretically the chapter uses the concept of oligopticon to interpret the empirical findings. The oligopticon has its roots in actor-network theory (ANT) but puts a specific focus on surveillance practices (Latour, 2005; Latour and Hermant, 2006). In particular, the concept is used to stress the networked character of surveillance. Thus an important insight is that the working of surveillance systems depends on a plethora of actors and that it sometimes can be difficult to align and coordinate these actors. In the process, surveillance itself becomes limited and fragile.

The oligopticon adds important nuances not only to folk theories of police use of CCTV but also to prevalent academic understandings of surveillance, most obviously perhaps to the concept of the panopticon developed by Jeremy Bentham in the 18th century (Bentham, 2011) but made famous by Michel Foucault (1991). As is well known, the panopticon is, in its original form, a model of a prison which is built in a way that makes it possible for a guard to watch the inmates, but the inmates cannot watch the guard. Accordingly the inmates assume that they are under constant surveillance, and this has, the theory states, disciplining effects.

The panopticon remains influential in academic discourse and has been at the centre of many interesting analyses within surveillance studies. The panopticon is an all-seeing and effective surveillance machine, and very little is heard about breakdowns in the machinery or the hard work that is put into maintaining the apparatus. However, where the panopticon is robust, the oligopticon is fragile. This does not entail that the oligopticon cannot be productive but it is always an achievement and a result of successful collaboration between actors (Gad and Lauritsen, 2009).

The chapter progresses in the following manner: First the folk theory of CCTV is sketched out in more detail, and two significant examples from the history of CCTV in Denmark are included to illustrate the folk theory. The second section focuses on how CCTV is used for solving crimes. The conclusion is that although CCTV is a valuable tool, it is not as smooth to use as many people seem to think. In the third section the concept of the oligopticon is introduced and used to interpret the empirical observations. I conclude by making clear that surveillance is (1) always carried out by a network, (2) limited in scope, and (3) often fragile.

A FOLK THEORY OF CCTV

According to Arie Rip, a folk theory "evolves in ongoing practices, and serves the purposes of that practice. [. . .] What characterizes folk theories is that they provide orientation for future action" (Rip, 2006, 349). Rip continues,

> Folk theories can be more or less explicit; this also depends on whether or not they are challenged. They are a form of expectations based in

> some experience, but not necessarily systematically checked. Their robustness derives from their being generally accepted, and thus part of a repertoire current in a group or in our culture more generally.
>
> (ibid., 349)

When it comes to the use of CCTV by the police a particular folk theory is clearly dominating at least in a Danish context. According to this theory, CCTV is an effective tool for fighting crime. The claim is not further developed or backed up by empirical data. Contrarily, the positive impact of CCTV in police work is presented as self-evident and self-explaining. For example, the minister of justice in 2009 stated that "it is my conception that CCTV can be an effective tool that can be used by the police for solving crime." Most leading politicians share this view, and surveys have consistently shown that the majority of the population is positive about increased use of CCTV (Det Kriminalpræventive Råd, 2005).

Perhaps surprisingly the theory of CCTV effectiveness has two opposing conclusions. In one variant the effectiveness of CCTV leads to the suggestion that it should be used even more, specifically in order to solve a range of problems ranging from terrorism, gangs, and rape to feelings of lack of safety in residential areas. The other variant of the theory does not disagree that CCTV is effective but warns that the technology has a flipside. According to this view the effectiveness of CCTV will not only lead to the capturing of more criminals, it will also lead to a more totalitarian and oppressive regime. Often Orwell's *1984* is used as a reference for this argument (Lauritsen, 2011). Most of the debate in Denmark can be traced back to these two opposite viewpoints. They are, however, basically expressing the same conviction that CCTV is a very effective tool. In the following I will give two examples that serve to show how the theory of effectiveness works.

The first example is from 1980, when private citizens in the town of Hobro installed CCTV in a street that for some time had experienced a lot of vandalism (Lauritsen and Feuerbach, 2015). In order to end this, a local trade organization, led by a businessman, installed CCTV in an attempt to identify the perpetrators. The CCTV system consisted of three or four (the sources disagree on this matter) cameras. No monitors were installed. If nothing happened the tapes would be deleted every morning. Otherwise they would be handed over to the police. However, after some months the cameras were removed. According to the businessman in charge of the project, this happened as the result of pressure from his employer (a bank)—they believed his engagement in the project hampered their image and could result in a loss of customers.

The installation of the cameras drew national attention, but politicians were divided on the subject. A high-ranking member of a right-wing party agreed that CCTV was unpleasant but found it necessary as long as there were not enough police on the streets. Other politicians were far more sceptical and made references to Orwell's *1984*, which was "just around the corner." In the end the prime minister promised that the government would make it illegal to use CCTV in public places, saying "the tendency is dangerous and must be stopped." Accordingly, a law was passed in which the first paragraph reads: "TV surveillance must not be used on a road, site or the like, that is used for ordinary coming and going."

The other example is from January 2008, when a young man was stabbed to death on the main pedestrian street in Copenhagen. Three young men demanded that the victim gave away his hat, and when he refused, he was killed. In the following days people tried to cope with the incident. How could such a thing happen in a country like Denmark, and who was responsible? The media looked for politicians that could be held accountable. A newspaper asked the Minister of Justice how she would prevent such a thing from happening again. Her answer was CCTV in public places. Apparently nobody noticed that surveillance cameras in fact had captured the killing of the young man without preventing the incident (Dahl and Bolther, 2012). In a matter of days everybody seemed to call for more surveillance cameras. Mayors, citizens, and members of Parliament all promised that CCTV would soon be in place in the major Danish cities. Of course CCTV was already there, for instance at the facades of banks and inside cafes and shops, but now everybody wanted the whole street to be filmed with new cameras operated by the police.

The examples clearly illustrate the theory of CCTV as effective. But one can also see the two opposite interpretations of this effectiveness at work. In the 1980s, politicians raised concern about the use of CCTV and passed legislation in order to bring surveillance under control. Almost 30 years later politicians actively pushed for more surveillance. Now the effectiveness of the technology was seen as something that should be used in the fight against crime.

Like other folk theories, the theory of 'CCTV as effective' lacks empirical support. There is, for instance, no empirical evidence that a few cameras in a small Danish town will lead to an Orwellian surveillance society, just as there is no evidence that a few more cameras operated by the police will prevent crime and ensure that the police will capture more criminals. However, as Mads Borup and colleagues state, "In the case of widely shared expectations [. . .] legitimation is hardly required" (Borup et al., 2006, 289). Also, the theory is clearly a vehicle for action. In the first example, politicians are prompted to constrain CCTV. In the other example, they encourage the use CCTV even more. Finally, it is interesting to note that the folk theory of surveillance is based on a rather strong technological determinism. Along these lines it is the cameras, although there are very few of them, which are seen to drive society in one direction or the other. This focus on technology has the implication that the context that is decisive for the working of the technology is left out of the picture. In a more general discussion of technology and expectations Borup and colleagues state, "Early technological expectations are in many cases technologically deterministic, downplaying the many organizational and cultural factors on which a technology's future may depend" (Borup et al., 2006, 290). As will become clear in the following, this is exactly what happens when it comes to the use of CCTV by the Danish police.

CCTV IN SOLVING CRIME

CCTV is a well-researched surveillance technology, and there is a vast literature on the topic. A significant part of the literature has tried to decide whether CCTV is preventing crime (Welsh and Farrington, 2007) or if the police solve more or fewer crimes when CCTV is put to use in certain areas (Ditton and Short, 1999). However, taken as a whole, this literature does not support the claim made by the folk theories that CCTV is an effective tool. In fact CCTV only seems to have very limited effect on preventing crime (Welsh and Farrington, 2007; see also Ditton and Short, 1999).

Although studies of the quantitative sort clearly are of relevance they do not shed light on how CCTV is integrated in police practices. In fact, practice is exactly what these studies try to eliminate in their attempt to isolate the effect of the cameras. An explicit focus on practice is, however, found in several interesting studies of operators in CCTV control rooms. Using observation as a primary method, these studies unravel new practices that have emerged as a result of CCTV. For example, it has been shown how suspicion is constructed in the control room and how collaboration between CCTV observers and members of the police force works—or rather does not work (MacHill and Norris, 2003; Goold, 2004).

These detailed studies of policing practices are interesting, but they reflect an important difference between the UK (and perhaps other countries) and Denmark. While control-room practices are widespread in some countries and almost have become the emblem of CCTV use, this is not the case in the work of the Danish police. Although they have the opportunity to watch CCTV pictures live in control rooms, they only do so on certain occasions—for example, in relation to soccer matches or huge demonstrations. As a senior police officer stated, "we cannot afford spending man hours on watching a screen where nothing happens. There is simply not enough action going on." However, the fact that Danish police only on some occasions invest resources in actually watching CCTV live does not mean that the use of CCTV footage is a marginal activity. In fact, the coverage of CCTV in Denmark is now so high that it is more than likely that pictures from surveillance cameras are included in the investigation. Thus one can be certain that the police look for CCTV footage when they arrive at a crime scene.

The following departs from most research on CCTV in police work as it investigates how CCTV is used by the police when solving crime. As part of the study I carried out fieldwork in several Danish police districts. Observations were made, and police officers were interviewed both formally and informally. In addition, various documents including media reports were collected. The fieldwork focused on two questions: (1) How do the police handle the process of installing CCTV in public areas and (2) How do they use CCTV footage in crime solving? It is experiences from the latter part that are presented here. Furthermore, I concentrate on the process that starts when the police collect footage from surveillance cameras and stops when the suspect is identified or the case is completed or left unsolved. How CCTV evidence becomes stronger or weaker through negotiations in court is an interesting topic, but it is not dealt with here.

The police officers I encountered had a highly nuanced understanding of CCTV. Nobody believed that CCTV can prevent serious crimes such as homicide, rape, or physical assault, especially not in the many instances in which these crimes are committed as an act of passion or desperation. Neither was it a widespread opinion that CCTV would make the public feel safer. But the police officers readily shared stories of how CCTV had helped in solving crime. In some instances, these stories showed how CCTV provided the police with high-quality "portraits" which made it possible to solve the case almost immediately:

> We have plenty of examples. There was this very unfortunate event where a young moped driver was out practicing with his driving school. He was run over in a traffic junction and killed. A witness saw that the people from the car jumped on a bus. But we got hold of CCTV footage from the bus and were thereby able to identify the culprits.

In this case pictures were used to identify the driver immediately, and the police could simply pick him up at his home address. However, the typical impression was that although useful and often described as a "highly valuable tool," the process was often more complicated than this. This can be seen in the following, in which a police officer presents an example in which he thinks the use of CCTV was a success.

> A person was stabbed to death . . . and at some point we get a hold of CCTV from a taxi. I looked at the footage, and I could see that there was a person sitting in the backseat. But it was only a dark spot because it was dark and the quality of the pictures was not good enough. But using a piece of software I analysed the footage frame by frame. And there was one single picture where the person did like this [shows how the suspect looks up]. But still one could only see a dark shadow. However, using photo-editing software we succeeded in developing a picture of the face of the person. We showed the portrait to the guys in our special unit and they said "We know this guy." And it is was in fact the killer.

To the police officer this is a story of success. It took time and skill to analyse the pictures, but in the end the killer was identified and captured. It is experiences like these that make most police officers conclude that CCTV is a valuable tool. However, as already indicated, the use of CCTV can be difficult and demanding. Often the process runs into obstacles that must be dealt with. Although the police are often successful in doing this, the effect of CCTV is uncertain. It cannot be taken for granted that the use of CCTV produces new evidence or helps much in identifying the perpetrator.

Whether the use of CCTV falls apart or turns out to be productive depends on many things, but in the following three important themes are discussed. The themes are at least partially overlapping, but they are all important to the police when using CCTV, as they all challenge the identification of the perpetrator.

How is the quality of the footage? One problem the police often face is that the surveillance pictures are of low technical quality. Also, cameras are sometimes out of order, or the incident happened outside the reach of the cameras and hence there are no pictures at all. A truck, leaves on the trees, or a marquee can hide the incident. In other situations the cameras may be old and unable to film at night. It is also a common experience that the perpetrator wears a hood or a mask and thus tries to avoid identification. In the same manner, license plates turn out to be stolen, or they are covered in one way or another.

Although surveillance pictures in low quality undoubtedly threaten the effectiveness of the surveillance system, one cannot conclude, however, that this necessarily makes the surveillance pictures useless. An experienced police officer states,

> Take the robbery of [the bank] for example. There you can see how they crash into the building. They drive a car through the fence and three people dash in. But the quality [of the CCTV footage] is very bad. But I improved contrast and lighting on a single picture and things like that. And then one could see parts of their clothing that matched clothing found at the place where the robbers shared the plunder.

Thus, surveillance pictures are sometimes used for other purposes than directly identifying the perpetrator. For example the police can get knowledge about how a sequence of events unfolded or if there were witnesses to the incident. Sometimes they obtain knowledge about the height and stature of the perpetrator and the clothes he is wearing. This may not lead to identification of the perpetrator in itself, but it can be important knowledge in linking, for instance, the clothes to the scene of crime, which can then strengthen the evidence found by DNA or other forensic analyses.

How can the footage be used? Even in situations in which the police have pictures of high quality of the face of the perpetrator, things can be difficult. Often the police do not know the identity of the person in the picture, and they have to find out. One option is then to ask the media to publish the picture. However, the police do not do this automatically; this is especially the case if they are uncertain that the picture in fact shows the perpetrator. They do not want to blame an innocent person for a serious crime. In other instances, the media are unwilling to publish a picture because they find the case too difficult to explain or too small. However, recently the police have started to distribute surveillance pictures using Twitter, but the impact of this strategy is still unknown. Another much-used strategy is to publish the pictures on the intranet of the police. Theoretically this will expose the picture to every police officer in the country, but some police officers admit that they seldom look at the pictures on the intranet. Knowing this, police officers with a picture of an unknown suspect often ask specific colleagues if they know the person. Often they do. Thus, according to the police, a number of crimes are solved because of the personal knowledge of police officers. They simply know the perpetrators. However, if the suspect is unknown things become more difficult. For example, in one instance, the police had very good pictures from a bank robbery. But after listening to the sound of the recording the police had reason to believe that the robbers were from a foreign country. This made the police conclude that the robbery most likely would not be solved, because it is often difficult to engage police authorities in other countries in solving crimes committed in Denmark.

How many resources can we invest? A third problem is related to resources. Often CCTV is discussed as either working or not working, but in the daily life of police practice, it is a common experience that CCTV in some situations can be made to work. For example, every gas station has CCTV capturing the license plates of the cars. Consequently a person driving away without paying for his or her gasoline can be identified quite easily. The police simply look up the license plate in the vehicle register and then call the driver. But if the plates are not clearly visible, or they are stolen from another vehicle, the police often choose not to investigate the incident. Thus the surveillance pictures are simply not used. The reason is that it would take too many resources to solve a rather harmless crime. Or, as a police officer stated, "You don't bring in Scotland Yard just because a person has stolen gasoline worth 300 kroner [40 Euros]." If however the driver continues to steal gas, an investigation would be opened. Thus when it comes to many minor crime incidents, CCTV is not 'working' because the police choose not to activate other technologies and personnel in order to make the technology work. If however a murder or a rape is committed, one can be certain that every surveillance camera near the crime scene is checked, even if there is only a remote chance that anything that can help finding the murderer has been captured on video. One such incident is described in the following:

> We had a couple of really serious incidents of rape. We didn't know who the rapist was but at some point we got hold of CCTV footage. And we got a picture of a man that matched the description, and we thought it was him. But we didn't know who he was; nobody knew him. Then we could see on the footage that he spat. We hurried to the scene and found

> the gob of spit. It showed that we had him in the DNA database, and then we took him in.

In this case, as in many others, the police often spend many hours looking at recordings without knowing precisely what they are looking for, but sometimes they actually find something that can be of help. In this case it is a gob of spit that enables the police to activate other resources, specifically their DNA database. It is this plethora of resources that identifies the perpetrator.

The question of resources is important. Like any other public institution, the police have to prioritize their resources, and they do not consider CCTV to be a technology that automatically makes police work more effective. In fact, CCTV is seen as something that generally requires resources, and therefore it should be used with caution. When for example a prominent Danish Islam critic was shot at, the police reported that they had looked through 1,400 hours of film without finding anything useful. When they were criticised for not getting hold of even more footage the police answered that it properly wouldn't be of much use since they were certain that the culprit wore a bicycle helmet in the attempt to disguise himself from the cameras. Of course the police didn't complain about spending many hours unsuccessfully. It was an attempted murder, and such cases get the highest priority. But the example questions the effectiveness of CCTV that is so often taken for granted.

CCTV AS OLIGOPTIC SURVEILLANCE

There is clearly a gap between the way the dominating folk theory and the ethnographic understanding developed above depict CCTV in police work. It is also obvious that the kind of surveillance practice described does not fit neatly into either the concept of Big Brother nor the concept of panoptic surveillance which dominates many academic discussions of surveillance. Thus, the practice described above is not about controlling or disciplining but about identifying subjects. This process of identification is not automatic and smooth running. Often it takes hard and complicated work that involves different kinds of resources, and still the result is uncertain. In some situations identifying a person is easy; in others it is difficult or even impossible.

The concept of oligopticon offers a performative understanding of surveillance that seems to fit much better with the way CCTV is actually used by the police. In an oligopticon surveillance is situated, specific, and limited, which at least to some extent puts the oligopticon in opposition to the panopticon:

> Oligoptica [. . .] do exactly the opposite of the panoptica: they see much too little to feed the megalomania of the inspector or the paranoia of the inspected, but what they see, they see it well.
>
> (Latour, 2005, 181)

The oligopticon has its theoretical roots in actor-network theory (ANT) and is thereby built on a "relational materiality" (Law, 1999). It holds that nothing exists outside of relations, that to exist is to be related. The consequence of this view is that reality (including technologies, science, power, agency, and of course surveillance) is constructed and maintained in networks of relations. It is these networks that produce agency and allow actors to act, hence the term *actor-network*. Importantly, these networks are furthermore heterogeneous—that is, they consist of human and non-human actors, who are made to work together.

Bruno Latour illustrates the workings of an oligopticon with the work of Mrs. Baysal (Latour and Hermant, 2006). Her job is to coordinate the teaching activities at the university by planning and booking rooms for lectures. She does this from the confined space of her office without ever attending lectures, only by consulting paper documents and computer files containing information about names of teachers, titles of lectures, and availability of rooms. These technologies participate in the construction of the situation and make it possible for Mrs. Baysal to inspect and intervene. But this happens in a very specific way. If a map is lost or an important document is missing the situation will break down or at least change. In this way oligoptica are fragile constructions. Or as Latour states, "From oligoptica, sturdy but extremely narrow views of the (connected) whole are made possible—as long as connections hold." However, "the tiniest bug can blind oligoptica" (Latour, 2005, 181). Thus, an oligopticon is a much more fragile construct than the panopticon. It consists of specific spaces that allow detailed observation, but only within a narrow frame. It involves, for instance, the use of maps, documents, or computer programs and is dependent on such technologies; if a technology malfunctions or stops working, the vision changes (Gad and Lauritsen, 2009).

Thus from a position in ANT, and in particular the oligopticon, it comes as no surprise that it is not CCTV in itself that identifies a perpetrator but a network in which CCTV is only one node. This network consists of cameras, police officers, different kinds of software, the DNA database, and so on. It is only in situations in which the work of these actors is coordinated in certain ways that identification is successful and hence CCTV is "a valuable tool."

The networked character of surveillance implies that the use of CCTV is fragile. If one of the actors does not perform as expected or simply stops working the vision of the police is challenged. They may literally become unable to see the perpetrator. This does not render CCTV useless, but in order to make identification possible, more resources and more work must be put into the process. Thus what the police gain from watching the CCTV footage is not a total or all-encompassing view. What they strive at is a much more limited and narrow view that is relevant for the task at hand, identifying the perpetrator.

CONCLUSION

This article has reported from fieldwork aimed at understanding the way Danish police use CCTV to identify perpetrators and hence solve crime. It showed how CCTV can be effective in some instances, but this only happens if a plethora of devices and actors act together and are coordinated in a certain way. In other instances CCTV is useless and leads to nothing else than a waste of resources. In between these extremes are, however, many situations in which CCTV is *made* to work by relating CCTV to other resources and actors.

Drawing on the concept of oligopticon the article offers three conclusions that are of more general relevance: First, it takes work to establish surveillance. Surveillance technologies do not work by themselves. They must be placed in a network, and they are depending on this network in order to work. Second, surveillance can be fragile. Many things can go wrong and disturb the picture. This does not deem CCTV useless, but it implies that we cannot take for granted that surveillance is a smooth-running machine without bugs and friction. Finally, surveillance is not necessarily about getting the big picture or establishing an all-encompassing situation of surveillance. When the police use CCTV they are not even interested in the big picture but in establishing a relevant vision. That is a situation that makes it possible to identify a suspect.

An understanding of surveillance as oligoptic has important implications also on a policy level. In Denmark, CCTV and other types of surveillance systems are applied to all sorts of problems partly because it is believed that it is rather easy to establish effective situations of surveillance. If, however, political debate and policy initiatives were based on the recognition that it is difficult and requires many resources to establish even fragile situations of surveillance, things would look different—and politicians might start to look for other relevant solutions to problems of security and safety.

REFERENCES

BENTHAM, J. (2011) *Pantoptikon—Magtens Øje*. Aarhus: Klim.

BORUP, M. et al. (2006) The Sociology of Expectations in Science and Technology. *Technology Analysis & Strategic Management*, 18(3/4). p. 285–298.

DAHL, O. & BOLTHER, S. (2012) *Drabschefen. Nye Sager*. København: Ekstrabladets Forlag.

DET KRIMINALPRÆVENTIVE RÅD. (2005) *Tv-overvågning. Fakta om Tv-overvågning i Danmark*. Glostrup: Det Kriminalpræventive Råd.

DITTON, J. & SHORT, E. (1999) Yes It Works, No It Doesn't: Comparing the Effects of Open-Street CCTV in Two Adjacent Scottish Town Centres. *Crime Prevention Studies*, 10. p. 201–223.

FOUCAULT, M. (1991) *Discipline and Punish. The Birth of the Prison*. London: Penguin Books.

GAD, C. & LAURITSEN, P. (2009) Situated Surveillance. An Ethnographic Study of Fisheries Inspection in Denmark. *Surveillance and Society*, 7(1). p. 49–57.

GOOLD, B.J. (2004) *CCTV and Policing: Public Area Surveillance ad Police Practices in Britain.* Oxford: Oxford University Press.
LATOUR, B. (2005) *Reassembling the Social: An Introduction to Actor-Network-Theory.* Oxford/New York: Oxford University Press.
LATOUR, B. & HERMANT, E. (2006) *Paris: Invisible City.* Available from www.bruno-latour.fr/sites/default/files/downloads/viii_paris-city-gb.pdf. Accessed 14–04–2013.
LAURITSEN, P. (2011) *Big Brother 2.0. Danmark som Overvågningssamfund.* København: Informations Forlag.
LAURITSEN, P. & FEUERBACH, A. (accepted 2015): CCTV in Denmark: 1954–1982. To appear in *Surveillance & Society.*
LAW, J. (1999) After ANT: Complexity, Naming and Topology. In Law, J. & Hassard, J. (eds.) *Actor Network Theory and After.* Oxford: Blackwell.
MCHILL, M. & NORRIS, C. (2003) *CCTV Systems in London. Their Structure and Practices.* Working Paper no. 10, Urbaneye.
RIP, A. (2006) Folk Theories of Nanotechnologists. *Science as Culture,* 15(4). p. 349–365.
WELSH, B.C. & FARRINGTON, D.P. (2007) *Closed-Circuit Television. Surveillance and Crime Prevention. A Systematic Review.* Stockholm: Swedish Council for Crime Prevention.

Part IV

On the Move

Migrants and Travellers

11 The Digital Evacuee
Mediation, 'Mobility Justice,' and the Politics of Evacuation

Peter Adey and Philip Kirby

INTRODUCTION

Two weeks before Hurricane Sandy devastated the Eastern Seaboard of the US, as well as Cuba and Jamaica, the New Jersey Office of Homeland Security and Preparedness announced that it had awarded a contract to the group Radiant RFID, who were commissioned to develop an 'evacuation solution.' This would work in advance of and during an emergency to track and therefore assist in the management of people, pets, vehicles and other emergency assets. Radiant's RFID tags were designed to surveil or trace these subjects and things across the cycle of evacuation mobility, as people moved from their homes, through processing by disaster officials, to temporary accommodation, and then, assuming all had gone to plan, back to their homes. Radiant's work in New Jersey was prefigured by their development of similar technology for the State of Texas (2011), and other states across America are currently in the process of developing such systems, too, including Colorado, Illinois, Louisiana, Ohio, and Virginia. The use of evacuation management software, integrated by ICTs, owe their particular origins to Texas, which we will trace. However, they are also of particular interest and importance. For, in tandem with other federal programmes, they represent part of a disparate series of bureaucracy, science, technologies, and surveillance systems from which the 'digital evacuee' has evolved.

In this chapter, we investigate evacuation as a particular form or way of watching over and governing mobility, that requires far more sustained study. Evacuation is noticeably absent from many of the diverse mobilities of humans, non-humans, and things that have been opened up to critical insight through the putative 'new mobilities turn' or 'paradigm' (although see Sheller, 2013, for an exceptional study of precisely those who could not evacuate). Indeed, for the few studies that have turned their attention to evacuation from this perspective, evacuation has been comprehended through a broader politics of mobility and meaning which elaborates precisely the depoliticisation of the term (see, for example, Cresswell, 2006). In other words, evacuation mobilities have often been approached and are often represented—as Cresswell shows—in such a way that they are bled of all social meaning, notably in the testimony of New Orleans' evacuation officials. To present evacuation as a purely technical act or engineering solution might be understood as a political move of closure. That is, mobility is naturalised as the only possible outcome that removes complicity, guilt, or a more distasteful politics of racial discrimination from its production. Notably, too, the involvement of surveillance practices in disaster and emergency contexts remains underinvestigated within the surveillance studies literature. This chapter seeks to delve far deeper into the practices and technologies of evacuation and its management.

First, the chapter sets out an approach by drawing together the insights of mobilities, STS, and conceptualisations of emergency and evacuation. It then traces a genealogy of evacuation surveillance, registration, and tracking as it emerged during the Second World War, with the latter's attendant evacuation of mass populations. Second, it explores how the earlier 'systems' failed in the chaos of modern emergency management, especially during Hurricane Katrina's uneven displacement of New Orleans residents in 2005, as well as those of Louisiana and the wider region. The chapter considers how those events provided the impetus for the construction of a nationwide federal system of evacuation registration and tracking, as well as a state system, with more parochial, perhaps even divisive, concerns.

EXPLORING EVACUATION MOBILITIES

In some ways, evacuation seems a poor fit for existing and more familiar categories of mobile subjects, such as 'the homeless,' 'refugees,' and/or 'migrants,' even if evacuation certainly touches upon these subjects. In others, including the ways that such categories direct state and non-state interventions toward certain people, it aligns much more precisely. Evacuation mobilities, for example, have traditionally been some of the most contentious and 'unknown' forms of mobility, demonstrated by the fact that, since the Second World War, numerous systems of governmental surveillance and registration have sought to manage their inherent plurality and unpredictability. More recently, 'the evacuee' has figured on the agendas of authorities pertaining to public health, transportation and highways, policing and emergency services, security, intelligence, and counter-terrorism, throughout the scales of local, state, and federal governance and supranational bodies, NGOs, and the aid sector, as well as a plethora of private companies. The evacuee is a subject moved away from harm. But the evacuee is also a mobile subject constituted as a figure by these various skeins of power, knowledge, technologies, and practices.

It is becoming increasingly important, therefore, to ask just what is at stake in the surveillance, categorisation, mobilisation, and treatment of the evacuated as it is a figure that seems to be moving across different grounds, approaches, institutions, and understandings, at some pace. Central to this are the ways in which the evacuee has been subjected to an extensive but uneven effort to render it as 'legible' (Scott, 1999) from its mobile and slippery condition through the administration of different forms of authority, bureaucracy, and technology. The primary means to do this have been the application of a series of techniques and technologies that make the evacuee visible and then sort, order, and manage that subject physically and within complex and multi-scalar systems of records and databases, accordingly. Opening up evacuation, then, requires the elaboration of several approaches from interdisciplinary research fields such as science and technology studies (STS), 'new mobilities,' and political-theoretical research on emergency.

First, the new mobilities paradigm shifts attention to take seriously life on the move orchestrated and experienced through different kinds of mobilities and infrastructures. Prior approaches to evacuation might tend to fetishize the locational start and end points of the internally displaced, or refugees, for example in migration and humanitarian studies. Engineering fields instead see evacuation as a more abstract technical object, perhaps obeying certain physical or social laws (Helbing, Farkas, Molnar and Vicsek, 2002). Approaches from within 'new mobilities' encourage the examination of movement as it is lived and experienced (Hannam, Sheller and Urry, 2006; Urry, 2007). That said, perspectives from mobilities studies have not tended to be brought to the study of emergencies or disasters until relatively recently to explore—in Cresswell—how evacuation mobilities are given particular meanings in Hurricane Katrina (Bartling, 2006; Tim Cresswell in Bergmann and Sager, 2008). And in Sheller's investigation of the humanitarian effort to deliver aid to Port-au-Prince following the earthquake in Haiti (Sheller, 2013), how evacuations falter through a power-geometry of mobility and immobility.

The approach taken in this chapter is to build on these insights but to also focus on the circulation of evacuation and the evacuee as a technical object, held together by various systems that surveil, categorise, sort, and manage mobilities (Aas, 2011). Surprisingly, the surveillance studies literature (Lyon, 2007) is remarkably absent from the fields of disaster management, becoming far more attuned to the quotidian uses of surveillance in the everyday, although see Monahan (2007) for an exception on intelligent transportation systems (ITS) and their role in emergency situations. More recently, Buscher (2013) suggests that the application of big data to emergency-management systems presents a new task to explore the potential ethical questions over how that data might be drawn, stored, and used appropriately and proportionately, especially over vulnerable populations. Extending these approaches therefore means asking questions about how the evacuee is shuttled between systems and software and representations, between practices held within different institutions and organisations, and is observed by different practices and technologies.

Third, practices of evacuation are closely associated with emergency politics, which create particularly susceptible conditions for the creep of 'security' and previously unpalatable (and maybe non-legal) measures. However, it is important that calls for the analysis of evacuation under an Agambenian 'state of exception' (Agamben, 1998) do not over-determine evacuation. In other words, and while we will certainly see evacuation emerging from emergency situations in which the normal rule of law and the separation of powers has been suspended, reading evacuation only in the context of exceptional measures and emergency or catastrophe politics forgets its routine operation inside the normal protections of liberal democratic systems (Lakoff, 2007; Collier and Lakoff, 2008).

These approaches are used to develop arguments and further questions around what we could call 'the politics of evacuated mobilities,' or what Mimi Sheller describes as an approach through 'mobilities justice.' Sheller's is a politics that attempts to develop the "capability of all [. . .] [to] access mobility in order to meet their own basic needs" (Sheller, 2013). What this particularly recognises is that mobility capabilities are highly and unevenly distributed across different spaces, subjects, and bodies. Such a distribution cannot be understood outside of vulnerability to the kinds of events evacuation is deployed to remove a populace from. This chapter explores the imperfect systems that record and manage evacuated populations, which have been made socially, technically, and legally indistinct and that do not enable but can prevent the very access to mobility that Sheller describes. It questions the injustice and sometimes violence associated with the process of 'becoming evacuee,' as well as the often halting motions and mobilities of returning. It unpicks the negotiation and ambiguity of identity as profiles and registration practices are continuously befuddled, escaped, and frequently gotten wrong. And it follows the consequences of all this for our mobile lives, made potentially more vulnerable by the very systems intended for our security.

GOVERNING THE EVACUEE

The current efforts we will explore try to turn the evacuee into a far more addressable subject through satellite systems, mobile technologies, social media, and interconnected systems. These advances, relying upon certain trigger moments, tipping points, or 'somatic markers' to facilitate political capital and technological will, have clearly not just happened on their own but in a broader and longer historical context. In this section we will draw something of a partial genealogy of the management and (pre)mediation of evacuee mobilities from the Second World War.

An Administration of Evacuation

Modern and, importantly, state-led evacuation measures developed in Western Europe in preparation for aerial bomber attack. The evacuation or 'billeting' of children from vulnerable urban areas and city centres to rural communities and the countryside is in many respects unlike the kinds of evacuation systems this chapter is concerned with. The eventual responsibility for a state for moving its people out of the way of disaster, however, was something of a novel thing. Adi Ophir (2007) locates this original intervention in the 1920s, finding that as late as 1900, even a hurricane hitting the port of Galveston, Texas, did not warrant the resolve of a state to step in in order to bring relief or defend its citizens from the repercussions of disaster. As Ophir writes,

> only at the end of the nineteenth century did the practice of saving lives become a profession, an art, and a science, as it was developed on the margins, and as an extension, of medicine, public health, the police, and the army, and it took a few more decades before this growing body of knowledge, techniques, and practices was integrated into the state apparatuses.
>
> (2007, 16)

This is not entirely accurate. The history of the European colonial imperial rivalries could well be a story of state and citizen evacuation following successions of territorial disputes overturning colonial outposts and stations. However, the natural disasters that might require evacuation and other measures of protection saw states beginning to relate to them no longer as inevitable catastrophes from which it (and its elites) would evacuate themselves to somewhere safer (as in the plague). Disaster instead became a providential moment for a state or sovereign to extend its powers to the protection of the population from harm.

Modern aerial war threatened populations like never before. In Britain, pre-war imaginaries heavily informed planning through the inter-war Committee of Imperial Defence, who were confronted with the first realities of aerial warfare and the difficulties in protecting the daily routines of a workforce so essential to public life (Adey, 2010) and the continuation of industrial production and services so essential to fighting a war. The evacuation of children was considered at length; the enormously complex process of moving almost 3 million people was coordinated by the Ministry of Health from vulnerable areas to 'reception' areas through a range of scheduled and organised transport to people's homes and buildings (O'Brien, 1955). Some of these were camp-like structures built for the purpose, while others were requisitioned. Some elderly and vulnerable people also followed in the children's footsteps.

In the United States, where much of this chapter focuses, the largest-scale evacuations took on quite a different and in some ways far more disturbing form than the population security intended to remove a valued life to safety. Instead, the Japanese attack on Pearl Harbor saw the increasing paranoia towards apparent 'enemy aliens' and 'disloyal citizens' become more intensively directed at the Japanese (of first- and second-generation migrants, notwithstanding that existing racial tensions already remained and manifested in protests over 'American' jobs). 120,000 people or effectively Americans of Japanese Ancestry under the executive 'evacuation' order 9066, signed by President Roosevelt, were removed from their constitutional and amendment rights wholesale. Those of Japanese descent were first voluntarily and then forcibly moved away from strategic 'vital' military exclusion zones created on America's West Coast, particularly around LA and San Francisco, following several very dubious assumptions based on the Census Bureau's detailed demographic data of the location of Japanese communities around sensitive locations (Ng, 2002).

The evacuees were eventually settled in internment camps in out of the way remote locations, perhaps most famously at Manzanar, California, nestled between the Sierra Nevada mountains, and in the Alabama foothills (Houston and Houston, 2002). Such a process involved a suitably large scale registration system conducted by the War Relocation Authority and the Western Defences Command based on initial registration of 'aliens' first by the Justice Department which required photography, fingerprinting, and relatively detailed registration data. Considerable information sharing also occurred with the FBI, who investigated suspects and made apprehensions of other individuals who were highlighted to them. Under categorisation as Japanese Citizens, Japanese-American Citizens, and Alien Enemies other than Japanese, the blanket order meant anyone inside these categories was subjected to evacuation from the designated military areas.

Like the diagrams of zones and stages of evacuation logistics routinely performed by militaries, civilian evacuation appeared a bureaucratic, administrative, and orderly affair of plans, sequences, and operations represented in link and node diagrams. Of course, these abstractions tell us much less about the lived experiences they represented or of their potential violence. In the wake of Pearl Harbour and other events of the war, outspoken public commentators and influential newssheets encouraged the wider public, as part of a broader effort, to seek out 'saboteurs,' 'fifth columnists,' and 'enemy aliens' resident in the United States. For the Japanese American experience, this meant overt forms of racial profiling through measures coloured by pseudo-patriotic racial suspicion to, for instance, discriminate between a person of Chinese and Japanese ancestry in order to 'shop' a potential evacuee to the authorities for questioning and eventual 'evacuation'/internment, first through assembly centers and then to one of the 10 'reception' or internment camps located away from the military exclusion zone that encircled many parts of California and the West Coast. Like many other forms of internment/registration, the evacuees were similarly given a number. Mine Okubo (1946), an artist who described and sketched her experiences of internment, titled her book *Citizen 13660*. The bureaucratic-militaristic and racially coded rendering of the Japanese 'evacuees' was thus a process of inscription: of representations, of tags and markers that individuated and abstracted those subjects for evacuation, processing, and internment.

Cold War Cultures of Simulation

For the period between the Second World War and the hinge point we want to focus on—that is evacuation management following Hurricane Katrina—it is impossible to do justice to the nuanced historical, political, and technological changes regarding evacuation. Evacuations have differed greatly by cause, by intensity, by temporality, by frequency, by planning (Cutter and Barnes, 1982). Neither is it adequate to detail the structural changes emergency evacuation responds to—a changing state system, post-war geopolitical shifts, and post-colonial moves resulting in mass evacuation movements, for example, in the formation of Israel and the partition of India that rendered dispossessed populations on the fault-lines of territory (Aguiar, 2011). What is clear, though, is that like the Japanese-American experience, populations have been moved under 'evacuation' as an almost euphemism. It is, however, important to acknowledge the emerging cultures of prediction, experimentation, and play that brought evacuation into a technical-imaginary domain of anticipatory simulation science (Ghamari-Tabrizi, 2009).

Geography's post-war academic complicity in this is becoming clearer, as historical geographers such as Trevor Barnes and Matthew Farish have outlined the role of the discipline in the deployment of operational research methods in the pursuit of evacuation planning, for example, of Bremerton, Washington, in the mid-1950s. As they argue, "Urban evacuation's lines of flight and the systemic grids of emergency response represented a rational ideal, but also the refined unreality of abstraction" (Barnes and Farish, 2006, 820). In this Cold War context, evacuation mobilities became the subject of increasingly complex stochastic models on the one hand—abstracted into the variables of a burgeoning positivist science—and on the other, the literal thought experiments of military intellectuals writing scenarios which inspired the more practical lived abstractions of evacuation war gaming. Those 'games' or 'exercises' were built primarily around the management and coordination of a displaced population leaving in response or in advance of nuclear attack.

In the late 1950s, however, strategy was famously balanced between shelter and dispersal. In America's cities, urban analysis was brought to vulnerability mapping. While in World War II in Britain as well as America this urban geography was attentive to understanding the movement of explosive blast through the channels of the urban landscape (Adey, 2010), post-war saw far finer-grain analysis of how those channels could permit the movement of evacuating people. The Federal Civil Defence Administration, learning the lessons of detailed analysis of Tokyo and Nagasaki, drew detailed maps and overlay tracings which would reimagine the urban landscape as a network of evacuation escape. These representations would overlay the identification of likely targets; the cities' probable distribution of civilians; and the overall defence pattern of the cities, including engineering department designs on traffic control and evacuation assembly (Collier and Lakoff,

2008). Building heights might determine whether they would be likely to block streets. Evacuation routes could thus be designed on much more coordinated basis. Even while these kinds of threats now seem far-fetched, and the threat was predominantly nuclear, the possibility of evacuation also drew on the lessons of other sorts of events of much less of an order than the disruption or loss of life predicted in nuclear apocalypse. For example, the Audrey Hurricane of 1957, which killed at least 500 people in Louisiana, Texas, and the Bolivar peninsula, brought evacuation to the public's attention as a credible measure of broader emergency planning, and response.

Preparing for evacuation composed a general strategy to pre-mediate emergency events in anticipation of their occurrence through a variety of representational analytical forms. The Federal Civil Defence Administration developed the formulaic and statistical modelling of evacuation motion to develop calculations of survival probability following a thermo-nuclear detonation. Variables included the speed of evacuation, the positioning of shelters along the evacuation route, and, notably, the critical relation to when the evacuation occurred. In this reasoning, an evacuee would be far safer taking shelter at the time of detonation than they would be travelling. On the other hand, should evacuees leave before detonation, and depending on the following radiation fallout, it could have a considerable effect on population survivability. Neither were these tactics immune from other cultures of (auto)mobility, despite some of the myths surrounding the automobile's centrality in US civil defence measures (Packer, 2008)—particularly the design of the interstate system. The ideal mobile unit to replace the individual, the burgeoning evacuation science began to privilege the automobile as an ideal vector of escape (an assumption that would come to feature high on the list of criticisms of the events in New Orleans in 2005; Bartling, 2006; Cresswell, 2006). And insofar as the involvement of figures such as Bertrand Klass, who conducted psychological surveys of reactions to bombing, and director of Stanford Research Institute's Applied Behavioural Science research division (and even wrote on subliminal advertising), could have guaranteed the significant study of the psychology of the individual or family, these approaches generally reduced the evacuee to an aggregation or as a line of flight. In these early models, the evacuee was simply a line of movement in a greater conglomeration of fleeing and semi-rational subjects (Orr, 2006).

Agents

Just as these approaches receded from military authorship following the height of Cold War nuclear dispersal planning which had found concrete form in the structural planning of backyard bunkers, large-scale post-war suburban development, highway planning, and inner-urban degradation, other fields took on the mantle of evacuation mobility studies in response to a wider set of threats, such as natural disasters, chemical accidents, and

Incident ____________________
Place ____________________
Year ____________________

I. Incident.

1. Nature: Natural ____________ Accident ____________ Exercise ____________
2. Description: ____

____

____

____

3. Build-up: Instant ____________ Hours ____________ Days ____________
4. Prior Warning: Of Possibility: No ______ Yes ______ When _____ How ____________
   Of Approach: No ______ Yes ______ When _____ How ____________
   Of Event: No ______ Yes ______ When _____ How ____________
5. Time of Event: Date ____________ Hour ____________

II. The Evacuation.

1. Area Evacuated: ____
2. Reception Area: ____
3. Number of Evacuees: ____________ Total Population ____________
4. Time of Evacuation: Start: Day ______ Hour ______ ; Finish: Day ______ Hour ______
5. Evacuation Order: By ____________ In Name of ____________
6. Spontaneous: No ______ Yes ______ Triggered By ____________
7. Movement Control: No ______ Yes ______ By ____________

III. The Preparation.

1. Plan: No ______ Yes ______ By ____________ Date ______
2. Publicized: No ______ Yes ______ By ____________ How ____________
3. Exercise: Government: No ______ Yes ______ Date ____________
   Public: No ______ Yes ______ Date ____________
4. previous Evacuations: No ______ Yes ______ Dates ____________

IV. Results: ____

1. Deaths: No ______ Yes ______ Number ____________
2. Injured: No ______ Yes ______ Number ____________
3. After-Incident Report: No ______ Yes ______ Findings ____________

____

____

Recommendations ____

____

V. Documentation: ____

____

Figure 11.1 Evacuation study sheet
Source: Strope et al., 1975.

fire. The concern of several evacuation scholars at the time was that longer-term analysis of the effectiveness of evacuation plans was particularly difficult to achieve given the inadequacy of effective record keeping during an evacuation and in after-action reports following an emergency (Strope, Devaney and Nehněvajsa, 1975). Insofar as the evacuee had been made known within earlier bureaucratic techniques, broader analytical metrics were not being recorded systematically to permit longer-term analysis across multiple-type emergencies.

As improved ways to record evacuation would develop along with techniques to register and process evacuees, advances in computing saw the new approaches reaching their finest resolution ever in the evolution from fluid-flow models that averaged out the uncertainty of individual behaviours (Henderson, 1974) towards the individual itself. The move in rapidly developing changes in personal computer use and far more sophisticated software transformed evacuation simulation. The finer granularity of 'agent-based' modelling techniques could assign a range of rule-based characteristics to agents that would simulate individual behaviour and what that might mean for aggregate crowd behaviour. This meant that for the first time, individuals could be simulated and visualised in evacuation scenarios. These simulations would be used especially for fire evacuations, for example, of major buildings such as airports and railway stations, and understandably for more routine forms of mobility, such as traffic flow.

In conclusion, evacuation techniques have evolved through a variety of bureaucratic means to manage large population groups. The evacuee has been subjected to increasing layers of abstraction and representation which has become, perhaps, increasingly distanced from the evacuee itself. So we see advances in cultures of anticipation and simulation informing the design of cities, built spaces, and evacuation plans with a sort of shadow evacuee in their models. In the following section, we explore how and some of the arguments why this distance is being foreshortened.

THE 'DIGITAL EVACUEE'

Hurricane Katrina formed over the Bahamas on August 23, 2005, and dissipated across the US's Great Lakes a week later. As has been well documented, over these 7 days, it inflicted more than $100 billion worth of damage, devastated New Orleans and parts of other states in its path, and claimed nearly 2,000 lives (Knabb, Rhome and Brown, 2006.). The storm also precipitated one of the largest evacuations in US history, with 1.2 million residents along the Gulf Coast subject to either voluntary or mandatory evacuation orders and nearly 800,000 eventually being displaced (FEMA, 2006). The effects of the hurricane were so devastating that, in its aftermath, the name 'Katrina' was retired by the World Meteorological Organization at the behest of the US government. Whether this was out of respect for the victims of the disaster or so that the government could avoid, rhetorically at least, 'another Katrina'-style catastrophic policy failure is debatable. Certainly, the failures of emergency management during Katrina were manifold, with the paucity of effective evacuee tracking one amongst many other ways that the evacuee failed to be truly grasped by the different emergency systems.

Grasping Evacuation

By following the evacuee tracking debacle, we can expound the crucial way Hurricane Katrina has led to sustained yet fragmented production of the digitally mediated and—especially—tracked evacuee. And through that, we can unpack how perhaps the failures of Katrina showed the evacuee up in the terms of what Jenny Edkins (2011) has called the 'person as such' as opposed to the person as a 'who.' In other words, the evacuation measures we will explore, in rendering the evacuee locatable and eventually digital, have tended to treat the evacuee as abstract coordinates rather than as fleshy, feeling, and complex mobile subjects.

Of the 1.2 million Americans who were issued with evacuation orders, only a small proportion were really all that known in any form of record keeping at the time, with a fuller picture of where this population dispersed emerging months, even years later (Groen and Polivka, 2008). Whilst, as we have seen, the US had already tackled certain evacuee issues of 'tracking' in earlier decades, the onus was more readily on anticipating and planning for where they would go and by what means. Being able to account for the location of evacuees on this scale was unheralded, with many of Katrina's victims slipping into the gaps between physical tagging, paper-based records recorded at 'rest centres,' and, more widely, the overlapping jurisdictions affected by the disaster and, more bluntly, between those who self-evacuated and those who required assistance and received it.

Paper-based tracking systems given to those who required city and state aid, the norm at the time, were simply unfit for the purpose (Pate, 2008). Material tagging like this functioned in theory, but only if persons retained their paperwork at all times or recalled the information it contained should the documentation be lost—problems we will examine in more detail below. Naturally, though, in the confusion after Katrina, what worked well on paper was less efficacious in practice. Ironically, the monitoring of the hurricane itself and its complex environmental effects was probably far more successful. Much more was known about the morphology of the hurricane's weather system by meteorological radar. The natural disaster itself was far easier to get a handle on than the social and technological disaster or 'complex humanitarian disaster' occurring (and produced) through the imperfect emergency response (Smith, 2006).

Perhaps the largest single failing pertaining to adequate registration, knowledge, and effective tracking of evacuation occurred during the disaster has been expressed in the strongest possible terms already. Naomi Klein (see Klein and Smith, 2008) referred to the 'ethnic cleansing' of the city by separation, as poor, vulnerable black communities were displaced and separated not merely by the hurricane, but by the practises that sought to manage the response.

The lack of effective tagging, record keeping, and information sharing meant that in many instances families who could not self-evacuate were divided, leaving parents unable to track down lost children and babies and other family members who could not be reunited for days, weeks, and in some cases months afterwards (Brandenburg, Watkins, Brandenburg and Schieche, 2007; Lindsay, 2010). Retrospective testimony of the events from the perspective of the military coordination reveals a certain kind of thinking in the 'heat' of the emergency moment, which help to explain the limitations of what seems to have been an 'exceptional' response, especially towards the respect of family ties and inter-personal associations, as above all, life came first (Graham, 2005). Accounts of survivors and local and state personnel reveal that some of the main problems in evacuating people away was that social groups, family units, friends, and other group dynamics were not properly envisaged or provided for in FEMA's and the city's emergency plans. It was as if the evacuee was treated as one of the disembodied agents in evac simulations or simply a flow to be redirected out of the way, as opposed to a subject who sustains and is maintained by subtle and vital but brittle relationships, fractured by the process of evacuation.

When people are evacuated, they often become more vulnerable because they are separated from formal and informal systems of care. Children separated from next of kin, siblings, and parents/guardians remained in a vulnerable state in relocation centers like Oklahoma's Camp Gruber. Those who were already known as homeless on the National Center for Missing and Exploited Children (NMEC) needed to be identified, too (Brandenburg et al., 2007). Patients that were given medical examinations at certain locations were unable to be treated at others because their diagnoses did not travel with them (Franco et al., 2006). There is now general consensus that of the some 1 million people displaced from New Orleans, very few were able to be effectively tied to their medical records, meaning that treatment, prescriptions, allergies, and prior medical history could not follow. Some hospitals taped patients' personal notes to their forearms before helicopters evacuated them elsewhere. The Veterans Association was one such exception, however, because the medical records of their members were electronic, which meant that those who were moved from Biloxi, Mississippi, and New Orleans could be effectively tracked as they moved around the country. Furthermore, 10 days after Katrina's landfall, a system was setup that would make private pharmacy data (such as those held at a Walmart) about an individual's repeat prescriptions available to doctors through a secure database.

Even those persons in custody within the criminal-justice system, including more than 2,000 'registered' sex offenders despite being, perhaps, the most visible, were just as problematically treated. Some were notably evacuated without pertinent judicial authorities being informed at the point of reception (Arlikatti, Kendra and Clark, 2012). But the prison system also presents an interesting case, because it is often held up as an area in which evacuation plans and technologies are usually the most comprehensive. Except in Katrina's case, the example of Orleans Parish prison presented one of the worst cases of the legal abandonment of evacuation plans, protocols, and civil rights, as the ACLU's documentary and written evidence has shown, and illustrated numerous abuses. Not to mention the fact that the Louisiana courts, their personnel, and the wide-spread mobility of the Louisiana judiciary during Katrina meant that the state was practically evacuated of its legal system (Guidry, 2009), the ACLU (2006; Metzger, 2006) have illustrated how forms of abandonment were effectively written into Louisiana law. All persons in custody of the Parish of New Orleans are to be released for a period of 10 days upon the declaration of emergency, disaster, or evacuation in the US or State or city of New Orleans, and asked to make their own way out of the disaster or register for city or state assistance.[1]

What we see in Katrina was the moment that the evacuee—as constituted in the various ways discussed—made its inadequacies so visible. Since World War II, many of the measures designed to track evacuees have concerned two contradictory populations: those 'at risk' (e.g. medical patients) and those 'posing risk' (felons). Whilst 'vulnerable' populations such as medical patients (to illness and special needs) and felons (to escape and potential reoffending) were subject to special, albeit faltering concern as we saw earlier during Katrina, the hurricane also presented challenges for a much wider population and long after the event. The existing systems prior to and during Katrina were unsophisticated by their imagination of the evacuee, who they were, what they needed, inadequately assessing their mobilities capabilities. Furthermore, they were performed in the almost complete absence of software or ICT despite the fact that so much of an evacuee's identity might have existed within several different sorts of organisations, bureaucracies, and sectors, from health to social security in electronic form. More often than not, it proved impossible to unite the actual evacuee fully with the less-than-fragmented digital imprint of him- or herself.

Since Katrina, and the ensuing political fallout, congressional inquiries and subsequent changes to the practice of emergency planning and response within the United States, the onus has been on the broadening of what we might call specific 'technologies of address' (Thrift, 2004, 585) through the development of different tracking programs. For Thrift, locatable or location-aware technologies are producing what he calls a "*'technological unconscious' whose content is the bending of bodies-with-environments to a specific set of addresses without the benefit of any cognitive inputs*" first evolving from the military arts of logistics. In evacuation management, this has meant seeking to produce legible evacuees so that they might be easily and automatically locatable in geographic space as well as within wider systems of records.

Such technologies have their own particular geographies and may result in the prioritisation of certain bodies. Like the reaction of the federal government to Katrina more broadly, we will explore how tracking after the hurricane was enmeshed in the politics of the mobile body, especially its abilities and disabilities, its material advantages and disadvantages, and perhaps, in the case of Texas' evacuee tracking system, even its 'racial' characteristics that have been tied into a broader migration politics of welfare provision and care.

Tracking the Evacuee

Some of the immediate changes following Katrina occurred through the Department of Transport, particularly as a means to survey, in real time, the kinds of mobility pathways evacuees could exploit during an emergency. Dedicated 'Evaculanes' form the basis of many city and state emergency plans, and these are now coupled with so-called 'smart roads,' which are now able to automatically monitor traffic conditions on relatively remote or rural roads by using radar, cameras, and video servers at strategic locations. Before Texas introduced a tracking system which is now being applied elsewhere by the federal government, FEMA began work on a nationwide effort, the National Mass Evacuation Tracking System (NMETS). The system, developed by FEMA's office of Geospatial Intelligence, was legislated by the Post Katrina Emergency Reform Act, and was designed "to assist States in tracking: Transportation-assisted evacuees [i.e. those requiring specialist transport, such as the disabled], household pets, luggage, medical equipment" (FEMA, 2010). In short, the system was intended to track vulnerable populations and their accoutrements. Since 2010, the NMETS software and training has been provided free of charge whilst states are responsible for the costs of equipment and maintenance.

NMETS demonstrated particularly well the disjuncture between traditional systems and what even basic technologies could accomplish. States wishing to adopt NMETS, either in whole or in part, could opt for one of three options: a stand-alone, paper-based system (Paper-based Evacuation Support Tool); a simple digital system (Low-tech Evacuation Support Tool); or a high-tech digital system (Advanced Technology Evacuation Support Tool; FEMA, 2010, 2012).

The paper-based system can be used alone and also as a backup should the more advanced systems fail. As a four-ply carbon copy, the form is an effective bureaucratic record of key information, including the following categories: name, address, gender, age, contact number, head of household, medical needs, caregiver contact details, parent/guardian or caregiver information, medical equipment, household pets, luggage, as well as transport mode, carrier, and details. The second option effectively turns this record into an entry within a Microsoft Access database, which means reports can be drawn in real time and shared quickly and easily allowing, for instance, the manifesting of a group to be evacuated by bus to be planned with some ease. The more advanced option means both RFID and barcode tags and more advanced software for RFID tethering, more advanced evacuee searches, and the export of the data in other formats.

All three systems promise to overcome the particular issue of separated families through the use of barcode wristbands which are given to evacuees and their important possessions. This means that all members of a household, including their things, are tied together in the system. The bands are then scanned at each site to record the evacuee's location and their departure/arrival times. From this information, responders can use the knowledge of where evacuees are and where they are likely to go to inform decision making. Furthermore, the system is designed to red-flag minors who are unaccompanied in order that they might be reported to the correct authorities and agencies before or during evacuation. The system also records evacuees with particular medical needs, recording whether they have sufficient medication and whether they require a caregiver.

In aggregate, NMETS is composed of both manual and computer-based elements, functioning through paper records, but also "the Internet, handheld scanners, laptop computers, tethered USB scanners and/or RFID readers" (FEMA, 2012). NMETS is a technological assemblage that addresses the evacuee, their body, identity, and correspondent records in a variety of ways and through a variety of pinch points. The system ultimately tries to correct the mistakes of Katrina in a way that imagines and records the evacuee as a potentially mobile body which is not abstracted from the things and relations they need.

Although FEMA pioneered this national response to the disaster, programmes like NMETS were also being implemented at lesser scales, and perhaps for more dubious reasons. Of all the states that received evacuees from New Orleans and the wider Louisiana area, Texas was foremost amongst them, receiving more than 250,000 persons, mostly in its largest city, Houston (Godoy, 2006). But the benevolence of the state and city was rewarded, at least in the opinion of some, by an increase in crime and antisocial behaviour, with police officers reporting a spike in emergency calls in those areas densely populated by evacuees, and the latter victims or suspects in about 20% of the city's murders, despite being less than 10% of the (new, total) population (this was reflected in mainstream national and local news CNN, 2006). As a result,

> Many of the evacuees who stayed on in Houston found the welcome mat quickly pulled . . . blamed for a rising crime rate, especially murders, and accused of playing the system—having their housing paid by the government while making little effort to find a job.
>
> (Buchanan, 2010)

Evacuation was threatening. Far from progressively destabilising many bounded senses of place, identity, and security, it seemed to reinforce them (Harvey, 1996), despite the fact that some studies have found really only very modest increases in crime (Varano, Schafer, Cancino, Decker and Greene, 2010).

Many evacuees appeared on the centralised federal databases of those entitled to housing benefit, and so requiring remuneration and welfare accordingly. Despite some of its own citizens being affected, the principal 'evacuee problem' encountered by Texas, and Houston, was the management of a neighbouring state's displaced persons. As Godoy (2006) reflected, a year after Katrina, "So many evacuees came to Texas and stayed that the state undertook its own accounting." Part of this 'accounting' was the development of the Special Needs Evacuation Tracking System (SNETS) in 2007, the country's putative first statewide citizen-evacuation system, which would use an array of technologies such as RFID, wireless, and mobile data to allow evacuees to be located in real time, with private-sector support from Radiant RFID, AT&T, and Intermedix, amongst others.

At first, as the name suggests, it focussed on vulnerable groups only, especially those with medical needs, but later this was broadened to include all segments of the population and the re-designation of the System as the Emergency Tracking Network (State of Texas, n.d.). We are faced, then, with the perhaps uncomfortable chain of causality that saw Texas house the majority of Katrina evacuees, followed by reportedly higher crime rates in cities such as Houston and the designation of 'problem evacuees,' followed by the state's adoption of an enhanced system for managing and tracking evacuees in the future. Whether the second on some level inspired the latter or whether the first link in this chain directly fed the last is a matter of speculation, but certainly the creation of the 'digital evacuee' remains bound up with issues of the most basic corporeality of what to do with bodies that require help and welfare.

Evacuation tracking has its own particular geographies and intensities, with bodies becoming more visible, physically and digitally, at certain nodes when moving through certain spaces. It is an assemblage that also works through multiple scales simultaneously, drawing together information from national, state, and local levels. A huge amount of work is still required to make systems at each level interoperable, reconciling the data collected from feeder points, such as hospitals, with centralised, national databases. Cross-cutting these geographical concerns are therefore issues of public and private stewardship over data (Lyon, 2003). In the wake of Katrina and the systems employed by Texas and FEMA, a host of private companies have emerged into the nascent evacuee tracking industry. In addition to Radiant RFID, Motorola and AT&T, who engineered the Texan system, Axcess International Inc., Disaster Management Systems, EVACTrak, Elliot Data Systems, LINSTAR, Med Media, Midwest Card and ID Solutions, Multicard US, Salamander Technologies, and Transition Works Software are all developing systems that will use RFID tags and other, more complex databases to keep track of evacuees. If this reflects the proliferation of tracking systems, it is also the addition of another layer in the increasing overlap between private and public security policies and solutions. But how will such an overlap be regulated and legislated? Who will maintain and service such systems, retrieve and store the information that they provide? While in one instance in Texas a federal judge was brought in to arbitrate the dispute behind a school's student tracking system on religious beliefs, such individual attention may not be possible as evacuee tracking systems multiply, expand, and institutionalise themselves into the apparatuses of state and federal governance over emergencies.

In the wake of these developments, the evolving inter-disciplinary fields of crisis and disaster informatics are providing other kinds of avenues for tracking potential evacuees and the displaced through more advanced forms of the collection and analysis of big data and social media networks. Crowd-sourcing community sentiment, for example, can provide more effective early warning of emerging threats or real-time disasters such as an earthquake quicker than the seismographs can transmit information (Hughes and Palen, 2009). They can also prove effective ways to establish where people are who might in need of evacuation, or, for example, to assess the welfare and well-being of evacuees once relocated. Unsurprisingly, this is not being led solely by the state. Civil society and activist groups such as Geeks without Bounds have proven the value of correlating information gathered through social media with geographical information system (GIS) –generated maps in Hurricane Sandy. But the newfound accessibility of people in emergencies through mobile technology can run up some different sets of questions. For example, Buscher (2013) has shown that the civilians who could not evacuate Utøya Island in Norway in 2011 became visible to the shooter Anders Behring Breivik because friends and relatives rang people's mobile phones who were hiding. Being locatable, in other words, can have some unlikely but devastating effects in particular emergencies.

The vulnerability of such bodies may well then be something constructed by the assemblage of digital technologies, if and when they enter it, as well as contemporary evacuee tracking systems. After Katrina, many displaced aliens avoided seeking government assistance, and certainly government tracking systems, because of their fears that the latter were being yoked together with the Department of Homeland Security's immigration databases (see Lindsay, 2011). In this instance, the state was already exercising control over the mobility and identification of individuals. The state claimed a stake in their future mobility by arrest, detention, even deportation should they be found as non-citizens. So we are left with the familiar question (albeit in different contexts) of what about those people more broadly that, even in emergencies, simply do not wish to be tracked and subjected to the scrutiny that comes with technologies of address? What if we object to the marking or 'tagging' of the body (Aas, 2006) through not only the concerns of privacy and civil liberties advocates but under religious freedoms. These questions portend to the issues with which evacuee tracking will need to contend in the future, especially if more far-reaching and compulsory evacuee tracking systems are promulgated going forward.

As detailed, the onus on evacuation planning appears to be to harmonise and join up previously distributed but siloed and fragmented databases and disparate registration systems and piloted tracking programmes held within a multitude of private providers, contractors, and local and federal government services. In this sense, the digital evacuee, like the passenger, finds itself mobile and interoperable across numerous systems of records that are being made to speak to each other in an albeit piecemeal fashion. In the future, for example, might it be possible for an airline reservation system to serve as a digital feeder point for a medical evacuee being transported through the secured, ordered mobilities of the airport? And how might this integrate with the myriad other non-governmental actors that provide assistance during emergencies, like the shelter registration programmes of the American Red Cross? To date, the privacy implications of such emergency management information systems (EMIS) have been given only limited attention, but as these systems proliferate and the technology behind them evolves, such concerns promise to move toward the forefront of critical agendas.

For Buscher, such practices may mean the obstruction or rendering "impossible lived practices of privacy boundary management." We also don't have to look to the United States to find examples of the potential implications of these practices or, conversely, when regulation intended to protect personal data is misapplied or abused. For instance, some of the very criticisms of the response effort to the 2005 7/7 attacks on London were the ways in which the 1998 Data Protection Act was applied in some cases overzealously that obstructed the efficient sharing of information about individuals between different emergency responders and organisations (Armstrong, Ashton and Thomas, 2007; Buscher, 2013).

CONCLUSION

It is important not to get ahead of ourselves. It is not all that clear how many of these systems are currently active and how many are dormant, awaiting the federal and/or state contracts that will warrant their implementation. At present, most evacuation systems, outside FEMA's and Texas' developments, draw on the kinds of hospital and prison technologies outlined previously, including low-tech tagging, to make an evacuee visible and readable via wristband and simple paper records to store their pertinent details and information. The material cultures of address of the past may be slated for supersession, but they are still required in current tracking methods. Indeed, the material dimension of tracking will never be completely lost, in that chips, cards, and other devices that can be read remotely will continue to be a part of the evacuee tracking assemblage, even if the records to which such materials pertain may increasingly become a part of the digital, rather than physical, landscape.

But even if the digital evacuee can ever perform the automated, interoperable, and joined-up dream that seems embedded within the projects of emergency planners, policy makers, and private industry, the contradiction always facing these bureaucracies and systems is how the evacuees they are seeking to address through processes of identification, tracking, and tracing evade the records and representations that stand in for them. It is not simply because the digital double or fragment of the evacuee is somehow incomplete. Rather, as Edkins has explored, there is a certain homology between "systems of registration, identification, and control and a process of objectification—the production of people as nothing but objects of administration" (2011, 7). In other words, for Edkins (2011), and as we've seen in evacuation, the intractable 'messy' person, with all their idiosyncrasies, their choices, their motivations, their friendships, and their complex associations and loves, 'gets in the way.'

NOTE

1. Municipal Court of Louisiana, 2007, En Banc Order, ACLU.

REFERENCES

ACLU. (2006) *Abandoned and Abused: Orleans Parish Prisoners in the Wake of Hurricane Katrina*. New York: ACLU, National Prisons Project.

AAS, K.F. (2006) "The Body Does Not Lie": Identity, Risk and Trust in Technoculture. *Crime, Media, Culture*, 2(2). p. 143–158.

AAS, K.F. (2011) "Crimmigrant" Bodies and Bona Fide Travelers: Surveillance, Citizenship and Global Governance. *Theoretical Criminology*, 15(3). p. 331–346.

ADEY, P. (2010) *Aerial Life: Spaces, Mobilities, Affects*. Oxford: Wiley.

AGAMBEN, G. (1998) *State of Exception*. Chicago: University of Chicago Press.

AGUIAR, M. (2011) *Tracking Modernity: India's Railway and the Culture of Mobility*. Minneapolis: University of Minnesota Press.

ARLIKATTI, S., KENDRA, J. & CLARK, N.A. (2012) Challenges for Multi-sector Organizations in Tracking and Sheltering Registered Sex Offenders in Disasters. *Journal of Homeland Security and Emergency Management*, 9(1). p. 1547–1573.

BARNES, T. J., & FARISH, M. (2006). Between Regions: Science, Militarism, and American Geography from World War to Cold War. *Annals of the Association of American Geographers*, 96 (4). p. 807–826.

BARTLING, H. (2006) Suburbia, Mobility, and Urban Calamities. *Space and Culture*, 9(1). p. 60–62.

BRANDENBURG, M.A., WATKINS, S.M, BRANDENBURG, K.L., SCHIECHE, C. (2007) Operation Child-ID: Reunifying Children with Their Guardians after Hurricane Katrina. *Disasters*, 31(3). p. 277–287.

BUCHANAN, M. (2010) Katrina Evacuees Found Welcome and Worries in Texas. BBC News Online. Available from www.bbc.co.uk/news/world-us-canada-11117607 [Accessed 23–11–2014]

BUSCHER, M. (2013) *A New Manhattan Project?: Interoperability and Ethics in Emergency Response Systems of Systems*. ISCRAM Conference, Baden-Baden, Germany, 12–15 May 2013.

COLLIER, S.J. & LAKOFF, A. (2008) Distributed Preparedness: The Spatial Logic of Domestic Security in The United States. *Environment and Planning. D, Society and Space*, 26(1). p. 7.

CRESSWELL, T. (2006) *On the Move: Mobility in the Modern Western World*. New York: Routledge.

CRESSWELL, T., BERGMANN, S. & SAGER, T. (2008) Understanding Mobility Holistically: The Case of Hurricane Katrina. In Bergmann S. & Sager, T. (eds.) *The Ethics of Mobilities: Rethinking Place, Exclusion, Freedom and Environment*. London: Ashgate, 129–140.

CUTTER, S. & BARNES, K. (1982) Evacuation Behavior and Three Mile Island. *Disasters*, 6(2). p. 116–124.

EDKINS, J. (2011) *Missing: Persons and Politics*. New York: Cornell University Press.

FEMA. (2006) *A Federal Response to Hurricane Katrina: Lessons Learned*. Washington (DC): FEMA

FEMA. (2010) *National Mass Evacuation Tracking Systems*. Washington (DC): FEMA.

FEMA. (2012) *Individual assistance: National Mass Evacuation Tracking System*. Washington (DC): FEMA.

FRANCO, C. et al. (2006) Systemic Collapse: Medical Care in the Aftermath of Hurricane Katrina. *Biosecurity and Bioterrorism: Biodefense Strategy, Practice, and Science*, 4(2). p. 135–146.

GHAMARI-TABRIZI, S. (2009) *The Worlds of Herman Kahn: The Intuitive Science of Thermonuclear War*. Cambridge, MA.: Harvard University Press.

GODOY, M. (2006) Katrina: One Year Later: Tracking the Katrina Diaspora: A Tricky Task *NPR News*: Available from http://www.npr.org/news/specials/katrina/oneyearlater/diaspora/ [Accessed 12–11–2013]

GRAHAM, S. (2005) Cities under Siege: Katrina and The Politics of Metropolitan America. Social Science Research Council: Understanding Katrina: Perspectives from the Social Sciences. Available from http://forums.ssrc.org/understandingkatrina/author/sgraham/ [Accessed 12–11–2013]

GROEN, J.A. & POLIVKA, A.E. (2008) Hurricane Katrina Evacuees: Who They Are, Where They Are, and How They Are Faring. *Monthly Labor Review*. 33(March). p. 32–51.

GUIDRY, G.G. (2009) Louisiana Judiciary: In the Wake of Destruction. The *LA Law Review*, 70. p. 1145.

HANNAM, K., SHELLER, M. & URRY, J. (2006) Editorial: Mobilities, Immobilities and Moorings. *Mobilities*, 1(1). p. 1–22.

HARVEY, D. (1996) *Justice, Nature and the Geography of Difference*. London: Wiley.

HELBING, D., FARKAS, I. J., MOLNAR, P., & VISEK, T. (2002) Simulation of Pedestrian Crowds in Normal and Evacuation Situations. *Pedestrian and Evacuation Dynamics*, 21. p. 21–58.

HENDERSON, L.F. (1974) On the Fluid Mechanics of Human Crowd Motion. *Transportation Research*, 8(6). p. 509–515.

HOUSTON, J.W. & HOUSTON, J.D. (2002) *Farewell to Manzanar: A True Story of Japanese American Experience During and After the World War II Internment*. New York: Houghton Mifflin.

HUGHES, A.L. & PALEN, L. (2009) Twitter Adoption and Use in Mass Convergence and Emergency Events. *International Journal of Emergency Management*, 6(3). p. 248–260.

KLEIN, N. & SMITH, N. (2008) The Shock Doctrine: A Discussion. *Environment and Planning. D, Society and Space*, 26(4). p. 582.

KNABB, R.D., RHOME, J.R. & BROWN, D.P. (2006) *Tropical Cyclone Report: Hurricane Katrina*. National Hurricane Center.

LAKOFF, A. (2007) Preparing for the Next Emergency. *Public Culture*, 19(2). p. 247.

LINDSAY, B.R. (2011) *Federal Evacuation Policy: Issues for Congress*. Washington (DC): DIANE Publishing.

LYON, D. (2003) *Surveillance After September 11*. London: Polity.

LYON, D. (2007) *Surveillance Studies: An Overview*. Cambridge (UK), Malden (MA): Polity.

METZGER, P.R. (2006) Doing Katrina Time. *Tul. L. Rev.*, 81. p. 1175.

MONAHAN, T. (2007) "War Rooms" of the Street: Surveillance Practices in Transportation Control Centers. *The Communication Review*, 10(4) p. 367–389.

NG, W.L. (2002) *Japanese American Internment During World War II: A History and Reference Guide*. Westport (CT): Greenwood Press.

O'BRIEN, T.H. (1955) *Civil Defence*. London: H.M. Stationery Off.

OKUBO, M. (1946) *Citizen 13660*. Seattle, Washington: University of Washington Press.

OPHIR, A. (2007) The Two-State Solution: Providence and Catastrophe. *Theoretical Inquiries in Law*, 8(1). p. 117–160.

ORR, J. (2006) *Panic Diaries: A Genealogy of Panic Disorder*. Durham (NC): Duke University Press.

PACKER, J. (2008) *Mobility without Mayhem: Safety, Cars, and Citizenship*. Durham (NC): Duke University Press.

PATE, B.L. (2008) Identifying and Tracking Disaster Victims: State-of-the-art Technology Review. *Family & Community Health*, 31(1). p. 23–34.

SCOTT, J.C. (1999) *Seeing Like a State: How Certain Schemes to Improve the Human Condition Have Failed*. Cambridge (MA): Yale University Press.

SHELLER, M. (2013) The Islanding Effect: Post-Disaster Mobility Systems and Humanitarian Logistics in Haiti. *Cultural Geographies*, 20(2). p. 185–204.

SMITH, N. (2006) There's No Such Thing As a Natural Disaster. Understanding Katrina: *Perspectives from the Social Sciences*, 11.

STROPE, W.E., DEVANEY, J.F. & NEHNĚVAJSA, J. (1975) *Importance of Preparatory Measures in Disaster Evacuations*. Stanford (CA): Stanford Research Institute.

THRIFT, N. (2004) Movement-Space: The Changing Domain of Thinking Resulting from the Development of New Kinds of Spatial Awareness. *Economy and Society*, 33(4). p. 582–604.

URRY, J. (2007) *Mobilities*. London: Polity.

VARANO, S.P., SCHAFER, J. A., CANCINO, J. M., DECKER, S. H., & GREENE, J. R. (2010) A Tale of Three Cities: Crime and Displacement after Hurricane Katrina. *Journal of Criminal Justice*, 38(1). p. 42–50.

12 The Datafication of Mobility and Migration Management

The Mediating State and Its Consequences

Dennis Broeders and Huub Dijstelbloem

MONITORING AND DATAFYING HUMAN MOBILITY

Modern technologies have increased the possibilities for governments to gather and process data and this has increased the variety and the depth of governmental observation and monitoring. This variety includes the data from new technologies such as radar, infrared, and satellite technology ('the eye in the sky') that allow for different forms of observation and detection, while depth can be added through technologies such as ICT, biometrics, GIS technology, and statistical risk calculation. The more recent development of big data analysis is now also finding its way into public policy making. The state's perception of reality thus becomes more technologically and statistically mediated and 'datafied.' Data of various types and sources are processed, combined, and connected through networked databases. Even though policymakers often claim that technology merely does the same job faster and better, technology also changes both the substance and the nature of policy. For one thing, it brings new actors to the scene. Baker (2008) described the work of what he calls a new class of 'numerati' that data mine vast databases for correlations and use these to plan for the future. He primarily emphasized the commercial brand of this class, but there are public counterparts in ever larger numbers in, for example, counterterrorism (Balzacq, 2008; Monahan and Palmer, 2009), youth care (Schinkel, 2011; Keymolen and Broeders, 2013), international development (Taylor, 2015; Taylor and Broeders, 2015), and crisis management (see Adey and Kirby, this volume). For another, the use of ever bigger datasets necessitates policy thinking in terms of risks and increasingly favours correlations over causalities (Mayer-Schönberger and Cukier, 2013).

The application of new technologies of surveillance and networked database technologies has been very prominent in the field of the management of migration and international mobility (Amoore, 2006; Broeders, 2007, Balzacq, 2008; Dijstelbloem and Meijer, 2011; Johnson et al., 2011). All the keywords apply: large populations in relation to which policy problems are increasingly defined in terms of risks (risk of international terrorism, transnational crime, and violations of immigration law and policy, i.e. irregular border crossing and settlement, multiple asylum claims, etc.) and an ever-expanding network of surveillance systems and databases aimed at visualising, registering, mapping, monitoring, and profiling mobile (sub)populations. The new technologies analysed in this chapter 'connect' the monitoring and management of human mobility in the territorial borderlands of Europe—the surveillance of the green and especially the blue borders of the EU—with the territorially detached manifestations of 'border surveillance' that work through the 'stretched screens' (Lyon, 2009) that connect an emerging European network of public border, immigration, and law enforcement officials and private 'unofficials.' In these stretched screens various sources of data come together, are weighed according to risk profiles and/or correlations, and are made part of decision trees (Meijer, 2011; Van der Ploeg and Sprenkels, 2011; Amoore, 2013).

A number of these developments—that will be elaborated on in the chapter—resonate with insights from literature on ontological perspectives on the relationships between politics and technology. The central role for data, calculus and risk assessment in the management of mobility resembles Latour's concept of the 'centre of calculation' (Latour, 1987, 1993). The integration of various kinds of new technologies and data sources makes the question what the role of 'non-human actors' in this field of policy entails a very relevant one (e.g. Dijstelbloem and Broeders, 2015). Moreover, these developments may also cast a different light on the role of the state itself, a subject to which we will turn our attention in the concluding section. The main question is whether adding a thicker layer of information and data to policymaking and the remarkable increase in speed and real-time exchange of data changes the nature of the state and the state's agency. Therefore, this chapter aims to show how new technologies shape the policy perception of problems of migration and mobility and looks at how the role of the state itself transforms both on a conceptual as well as on an empirical level.

This chapter is structured in the following way. The first section sketches a theoretical view on the use of technologies and data applied to the matter of managing migration and mobility at the national and especially the European level. The following section investigates the way in which new technologies are applied in European border management—especially through the Eurosur programme—and concludes that the migrant's environment and the migration process have become increasingly datafied: all sorts of data from a myriad of sources are mashed to create a new 'situational awareness.' Next, we turn our attention to the way that migrants and travellers *themselves* have become datafied. The individual migrant and traveller are entered into various biometric databases, with an increasing number of data points to facilitate identification and, in the aggregate, data mining and profiling. Finally, we discuss the consequences of these developments for the position of the state and the state's agency. How can we interpret the process of datafication in migration and mobility management, and how does it influence the policy perspectives and implementation? How does it influence the status of the state as an actor in a technological network? What are the consequences of the state's role in collecting, displacing and transforming information for the materialization of legitimate decisions about citizens, travellers, and migrants?

HUMAN MOBILITY REGISTERED, CATEGORISED, AND DATAFIED

The sheer numbers of international mobility and the fast developments in modern surveillance technologies have changed the way states register, monitor, and deal with human mobility and migration. The nature of the border has changed drastically and is now 'everywhere' (Lyon, 2005), has become 'virtual' (Johnson et al., 2011), or has changed into a 'border security continuum' (Vaughan-Williams, 2010). New technologies of surveillance and the digitisation of information have drastically enhanced, intensified, and changed immigration and border policies. Many new technologies of visualisation, detection, and registration have been added to the policy instruments that governments and international organizations use to deal with human mobility in various places and stages of the migratory process (Düvell and Vollmer, 2011). Some technologies only yield direct operational information—think of infra-red or carbon dioxide scanners—but most (also) generate data on patterns of mobility and characteristics of the mobile populations. So eventually, most information, irrespective of its original technological nature ends up in the great information equalizer that is the database. Data from various different sources are broken down into bits and bytes and reassembled in databases that have become a cornerstone of modern migration policy, which is organized and executed through the 'stretched screens' (Lyon, 2009) of the immigration official. Increasingly the Internet has become the 'backbone of backbones' (Choucri, 2012, 151) that ties the various sources together and makes them accessible worldwide and in real time. Some of these new technologies then are very different from earlier forms of border and migration control. Data management, the calculation of risk factors, and the global use of biometric databases, profile, and digital watch lists that are able to link border control posts, embassies, consulates and field officers in refugee situations with and through the digital back offices of mobility monitoring and management. Whereas before migration officials primarily relied on their tacit knowledge—who is taken out of the queue for closer inspection—and a necessarily very limited 'watch list of people to look out for' in their direct surveillance of border flows, the gathering and analysis of data and the application of new technologies in passports and visas—chips and biometrics—for example, have shifted their attention in part to data flows rather than the actual moving bodies. More and more data is informing policy making and feeds into policy execution. Monitoring mobility and migration have changed drastically in the digital age.

As a result, the modern-day problem of immigration authorities lies in the governance of international mobility. According to Koslowski (2008, 105), "migration [is] not the 'new security issue'; it is increasing global mobility, which is primarily tourism and business travel." Indeed, the volume of international mobility is staggering (see Table 12.1). The number of people that annually pass the borders of the average OECD country is vast and dwarfs the numbers that are covered under the subheading of 'immigration.' Moreover, the risks and problems that haunt policy makers today—international terrorism, illegal migration, and transnational crime—are much more likely to be enveloped in the flow of human mobility than in the much smaller and more tightly regulated sub-flow of immigration and settlement.

Mobility has in the past decades become an integral part of modern life. Cresswell (2010, 27) places mobility at 'the heart of what it is to be modern.' At the same time, mobility is not for everyone: There is a politics of mobility in which the differential distribution of mobility produces some of the starkest differences today (Sparke, 2006; Cresswell, 2010). In short, international mobility is about (international) power relations and about separating the privileged from the non-privileged (Bauman, 1998). Lyon (2003, 142) states that surveillance has always been about 'social sorting', about the classification of populations as a precursor to differential treatment. Whether this is done using traditional technologies and techniques—such as 'classical' statistics—or through the use of new technologies and surveillance systems, the aim remains social sorting. Lyon (2007, 3) also noted that surveillance always moves somewhere on the continuum between care and control. Surveillance, visualisation, and categorisation are not a priori negative or positive for those subjected to them. Their effects are to a large part dependent on the policy aims that are underlying surveillance, although it will also be argued in this paper that the use of modern technologies alters policies themselves too. Technological instruments are, like

Table 12.1 International tourist arrivals 1995–2009 (in millions)

	1995	2000	2005	2007	2008	2009
World	533	683	802	901	919	880
• Advanced economies	339	423	451	496	494	470
• Emerging economies	194	260	351	405	425	410
United States	43.5	51.2	49.2	56	57.9	54.9
Europe	309.1	392.2	441	485.4	487.2	459.7
• France	60	77.2	75.9	80.8	79.2	74.2
• Spain	34.9	47.9	55.9	58.7	57.2	52.2
• Italy	31.1	41.2	36.5	43.7	42.7	43.2
• United Kingdom	23.5	25.2	28	30.9	30.1	28

Source: UNWTO 2009 and 2010.

other policy instruments, instruments of power. For states the monitoring of international mobility aims to 'filter out' those that desperately wish to remain unseen or, at the very least, to remain unidentified: terrorists, irregular migrants, and criminals. But it also serves to locate, categorize, and identify those that need to be found, recognized, and categorized in order to protect and aid populations such as refugees and internally displaced persons. Both categorization—identifying people as part of a group, or at least ascribing membership to them—and identification are vital for the digital monitoring and management of human mobility.

For one thing, risk, categorisation, and databases determine the options and treatment of travellers and migrants. According to Rose (2001, 7), risk can be understood as a "family of ways of thinking and acting, involving calculations about probable futures in the present followed by interventions into the present in order to control that potential future." Defining and calculating risks then determines, literally, how the state will watch its subjects, migrants, and visitors, what it will see and what it will 'think' of that. Risk categories, Jones (2009, 177) argues on the basis of Foucault, create power by "obscuring difference by forcing the multiple into manageable units (categories) with solid separations (boundaries) between them." Today, with risk calculation, categorisation, and networked databases taking centre stage in the monitoring and management of human mobility, the creation and the operational use of new digitally constructed facts has taken a quantum leap. Surveillance is about tracking flows and in these technologically mediated times, "the whole process shifts from being focused on persons to being focused on codes" (Brighenti, 2007 337).

In this respect, the state's organizations that are responsible for executing these policies resemble what Latour (1987, 1993) has called 'centers of calculation.' Centers of calculation are specific spots where experiments, expeditions, and data collection take place and where observations, information and knowledge are combined. They can be any site, a laboratory, a statistical institution, a data bank, and so forth (1999, 304). Characteristic to these sites is that the objects under study—in the case of border management, for example, travellers and migrants, but also routes, intermediaries, and various contexts—are represented into a sign, an archive, a document, a piece of paper, a trace (1999, 306). For example, since 2010 the UK operates a National Border Targeting Centre (as part of its eBorders programme to analyse passenger data on a number of high-risk routes; see Broeders and Hampshire, 2013). In the United States the Department of Homeland Security has been setting up a network of 'data fusion centres' that are primarily concerned with data flows connected to national security, though this has been known to be affected by function creep (Monahan and Palmer, 2009).

With new technologies of visualisation and the digitization of migration policies, the policy process and the implementation of policies change, too. Digitization does not come without consequences. A new class of policy makers increasingly makes the most important decisions in terms of migration policy—who fits into what category. Johnson and colleagues (2011, 62) point out that "the sovereign decisions of the border are as likely to be made by programmers and mathematicians who write computer code as they are by uniformed border agents." In other words, the *numerati* (Baker, 2008) that design and construct the digital tools for governments have become much more important in shaping policy because it falls to them to translate political priorities and decisions into the algorithms and decision trees that run and organize the data in databases. As a result, the people—Lyon calls them the 'others' in the following quote—that are digitally categorized essentially ebb and flow with changes in algorithms and the settings of the system. "One difficulty of such others, in current identification regimes, is that their ranks may expand at will—or whim—through slight statistical adjustments expressed in the algorithms controlling for entry and eligibility" (Lyon, 2009, 148). Political and policy decisions about risks and categorizations and changes therein cause ripples in the mass of data that is collected and stored about travellers and migrants once they are translated into the software. Categories do indeed have politics. Aradau and associates (2008, 152; see also Salter, 2008) underscore the consequences of risk-based database systems: "'Who decides?' is supplemented by 'Who gets to imagine the future?' The imagination of the future has become one of the main political stakes."

MONITORING THE BORDERLANDS OF EUROPE

The different modalities of today's borders intervene in human mobility in complex ways. Even though borders are now 'everywhere,' there are still lines on the map that separate countries from each other and are patrolled by border guards. The—at places—heavily fenced and patrolled border between Mexico and the US resembles parts of the EU's external border, both in its selectiveness of enforcement and in its appearance characterised by militarised fences and watchtowers. In the 'Schengen land' without internal borders the emphasis has shifted to the communal external borders. The basic data on these borders are daunting: 27 member states are responsible for roughly 10,000 kilometres of green borders, 50,000 kilometres of blue borders, and 1,800 official ports of entry into the EU (Hobbing, 2010). Unsurprisingly, guarding the border has increasingly become a technological affair. Much has been invested in new technologies of border surveillance, driven by both political aspirations to 'control' borders and by the 'homeland security industry' to create and expand new markets for surveillance technology (Hayes, 2009; Broeders, 2011b; Düvell and Vollmer, 2011).

The green Eastern borders of the EU combine a mix of traditional border patrol and technology (Düvell and Vollmer, 2011). At border crossings heartbeat and mobile carbon dioxide detectors are used to detect irregular immigrants hidden in carriers or cargo. Also, border controls are supplemented by fixed and mobile document examination systems, CCTV, night-vision equipment, thermal cameras, and movement detectors. At the blue borders of the Mediterranean, new technologies of visualisation are set to play an even greater role and include the use of satellites, drones (UAVs), and the data mining of various sources of public and operational data (Hayes and Vermeulen, 2012). Especially through the FRONTEX agency and programmes such as Eurosur, the EU aims to transform the Mediterranean into a digital moat shielding the south of the Union against illegal immigration especially. The dangerous water barrier between North Africa and Southern Europe has attracted many irregular migrants to seek entry to the EU under very harsh conditions and claimed many of their lives (Carling, 2007; Spijkerboer 2007).

Spain, separated from Africa only by the narrow Straits of Gibraltar, was one of the first EU countries to turn to new surveillance systems to deal with (illegal) migration. As early as 2002, Spain began to introduce a maritime surveillance system, the Integrated External Policing System, for its external borders (*Sistema Integrado de Vigilancia Exterior*, SIVE), to deal with the rise in illegal immigration (Düvell and Vollmer, 2011, 10). Systems like the Spanish one were precursors to more encompassing ambitions laid out by the European Commission in 2008. In that year EU Justice and Home Affairs Commissioner Franco Frattini launched his so-called 'border package,' a vision for the management of the EU's external borders (Commission of the European Communities, 2008). This package consisted of three communications: one on the use of database technology, including the intention to create the EU–wide Entry/Exit System; one on the future of FRONTEX; and one Communication examining the establishment of a satellite-based border surveillance system called Eurosur (Guild et al., 2008). Hobbing considers the border package to be a paradigm shift for the EU:

> All that seemed of doubtful value before, such as fully automated border checks, comprehensive systems of entry-exit control, air passenger surveillance and electronic travel authorisation, hi-tech border installations including virtual fences, has all of a sudden become part of the EU's vision for the 21st century.
>
> (Hobbing, 2010, 68)

After the 2011 Arab Spring and the (in retrospect, small) numbers of irregular migrants heading for Europe that followed those events, the EU has pushed forward with the plans for Eurosur and the EU's smart borders. In terms of the technological management of migration flows the Eurosur plan is most interesting, as it aims to create an EU–wide mechanism for the deployment of surveillance systems 'at or beyond the geographical external borders.' The plan involves 'pooling' all sorts of surveillance technologies that the member states use at the border and should "ultimately lead to the establishment of a 'common monitoring and information sharing environment'" under the direction of FRONTEX (EC quoted in Jeandesboz, 2008, 9). The result should be a 'system of systems.' So initially, the aim is to pool national systems such as Spanish SIVE operated by the Guardia Civil (Carling and Hernandez-Carretero, 2011), for common use. The main aims are to reduce illegal migration into the EU, to prevent cross-border crime, and to enhance search and rescue capacity.

Investments in both the hardware of border surveillance as well as in software and information management systems are steadily growing. The big companies involved in the migration management and security industry pushing for the introduction of such new technologies have found a receptive partner in the EU. Hayes (2009) speaks of a 'security-industrial complex' and documents the extensive links between the industry and the EU's research programme, which funds substantive R&D in this area—not in the least for technologies for migration surveillance such as robotics, unmanned aerial surveillance, and satellite tracking technology.

But the investments in the data-analytical or 'informational' parts of the Eurosur programme are also growing. The idea and aim is that FRONTEX will produce all sorts of risk analyses and tap into all data from the various surveillance systems to make 'intelligence-led' border patrolling possible (Léonard, 2010) and coordinate efforts at the border. Risk analysis, according to FRONTEX's website, is the starting point for all FRONTEX activities, from joint operations through training to research studies, and relies on all possible sources of data:

> In order to identify short—medium—and long-term trends, a wealth of data needs to be gathered and analysed. For this, FRONTEX monitors the global security environment, especially those political, economic, social, technological, legal and environmental factors which could affect border security.[1]

FRONTEX's Eurosur programme will have three layers of data: the *events layer*—including migratory flows, an *operational information layer* showing what member states are doing, and an *analysis layer* to determine how risks are assessed and translated into operational responses.[2] This should create a 'situational awareness' and an accurate 'situational picture' for border guards to work with. The legal definitions for 'situational awareness' and other key concepts in the regulation are simultaneously detailed as well as wide ranging and defined in the broadest possible terms (Hayes and Vermeulen, 2012). For example, Article 3 (d) of the Eurosur regulation reads:

> 'situational picture' means a graphical interface to present near-real-time data and information received from different authorities, sensors, platforms and other sources, which is shared across communication and information channels with other authorities in order to achieve

> situational awareness and support the reaction capability along the external borders and the pre-frontier area.
>
> (European Union, 2013, 13)

In other words, the data gathering, mining, and analysis under the flag of Eurosur is wide ranging and may draw on many and relatively unspecified sources. Even though this data is subject to the EU regime of data protection and the protection of fundamental rights, it is unclear how oversight on this data gathering is organised. In the run-up to the European Day for Border Guards 2013, there was a call to industry and researchers to showcase their wares on the 'technology exhibition' that was held in parallel. In addition to calls for various kinds of surveillance hardware, FRONTEX was also very interested in ideas and products of technology for 'information sharing and interoperability' and 'information acquisition and fusion.' Especially the latter category, calling for applications that can deal with "real time data mining for processing vast amounts of heterogeneous data" and the use of "new sources of information (on line news and social media) for intelligence gathering" (FRONTEX, 2013) shows a new interest in the datafication of border management. This datafication goes well beyond the data gathered by public officials in migration management themselves and seems set to take in all accessible information that may prove useful. It is a datafication of the migrants' and travellers' environment in the broadest sense. The fact that EUROSUR will also hook up with the EU–wide Common Information Sharing Environment as 'its border control function' (Hayes and Vermeulen, 2012) underlines that the data gathered here will also reach stretched screens across Europe that are not involved in migration management directly.

MOBILITY MANAGEMENT THROUGH 'STRETCHED SCREENS'

Where the previous section illustrated how the border environment has become datafied—the 'situational awareness' is pieced together from a myriad of sources—this section turns to the datafication of the individual migrant and traveller. New technology has made it easier and more convenient for migration control to move away from the actual border and has partially become 'remote control' (Zolberg, 2003). *At* the border (see previous section), the notion of a border is already stretched by using remote sensing technology and open sources, but within the procedures regulating mobility and migration this goes double. The aim is "for borders to increasingly exist *de facto* in cyberspace, i.e., become 'virtual borders'" (Hobbing and Koslowski, 2009, 14). Mobility management in the digital age is preferably organised in such a way that decisions on entry and eligibility are taken as far away from the territorial border as possible. Migrants and travellers are monitored through data, data mining, profiles, and risk calculation. The vast numbers of the flows of migration and mobility are increasingly matched by the vast numbers that are registered, categorised, and data mined. Databases and the 'screens' of the terminals of migration officials everywhere shape the image of migrants and the opportunities they have or lack (Amoore, 2009; Lyon, 2009).

In recent years many Western countries have been constructing migration database systems to register and manage especially three categories of migrants: asylum seekers, migrants on (short-term) visas, and irregular migrants. In the EU this has translated into a new digital border of the EU consisting initially of the Schengen Information System (SIS) and the Eurodac system. In October 2011 the Visa Information System (VIS) became operational, and in April 2013 the second generation of the Schengen System (SIS II) went live. Plans for an EU–wide Entry/Exit System and smart border programmes have been on the EU's agenda since 2008 (Broeders, 2007, 2009, 2011) and gained renewed traction after the migratory movements in the wake of the Arab Spring in 2011 (Hayes and Vermeulen, 2012). The EU's investment in these programmes is considerable. The budget for Home Affairs 2014 to 2020 reserves 822 million euros for existing large scale IT programmes. The recently created EU Agency for IT in Justice and Home Affairs and an unknown portion of 4,648 million euros reserved for internal security funds are earmarked for the development of new large-scale IT systems (Comission of the European Communities, 2011, 4). These funds primarily flow towards both privately contracted and the EU's own technical experts, developers, and the operators of data systems working with mobility-related data flows.

These systems all chart and monitor mobility, store vast amounts of personal data and biometrics and, in the case of the EU systems, can give insight into the primary and secondary dispersal of migration flows over the member states of the EU. For example, the Eurodac system, a central register of the fingerprints of all asylum applicants in the EU, charts the distribution of asylum migration across Europe and detects multiple asylum claims in the EU. Through the registration of multiple claims—someone has filed a claim for asylum in various member states at various times—the system also gives some indication of secondary movement. The VIS (Visa Information System) connects the EU member states' immigration authorities and consular posts all over the world. Its central database details the personal and biometric information of all visa applicants to the EU and the dates on which visas were applied for, granted, refused, cancelled, withdrawn, or extended. This means the VIS will generate aggregated information on shifts and trends in visa-based mobility from certain countries and regions. The Entry/Exit system, if and when it will be implemented, will be able to generate even more information on migration processes in the EU as it registers data on all travellers entering and exiting the EU (however, see Jeandesbosz et al., 2013, for a critical analysis of the technological and financial feasibility of the scheme). The main emphasis in all these systems shifts to identification.

All the systems mentioned have become 'identity technologies' and revolve around biometrics—usually fingerprints and/or iris and facial recognition—as a unique identifier that ties all the data in these systems to one registered individual (Broeders, 2007). As a result of the use of surveillance technologies in the adjacent policy terrain of counter-terrorism and mobility, other systems, data exchanges, and databases such as PNR data exchange, Advance Passenger Information, and many watch lists, supplement—and sometimes interact with—the migration surveillance systems (Balzacq, 2008; De Hert and Bellanova, 2011). The closer to national security one gets, the bigger the data sets available, as we have learned from the recent disclosures about the American PRISM programme (Bigo et al., 2013), and the more various sources can and will be combined.

With the bulk of data contained in these various systems, categorisation becomes a prerequisite for a pre-emptive line of sight in migration policy (Amoore, 2009). Two trends stand out in the development of migration databases. The first is the shift from reactive to pre-emptive databases. Whereas the SIS, for example, only registered persons who had 'done' something (violated migration law, for example), most other systems register people because they may do something in the future (people are registered in Eurodac because they applied for asylum but also because they *may* apply in multiple countries and *may* become irregular migrants). This explains why new and proposed systems—such as the EU's Entry/Exit system in combination with biometric passports and automated border controls—aim to register and fingerprint all travellers that will cross the external border: citizens, visa-free travellers, and those travelling on a visa alike. The digital haystack is collected to pinpoint the needle later. Lyon (2003) calls this 'dragnet policies' in which large quantities of data on as many people as possible are stored in order to trace an (infinitely smaller) policy-relevant subpopulation. Overall, the pre-emptive governance of mobility through databases is organised around the logic of blacklisting, green-listing, and grey-listing the mobile populations that are heading towards the EU (cf. Broeders and Hampshire, 2013). Those who are blacklisted should be stopped well before they reach a territorial border, those who are green-listed are fast-tracked for easy border passage, and those who are grey-listed are labelled 'suspect' and require further scrutiny at the border or, preferably, before embarking on their journey. The value attributed to the various data points that make up a category determines the colour and the shades of grey (for a more detailed analysis, see Broeders and Hampshire, 2013).

The second trend is that categorisation becomes technologically mediated and datafied. The classic state view on migration and international mobility is characterised by countries and visa; the citizens of some countries are suspect in terms of the (perceived) risk of illegal migration, refugee flows (perceived to be bogus or real), and forged identity documents. This view was based on countries and nationalities, and visa policy is the means to regulate. New technologies build on this classic view and also go beyond it. The EU's border package, for example, aims to create different flows of people at the airport on the basis of risk assessment. These flows are organised through databases and separate systems for registration and passage at the border itself. The language is important here: The systems and programmes for fast-track procedures are those for 'trusted travellers.' In the original plans the Commission even used the unfortunately chosen label of 'bona fide' travellers, suggesting that those travelling on a visa were collectively regarded to be of 'bad faith' (Mitsilegas, 2009). The trend in the new systems is to increase the data points on individuals to make more fine-grained analysis and categorisations possible. The original Schengen Information System resembled the traditional paper watch lists most closely: The information that was permitted into this database was limited and almost austere.[3] In comparison the Visa Information System registers a wealth of information about the applicant himself, his visa-history, and the people or organisations that support the application. New systems and databases come with formal policy categorisations but also more informal labels that affect how groups of travellers and individual travellers are perceived by immigration officials and those who enact policies 'on behalf of' the state such as private visa application centres who run the visa procedures for many OECD countries and carriers such as airlines and shipping companies (Broeders and Hampshire, 2013). Over the years carrier sanctions have been enacted and severely tightened in many Western countries (Menz, 2011), increasing the incentives of airlines to only accept immaculate paperwork and digital registrations. Just beyond the horizon new technologies for tracking and tracing migration and mobility are already in play outside the realm of European migration policy. For example, in situations with refugee flows and disaster management aid organisations and governments are increasingly using cell phone data (Broeders, 2011b; Taylor, 2015) and other sources of available data, sometimes even crowd-sourced data (Zook et al., 2010). Although these innovations will not be integrated into the European stretched screens anytime soon—though some of these may already be in the monitoring of the borderlands—the drive to increase the number of data points in migration policy may in time lead to the integration of new sources of information.

Mobility management is increasingly operated through the stretched screens that connect border and immigration officials to a network of national and international databases that contain data on travellers that have been registered, categorised, and in some cases 'tagged' for further action. In these databases—and because of the volume of data collected—some categorisations now move away to some extent from the rather blunt categories of nationality towards being based on characteristics of (aggregated) individuals. De Hert and Bellanova (2011, 1) observe that "Governments once based the intensity of screening primarily on a traveller's nationality ('sorting countries'), but new sources of information allow them to focus more directly on personal characteristics ('sorting individuals')." Managing migration flows through the prism of a database then becomes a technologically mediated combination of individual characteristics and the profiling and data mining of aggregate individual characteristics. The result is that travellers become screened in the form of their data doubles (Haggerty and Ericson, 2000), which are consequently judged to be 'bona fide' or 'mala fide' and treated accordingly. Or, as Louise Amoore (2009, 24) writes "the migrant or traveller is both targeted and anticipated—identified via their personal data and projected forward so that their digital shadow arrives at the border before they do."

THE DATAFICATION OF MOBILITY AND MIGRATION MANAGEMENT: CONSEQUENCES FOR THE STATE

An interesting question is whether adding a thicker layer of information and data to policy making and the remarkable increase in speed and real-time exchange of data that we have seen in this policy area changes the nature of the state and the state's agency. Callon and Latour (1981) have proposed a certain analogy between science and politics and between the function of the laboratory and the state. Not unlike laboratories, states consist of various heterogeneous actors capable of mobilizing each other and forming associations to execute specific tasks (Latour, 1983). States have to split themselves up, move towards different locations, and start field projects to test their own programmes and connect the internal to the external world. As Passoth and Rowland (2010, 832) conclude, "if the lab is not a place, but a setting in which problems are scaled up and down, then states are not containers for political action, but registers of political actors, networks and actions." In the migration-control literature similar ideas about the changing nature of migration governance have been captured under the notion of "remote control" (Zolberg, 2003) and shifting migration control "upwards, downwards and outwards" (Lahav and Guiraudon, 2000).

The analogy with the laboratory envisages the state as a *mediator* able to enrol a network of instruments. Here, the state does not mediate between unhappy spouses; the mediation at hand consists of the creation and transformation of all kinds of data and information into reliable facts. These facts are used to make certain risk assessments and support decision-making processes. This process of mediation has three aspects: *place, time*, and *meaning*.

First, the mediating role of the state is continuously concerned with transferring data, information, and knowledge from one place to the other. This gathering of information and coordination between different places does not take place by simply copying reality and turning it into a representation. Instead, the "mediation work" (Latour, 1993) can be characterized as "circulating reference." As Latour has clarified, "reference" comes from the Latin *referre*, "to bring back" (1999, 32). Going out, bringing back and combining all kinds of data is pretty much what the aforementioned "stretched screens" aim to do. For example, the VIS will connect the EU member states' immigration authorities and consular posts all over the world. Its central database details the personal and biometric information of all visa applicants to the EU and the dates on which visas were applied for, granted, refused, cancelled, withdrawn, or extended. In addition, VIS will be able to generate aggregated information on shifts and trends in visa-based mobility from certain countries and regions. Moreover, the longstanding and reliable tendency of policy makers to connect various (migration) databases and add more uses for the data—in a process of function or surveillance creep—will make sure that the merging of information from various sources continues (cf. Prins et al., 2011; Broeders, 2011c). It also means that new ways have to be found to strengthen what is usually referred to as the 'interoperability' of these systems.

Second, the state as consisting of a network of centres of calculation is increasingly involved with connecting knowledge of the past, the present, and the future. Risk calculations and categorizations as sketched in the previous sections link the aggregate past to images of the future in order to deal with the present. Schinkel (2011, 378) argues that such risk-based registry systems, "which record and recode the past, are first and foremost relevant in the present by sketching the contours (under the name of 'prevention') of a statistically constructed future."

According to him they, in a sense, 'visualize society' along lines that favour governing. In doing so, boundaries become fixed, and categories become harder and are more and more perceived to be 'real.' At the aggregate level, FRONTEX is merging all its surveillance data into a common monitoring and information-sharing environment and also taps into various other sources of (open) data to enrich its information position and add more and more data to its analyses. The aggregate past and present steer the present and future operations of the border agency. At the individual level, many of the migration databases operated by the EU (also) serve to reconnect migrants to their migration histories. Unidentified—often irregular—migrants are traced back to a visa application or asylum claim through the fingerprints left in the SIS, VIS, or Eurodac in order to help re-identify them with a view to expulsion (see Broeders, 2009). In these cases the past is literally catching up with the present.

Third, the mediating role of the state is concerned with transforming meaning. In order to operate effectively centers of calculation blur the distinction between the inside and the outside of a laboratory or a state agency or any other site which gathers and merges information. Laboratories have consequences outside their walls. The theories that are developed there are not just deemed applicable in experimental settings but are of influence on the external world (Latour, 1987). Information collected at different practices, control posts, and points of entry will have to be standardized and made communicable to be gathered together and related at specific nodes.

As such, the parts of the outside world that are under surveillance have to be transformed into a kind of 'proto-laboratory' to make information extracted from different settings compatible.

These three characteristics of mediation processes have severe consequences for the position of the state and the justification of the state's role in the datafication of mobility and migration management. Crucial to the technologies that are deployed is that they aim to deliver data, information, and facts on the basis of which *decisions* are to be taken. These are, in some cases, the sovereign decisions of the state on entry and non-entry, eligibility and non-eligibility. As Latour and Woolgar (1979) have shown, central to the "construction of scientific facts" is the erasing of traces. Facts are constructed in long and messy processes, but the trajectory that leads to their institutionalization is hardly referred to in scientific publications. Similarly, Brighenti (2007, 338) notes that "the legibility of social phenomena is often achieved at the expense of the recognition of their richness." Once considered a fact, it is presented as a 'fait accompli.' Policy decisions require a similar kind of unequivocal categorization, not in the least in migration policy, which is ultimately about inclusion and exclusion. 'Faits accomplis' are crucial to socio-technological practices in which decisions have to be taken. On a more general level, the erasing of traces can be understood as a process of 'purification.' Modernity, according to Latour (1993), is overwhelmingly inhibited by 'hybrids'—marriages between subjects and objects, humans and humans—as is the case in the socio-technological systems which are used for mobility management and border control. However, hybrids are likely to be denied a legitimate place in the modern order. Instead, they are brought back to a binary position. They are either a subject or an object, not anything in between. The implication is that the erasing of traces serves to mask the constructed nature of what are supposed to be clear-cut subjects or objects. A fact can only speak for itself once it is declared independent of human actions.

In a similar vein, the state's information management is aimed at the creation of undisputable facts. Interestingly, the process of datafication starts off by vastly increasing the hybridization of the available data and information. The size of the intake of data from increasingly varied sources is growing fast—there is a reason the debate is about big data—making the resulting data set a fuzzy mashup. However, information networks and 'centers of calculation' then transform bits of information by selecting and connecting them and build a workable image of reality, similar to what Deleuze described as the creation of virtual date doubles, some of which are considered 'green,' some 'black,' and some 'grey,' with the latter category being an transit category—that is, being on its way to become at least temporarily one of the former. However, there is no natural correspondence between these representations and the outside world. To make them correspond, the intermediary steps that connect them must be made invisible in the end. If messy and hybrid, the constructed nature of fact would come to light and undermine the rational justification of decisions. The mediating role of the state, it can be concluded, works out in two directions. On the one hand, it relates, collects, and transforms all kinds of data and information to gather them together and turn into robust facts. On the other hand, it evades the traces of this process to purify the outcome and to present it as an objective, undisputable ground for decision making.

NOTES

1. See FRONTEX website under the heading of Risk analysis: http://frontex.europa.eu/intelligence/risk-analysis. Accessed 17 March 2014.
2. Klaus Roesler, Director of Operations division, FRONTEX. Report of Panel Discussion III—Eurosur and the future of Border Management. European Day for Border Guards, 23 May 2013, Warsaw, Poland.
3. The data included in SIS were: first name and surname, known aliases, first initial of the second or middle name, date and place of birth, distinguishing physical features, gender, nationality, whether the person may be considered to be armed and/or dangerous, the reasons for the SIS report, and the measures that need to be taken.

REFERENCES

AMOORE, L. (2006) Biometric Borders: Governing Mobilities in the War on Terror. *Political Geography*, 25(3). p. 336–351.

AMOORE, L. (2009) Lines of Sight: On the Visualization of Unknown Futures. *Citizenship Studies*, 13(1). p. 17–30.

AMOORE, L. (2013) *The Politics of Possibility. Risk and Security Beyond Probability*. Durham (NC) and London: Duke University Press.

ARADAU, C., LOBO-GEURRO, L. & VAN MUNSTER, R. (2008) Security, Technologies of Risk, and the Political: Guest Editors' Introduction. *Security Dialogue*, 29(2–3). p. 147–154.

BAKER, S. (2008) *The Numerati*. Boston/New York: Houghton Mifflin Company.

BALZACQ, T. (2008) The Policy Tools of Securitization. Exchange, EU Foreign and Interior Policies. *Journal of Common Market Studies*, 46(1). p. 75–100.

BAUMAN, Z. (1998) *Globalization. The Human Consequences*. Cambridge: Polity Press.

BIGO, D. et al. (2013) Open Season for Data Fishing on the Web. The Challenges of the US PRISM Programme for the EU. *CEPS Policy Brief*, 293, June 2013

BRIGHENTI, A. (2007) Visibility: A Category for the Social Sciences. *Current Sociology*, 55(3). p. 323–342.

BROEDERS, D. (2007) The New Digital Borders of Europe: EU Databases and the Surveillance of Irregular Migrants. *International Sociology*, 22(1). p. 71–92.

BROEDERS, D. (2009) *Breaking Down Anonymity: Digital Surveillance of Irregular Migrants in Germany and the Netherlands*. Amsterdam: Amsterdam University Press.

BROEDERS, D. (2011) A European 'Border' Surveillance System under Construction. In Dijstelbloem, H. & Meijer, A. (eds.) *Migration and the New Technological Borders of Europe*. Houndmills, Basingstoke, and Hampshire (UK): Palgrave, 40–67.

BROEDERS, D. & HAMPSHIRE, J. (2013) Dreaming of Seamless Borders: ICTs and the Pre-Emptive Governance of Mobility in Europe. *Journal of Ethnic and Migration Studies*, 39(8). p. 1201–1218.

CALLON, M. & LATOUR, B. (1981) Unscrewing the Big Leviathan: How Actors Macro-structure Reality and How Sociologists Help Them To Do So. In Knorr Cetina, K. & Cicourel, A. V. (eds.) *Advances in Social Theory and Methodology. Toward an Integration of Micro- and Macro-Sociologies*. London: Routledge & Kegan Paul, 277–303.

CARLING, J. (2007) Migration Control and Migrant Fatalities at the Spanish-African Borders. *International Migration Review*, 41(2). p. 316–343.

CARLING, J. & HERNÁNDEZ-CARRETERO, M. (2011) Protecting Europe and Protecting Migrants? Strategies for Managing Unauthorised Migration from Africa. *The British Journal of Politics and International Relations*, 13. p. 42–58.

CHOUCRI, N. (2012) *Cyberpolitics in International Relations*. Cambridge: The MIT Press.

COMMISSION OF THE EUROPEAN COMMUNITIES. (2008) *Communication from the Commission to the European Parliament, the Council, the European Economic and Social Committee and the Committee of the Regions. Preparing the Next Steps in the Border Management in the European Union*. Com (2008) 69 final. Brussels, 13.2.2008.

COMMISSION OF THE EUROPEAN COMMUNITIES. (2011) *Building an Open and Secure Europe: The Home Affairs Budget for 2014–2020*. COM(2011) 749 final, Brussels, 15.11.2011.

CRESSWELL, T. (2010) Towards a Politics of Mobility. *Environment and Planning D: Society and Space*, 28. p. 17–31.

DE HERT, P. & BELLANOVA, R. (2011) *Transatlantic Cooperation on Traveler's Data Processing: From Sorting Countries to Sorting Individuals*. Washington (DC): Migration Policy Institute.

DIJSTELBLOEM, H. & BROEDERS, D. (2015) Border Surveillance, Mobility Management and the Shaping of Non-Publics in Europe. *European Journal of Social Theory*. 18(1), p. 21–38.

DIJSTELBLOEM, H. & MEIJER, A. (eds.) (2011) *Migration and the New Technological Borders of Europe*. Houndmills, Basingstoke, and Hampshire (UK): Palgrave.

DÜVELL, F. & VOLLMER, B. (2011) *European Security Challenges. Background paper 'Improving EU and US Immigration Systems,' 2011/01*, Robert Schuman Centre for Advanced Studies, San Domenico di Fiesole (FI): European University Institute.

EUROPEAN UNION. (2013) *Regulation of the European Parliament and of the Council Establishing the European Border Surveillance System (EUROSUR)*. PE-CONS 56/13. Brussels, 11.10.2013

FRONTEX. (2013) *Invitation to Industry/Researchers to Showcase during the European Day for Border Guards*, 28.1.2013. Available from: www.frontex.europa.eu/news/invitation-to-industry-researchers-to-showcase-during-the-european-day-for-border-guards-m4VuuC. [Accessed 19.8.2013]

GUILD, E., CARRERA, S. & GEYER, F. (2008) The Commission's New Border Package. Does It Take Us One Step Closer to a 'Cyber-Fortress Europe?' *CEPS Policy Brief*, nr. 154, March 2008.

HAGGERTY, K. & ERICSON, R. (2000) The Surveillant Assemblage. *British Journal of Sociology*, 51(4). p. 605–622.

HAYES, B. (2009) *Neoconopticon: The EU Security-Industrial Complex*. Transnational Institute/Statewatch.

HAYES, B. & VERMEULEN, M. (2012) *Borderline: The EU's New Border Surveillance Initiatives. Assessing the Costs and Fundamental Rights Implications of EUROSUR and the 'Smart Borders' Proposals*. Berlin: Heinrich Böll Foundation.

HOBBING, P. (2010) The Management of the EU's External Borders. From the Customs Union to FRONTEX and E-Borders. In Guild, E., Carrera, S. & Eggenschwiler, A. (eds.) *The Area of Freedom, Security and Justice Ten Years On. Successes and Future Challenges under the Stockholm Programme*. Brussels: CEPS, 63–72.

HOBBING, P. & KOSLOWSKI, R. (2009) *The Tools Called to Support the 'Delivery' of Freedom, Security and Justice: A Comparison of Border Security System in the EU and in the US*. Ad Hoc Briefing Paper. Brussels: European Parliament, Directorate-General Internal Policies, Policy Department C, Citizens' Rights and Constitutional Affairs, Committee on Civil Liberties, Justice and Home Affairs, PE 410.681, February 2009.

JEANDESBOZ, J. (2008) Reinforcing the Surveillance of EU Borders. The Future Development *of FRONTEX and EUROSUR. Challenge Research Paper* 11. Brussels: CEPS.

JEANDESBOZ, J. et al. (2013) The Commission's Legislative Proposals on Smart Borders: *Their Feasibility and Costs. A Study for: Directorate General for Internal Policies. Policy Department C: Citizens' Rights and Constitutional Affairs*. Brussels: EU.

JONES, R. (2009) Categories, Borders and Boundaries, *Progress in Human Geography*, 33(2). p. 174–189.

JOHNSON, C. et al. (2011) Interventions on Rethinking "The Border" in Border Studies. *Political Geography*, 30(2). p. 61–69.

KEYMOLEN, E. & BROEDERS, D. (2013) Innocence Lost? Care and Control in Dutch Digital Youth Care. *The British Journal of Social Work*, 43(1). p. 41–63.

KOSLOWSKI, R. (2008) Global Mobility and the Quest for an International Migration Regime. In Chamie, J. & Dall'Oglio, L. (eds.) *International Migration and Development: Continuing the Dialogue: Legal and Policy Perspectives*. Geneva: International Organization for Migration, 103–143.

LAHAV, G. & GUIRAUDON, V. (2000) Comparative Perspectives on Border Control: Away from The Border and outside The State. In Andreas, P. & Snyder, T. (eds.) *The Wall around the West. State Borders and Immigration Controls in North America and Europe*. Lanham (MD): Rowman and Littlefield Publishers, 55–77.

LATOUR, B. (1983) Give me a Laboratory and I will Raise the World. In Knorr-Cetina, K. & Mulkay, M. (eds.) *Science Observed. Perspectives on the Social Study of Science*. London: SAGE, 141–170.

LATOUR, B. (1987) *Science in Action*. Cambridge (MA): Harvard University Press.

LATOUR, B. (1993) *We Have Never Been Modern*. Cambridge (MA): Harvard University Press.

LATOUR, B. and WOOLGAR, S. (1979) Laboratory Life: The Construction of Scientific Facts. Beverly Hills: Sage.

LÉONARD, S. (2010) EU Border Security and Migration into the European Union: FRONTEX and Securitisation through Practices. *European Security*, 19(2). p. 231–254.

LYON, D. (2003) *Surveillance after September 11*. Cambridge: Polity Press.

LYON, D. (2005) The Border Is Everywhere: ID Cards, Surveillance and the Other. In Zureik, E. & Salter, M. (eds.) *Global Surveillance and Policing. Borders, Security, Identity*. Cullompton (UK): Willan Publishing, pp. 66–82.

LYON, D. (2007) *Surveillance Studies. An Overview*. Cambridge: Polity Press.

LYON, D. (2009) *Identifying Citizens. ID Cards as Surveillance*. Cambridge: Polity Press.

MAYER-SCHÖNBERGER, V. & CUKIER, K. (2013) *Big Data. A Revolution That Will Transform How We Live, Work and Think*. Boston/New York: Houghton Mifflin Harcourt.

MEIJER, A. (2011) Migration Technology and Public Responsibility. In Dijstelbloem, H. & Meijer, A. (eds.) *Migration and the New Technological Borders of Europe*. Houndmills, Basingstoke and Hampshire (UK): Palgrave, 105–133.

MENZ, G. (2011) Neo-liberalism, Privatization and the Outsourcing of Migration Management: A Five-Country Comparison. *Competition and Change*, 15(2). p. 116–135.

MITSILEGAS, V. (2009) The Borders Paradox. The Surveillance of Movement in a Union without Internal Frontiers. In Lindahl, H. (ed.) *A Right to Inclusion and Exclusion? Normative Faultlines of the EU's Area of Freedom, Security and Justice*. Oxford: Hart Publishing, 33–64.

MONAHAN, T. & PALMER, N. (2009) The Emerging Politics of DHS Fusion Centers. *Security Dialogue*, 40(6). p. 617–636.

PASSOT, J. H. & ROWLAND, N. J. (2010) Actor-Network State: Integrating Actor-Network Theory and State Theory. *International Sociology*, 25(6). p. 818–841.

PRINS, C. et al. (2011) *iGovernment*. Amsterdam: Amsterdam University Press.

ROSE, N. (2001) The Politics of Life Itself. *Theory, Culture and Society*, 18(6). p. 1–30.

SALTER, M. (2008) Imagining Numbers: Risk, Quantification and Aviation Security. *Security Dialogue*, 39(2–3). p. 243–266.

SCHINKEL, W. (2011) Prepression: The Actuarial Archive and New Technologies of Security. *Theoretical Criminology*, 15(4). p. 365–380.

SPARKE, M. (2006) A Neoliberal Nexus: Economy, Security, and the Biopolitics of Citizenship on the Border. *Political Geography*, 25(4). p. 151–180.

SPIJKERBOER, T. (2007) The Human Costs of Border Control. *European Journal of Migration and Law*, 9(1). p. 127–139.

TAYLOR, L. (2015) No Place to Hide? The Ethics and Analytics of Tracking Mobility Using African Mobile Phone Data. *Environment and Planning D: Society and Space*. Available from www.academia.edu/4785050/No_place_to_hide_The_ethics_and_analytics_of_tracking_mobility_using_African_mobile_phone_data. [Accessed 25-8-2013]

TAYLOR, L. & BROEDERS, D. (2015) In the Name of Development: Power, Profit and the Datafication of the Global South. *Geoforum*, 64(August 2015), p. 229–237.

UNWTO. (2009) *Tourism Highlights 2009 Edition*. Madrid: UNWTO.

UNWTO. (2010) *Tourism Highlights 2010 Edition*. Madrid: UNWTO.

VAUGHN-WILLIAMS, N. (2010) The UK Border Security Continuum: Virtual Biopolitics and the Simulation of the Sovereign Ban. *Environment and Planning D: Society and Space*, 28(1). p. 1071–1083.

VAN DER PLOEG, I. & SPRENKELS, I. (2011) Migration and the Machine-Readable Body: Identification and Biometrics. In Dijstelbloem, H. & Meijer, A. (eds.) *Migration and the New Technological Borders of Europe*. Houndmills, Basingstoke and Hampshire (UK): Palgrave, 68–104.

ZOLBERG, A. (2003) The Archaeology of 'Remote Control. In Fahrmeir, A., Faron, O. & Weil, P. (eds.) *Migration Control in the North Atlantic World: The Evolution of State Practices in Europe and the United States from the French Revolution to the Inter-War Period*. Oxford: Berghahn, 195–222.

ZOOK, M. et al. (2010) Volunteered Geographic Information and Crowdsourcing Disaster Relief: A Case Study of the Haitian Earthquake. *World Medical & Health Policy*, 2(2). p. 7–33.

13 Migrants at/as Risk

Identity Verification and Risk-Assessment Technologies in the Netherlands

Karolina La Fors-Owczynik and Irma van der Ploeg

INTRODUCTION

European policy discourse on migration shows a tendency to prioritize the security of EU citizens over securing migrants (Tsianos and Kuster, 2010). Practices geared toward the sorting out of entitlements to access and residence of migrants mobilize a discourse that increasingly frames them as *posing risks* to the societies of their host countries (Ministerie van Binnenlandse Zaken en Koninkrijksrelaties, 2011, 2012a, 2012b) notwithstanding the fact that only a small minority of migrants are associated with criminal offences, for example, organized crime, illegal entry, human trafficking, or terrorism. Generally, migrants with refugee or asylum status, as well as those seeking this designation, arrive as a consequence of wars, natural disasters, political or economic unrest, poverty, human trafficking, international crime, or a combination thereof. These immigrants can be regarded as being *at* risk. Although technological systems of migration and border control are generally installed to prevent threats to a country's inhabitants, including threats associated with migrants, countries also have a human rights obligation to assist and protect vulnerable migrants. Today, the perspective on migrants as vulnerable and at risk, rendered acute with the current refugee crises in the Middle East and on the Mediterranean Sea, seems increasingly at odds with the perspective dominating border-management policies and technologies (European Commission, 2006; Council of the European Union, 2012; European Parliament, 2012).

This chapter discusses how migrants and travellers are increasingly framed as posing a risk to the Netherlands. More specifically, we analyse the way that modes of prevention (Bigo and Guild, 2005; Broeders, 2009) and their associated risk assessment systems have come to focus on translating specific problems around migrants into problems of identity fraud, illegal entry, and illegal residence. The ways in which these problems are defined and managed has directed attention towards improving the establishment and the management of '*identity*.'[1] These identification practices have ethical implications because they may be instrumental in discriminative exclusion and inclusion. For this reason, we focus in particular on identification and risk-assessment practices performed by border control, migration, and law enforcement agencies.

In the Netherlands, the constellation of border and immigration agencies is known as the 'alien chain,' and that of law enforcement agencies as the 'criminal justice chain.' Establishing migrants' and travellers' identities and organizing fraud-proof identity management systems have high priority within both chains. This is pursued by elaborate risk-profiling practices, identity-management systems, and sharing of information along and between the range of agencies within the chains, such as the Alien Police, the Royal Military Police, and the Immigration and Naturalization Service (IND).

Whereas terms such as 'identity,' 'prevention,' and 'risk' concerning migrants suggest a certain self-evidence at first sight, these terms derive their meaning from complex arrangements of local, national, and international institutions, digital technologies, legal settings, and professional practices. This is also evident in the international commitments. The Netherlands has a broad range of information exchange tasks, including information on migrants and travellers. As part of the European Union, the Netherlands is, for instance, committed to performing policing tasks through using the national database of the Schengen Information System (SIS[2]) and exchanging data within the pan-European law enforcement organization, Europol.[3] The Netherlands is also obliged to enforce the Dublin convention,[4] which prescribes member states to determine whether an asylum seeker has submitted a prior application in another member state. As part of these assessments, the fingerprint database EURODAC[5] is consulted. Another obligation for the Dutch government is the exchange of visa data on migrants through the Visa Information System (VIS[6]). Given that the Dutch sea border also constitutes part of the EU's external border, the Netherlands actively participates within the EU's border management organization FRONTEX.[7] For example, the Dutch also aggregate and share data on illegal entry through the EU's border surveillance system, EUROSUR.[8] Beyond these European organizations and systems, a large variety of national and local organizations exist in the Netherlands that deploy local border control, immigration, and law enforcement procedures. The two identification systems, as well as the risk-profiling system analysed in this chapter, are embedded within these European and Dutch regulatory and technological settings, yet operated solely in the Netherlands.

These three systems are the following: first, the identification and verification console of the Dutch Immigration and Naturalisation Service, the INS console, second the console of the information provision program (in Dutch: Programma Informatievoorziening Strafrechtsketen) within the Dutch criminal law chain, the PROGIS console, and the Advanced Passenger Information-System, the API system. Although they differ significantly, as they are situated in different practices and operated for different purposes, this chapter aims to articulate some shared characteristics and implications of their use. We suggest that all three systems contribute to a shift that increasingly frames migrants as *posing* a risk, as opposed to potentially being *at* risk. Moreover, we aim to show how the quest for 'accurate identity' and the technologies used to approach this goal transform the problem in specific ways and, in the process, create new uncertainties and risks for those subjected to them. We argue that this happens because of the particular way problems of identity fraud and illegal entry are translated (Latour, 1987) into specific technological solutions.

To illustrate this dynamic, the next section first introduces the systems under study and briefly describes how identity verification of certain categories of migrants and risk profiling of travellers is enabled by these systems. The third section discusses how the 'accuracy of identity' and an accurate 'risk profile' are produced by focusing on the development of 'risk indicators.' The fourth section looks a bit deeper into the functioning of the systems in practice and identifies a number of pitfalls in the socio-technical production of 'identity' and 'risk.' The analysis is based on empirical data from interviews with professional users of these systems within the alien and law enforcement chains and guided by actor-network theory (Akrich, 1992; Latour, 1987) and a material semiotics–informed approach (Law, 2008). The final section draws the arguments together and concludes that the technological quest for 'accurate identification' and risk prevention introduces a range of new risks for migrants.

PREVENTION SYSTEMS IN DUTCH IMMIGRATION, LAW ENFORCEMENT, AND BORDER MANAGEMENT

'Risk prevention' with regard to identity fraud, illegal entry, and international crime has a high priority in Dutch immigration policy (Ministerie van Binnenlandse Zaken en Koninkrijksrelaties, 2012a). In the discourse on improving this prevention, visual metaphors dominate: Migrants and their associated risks need to be made "more visible" (Prins et al., 2011), and there is a need for more 'complete and accurate pictures' of migrants. A report by the Dutch Advisory Committee on Alien Affairs, for instance, describes a need for acquiring a "better view on asylum seekers" (Tweede Kamer, 2005), and another report from the Ministry for Foreign Affairs similarly emphasizes the need for a more "comprehensive picture" of migrants (Zijderveld et al., 2013). The need for improving this 'visibility' is invariably addressed through the introduction of advanced digital technologies for identity-verification and risk-assessment purposes. The INS console, the PROGIS console, and the API system exemplify such technologies.

The INS Console

The INS console is a biometric fingerprint scanning and facial photographing system employed by the Immigration and Naturalization Service (INS, in Dutch: *Immigratie en Naturalisatie Dienst*) of the Dutch Ministry of

Interior Affairs. The European Council Regulation (EC) No. 380/2008 prescribes that all EU member states, including the Netherlands, register "a *photograph [. . .] and two fingerprints taken flat and digitally captured*" in each residence permit issued to a third-country national. 'INS consoles' have been installed specifically to meet this regulation by producing facial photographs and 'high-quality' digitally scanned fingerprints. These data are then incorporated into the residence permits of non–EU migrants (Immigratie en Naturalisatiedienst, 2013). First, it was only allowed to register scanned fingerprints and personal photographs on the residence permits. But as of 1 March 2014, a legal change allows for the registration of the mentioned biometric features in a central database, in the Basic Facility for Aliens.[9] During every subsequent verification process, the residence permit holder places his/her fingers on a reader, and the images are compared with the fingerprints stored on the permit. Residence permits furnished with these biometric features are considered to increase certainty about the permit holder's identity and that the document truly belongs to the immigrant to whom it has been issued (Teeven, 2013). Enrolment in the system will eventually include all third-country nationals acquiring a residence permit. However, when the interviews used in this chapter took place, the INS had only begun enrolling asylum seekers. Our analysis in subsequent sections of the ways in which 'identity' and 'risk' are translated and performed within this system, thereby reinforcing the trend of shifting perceptions from seeing them being *at* risk to seeing them *as* risk, therefore pertains only to this particular subgroup of migrants.

The digital fingerprint scanning by the INS console is considered an improvement upon previous enrolment procedures for asylum seekers. That procedure involved rolling the applicant's 10 fingers in ink and producing prints on paper, the so-called *dactyslips*. All original dactyslips are archived in the Dutch National Investigation Information Service (DNRI). Copies of these sheets are subsequently transferred to a central European system called Eurodac, where they are checked against those already registered. In case of a 'no-hit,' the fingerprints are registered, and the application will be processed. In case of a 'hit,' this is taken as evidence of 'asylum shopping,' or at least as evidence that an earlier application has been submitted by the same person in another EU country. Eurodac is the main tool for the execution of the Dublin Convention (Council Regulation (EC) No 2725/2000) that determined that one cannot apply for asylum in more than one of the EU member states and that the country of first application remains responsible for that person and their application (Van der Ploeg, 1999). In addition to checking in Eurodac, copies of applicants' dactyslips are registered in the Basic Facility for Aliens (Basis Voorziening Vreemdelingen), an IND database containing data on all migrants in the Netherlands, and in the law enforcement database HAVANK (Het Automatisch Vingerafdrukkensysteem Nederlandse Kollektie, or Automated Fingerprint system Dutch Collection).

PROGIS System

Prevention of identity fraud by convicted criminals is a key target within the Dutch law enforcement chain. Although this particular issue is part of a much wider concern, it has recently been pushed to the forefront after several prisoners were found to be others than those who were actually sentenced. Therefore, the Dutch Act on Identification of suspects, convicts, and witnesses (Wet identiteitsvaststelling verdachten, veroordeelden en getuigen, 2009) prescribes law enforcement authorities to 'establish the identity' of suspects, convicts, and witnesses to crimes by taking their digital fingerprints and facial photographs.

In line with this law, the police and other judicial authorities introduced a new[10] biometric system, the PROGIS console (PROGIS), to guarantee that 'the right person' is punished. At the end of an identity-verification and enrolment process, which involves taking a facial photograph and scanning 10 fingers, a so-called 'ID state' is produced. This ID state meets the objective of the Dutch Ministry of Security and Justice in acquiring a "more integrated, criminal person image" (in Dutch: *integraal strafrechtelijk persoonsbeeld*) in that it is claimed to ensure a person's identity during criminal investigations.

The enrolment of suspects and witnesses in PROGIS constitutes the entry point to the Dutch criminal justice system. From that point on, the 'established identity' on the ID state becomes the reference point against which all fingerprints and facial images taken at later moments in the procedure are cross-checked and verified. In order to use the same person's file between criminal justice agencies, each PROGIS ID state is linked to a so-called criminal justice chain number (CJCN, in Dutch: *strafrechtsketennummer*—SKN) and stored in a central database, the Criminal Justice Chain Database (CJCD). The CJCN is meant to harmonize the administration of cases among agencies. In case of recidivism, this database allows for updating a criminal record. This occurs when separate criminal cases become associated with the same person through one CJCN.

Remarkably, it has been the Dutch Alien police that was tasked with operating PROGIS for the criminal justice chain, primarily because of the experience and expertise they acquired through conducting identity research[11] on migrants within the alien chain. However, biometric data produced by PROGIS is only used by partners within the criminal justice chain to verify whether a person's data is already registered in the CJCD. Therefore, if an immigrant offends or becomes a criminal suspect, they would be enrolled in PROGIS the same as anyone else in the Netherlands. We are less interested here in the specific framing of an immigrant as posing a risk in the sense of being a suspect in the context of a particular crime investigation.[12] Our concern here regards the particular framing as risk that is performed with the very enrolment—either as a suspect or a witness—in PROGIS. The likelihood for a migrant to become suspected of identity fraud, for instance, is higher than for 'regular' residents, since the identification process for immigrants is in general far more complicated than that for Dutch citizens and therefore more prone to error. Along this line, we highlight below how the very use of PROGIS can increase the chances for a migrant to be framed as *identity fraudster*.

The Advanced Passenger Information System (API)

Within the context of border control, travellers from non–EU states are routinely assessed against risks of illegal entry (e.g. fraudulent visa or passport), international criminal activity, or threats to national security (e.g. terrorism). All these problems have contributed to the development of more orchestrated risk profiling practices of passengers internationally. Problems of international crime and terrorism generated new modes of data exchange, as EU agreements on the exchange of Passenger Name Records (PNR) of travellers with the US (2012), Canada (2006), and Australia (2012) exemplify. In fact, airports transformed into ever-more-advanced security checkpoints (Schouten, 2014), where, beyond facilitating the mobility of travellers, the filtering out of 'untrustworthy' passengers grew into a top priority.

The Advanced Passenger Information project (henceforth API) is situated at Schiphol Airport and is part of a larger programme called Sustained Border Management[13] (in Dutch: *Verbeterd Grensmanagement*) in the Netherlands. API has been developed to meet EU (EC, 2004/82/EG) and national regulations for the sole purpose of preventing *illegal entry* into the Netherlands and is used by Dutch border control and immigration authorities to check all travellers moving through Schiphol Airport against 'API profiles.' A wide range of passenger attributes, including behavioural characteristics, air travel histories, modes of plane ticket purchase, and classifications of personal belongings, are assessed against these API profiles.

In 2010, the International Civil Aviation Organization (ICAO), the World Customs Organization (WCO), and the International Air Transport Association (IATA) revised the guidelines for API. According to these guidelines, part of the flight information from the 'departure control system' (DCS) of airlines and individual passengers' data from the machine-readable zone of the travel document and passengers' seat and baggage information need to be included in the API dataset. This dataset can be extended to include a maximum of 39 items (depending on country-specific legislation). The EU also follows the international API guidelines. Carriers of incoming and outbound flights in the EU are obliged by Directive 2004/82/EC to submit information on passengers to border-control authorities prior to their departure, which also applies to the Netherlands. Such data may be kept by these authorities for a maximum of 24 hours. The Minister for Immigration suggests in a policy analysis about the work of the Dutch Royal Military Police, Dutch Customs Services,

General Intelligence and Security Service, and the Immigration and Naturalisation Service, as well as test results of the API project, that if these agencies could gain access to passengers' travel document data and check that data against API risk profiles before travellers cross the border, this would foster security and more efficient processes by agencies, as well as smoother border crossing of travellers (Ministerie van Binnenlandse Zaken en Koninkrijksrelaties, 2011).

API data and profiling are perceived as pivotal elements in apprehending migrants involved in human trafficking. While on the one hand being construed as useful in the protection of potential victims, by identifying those 'at risk' of this and other, related crimes (e.g. prostitution or exploitation of illegal workers), API data are, on the other hand, also considered useful in identifying those *posing* a risk, in particular regarding illegal entry. Our analysis below will indicate how both uses of API profiles can, in fact, merge into each other, thus casting doubt on the proclaimed affectivity of each.

DOING RISK: BUILDING 'INDICATORS'

The prevention of potential problems associated with migrants hinges in part upon the sharing of information among practitioners, organizations, and technological systems. Both the prevention of identity fraud through identity documents and of *illegal entry* through risk-profiling methods are shaped by the ways in which classifications, standards, watch lists, and other tools are implemented. This 'operationalisation,' in turn, takes the form of marking specific personal and other characteristics as 'indicators.' Although such indicators are seemingly straightforward characteristics, they are in fact the result of a considerable amount of work (La Fors-Owczynik and Valkenburg, this volume). Moreover, framing risks, that is, a *possible* future occurrence, as something detectable in the present, requires an *expectation* to be translated into observable categories, which, at the same time, renders these risks more 'real.' In addition, and despite their apparent simplicity, risk indicators need to be continually interpreted by professionals. The efforts to determine and interpret risk indicators involve an opaque set of problem transformations by different actors that introduce a range of ambiguities concerning the functioning of the technologies.

Establishing 'Proof' of Identity: Revisiting the 'Entry-Point Paradox'

Ambiguities around what constitutes a risk of identity fraud also emerge in the ways in which 'identity' is established within the configuration of PROGIS. Although this system is intended to provide more accurate ways of identifying persons by biometric and other technologies, thus to prevent the risk of identity fraud, enrolment in the system requires prior 'proof' of identity:

> PROGIS-consoles do not check the authenticity of ID documents before a person becomes enrolled. [. . .] so, professionals must know IDs. New European documents are all made of polycarbonate, such as Polish IDs, for instance. If you drop one, you hear a tinny sound. Therefore, while being busy with someone, policemen often let documents 'accidentally' fall. If a document sounds dull, that indicates fakeness.
>
> (PROGIS professional, city A)

This quote exemplifies two points. First, ID documents are not checked for authenticity by PROGIS; instead, professionals must decide whether an ID document used at enrolment is genuine or fake. Second, the potential problem of identity fraud is transformed into observable indicators, such as, in this particular example, *the sound of a falling ID card*. Thus, a general problem of identification, one that Roger Clarke (1994) labelled the '*entry-point paradox*,' resurfaces here: the accuracy of each digital identification or verification system, however sophisticated, is only as strong as its weakest link, which often lies right at the start of the whole procedure, the authenticity of 'breeder documents' (e.g. IDs, birth certificates). This clearly is an issue in PROGIS, where its claimed technologically enhanced accuracy, in practice, may depend upon an improvised trick that is anything but high tech or accurate.

In a similar vein, the INS console is claimed to provide an 'accurate identity' for migrants while also requiring prior 'identity proof' from them. A professional identifying so-called 'invited refugees'[14] via a mobile INS console in refugee camps explains:

> I: How can you be sure that the [undocumented] person you want to identify with the INS-console is the one he/she claims to be?
>
> P: That you never know. I can give you a basic answer: I can only hope that the person who said something about him/herself to me, said the same thing to our UNHCR[15] colleagues. It can be two times a lie, but since I cannot figure this out, I must be satisfied with the consistency of the refugee's story.
>
> (INS professional, city D)

The above excerpt indicates once more the 'clay feet' of many high-tech identification and verification systems today. Sometimes all one has to go on at enrolment is a minimum level of consistency in a claimed identity, life, or flight story. In the final analysis, it is still the experienced worker 'in the field' whose judgement about the credibility of someone's personal account carries weight. Whether this is to be seen as a strength or a weakness—some may find this remaining human element reassuring—it is a key element in the functioning of such systems that is usually left out of the accounts of technological accuracy and their role in combating identity fraud.

Turning Attributes into Indicators for 'Illegal Entry'

Building risk profiles from indicators visible in the Advanced Passenger Information system shows similar shifts in localization of the problem. The problem here is 'illegal entry,' and the localization may be quite literal, in the sense that geographical locations and travelling routes may become part of a particular risk profile:

> Ultimately, you want to focus on every flight, but you need to build this up gradually. Where does our first priority lie? [. . .] if other partners also have problems with flights from a given country, than there must be something wrong with those flights. If 5 professionals from different organizations say the same about 3 places, than there is something risky with those flights.
>
> (API professional, city A)

The same professional explains how a range or a combination of rather generic attributes and characteristics of passengers on flagged flights are turned into risk indicators.

> You can discover that [. . .] 'facts' about persons traveling from those risk flagged places are also important, these help you learn the type of persons you look for. [. . .] you often search for particular men or women of a certain age, behaviour, clothing or travel companions. I often check passengers against such indicators.

As indicated earlier, API profiles are also used to prevent illegal entry connected to international crime like human trafficking. An IND official, who also manages API, describes how particular instances of this crime are sometimes spotted through the API profiling:

> We did quite well with that profile and stopped many women who were glad and grateful for what we did. We were also happy we could protect them from becoming prostitutes. [. . .] The funny thing is that a month after we started to screen flights against the profile, trafficked women no longer travelled directly to Madrid, but took the route: Amsterdam—Paris—Barcelona—Madrid. The change in the route assured us that the profile was good, and that criminal organizations are well informed. The API profile [. . .] did well. This allowed us to indicate for the minister the usefulness of API data and the importance of binding several issues together in one profile.
>
> (API manager, city A)

Interestingly, this quote illustrates as well how the API system–based profiling may contribute to the convergence, if not conflation, of protecting migrants *at* risk (of trafficking and sexual exploitation) with prevention of travellers *posing* a risk (of illegal entry). There is no need to doubt the intentions of border guards in any way in order to legitimately raise the question whether stopping someone at the border casts them as victim or as perpetrator, as it is unclear whether this is followed by sending them back, prosecuting them, or really helping them. The fact of traffickers changing their routes is taken as a sign of success of the profile and could indicate that it is above all the mere prevention of illegal entry that counts.

It is also clear that professionals do not merely follow standardized protocols or automated decision processes. Seeing certain attributes of travellers as risk indicators can also be based on tacit knowledge and acquired experience:

> If I only consider what is registered in the system, I would only follow the system. The moment I look at my quantitative data analysis and indicators suggest that persons who smuggle others always have a red cap on, I also start 'qualitative research.' If I only focus on persons with red caps I would not see if someone is smuggling people in yellow rain boots, for instance. You have to rely on your senses [. . .] and adjust your profile.
>
> (API professional, city A)

We repeatedly heard about professionals' 'gut feelings' being the reason for modifying risk profiles and introducing new indicators. Thus a shared or hybrid agency exists between human actors and automated systems that makes the process leading up to the decision who will be assigned a risk qualification and who will be stopped for further inspection rather obscure. The constant need to amend API profiles and the flexible conception of indicators renders the process even more elusive.

A major part of the work in identifying risk-associated migrants is about fixing the ambiguities, uncertainties, and (im)probabilities concerning what, in practice, constitutes such risk. Yet the whole idea of detecting and preventing risk in this context requires the presumption that risks are somehow observable, a presumption that lies at the basis of the efforts to develop indicators for them. This section, however, gave examples suggesting that the particular indicators used within the operation of the INS console, the PROGIS console, and the API system sometimes increase ambiguities and uncertainties about risks. Moreover, as the next section aims to make clear, the very use of these three systems generates a proliferation of such 'indicators' and requires workarounds to make them function, that, together, have the ironic effect of increasing the perception rather than the prevention of risk.

PITFALLS OF MAKING RISKS 'VISIBLE'

To distinguish those entitled to enter the country, obtain employment, or receive government support from those who pose a security risk has always been a politically laden process. Pivotal in this is the conceptualization of identity as something fixed and verifiable. As Caplan and Torpey (2001) argue, identification processes transform the 'who' question into 'what kind' of a person someone is. This shifts the search for identity towards the classification of personal characteristics into categories. Similarly, Btihaj argues that "this collapse of the 'who' into the 'what' [. . .] indicates their [identification modes] inherent limitations in capturing the ambiguity of identity and the complexity of the lived experience" (Btihaj, 2010, 6).

Technological innovations like machine-readable passports, e-IDs, and biometric identification systems exemplify efforts for producing certainty about a person's identity (Holowitz and Noiriel, 1992; Caplan and Torpey, 2001; Bigo and Guild, 2005; Lyon, 2009). However, this certainty rests on the acceptance of a series of problem translations that remain unexamined by those operating the systems but that nonetheless each introduce uncertainty and possibility of error (Van der Ploeg and Sprenkels, 2011).

Continuing this line of thought, in this section we argue that efforts to make the risks of identity fraud and illegal entry visible requires a particular type of visibility, one that always could have been otherwise. Moreover, we show how the particular visualization of risk produced by the INS and PROGIS consoles and the API system inscribes these risks onto material objects such as clothing or personal belongings and body parts.

The practices within which these systems are used exemplify that 'identity' and 'risk' are increasingly constitutive of each other: To identify immigrants presupposes risk assessments, and to assess immigrants against risks involves practices of identification and identity verification. As much as identification practices are increasingly about extensive categorization and registration of personal attributes and modes to verify these, risk assessments of immigrants are increasingly about cataloguing a growing number of personal attributes as risk indicators. That is to say, if an immigrant's 'identity' does not conform to a norm during a verification process by the INS or PROGIS console, or if certain attributes of an immigrant match with an API risk profile, that identifies them as a 'risky migrant.'

In the following we highlight how operating the systems discussed creates additional 'risks.' The systems all have their weaknesses and fallibilities that may be exacerbated when agencies exchange information and repeat procedures in different systems. The next section demonstrates how this occurs in the field and provides further examples of how problems of identity fraud, illegal entry, or related crimes by immigrants become translated into other issues within the configurations of the INS, PROGIS console, and API system.

False Positives and False Negatives

The INS console was intended to provide 'improved' biometric data for verification by skipping a translation step within the fingerprinting processes (see above). In the new system, fingerprints are directly digitally scanned, so the scanning of the ink-based dactyslips is no longer necessary.

> P: The problem was that if you take a dactyslip [. . .] a fingerprint consists of lines. If you put here a magnifying glass, then you see that the lines consist of stripes and points, that's a print of a scanned fingerprint. What happens now with the Dactyslip is that the sheets [of the inked fingerprints] become digitalized and the lines of your fingerprint are transformed into stripes and points. So, you have a large quality loss. The moment you scan fingerprints by the INS-console, the quality becomes in any case higher. A bad digital fingerprint scan is probably still better than the best photocopy of an original dactyslip.
>
> (INS console operator, city A)

However, the improved quality and matching rates turn out not to be as straightforward as this. In order to attain the expected accuracy of verification, significant workarounds are needed that show how risk assessment and identity verifications still rely on assessments independent of the system:

> I: How about the lady with whom it went wrong?
>
> P: [. . .] the system says 'no match' for her fingers [. . .] Are we going to refuse that lady a residence permit, because the prints might not be hers? [. . .] The lady was a Somali national, and although Somalis do that, she had not mutilated her fingerprints [. . .], I checked her fingers myself. Then I took her prints and got a 40 % result. I was like: what is this? [. . .] if you clean your fingers, then the prints are worse, if they are greasy, you gain better prints. What are the oily spots on your skin? It is here [points to side of nose] and on your forehead. So, to get good prints we ask people to rub these spots [. . .]. Yet, these techniques were not helpful. Finally, the project manager said, put her four fingers on the scanner and fold them a little around the table, then you have the right pressure. It was not easy, but we improved the fingerprint quality. We achieved 80%; that was good quality.
>
> (INS officer, city A)

What we see in this excerpt is how the accuracy of the system is in fact something that takes a lot of effort and additional 'techniques' to achieve. More specifically, the system is made to perform well because the actual risk assessment is done differently and turned out negative ('no risk'): When her fingerprints fail to give a match, an asylum-seeking woman from Somalia is first suspected of perhaps trying to sabotage the verification process by mutilating her fingertips because she is Somali ("Somalis do that"). The specific risk indicator for that type of sabotage (having mutilated fingertips) is subsequently checked visually by the IND officer ("I checked her fingers myself"). After satisfying himself this way that no fraud is attempted, the negative verdict of the system is not believed, and all effort goes into the production of a better fingerprint scan. The belief in the first assessment is so strong that even if all this fails, the project manager is asked to step in and help out to achieve a positive verification.

The other side of this is that any reliance on such a system introduces significant new risks for those whose fate depends on being believed and whose identity claim of being at risk. That is, a recognised refugee with right of stay is 'verified' this way. Instead of the promised accuracy and certainty of digitalized biometric identity verification, a number of highly contingent factors determine whether a person passes this verification test, including the assessment by the operator, the manager, and the availability of the right levels of pressure and greasiness of the fingers to be scanned.

But often enough, if a person's fingerprints turn out to be unreadable within the configuration of a digital biometric system, this is perceived as an indicator of potential identity fraud. Consequently, the owner of the fingerprint becomes suspect and changes from a person claiming to be at risk into one that is perceived as risk. This is the case even though it is known that there are more problems with the fingerprinting systems.

For example, the PROGIS console, although equally intended to improve accuracy, is acknowledged to have an in-built risk of failure, stemming from a weaker predecessor system:

> Webfit is the predecessor of PROGIS, and was the first program using fingerprints that were taken digitally. In Ter Apel, the Alien Police said: we tried out Webfit, but it did not work for us and it took too much time to work with it. The program of Webfit was actually installed in such a way that it always delivered negative results for asylum seekers when verifying their fingerprints. Webfit turned out to have only been tested on Dutch fingers [. . .]; despite updates, the basis for PROGIS is still Webfit.
>
> (INS professional about PROGIS)

Ironically, a system intended for the highly diverse population of international refugees and asylum seekers had been tested on a relatively homogeneous population ('Dutch fingers'), thus rendering it basically unsuitable for its purpose.

Here we see the rather paradoxical conception of the body underlying the very idea of biometric technologies as automated identification and authentication tools playing out (Van der Ploeg, 2011) on the one hand; biometrics is based on the biological fact that every individual is physically unique. No two fingerprints are identical, everybody's irises are different from those of another, the same way that no two faces, voices, or retinas are exactly the same. This is the condition of possibility of the very idea of biometric technologies as identification tools.

On the other hand, however, there is a simultaneous assumption of *similarity*: every human person is assumed to have a clearly audible voice, a set of 10 fingerprints, two irises, a recognizable face, and so on. Though hardly ever mentioned as such, this assumption of similarity is as crucial to the functioning of biometric systems as is the assumption of uniqueness.

With respect to the human bodily features used in biometrics, this means that there is an assumption of normality that is defined as a range of variations that constitute 'the normal.' Such notions of normality are built into the equipment: hand scanners have particular shapes and sizes, with designated places to put the fingers; fingerprint systems are designed for the registration and comparison of a particular number of fingerprints (most systems use 1, 2, or 10) and a particular range of ridge definition; cameras to scan faces are directed at a specific height, and the accompanying face-recognition software often works best for a particular shade range of skin colour, and so on. In the case of PROGIS and its underlying legacy software Webfit, it is this assumed similarity that turns out to be unwarranted and causing trouble.

The question is, however, for whom it causes trouble. The quote shows operators disqualifying the system: it does not work for them, and it takes too much time to operate. The other side of the coin, however, is that an unsuccessful enrolment or verification may equally well be attributed to the asylum seeker, casting suspicion on them. In a context in which policy aims at limiting admittance of refugees, and prevailing distrust of migrants' identity claims is the very reason for introducing technologies that come with the promise of accuracy and certainty, one may wonder who will get the benefit of doubt in any concrete instance of failed recognition on the work floor. This is why we suggest that these systems introduce new risks for the people subjected to them.

In a different way, and for a different set of travellers and migrants, the API system–based profiles constitute new risks as well. As described earlier, a traveller can become framed as 'risk' if a match emerges between the attributes of this passenger and an API profile:

> We were informed by Madrid that a gang is trafficking women from South- and Central America for prostitution. [. . .] We learnt that these women use Amsterdam as a transit; therefore we built a profile on flights from South and Central-America. We wanted to see all the women, in the age group of 18–24 years, travelling through Amsterdam to Madrid. If a match emerged on these four criteria, then the system signalled that passenger. Since not all female passengers were being trafficked, you had to ask what travel purpose a passenger had. [. . .] there were often no reasons for a stopping, but these are indicators you base your profile on.

What the above illustrates, however, is how a particular combination of rather general attributes renders a person suspect if a match with the API profile occurs. The very generality of the attributes mentioned—a certain age range or gender—demonstrates the limitations of risk assessments by API. False positives are certain to be many. This highlights that an API profile, and the indicators it is built on, do not really 'capture' risks but rather mediate and displace the ambiguities and inherent uncertainties of risk.

Organizational Boundaries and Information Exchange

Visualization of risk is also done by information exchange between different agencies within the alien and law enforcement chains. This information exchange implies a certain "partiality of professional knowledge" (La Fors-Owczynik and Valkenburg, this volume) as each profession focuses on different things, and digital technologies are perceived to overcome interagency boundaries among immigration, border control, and law enforcement practices. The following interview excerpt demonstrates that during these communications, professional and organizational boundaries are actively maintained. This is in part a consequence of the ways in which knowledge exchange brings along overlap of tasks between separate local practices. The different identification tasks of the Alien Police for law enforcement and immigration demonstrate that intensive efforts—or 'boundary work' (Gieryn, 1983)—are undertaken to protect the integrity of the immigration and law enforcement chains. Yet these same efforts make cooperation possible among these professions:

P: INS is a distant chain partner of the Aliens Police, but not one that can access the criminal justice database [database for PROGIS-data]. That is separate.

K: Yes, but the INS also does identification.

P: Yes, [. . .] the INS very often contacts the Aliens Police, and explains: "Listen, we have someone in detention, but we would like to present him/her [at the embassy]." Then we [Alien Police] start an identity investigation, but not at the PROGIS-console, but according to our identity investigation task on aliens within the alien chain. So we put the whole PROGIS issue aside. As you see cooperation [with the INS] is there.

(PROGIS professional, city B)

The distinct functions of the Alien Police in establishing persons' identities within the law enforcement chain via PROGIS and within the alien chain by comprehensive investigations on 'undocumented' migrants draw boundaries between the law enforcement and immigration chains. Although these boundaries serve to maintain legally underpinned distributions of work, authority, and responsibility, they also frustrate the INS and PROGIS console operators:

> We both have the same goal to prevent identity fraud, and one-time registration, and multiple use. And then, of course, legislation should also cooperate in this, a new bill is in progress [. . .]. But now there are two parallel trajectories and I hope they will meet in the best interest of the alien. Because currently assessments are done double, and why? Why don't you look for cooperation?
>
> (INS console operator, city A)

As "assessments are done double" through enrolment in the PROGIS and INS consoles sometimes, the risk of something going wrong and someone's identity thereby becoming suspect increases. Risks are "situated" entities in the bodies of knowledge upon which they are based (Suchman, 2009) and contingent upon the different socio-technical network within which they emerge. The introduction of new systems, the double use of systems, and the information exchange between them and the organizations that operate them thus all generate additional risks of error, the burden of which will fall on the people subjected to them. The new legislation currently underway referred to in the quote is presented to reduce the occurrence of this problem by proposing to have one central database for all biometric data used in the alien chain, the BVV mentioned above; at the same time, however, the use of biometrics throughout the various IND and border management procedures is significantly extended, as are the number of agencies that will be legally entitled to enter data or access this database. The Privacy Impact Assessment conducted on this new legislation, conducted by the Ministry of the Interior, identifies a range of 'risks' connected to the new network of systems, such as, for instance, a risk of 'data overload,' and emphasises the need for a range of risk-reduction measures (Ministerie van Veiligheid en Justitie, 2013).

CONCLUSION: TECHNOLOGY SHIFTS AND PROLIFERATES 'RISKS'

Dutch efforts to reduce identity fraud and illegal entry in the context of migration have come to concentrate on prevention in recent years. Policy makers were calling for a 'better, more complete picture' of migrants in order to enable effective risk assessment of migrants and travelers entering the country. This led to an increased reliance on information systems and digital identification. This chapter has focused on three recently introduced systems for identifying and verifying those posing a risk: the Advanced Passenger Information system for profiling travelers and the biometrics-based identity verification systems within the alien and law enforcement chains, the INS console and the PROGIS console.

Our analysis has highlighted how none of the socio-technical configurations of these technologies delivers the flawless accuracy hoped for. While in some respects improvements regarding the prevention of identity fraud and illegal entry by travelers and migrants may have been achieved, a closer look into the way these systems work in practice has shown how a range of potential system fallibilities lead to a shift in localization of the problems rather than a solution.

With the use of the systems, new risk indicators are developed that amount to new norms concerning what a valid identity is and, hence, what a trustworthy migrant is. Conforming to these new norms is a challenge also for legitimate migrants and travelers involving aspects trivial outside the context of digital identification: the 'machine readability' and greasiness of one's fingertips or the age at which one travels a particular route at a particular moment. The (in)ability to produce readable fingerprints or a particular combination of rather general attributes such as country of origin and age/gender may come to inspire distrust in a particular traveller's identity claim. This happens despite the fact that most of these systems, to some extent at least, are built on clay feet: To enter one of the systems for identity verification, one needs to provide a primary proof of identity, the validity of which cannot be checked by the system itself. Hence, a range of tricks, experiential knowledge, and trust comes into play in order to assess the reference identity proofs on which all later translations and verifications come to rely.

The consequences of this are twofold. On the one hand, it seriously undermines the trust put into the technology and the belief that the latest technology delivers what it promises: accurate and strong verification and identification of those migrants posing a risk of fraud or becoming illegal residents. In this sense, these technologies may foster a false sense of control, security, and successful 'prevention.'

On the other hand, however, these 'clay feet' may cause a failure of protection of those most in need of it: From being a refugee fleeing from risk for life and limbs, an asylum seeker confronted with the systems set up to keep out those deemed non-eligible for the protection offered by asylum status may find themselves being recast as *posing* a risk; a failure to enrol may be met with suspicion of a deliberate attempt to avoid successful registration; a false negative during subsequent verification may cast them as identity fraudster. They may chance upon operators, who, for some reason, and unlike the ones interviewed for this chapter, are little inclined to guide them carefully through either the enrolment or the later verification processes with the range of workarounds required to make the system perform. In this sense, these systems and the belief in them actually pose new risks for those coming to our borders for protection against risk.

The Privacy Impact Assessment on the new legislation mentioned above, with its extensive enumeration of 'risks' to migrants' rights posed by the increased reliance on and extended use of biometrics throughout the alien chain proposed in the new bill within the Netherlands' legislature, underscores this view. Even though it includes a range of risk-mitigating measures—for this issue of false negatives, that is, a failure of the systems to match two sets of fingerprints from the same person, for example, it proposes a mandatory check by a dactyloscopic expert in case of mismatch—it remains to be seen how effective and feasible these will turn out to be. The proliferation of 'risks' when using the INS and PROGIS consoles and the API profiles underlines the pivotal need for all involved to remain reflective about the pitfalls the use of these systems can bring along for the lives of persons assessed by them.

NOTES

1. In opposition to the identity-management discourse, where 'digital identity' is often equated with a collection of personal data, this chapter regards identity as a 'multi-layered concept,' as something "interactive, mediated, relational, and dynamic, as opposed to something pre-given to be 'expressed' or 'registered'" (Van der Ploeg, 1999).
2. SIS—http://ec.europa.eu/dgs/home-affairs/what-we-do/policies/borders-and-visas/schengen-information-system/index_en.htm
3. Europol—www.europol.europa.eu/content/page/about-us
4. Dublin Convention—http://europa.eu/legislation_summaries/justice_freedom_security/free_movement_of_persons_asylum_immigration/l33153_en.htm
5. EURODAC—http://ec.europa.eu/dgs/home-affairs/what-we-do/policies/asylum/identification-of-applicants/index_en.htm
6. VIS—https://secure.edps.europa.eu/EDPSWEB/edps/Supervision/VIS
7. FRONTEX—http://frontex.europa.eu/
8. EUROSUR—http://frontex.europa.eu/intelligence/eurosur
9. The new bill also enables a significant extension of use of biometrics throughout the alien chain (Ministerie van Veiligheid en Jusitie, 2014).
10. The digital fingerprint scanning via PROGIS is new compared to the classical dactyloscopy routine of law enforcement practices. This entails the ink-based fingerprinting of suspects in remand and convicted criminals, and the production of dactyslips. Dactyslips are digitally copied and saved in two major police databases: in AFDC and in the Facility for Verification and Identification (FVI, in Dutch: *Voorziening voor Verificatie en Identificatie*, VVI; Ministerie. van Veiligheid en Justitie, 2011). (The original sheets are submitted to and archived by the Dutch National Research Information Service/dNRI/.) The fingerprints taken by PROGIS during the identification process are regularly compared with fingerprints stored in AFDC. If fingerprints have not been registered yet, dactyslips are produced and their copies transferred to AFDC. In case a suspect is an alien, fingerprints are also compared with the BFA.
11. The Dutch Alien Police operates PROGIS from the back office, including an extra control function. Back-office tasks were granted to the Dutch Alien Police based on the already-accumulated experience of this unit in conducting identity research on immigrants within the alien chain. These tasks include establishing the identity of suspects by PROGIS, which can involve 'identity research' on immigrants (Ministerie van Binnenlandse Zaken en Koninkrijksrelaties, 2011).

12. Immigrants who overstay their visa, who are not part of an asylum-seeking process, or who have simply no identity documents all are enrolled in PROGIS as illegal residents.
13. The Dutch Sustained Border Management programme is coordinated by the Department of Identity Management and Immigration of the Ministry of Interior Affairs. This includes four sub-projects: Passenger Related Data Exchange (PARDEX), Advanced Passenger Information (API), no queue (No-Q), and a Registered Traveller (RT) programme. PARDEX is a central system intended for sharing passengers' information (acquired prior to their travel) with law enforcement agencies. The No-Q and RT are aimed at fostering automated border passage for all EU passengers based on machine readability of travel documents.
14. Most countries have signed agreements about inviting a given number of refugees. The Netherlands invites a maximum 500 refugees yearly. INS professionals select these refugees by visiting camps and conducting research about who shall become entitled to an invitation.
15. Refugee camps are generally run by UNHCR and local authorities.

BIBLIOGRAPHY

AKRICH, M. (1992) The De-scription of Technical Objects. In Bijker, W. & Law, J. (Eds.) *Shaping Technology/Building Society: Studies in Sociotechnical Change.* Cambridge (MA): MIT Press, 205–224.

BIGO, D. & GUILD, E. (Eds.) (2005) *Controlling Frontiers: Free Movement into and within Europe.* London: Ashgate.

BROEDERS, D. (2009) *Breaking Down Anonymity. Digital Surveillance on Irregular Migrants in Germany and the Netherlands.* Amsterdam: Amsterdam University Press.

BTIHAJ, A. (2010) Recombinant Identities: Biometrics and Narrative Bioethics. *Journal of Bioethical Inquiry*, 7(2). p. 237–258.

CAPLAN, J. & TORPEY, J. (Eds.) (2001) *Documenting Individual Identity: The Development of State Practices in the Modern World.* Princeton (NJ): Princeton University Press.

CLARKE, R. (1994) Human Identification in Information Systems: Management Challenges and Public Policy Issues. *The Information Society*, 7(4). p. 6–37.

COUNCIL OF THE EUROPEAN UNION. (2000) Council Regulation (EC) No 2725/2000 Concerning the Establishment of "Eurodac" for the Comparison of Fingerprints for the Effective Application of the Dublin Convention. *Official Journal of the European Union*, 43(L316). p. 1–10.

COUNCIL OF THE EUROPEAN UNION. (2004) Council Directive 2004/82/EC on the Obligation of Carriers to Communicate Passenger Data. *Official Journal of the European Union*, 47(L261). p. 24–27.

COUNCIL OF THE EUROPEAN UNION. (2008) Regulation (EC) No. 380/2008 of 18 April 2008 Amending Regulation (EC) No 1030/2002 Laying Down a Uniform Format for Residence Permits for Third-Country Nationals. *Official Journal of the European Union*, 51(L115). p. 1–7.

COUNCIL OF THE EUROPEAN UNION. (2012) Council Decision of 22 September 2011 on the Signing, on Behalf of the Union, of the Agreement between the European Union and Australia on the Processing and Transfer of Passenger Name Record (PNR) Data by Air Carriers to the Australian Customs and Border Protection Service. *Official Journal of the European Union*, 55(L186). p. 1–12.

EUROPEAN COMMISSION. (2006) Commission Decision of 6 September 2005 on the Adequate Protection of Personal Data Contained in the Passenger Name Record of Air Passengers Transferred to the Canada Border Services Agency. *Official Journal of the European Union*, 49(L91). p. 49–60.

EUROPEAN PARLIAMENT. (2012) Agreement between the United States of America and the European Union on the Use and Transfer of Passenger Name Records to the United States Department of Homeland Security. *Official Journal of the European Union*, 55(L215). p. 5–14.

GIERYN, T. F. (1983) Boundary-Work and the Demarcation of Science from Non-Science: Strains and Interests in Professional Ideologies of Scientists. *American Sociological Review*, 48(6). p. 781–795.

HOLOWITZ, D. & NOIRIEL, G. (1992) *Immigrants in Two Democracies: French and American Experiences*. New York: NYU Press.

IMMIGRATIE EN NATURALISATIEDIENST. (2013) *Vingerafdrukken op Verblijfsdocumenten—Geen Fotokaart Meer*. Online Newsletter IND. Available from www.ind.nl/Nieuws/Pages/Vingerafdrukkenopverblijfsdocumenten.aspx. [Accessed 28–11–2013]

LATOUR, B. (1987) *Science in Action: How to Follow Scientists and Engineers through Society*. Cambridge (MA): Harvard University Press.

LAW, J. (2008) Actor Network Theory and Material Semiotics. In Turner, B. S. (ed.) *The New Blackwell Companion to Social Theory*. Oxford: Blackwell, 141–158.

LYON, D. (2009) *Identifying Citizens: ID Cards as Surveillance*. Cambridge, Malden: Polity Press.

MINISTERIE VAN BINNENLANDSE ZAKEN EN KONINKRIJKSRELATIES (BZK) (2011) Kamerbrief over de Aanpak van Illegaal Verblijf in Reactie op het WODC-Rapport Illegalenschatting 2009. *Kamerstukken*, II 2010–2011, 31 594(10). p. 1–11.

MINISTERIE VAN BINNENLANDSE ZAKEN EN KONINKRIJKSRELATIES. (BZK) (2012a) *Het Gebruik van Passagiergegevens in het Grensbeheer*, Den Haag, Kamerbrief 2012–0000143248, p. 1–8.

MINISTERIE VAN BINNENLANDSE ZAKEN EN KONINKRIJKSRELATIES (BZK) (2012b) *Notitie inzake Openbare Orde Bevoegdheid Burgermeester*. Den Haag, April 26th.

MINISTERIE VAN VEILIGHEID EN JUSTITIE. (2011a) *Het Fundament Progis*. Available from www.vka.nl/sites/default/files/downloads/Boekje Progis Het Fundament.pdf. [Accessed 13–11–2013]

MINISTERIE VAN VEILIGHEID EN JUSTITIE. (2011b) *Protocol Identiteitsvaststelling Strafrechtsketen* (pp. 1–36). Available from www.rijksoverheid.nl/documenten-en-publicaties/brochures/2011/12/22/protocol-identiteitsvaststelling.html. [Accessed 25–04–2013]

MINISTERIE VAN VEILIGHEID EN JUSTITIE. (2013) *Privacy Impact Assessment met betrekking tot de Wijziging van de Vreemdelingenwet 2000*. The Hague, p. 1–15.

MINISTERIE VAN VEILIGHEID EN JUSTITIE. (2014) Besluit van 21 Januari 2014 tot Wijziging van het Vreemdelingenbesluit 2000 in Verband met de Uitbreiding van het Gebruik van Biometrische Kenmerken in de Vreemdelingenketen. *Staatsblad van het Koninkrijk der Nederlanden*, 44, pp. 1–23.

PRINS, C. et al. (2011) *iOverheid*. Amsterdam: Amsterdam University Press/WRR.

SCHOUTEN, P. (2014) Security as Controversy: Reassembling Security at Amsterdam Airport. *Security Dialogue*, 45(1). p. 23–42.

SUCHMAN, L. (2009) Embodied Practices of Engineering Work. *Mind, Culture, and Activity*, 7(10). p. 4–18.

TEEVEN, F. (2013) *Reactie op de brief van de Commissie Meijers van 24 januari 2013 over het EURODAC-voorstel*. The Hague: JBZ Raad, 1–6.

TSIANOS, V. & KUSTER, B. (2010) *Transnational Digital Networks, Migration and Gender, Mig@net Project Deliverable No. 6: Thematic Report "Border Crossings."* Available from https://mignetproject.eu. [Accessed 12–03–2015]

TWEEDE KAMER DER STATEN-GENERAAL. (2005) Terugkeerbeleid. Verslag van een Algemeen Overleg. *Kamerstuk*, 29344 (47). Available from www.zoek.officielebekendmakingen.nl. [Accessed 22–05–2013]

VAN DER PLOEG, I. (1999) The Illegal Body: "Eurodac" and the Politics of Biometric Identification. *Ethics and Information Technology*, 1(4). p. 295–302.

VAN DER PLOEG, I. (2011) Normative Assumptions in Biometrics: On Bodily Differences and Automated Classifications. In Van der Hof, S. & Groothuis, M. (eds.) *Innovating Government—Normative, Policy and Technological Dimensions of Modern Government*. The Hague: IT & Law Series, T.M.C. Asser Press, Springer, 29–40.

VAN DER PLOEG, I. & SPRENKELS, I. (2011) Migration and the Machine-Readable Body. Dijstelbloem, H. & Meijer, A. (eds.) *Migration and the New Technological Borders of Europe*. London: Palgrave Macmillan, 68–104.

ZIJDERVELD, M., RIDDERHOF, W. & BRATTINGA, M. (2013) *Basis Start Architectuur van de Vreemdelingenketen: Kennis Delen, Informatie Gebruiken, Samen Doen*. Den Haag: Ministerie van Binnenlandse Zaken en Koninkrijksrelaties.

Contributors

Irma van der Ploeg is a Senior Research Fellow at UNU-MERIT, Maastricht University, where she coordinates the research programme on Social and Ethical Aspects of ICT-based Innovation. She holds a degree in philosophy from the University of Groningen and received her PhD from Maastricht University. She has published extensively on philosophical, normative, social, and ethical aspects of medical technologies and ICTs. She has been involved in a range of research projects for several Dutch ministries, the Netherlands Organization for Scientific Research, the Advisory Council for Science, Technology and Innovation, the Rathenau Institute, and the European Commission (FP6, FP7). She was principal investigator of the DigIDeas project 'Social and Ethical Aspects of Digital Identities. Towards a Value Sensitive Identity Management', for which she received a Starting Grant from the European Research Council. Her current research interests include STS approaches to social and ethical aspects of ICTs, in particular security, surveillance, and identification technologies; responsible innovation through ICTs; and the informatisation of the body.

Jason Pridmore is an Assistant Professor in the Department of Media and Communication at Erasmus University Rotterdam. His research interests are focused primarily on surveillance and consumption, specifically new media and marketing and the performativity of markets. His research further examines how these connect with personal identity and practices of identification and their implications for issues of security. His previous work has focused on marketing techniques such as the use of loyalty cards and social media integration as forms of collaborative surveillance. He is the author of numerous texts on the subject of consumer surveillance, including the entry on consumer surveillance in the *Routledge Handbook of Surveillance Studies* (2012) and the expert report on the surveillance of consumers and consumption, part of the report on the surveillance society commissioned by the British Information Commissioner in 2006. Jason received his PhD from the Department of Sociology at Queen's University, Canada, in 2008. Before working at Erasmus University, he was Senior Researcher on the DigIDeas project based in Maastricht, the Netherlands, and a Post-Doctoral fellow for the New Transparency Project within the Surveillance Studies Centre at Queen's University.

Peter Adey is professor of geography at Royal Holloway University of London. His work lies at the intersection between space, security, and mobility and the blurring boundaries between cultural and political geography. He has worked at Royal Holloway since 2012, leading the geopolitics and security Masters of Science programme with politics and international relations. He is also chair of the Social and Cultural Geography Research Group, one of the largest research groups of the Royal Geographical Society. In 2011, he was awarded a Philip Leverhulme Prize for his contributions to human geography, and his research focuses on the putative 'new mobilities paradigm.' He is the author of the *Mobility* (2009) and co-editor of the *Handbook of Mobilities* (2014).

Anders Albrechtslund is an Associate Professor at Aarhus University, Denmark. He received his PhD from Aalborg University (2008) and is currently working on a book about online social networking and self-surveillance. Recent publications are on topics such as surveillance, technologies, and Internet practices.

Anne-Mette Albrechtslund is an Assistant Professor at Aalborg University, Denmark. Her research interests include online communication, digital identities, and fiction and culture in everyday life. She has published work about these interests, including the PhD dissertation *Storytelling and Identity in Online Gaming Communities: Exploring Online Culture and Communication as Narrative Practices* (2011).

Dennis Broeders is a Senior Research Fellow at the Dutch Scientific Council for Government Policy (WRR), an advisory body to the Dutch government located within the prime minister's department, and professor of technology and society at the department of Sociology of the Erasmus University Rotterdam. His research broadly focuses on the interaction between technology and policy, with specific areas of interest in cybersecurity governance and Internet governance as well as surveillance, databases, and migration control. At the council, he is currently heading a project on 'Big Data, Privacy and Security.' He was previously project coordinator of the council's report on the future of government digitisation (*iGovernment*, Amsterdam University Press, 2011) and recently published *The Public Core of the Internet: Towards a New International Agenda for Internet Governance* (2015, Amsterdam University Press). He has held visiting research fellowships at the Social Science Research Centre Berlin (WZB) in 2008 and at the Oxford Internet Institute at the University of Oxford in 2011. He has published articles in various internationally leading journals in the fields of sociology, political science, and criminology.

Huub Dijstelbloem is Professor of philosophy of science and politics at the University of Amsterdam (UvA) and Senior Research Fellow at the Netherlands Scientific Council for Government Policy (WRR) in The Hague. Bringing together the fields of philosophy of science and political philosophy, his research employs a combination of conceptual, normative, and empirical approaches. He has published on issues relating to border control and surveillance technologies, on the science–democracy debate, and on philosophical pragmatism. He is a member of the Advisory Board of the UvA's Institute for Interdisciplinary Studies (IIS) and a board member of the Netherlands Graduate Research School of Science, Technology and Modern Culture (WTMC). He was previously also a member of the editorial board of *Krisis*, an open-access, peer-reviewed journal for current issues in philosophy. He has been affiliated to University of California San Diego and the Eduardo Mondlane University in Maputo, Centre for Policy Analysis, Mozambique. He is one of the initiators of Science in Transition, a movement that aims to reflect on the organization of quality assessment and social impact of the sciences and on science policy.

Francisca Grommé is a post-doctoral researcher at the Department of Sociology, Goldsmiths, University of London. Her area of interest is the introduction of technologies for collecting data about citizens and consumers in a variety of governmental practices. As a researcher within the ERC–funded project Peopling Europe: How Data Make a People (ARITHMUS), she is currently studying changes in the production of official statistics by national statistical institutes, mainly the census. She is also completing her doctoral dissertation on the introduction of surveillance technologies in Dutch crime control at the University of Amsterdam, Departments of Anthropology and Political Science.

Philip Kirby completed his PhD on US homeland security policy at the Geography Department at Royal Holloway, University of London, before taking a research position at the Geography Department at the University of Exeter. He is currently Research Fellow at the Sutton Trust, a think tank in London, which seeks to improve social mobility through education. His research interests include US homeland security policy, critical geopolitics, and the politics of UK education.

Karolina La Fors-Owczynik is an external PhD researcher at Tilburg Institute for Law, Technology and Society (TILT) at Tilburg University in the Netherlands. She earned her MPhil and LLM degrees from the Faculty of Law at Tilburg University and her MA in international relations from Corvinus University in Budapest, Hungary. Her work deals with the controversies inherent in the construction and daily use of digital risk profiles or 'risk identities' that are implemented for a variety of preventative assessment purposes concerning children and migrants in the Netherlands. Previously, Karolina has been involved as a junior researcher and later PhD candidate with the ERC–funded DigIDeas research project Social and Ethical Aspects of Digital Identities Towards a Value-Sensitive Design. Furthermore, she participated in the FP7 research projects HIDE, FIDIS, and STORK, all of which dealt with the ethical, legal, and societal implications of identity management technologies.

Peter Lauritsen is an Associate Professor in information studies at Aarhus University, Denmark. Amongst his research areas are the use of CCTV by the Danish police force as well as the use of civic registration numbers in surveillance practices. He was the head of the project Surveillance in Denmark (2010–2015), which investigated various aspects of the Danish surveillance culture, drawing on theoretical concepts from actor-network theory and post-phenomenology. He is currently working on a new project focused on how surveillance and social welfare are intertwined. This includes research on privacy, public perceptions on surveillance, and surveillance as infrastructure. Peter Lauritsen has written several articles on surveillance as well as the book *Big Brother 2.0* (2011). Peter Lauritsen is an active participant in the public debate on surveillance in Denmark and serves as columnist for the newspaper *Information*.

Vlad Niculescu-Dinca is a lecturer in the media and communication department of the Erasmus School of History, Culture & Communication in Rotterdam, the Netherlands. Previously, he participated as a PhD student in the ERC–funded DigIDeas project Social and Ethical Aspects of Digital Identities. Towards a Value Sensitive Identity Management. In this context, he examines contemporary technologically mediated policing (social media surveillance, sensing technologies, mobile communications, geographic information systems) with an STS–inspired approach. He draws from ethnographic research, which he previously performed at several police organizations within the EU. Vlad's research interests include qualitative research approaches to surveillance, privacy, and suspicion and social and ethical aspects of new information technologies' design and use. Vlad holds a master's degree from the University of Twente in philosophy of technology and society, where he investigated the structure of ethical debates around new and emerging technologies. He holds degrees in software engineering from the Technical Universities of Eindhoven (PDeng) and Bucharest (BSc).

Isolde Sprenkels studied philosophy at Tilburg University and is currently an external PhD candidate at Maastricht University. Her work concerns socio-technical configurations in which children's identities as consumers in a digitizing society are enacted. In addition, she is a lecturer at Avans

University of Applied Sciences, Academy of Marketing and Business Management, where she also participates in the Centre of Expertise Sustainable Business. Previously, Isolde worked as a teacher in secondary school and as a junior researcher at the Infonomics and New Media Research Centre at Zuyd University of Applied Sciences. She conducted research on digital identities and identity management systems and co-developed and taught a minor on digital identity and on marketing and new media. She contributed to publications on social and ethical aspects of identification technologies such as biometrics used in migration and border management. Furthermore, she participated as a PhD student in the ERC–funded DigIDeas project Social and Ethical Aspects of Digital Identities: Towards a Value Sensitive Identity Management.

Valerie Steeves, BA, JD, PhD, is an Associate Professor in the Department of Criminology at the University of Ottawa in Ottawa, Canada. She is the lead researcher on MediaSmart's Young Canadians in a Wired World project (YCWW), which has been tracking young people's use of new media since 1999. With Jane Bailey, she co-leads the eGirls Project, an examination of the performance of gender on social media. She is also a co-editor of *Transparent Lives: Surveillance in Canada*, a 2014 multi-disciplinary report that maps out seven main trends in emerging surveillance practices. Professor Steeves received her JD from the University of Toronto and was called to the Bar of Ontario in 1984.

Tsjalling Swierstra studied philosophy and political science and received his PhD in philosophy in Groningen; he worked at the technical university of Twente until being appointed full professor in Maastricht, where he now heads the philosophy department. He is a member of the Maastricht University Science and Technology Studies (MUSTS) research programme. He is director of the centre for Ethics and Politics of Emerging Technologies, a member of the Advisory Committee on Health Research, and a member of the Program Committee of the Responsible Innovation program funded by the Dutch Research Council NWO. He has published widely on the ethics of new and emerging science and technology (NEST ethics) and on the mutual shaping of science and technology and morals (technomoral change) in numerous books and in journals like *Krisis*, *Technology and Human Values*, *Technology in Society*, *Nano-Ethics*, and *Futures*.

Daniel Trottier is an Assistant Professor in the Department of Media and Communication at Erasmus University Rotterdam. His current research considers the use of social media by police and intelligence agencies, as well as other forms of policing that occur on these platforms. As part of this research, he has participated in two European Commission projects on security, privacy, and digital media. Daniel has authored several articles in peer-reviewed journals on this and other topics, as well as *Social Media as Surveillance* (Ashgate, 2012), *Identity Problems in the Facebook Era* (Routledge, 2013), and *Social Media, Politics and the State* (co-edited with Christian Fuchs; Routledge, 2014). Daniel previously held postdoctoral fellowships at the Communication and Media Research Institute (CAMRI), University of Westminster, the Department of Informatics and Media at Uppsala University Sweden, and the Department of Sociology at the University of Alberta, Canada. Daniel completed a PhD in sociology at Queen's University in Kingston, Canada, as part of the Surveillance Studies Research Centre.

Govert Valkenburg is currently a Postdoctoral Research Fellow at the Maastricht University Science, Technology and Society (MUSTS) research programme. His work has concerned social and political aspects of a wide range of technologies. These technologies have ranged from human genomics to privacy and security technologies and energy and sustainability technologies. He has analysed these technologies through political-theoretical lenses such as public reason, citizenship, and notions of the political, as well as through lenses from constructivist science and technology studies, such as actor-network theory and critical theories of technology. He is currently working on the conceptualization of modes of governance that can be used in the societal management of sustainable transitions. Additionally, the mobilization of expertise in the democratic governance of technological societies is one of his research topics. His teaching has included social, cultural, and political theory. He is currently one of the programme coordinators of the Dutch Graduate School of Science, Technology and Modern Society WTMC.

Sally Wyatt is Professor of digital cultures in development, Maastricht University, and programme leader of the eHumanities Group, Royal Netherlands Academy of Arts and Sciences (KNAW). She originally studied economics (BA McGill, 1976; MA Sussex, 1979) but later did a PhD in science and technology studies (Maastricht, 1998), which focused on different ways of transmitting data over networks. She has more than thirty years of experience in teaching and research about technology policy and about the relationship between technological and social change, focusing particularly on issues of social exclusion and inequality. Her current research interests include digital media in the production of knowledge in the humanities and the social sciences and the ways in which people incorporate the Internet into their practices for finding health information. She is one of the co-editors (together with Paul Wouters, Anne Beaulieu, and Andrea Scharnhorst) of *Virtual Knowledge. Experimenting in the Humanities and the Social Sciences* (MIT Press, 2013).

Index

For Product Safety Concerns and Information please contact our EU representative GPSR@taylorandfrancis.com
Taylor & Francis Verlag GmbH, Kaufingerstraße 24, 80331 München, Germany

www.ingramcontent.com/pod-product-compliance
Lightning Source LLC
Chambersburg PA
CBHW070239290326
41929CB00046B/2056

* 9 7 8 0 3 6 7 5 9 7 6 5 8 *